Grammars with
Context Conditions
and Their Applications

Grammars with Context Conditions and Their Applications

Alexander Meduna

Martin Švec

Brno University of Technology
Faculty of Information Technology
Brno, Czech Republic

WILEY-
INTERSCIENCE

A JOHN WILEY & SONS, INC., PUBLICATION

Library of Congress Cataloging-in-Publication Data:

Meduna, Alexander, 1957–
    Grammars with context conditions and their applications / by Alexander Meduna and Martin Švec.
        p. cm.
    Includes bibliographical references (p.) and indexes.
    ISBN 0-471-71831-9 (acid-free paper)
    1. Generative grammar.   2. Context (Linguistics)   3. Grammar, Comparative and general—Conditionals.   4. Computational linguistics.   5. Formal languages.   I. Svec, Martin.   II. Title.
P158.M43 2005
415—dc22   2004028737

Printed in the United States of America.

10 9 8 7 6 5 4 3 2 1

To Professor Miroslav Novotný

Contents

Preface

The investigation of grammars with context conditions represents an exciting trend within the formal language theory. Although this investigation has introduced a number of new grammatical concepts and brought many remarkable results, all these concepts and results are scattered in various journal papers. In effect, the formal language theory lacks any monograph systematically and compactly summarizing this important trend. The primary goal of the present book is to provide such a monograph.

According to the types of context conditions, the present book classifies the grammars into three classes and sums up the crucial results about them. Specifically, this classification comes from the distinction between context conditions placed on (1) the domains of grammatical derivations, (2) the use of grammatical productions, and (3) the neighborhood of the rewritten symbols. In all three cases, the main attention is on establishing the grammatical generative power and important properties. In particular, this book studies how to reduce these grammars with respect to some of their components, such as the number of grammatical symbols or productions, in order to make the grammars small, succinct, and therefore easy to use. To demonstrate this practical use, it also discusses the applications and implementation of grammars with context conditions. Most of the applications are related to microbiology, which definitely belongs to the central application areas of computer science today.

No previous knowledge concerning the subject of this book is assumed on the part of the reader. Indeed, this book is self-contained in the sense that no other sources are needed for understanding all the presented material. Almost every new concept defined in the text is immediately illustrated by some examples to give it grasp. Every complicated mathematical passage is preceded by its intuitive explanation, so the reader should easily follow every proof in the book. All the applications given in the book are explained in a realistic way to clearly demonstrate the strong relation between the theoretical concept and its use in practice. Additional information found at http://www.fit.vutbr.cz/~meduna/books/gwcc/.en.

Acknowledgments

We are indebted to many people for their assistance in various aspects of creating this book. We greatly benefited from conversations with our colleagues at the Brno University of Technology. Our special thanks go to Vladimír Čech. We are grateful to our Editor, Val Molière and Editorial Assistant, Emily Simmons at John Wiley & Sons, who were very encouraging and helpful during the preparation of this book. We gladly acknowledge support of GACR grant 201/04/0441. Most important, we thank our families for their constant patience and encouragement.

Alexander Meduna and Martin Švec.

Chapter 1

Introduction

Formal languages fulfill a crucial role in many computer science areas, ranging from compilers through mathematical linguistics to molecular genetics. In dealing with these languages, we face the problem of choosing appropriate models in order to capture their structure elegantly and precisely. By analogy with the specification of natural languages, we often base these models on suitable grammars.

A grammar generates its language by performing derivation steps that change strings, called sentential forms, to other strings according to its grammatical productions. During a derivation step, the grammar rewrites a part of its current sentential form with a string according to one of its productions. If in this way it can make a sequence of derivation steps from its start symbol to a sentential form consisting of terminal symbols—that is, the symbols over which the language is defined—the resulting sentential form is called a sentence and belongs to the generated language. The set of all sentences made in this way is the language generated by the grammar.

In classical formal language theory, we can divide grammatical productions into context-dependent and context-independent productions. Based on this division, we can make a natural distinction between context-dependent grammars, such as phrase-structure grammars, and context-independent grammars, such as context-free grammars. The derivation step by context-dependent productions depends on rather strict conditions, usually placed on the context surrounding the rewritten symbol, while the derivation step by context-independent productions does not have any restrictions. For this reason, we tend to use context-independent grammars. Unfortunately, compared to context-dependent grammars, context-independent grammars are far less powerful; in fact, most of these grammars are incapable of grasping some basic aspects of common programming languages. On the other hand, most context-dependent grammars are as powerful as the Turing machines, and this remarkable power gives them an indisputable advantage.

From a realistic point of view, the classical context-independent and context-dependent grammars have some other disadvantages. Consider, for instance, English. Context-independent grammars are obviously incapable of capturing all the contextual dependencies in this complex language. However, we may find even the classical context-dependent grammars clumsy for this purpose. To illustrate, in an English sentence, the proper form of verb usually depends on the form of the subject. For instance, we write *I do it*, not *I ~~does~~ it*, and it is the subject, *I*, that implies the proper form of *do*. Of course, there may occur several words, such as adverbs, between the subject and the verb. We could extend *I do it* to *I often do it*, *I very often do it* and infinitely many other sentences in this way. At this point, however, the classical context-dependent productions, whose conditions are placed on the context surrounding the rewritten symbol, are hardly of any use. The proper form of the verb follows from a subject that does not surround the verb at all; it can occur many words ahead of the verb.

To overcome the difficulties and, at the same time, maintain the advantages described above, modern language theory has introduced some new grammars that simultaneously satisfy these three properties:

- They are based on context-independent productions.

- Their context conditions are signficantly more simple and flexible than the strict condition placed on the context surrounding the rewritten symbol in the classical context-dependent grammars.

- They are as powerful as classical context-dependent grammars.

In the present book, we give an overview of the most essential types of these grammars. Their alternative context conditions can be classified into these three categories:

- Context conditions placed on derivation domains.

- Context conditions placed on the use of productions.

- Context conditions placed on the neighborhood of the rewritten symbols.

As already pointed out, we want the context conditions to be as small as possible. For this reason, we pay a lot of attention to the reduction of context conditions in this book. Specifically, we reduce the number of their components, such as the number of nonterminals or productions. We study how to achieve this reduction without any decrease of their generative power, which coincides with the power of the Turing machines. By achieving this reduction, we actually make the grammars with context conditions more succinct and economical, and these properties are obviously highly appreciated both from a practical and theoretical standpoint. Regarding each of the dicussed grammars, we introduce and study their parallel and sequential versions, which represent two basic approaches to grammatical generation of languages in today's formal language theory. To be more specific, during a sequential derivation step, a grammar rewrites a single symbol in the current sentential form whereas during a parallel derivation step, a grammar rewrites all symbols. As context-free and E0L grammars represent perhaps the most fundamental sequential and parallel grammars, respectively, we usually base the discussion of sequential and parallel generation of languages on them.

Organization

The text consists of the following chapters:

Chapter 2 gives an introduction to formal languages and their grammars.

Chapter 3 restricts grammatical derivation domains in a very simple and natural way. Under these restrictions, both sequential and parallel context-independent grammars characterize the family of recursively enumerable languages, which are defined by the Turing machines.

Chapter 4 studies grammars with conditional use of productions. In these grammars, productions may be applied on condition that some symbols occur in the current sentential form and some others do not. We discuss many sequential and parallel versions of these grammars in detail. Most important, new characterizations of some well-known families of L languages, such as the family of ET0L languages, are obtained.

Chapter 5 studies grammars with context conditions placed on the neighborhood of rewritten symbols. We distinguish between scattered and continuous context neighborhood. The latter strictly requires that the neighborhood of the rewritten symbols forms a continuous part of the sentential form while the former drops this requirement of continuity.

Chapter 6 takes a closer look at grammatical transformations, many of which are mentioned in the previous chapters. Specifically, it studies how to transform grammars with context-conditions to some other equivalent grammars so that both the input grammars and the transformed grammars generate their languages in a very similar way.

Chapter 7 demostrates the use of grammars with context conditions by several applications related to biology.

Chapter 8 summarizes the main results of this book and presents several open problems. It makes historical notes and suggests some general references regarding the theoretical background of grammars with context conditions. In addition, it proposes new directions in the investigation of these grammars.

Approach

This book is theoretically oriented in its treatment of the grammars. It presents the formalism concerning grammars with enough rigor to make all results quite clear and valid. Every complicated mathematical passage is preceded by its intuitive explanation so that even the most complex parts of the book are easy to grasp. As most proofs of the results contain some transformations of grammars, the present book also provides an algorithmical approach to the gramatical models under discussion and shows how they are used in practice. Several worked-out examples and real-world applications give further illustrations of the theoretical notions.

Use

This book can be used by every computer scientist interested in formal languages and their grammatically based models as discussed in today's theoretical computer science curricula. It can also be used as a textbook for advanced courses in theoretical computer science at the senior levels; the text allows the flexibility needed to pick and choose different topics for discussion.

Chapter 2

Preliminaries and Definitions

2.1 Basic Definitions

This section reviews fundamental notions concerning sets, languages, and relations.

A *set* Σ is a collection of elements taken from some prespecified universe. If Σ contains an element a, then we symbolically write $a \in \Sigma$ and refer to a as a member of Σ. On the other hand, if a is not in Σ, we write $a \notin \Sigma$. The cardinality of Σ, $|\Sigma|$, is the number of Σ's members. The set that has no member is the *empty set*, denoted $\emptyset$; note that $|\emptyset| = 0$. If Σ has a finite number of members, then Σ is a *finite set*; otherwise, Σ is an *infinite set*.

A finite set Σ is customarily specified by listing its members; that is,

$$\Sigma = \{a_1, a_2, \ldots, a_n\},$$

where a_1 through a_n are all members of Σ. An infinite set Ω is usually specified by a property π, so that Ω contains all elements satisfying π; in symbols, this specification has the following general format:

$$\Omega = \{a : \ \pi(a)\}.$$

Sets whose members are other sets are usually called *families of sets* rather than sets of sets.

Let Σ and Ω be two sets. Σ is a *subset* of Ω, symbolically written as $\Sigma \subseteq \Omega$, if each member of Σ also belongs to Ω. Σ is a *proper subset* of Ω, written as $\Sigma \subset \Omega$, if $\Sigma \subset \Omega$ and Ω contains an element that is not in Σ. If $\Sigma \subseteq \Omega$ and $\Omega \subseteq \Sigma$, Σ equals Ω, denoted by $\Sigma = \Omega$. The *power set* of Σ, denoted by 2^Σ, is the set of all subsets of Σ. For two sets Σ and Ω, their union, intersection, and difference are denoted by $\Sigma \cup \Omega$, $\Sigma \cap \Omega$, and $\Sigma - \Omega$, respectively, and defined as

$$\Sigma \cup \Omega = \{a : \ a \in \Sigma \text{ or } a \in \Omega\},$$

$$\Sigma \cap \Omega = \{a : \ a \in \Sigma \text{ and } a \in \Omega\},$$

and

$$\Sigma - \Omega = \{a : \ a \in \Sigma \text{ and } a \notin \Omega\}.$$

For a set Σ over a universe U, the *complement* of Σ is denoted by $\overline{\Sigma}$ and defined as $\overline{\Sigma} = U - \Sigma$. A *sequence* is a list of elements from some universe. A sequence is *finite* if it represents a finite list of elements; otherwise, it is *infinite*. The *length* of a finite sequence x, denoted by $|x|$, is the number of elements in x. The empty sequence, denoted by ε, is the sequence consisting of no element; that is, $|\varepsilon| = 0$. A finite sequence is usually specified by listing its elements. For instance, consider a finite sequence x specified as $x = 0, 1, 0, 0$, and observe that $|x| = 4$.

An *alphabet* T is a finite, nonempty set, whose members are called *symbols*. A finite sequence of symbols from T is a *string* or, synonymously, a *word* over T; specifically, ε is referred to as the *empty string*. By T^*, we denote the set of all strings over T; $T^+ = T^* - \{\varepsilon\}$. Any subset $T \subseteq T^*$ is a *language* over T. If L represents a finite set of strings, L is a *finite language*; otherwise, L is an *infinite language*. For instance, T^*, called the universal language over T, is an infinite language while $\emptyset$ and $\{\varepsilon\}$ are finite; notably, $\emptyset \neq \{\varepsilon\}$ because $|\emptyset| = 0 \neq |\{\varepsilon\}| = 1$. For a finite language L, $\max(L)$ denotes the length of the longest word in L. By analogy with the set theory, sets whose members are languages are called *families of languages*.

By convention, we omit all separating commas in strings. That is, we write $a_1 a_2 \ldots a_n$ rather than $a_1, a_2, \ldots, a_n$.

Let $x, y \in T^*$ be two strings over an alphabet, T, and let $L, K \subseteq T^*$ be two languages over T. As languages are defined as sets, all set operations apply to them. Specifically, $L \cup K$, $L \cap K$, and $L - K$ denote the union, intersection, and difference of languages L and K, respectively. Perhaps most important, the *concatenation* of x with y, denoted by xy, is the string obtained by appending y to x. Notice that from an algebraic point of view, T^* and T^+ are the *free monoid* and *free semigroup*, respectively, generated under the operation of concatenation. Observe that for every $w \in T^*$, $w\varepsilon = \varepsilon w = w$. The concatenation of L and K, denoted by LK, is defined as

$$LK = \{xy : x \in L, \ y \in K\}.$$

Apart from binary operations, we also make some unary operations with strings and languages. Let $x \in T^*$ and $L \subseteq T^*$. The *complement* of L is denoted by $\overline{L}$ and defined as $\overline{L} = T^* - L$. The *reversal* of x, denoted by $\mathrm{rev}(x)$, is x written in the reverse order, and the *reversal* of L, $\mathrm{rev}(L)$, is defined as

$$\mathrm{rev}(L) = \{\mathrm{rev}(x) : x \in L\}.$$

For all $i \geq 0$ the ith *power of x*, denoted by x^i, is recursively defined as (1) $x^0 = \varepsilon$ and (2) $x^i = xx^{i-1}$, for $i \geq 1$. Observe that this definition is based on the recursive definitional method. To demonstrate the recursive aspect, consider, for instance, the ith power of x^i with $i = 3$. By the second part of the definition, $x^3 = xx^2$. By applying the second part to x^2, we obtain $x^2 = xx^1$. By another application of this part to x^1, $x^1 = xx^0$. By the first part of this definition, $x^0 = \varepsilon$. Thus, $x^1 = xx^0 = x\varepsilon = x$. Hence, $x^2 = xx^1 = xx$. Finally, $x^3 = xx^2 = xxx$. By this recursive method, we frequently introduce new notions, including the ith power of L, L^i, which is defined as (1) $L^0 = \{\varepsilon\}$ and (2) $L^i = LL^{i-1}$, for $i \geq 1$. The *closure* of L, L^*, is defined as

$$L^* = \bigcup_{i \geq 0} L^i,$$

and the *positive closure* of L, L^+, is defined as

$$L^+ = \bigcup_{i \geq 1} L^i.$$

Notice that

$$L^+ = LL^* = L^*L$$

and

$$L^* = L^+ \cup \{\varepsilon\}.$$

If there is $z \in T^*$ such that $xz = y$, x is a *prefix* of y; in addition, if $x \notin \{\varepsilon, y\}$, x is a *proper prefix* of y. By prefix(y), we denote the set of all prefixes of y. Set

$$\text{prefix}(L) = \{x : x \in \text{prefix}(w) \text{ for some } w \in L\}.$$

If there is $z \in T^*$ such that $zx = y$, x is a *suffix* of y; in addition, if $x \notin \{\varepsilon, y\}$, x is a *proper suffix* of y. By suffix(y), we denote the set of all suffixes of y. Set

$$\text{suffix}(L) = \{x : x \in \text{suffix}(w) \text{ for some } w \in L\}.$$

If there is $u, v \in T^*$ such that $uxv = y$, x is a *substring* or a *subword* of y; in addition, if $x \notin \{\varepsilon, y\}$, x is a *proper substring* or a *proper subword* of y. By sub(y), we denote the set of all substrings of y. Moreover,

$$\text{sub}(y, k) = \{x : x \in \text{sub}(y), |x| \leq k\}.$$

Observe that for every word w, prefix(w) $\subseteq$ sub(w), suffix(w) $\subseteq$ sub(w), and $\{\varepsilon, w\} \subseteq$ prefix(w) $\cap$ suffix(w) $\cap$ sub(w). Set

$$\text{sub}(L) = \{x : x \in \text{sub}(w) \text{ for some } w \in L\}.$$

Let w be a nonempty word; then, first(w) denotes the left-most symbol of w. Given a word w, alph(w) is the set of all symbols occurring in w. Set

$$\text{alph}(L) = \bigcup_{y \in L} \text{alph}(y).$$

For two words x and y, where $|y| \geq 1$, $\#_y x$ denotes the number of occurrences of y in x. A generalized form $\#_W x$, where W is a finite language, $\varepsilon \notin W$, denotes the number of all occurrences of x's subwords that belong to W. Let $w = a_1 \ldots a_n$ with $a_i \in T$ for some $n \geq 0$. The *set of permutations* of w, $\Pi(w)$, is defined as

$$\Pi(w) = \{v : v = b_1 \ldots b_n \text{ with } b_i \in \text{alph}(w) \text{ for } i = 1, \ldots, n,$$
$$\text{and } (b_1, \ldots, b_n) \text{ is a permutation of } (a_1, \ldots, a_n)\}.$$

For two objects a and b, (a, b) denotes the *ordered pair* consisting of a and b in this order. Let A and B be two sets. The Cartesian product of A and B, $A \times B$, is defined as

$$A \times B = \{(a, b) : a \in A \text{ and } b \in B\}.$$

A *binary relation* or, briefly, a *relation* ρ from A to B is any subset of $A \times B$; that is,

$$\rho \subseteq A \times B.$$

The *domain* of ρ, denoted by domain(ρ), and the *range* of ρ, denoted by range(ρ), are defined by

$$\text{domain}(\rho) = \{a : (a,b) \in \rho \text{ for some } b \in B\}$$

and

$$\text{range}(\rho) = \{b : (a,b) \in \rho \text{ for some } a \in A\}.$$

If $A = B$, then ρ is a *relation on A*. A relation σ is a *subrelation* of ρ if σ represents a subset of ρ. The *inverse* of ρ, denoted by ρ^{-1}, is defined as

$$\rho^{-1} = \{(b,a) : (a,b) \in \rho\}.$$

A *function* or, synonymously, a *mapping* from A to B is a relation ϕ from A to B such that for every $a \in A$,

$$|\{b : b \in B, (a,b) \in \phi\}| \leq 1.$$

Let ϕ be a function from A to B. If domain(ϕ) $= A$, ϕ is *total*; otherwise, ϕ is *partial*. If for every $b \in B$, $|\{a : a \in A, (a,b) \in \phi\}| \leq 1$, ϕ is an *injection*. If for every $b \in B$, $|\{a : a \in A, (a,b) \in \phi\}| \geq 1$, ϕ is a *surjection*. If ϕ is both a surjection and an injection, ϕ represents a *bijection*.

Instead of $(a,b) \in \rho$, we often write $a \in \rho(b)$ or $a\rho b$; in other words, $(a,b) \in \rho$, $a\rho b$, and $a \in \rho(b)$ are used interchangeably. If ρ is a function, we usually write $a = \rho(b)$.

Let ρ be a relation over a set, A. For $k \geq 1$, the *k-fold product* of ρ, ρ^k, is recursively defined as (1) $a\rho^1 b$ if and only if $a\rho b$, and (2) $a\rho^k b$ if and only if $a\rho c$ and $c\rho^{k-1}b$, for some c and $k \geq 2$. The *transitive closure* of ρ, ρ^+, is defined as $a\rho^+ b$ if and only if $a\rho^k b$ for some $k \geq 1$, and the *reflexive and transitive closure* of ρ, ρ^*, is defined as $a\rho^* b$ if and only if $a\rho^k b$ for some $k \geq 0$.

Let T and U be two alphabets. A total function τ from T^* to 2^{U^*} such that $\tau(uv) = \tau(u)\tau(v)$ for every $u,v \in T^*$ is a *substitution* from T^* to U^*. By this definition, $\tau(\varepsilon) = \varepsilon$ and $\tau(a_1a_2 \ldots a_n) = \tau(a_1)\tau(a_2) \ldots \tau(a_n)$, where $a_i \in T$, $1 \leq i \leq n$, for some $n \geq 1$, so τ is completely specified by defining $\tau(a)$ for every $a \in T$. A total function χ from T^* to U^* such that $\chi(uv) = \chi(u)\chi(v)$ for every $u,v \in T^*$ is a *homomorphism* or, synonymously and briefly, a *morphism* from T^* to U^*. As any homomorphism is obviously a special case of a substitution, we specify χ by analogy with the specification of τ. If χ is an injection, χ is called an *injective homomorphism*.

2.2 Grammars

This section reviews the basics of grammars. Specifically, it provides definitions of context-free, context-sensitive, and phrase-structure grammars along with some related notions and basic results which are used throughout the book.

Definition 1. A *phrase-structure* grammar is a quadruple

$$G = (V, T, P, S),$$

where

V is the *total alphabet*,

T is the set of *terminals* $(T \subset V)$,

$P \subseteq V^*(V - T)V^* \times V^*$ is a finite relation,

$S \in V - T$ is the *axiom* of G.

The symbols in $V - T$ are referred to as *nonterminals*. In what follows, each $(x, y) \in P$ is called a *production* or a *rule* and written as

$$x \to y \in P;$$

accordingly, P is called the *set of productions* in G. Given a production $p = x \to y \in P$, we set $\mathrm{lhs}(p) = x$ and $\mathrm{rhs}(p) = y$. The relation of a *direct derivation* in G is a binary relation over V^* denoted by $\Rightarrow_G$ and defined in the following way. Let $x \to y \in P$, $u, v, z_1, z_2 \in V^*$, and $u = z_1 x z_2$, $v = z_1 y z_2$; then,

$$u \Rightarrow_G v \; [x \to y].$$

When no confusion exists, we simplify $u \Rightarrow_G v \; [x \to y]$ to $u \Rightarrow_G v$. By $\Rightarrow_G^k$, we denote the k-fold product of $\Rightarrow_G$. Furthermore, let $\Rightarrow_G^+$ and $\Rightarrow_G^*$ denote the transitive closure of $\Rightarrow_G$ and the transitive and reflexive closure of $\Rightarrow_G$, respectively. If $S \Rightarrow_G^* x$ for some $x \in V^*$, x is called a *sentential form*. Set

$$F(G) = \{x \in V^* : \; S \Rightarrow_G^+ x\}$$

and

$$\Delta(G) = \{x \in V^* : \; S \Rightarrow_G^+ x \Rightarrow_G^* y, \; y \in T^*\}.$$

If $S \Rightarrow_G^* w$, where $w \in T^*$, $S \Rightarrow_G^* w$ is said to be a *successful derivation* of G. The *language of G*, denoted by $L(G)$, is defined as

$$L(G) = \{w \in T^* : \; S \Rightarrow_G^* w\}.$$

In the literature, the phrase-structure grammars are also often defined with productions of the form

$$xAy \to xuy,$$

where $u, x, y \in V^*$, $A \in V - T$ (see [81]). Both definitions are interchangeable in the sense that the grammars defined in these two ways generate the same family of languages—the family of *recursively enumerable languages*, denoted by **RE**.

Definition 2. A *context-sensitive grammar* is a phrase-structure grammar,

$$G = (V, T, P, S),$$

such that each production in P is of the form

$$xAy \to xuy,$$

where $A \in V - T$, $u \in V^+$, $x, y \in V^*$. A *context-sensitive language* is a language generated by a context-sensitive grammar. The family of context-sensitive languages is denoted by **CS**.

Definition 3. A *context-free grammar* is a phrase-structure grammar,

$$G = (V, T, P, S),$$

such that each production $x \to y \in P$ satisfies $x \in V - T$. A *context-free language* is a language generated by a context-free grammar. The family of context-free languages is denoted by **CF**.

For the families of languages generated by context-free, context-sensitive and phrase-structure grammars, it holds:

Theorem 1 (see [118]). $\mathbf{CF} \subset \mathbf{CS} \subset \mathbf{RE}$.

Lemma 1 (Chomsky Normal Form of Context-Free Grammars). *Let* $L \in$ **CF**, $\varepsilon \notin L$. *Then, there exists a context-free grammar,* $G = (V, T, P, S)$, *such that* $L = L(G)$ *and every production in* P *is either of the form* $A \to BC$ *or* $A \to a$, *where* $A, B, C \in V - T$ *and* $a \in T$.

Lemma 2 (Penttonen Normal Form of Context-Sensitive Grammars, see [147]). *Let* L *be a context-sensitive language. Then, there exists a context-sensitive grammar,* $G = (V, T, P, S)$, *such that* $L = L(G)$ *and every production in* P *is either of the form* $AB \to AC$ *or* $A \to x$, *where* $A, B, C \in V - T$, $x \in T \cup (V - T)^2$.

Lemma 3 (Penttonen Normal Form of Phrase-Structure Grammars, see [147]). *Let* L *be a recursively enumerable language. Then, there exists a phrase-structure grammar,* $G = (V, T, P, S)$, *such that* $L = L(G)$ *and every production in* P *is either of the form* $AB \to AC$ *or* $A \to x$, *where* $A, B, C \in V - T$, $x \in \{\varepsilon\} \cup T \cup (V - T)^2$.

Lemmas 2 and 3 can be further modified so that for every context-sensitive production of the form $AB \to AC \in P$, $A, B, C \in V - T$, there exist no $B \to x$ or $BD \to BE$ in P for any $x \in V^*$, $D, E \in V - T$:

Lemma 4. *Every* $L \in$ **CS** *can be generated by a context-sensitive grammar* $G = (N_{CF} \cup N_{CS} \cup T, T, P, S)$, *where* N_{CF}, N_{CS}, *and* T *are pairwise disjoint alphabets, and every production in* P *is either of the form* $AB \to AC$, *where* $B \in N_{CS}$, $A, C \in N_{CF}$, *or of the form* $A \to x$, *where* $A \in N_{CF}$, $x \in N_{CS} \cup T \cup N_{CF}^2$.

Proof. Let

$$G' = (V, T, P', S)$$

be a context-sensitive grammar in Penttonen normal form (see Lemma 2) so that $L = L(G)$. Then, let

$$G = (N_{CF} \cup N_{CS} \cup T, T, P, S)$$

be the context-sensitive grammar defined as follows:

$$
\begin{aligned}
N_{CF} &= V - T, \\
N_{CS} &= \{\widetilde{B} : AB \to AC \in P', \ A, B, C \in V - T\}, \\
P &= \{A \to x : \ A \to x \in P', \ A \in V - T, \ x \in T \cup (V - T)^2\} \ \cup \\
&\quad \{B \to \widetilde{B}, A\widetilde{B} \to AC : \ AB \to AC \in P', \ A, B, C \in V - T\}.
\end{aligned}
$$

Obviously, $L(G') = L(G)$ and G is of the required form. □

Lemma 5. *Every $L \in \mathbf{RE}$ can be generated by a phrase-structure grammar $G = (N_{CF} \cup N_{CS} \cup T, T, P, S)$, where N_{CF}, N_{CS}, and T are pairwise disjoint alphabets and every production in P is either of the form $AB \to AC$, where $B \in N_{CS}$, $A, C \in N_{CF}$, or of the form $A \to x$, where $A \in N_{CF}$, $x \in \{\varepsilon\} \cup N_{CS} \cup T \cup N_{CF}^2$.*

Proof. The reader can prove this lemma by analogy with Lemma 4. □

Besides context-free, context-sensitive and phrase-structure grammars, we also discuss ET0L grammars, EIL grammars and queue grammars in this book.

Definition 4. An *ET0L grammar* (see [155], [156]) is a $t+3$-tuple,

$$G = (V, T, P_1, \ldots, P_t, S),$$

where $t \geq 1$, and V, T, and S are the total alphabet, the terminal alphabet $(T \subset V)$, and the axiom $(S \in V - T)$, respectively. Each P_i is a finite set of productions of the form

$$a \to x,$$

where $a \in V$ and $x \in V^*$. If $a \to x \in P_i$ implies $x \neq \varepsilon$ for all $i \in \{1, \ldots, t\}$, G is said to be *propagating* (an *EPT0L grammar* for short). Let $u, v \in V^*$, $u = a_1 a_2 \ldots a_q$, $v = v_1 v_2 \ldots v_q$, $q = |u|$, $a_j \in V$, $v_j \in V^*$, and $p_1, p_2, \ldots, p_q$ is a sequence of productions of the form $p_j = a_j \to v_j \in P_i$ for all $j = 1, \ldots, q$, for some $i \in \{1, \ldots, t\}$. Then, u *directly derives* v according to the productions p_1 through p_q, denoted by

$$u \Rightarrow_G v \ [p_1, p_2, \ldots, p_q].$$

In the standard manner, we define the relations $\Rightarrow_G^k$ $(k \geq 0)$, $\Rightarrow_G^+$, and $\Rightarrow_G^*$. The language of G, denoted by $L(G)$, is defined as

$$L(G) = \{w \in T^* : S \Rightarrow_G^* w\}.$$

The families of languages generated by ET0L and EPT0L grammars are denoted by **ET0L** and **EPT0L**, respectively.

Let $G = (V, T, P_1, \ldots, P_t, S)$ be an ET0L grammar. If $t = 1$, G is called an *E0L grammar*. We denote the families of languages generated by E0L and propagating E0L grammars (EP0L grammars for short) by **E0L** and **EP0L**, respectively.

An *0L grammar* is defined by analogy with an E0L grammar except that $V = T$ and $S \in T^*$. For simplicity, as $V = T$, we specify an 0L grammar as a triple $G = (T, P, S)$ rather than a quadruple $G = (T, T, P, S)$. By **0L**, we denote the family of languages generated by 0L grammars.

Theorem 2 (see [155]).

$$\textbf{CF}$$
$$\subset$$
$$\textbf{E0L} = \textbf{EP0L}$$
$$\subset$$
$$\textbf{ET0L} = \textbf{EPT0L}$$
$$\subset$$
$$\textbf{CS}.$$

Definition 5. Given integers $m, n \geq 0$, an *E(m, n)L grammar* (see [155], [156]) is defined as a quadruple

$$G = (V, T, P, s),$$

where V, T, and s are the total alphabet, the terminal alphabet $T \subseteq V$, and the axiom $s \in V$, respectively. P is a finite set of productions of the form

$$(u, a, v) \to y$$

such that $a \in V$, $u, v, y \in V^*$, $0 \leq |u| \leq m$, and $0 \leq |v| \leq n$. Let $x, y \in V^*$. Then, x *directly derives* y in G, written as

$$x \Rightarrow_G y,$$

provided that $x = a_1 a_2 \ldots a_k$, $y = y_1 y_2 \ldots y_k$, $k \geq 1$, and for all i, $1 \leq i \leq k$,

$$(a_{i-m} \ldots a_{i-1}, a_i, a_{i+1} \ldots a_{i+n}) \to y_i \in P.$$

We assume $a_j = \varepsilon$ for all $j \leq 0$ or $j \geq k + 1$. In the standard way, $\Rightarrow_G^i$, $\Rightarrow_G^+$, and $\Rightarrow_G^*$ denote the i-fold product of $\Rightarrow_G$, $i \geq 0$, the transitive closure of $\Rightarrow_G$, and the transitive and reflexive closure of $\Rightarrow_G$, respectively. The language of G, $L(G)$, is defined as

$$L(G) = \{w \in T^* : s \Rightarrow_G^* w\}.$$

Let $G = (V, T, P, s)$ be an E(0, n)L grammar, $n \geq 0$, and $p = (\varepsilon, A, v) \to y \in P$. We simplify the notation of p so that $p = (A, v) \to y$ throughout this book. By *EIL grammars*, we refer to E(m, n)L grammars for all $m, n \geq 0$.

Definition 6. A *queue grammar* (see [88]) is a sixtuple,

$$Q = (V, T, W, F, R, g),$$

where V and W are alphabets satisfying $V \cap W = \emptyset$, $T \subseteq V$, $F \subseteq W$, $R \in (V - T)(W - F)$, and

$$g \subseteq (V \times (W - F)) \times (V^* \times W)$$

is a finite relation such that for any $a \in V$, there exists an element $(a, b, x, c) \in g$. If there exist $u, v \in V^*W$, $a \in V$, $r, z \in V^*$, and $b, c \in W$ such that $(a, b, z, c) \in g$, $u = arb$, and $v = rzc$, then u *directly derives* v according to (a, b, z, c) in Q,

$$u \Rightarrow_Q v \; [(a, b, z, c)].$$

Define $\Rightarrow_Q^k$ $(k \geq 0)$, $\Rightarrow_Q^+$, and $\Rightarrow_Q^*$ in the standard way. The *language of* Q, $L(Q)$, is defined as

$$L(Q) = \{w \in T^* : \; R \Rightarrow_Q^+ wf, \; f \in F\}.$$

Theorem 3 (see [88]). *Every language in* **RE** *is generated by a queue grammar.*

If some grammars define the same language, they are referred to as *equivalent grammars*. This equivalence is central to this book because we often discuss how to transform some grammars to some other grammars so that both the original grammars and the transformed grammars are equivalent.

Chapter 3

Context Conditions Placed on Derivation Domains

In the formal language theory, the relation of a direct derivation, $\Rightarrow$, is introduced over V^*, where V is the total alphabet of a grammar. Algebraically speaking, $\Rightarrow$ is thus defined over the free monoid whose generators are symbols. In this chapter, we modify this definition by using strings rather than symbols as the generators. More precisely, we introduce this relation over the free monoid generated by a finite set of strings; in symbols, $\Rightarrow$ is defined over W^*, where W is a finite language. As a result, this modification represents a very natural context condition: a derivation step is performed on the condition that the rewritten sentential form occurs in W^*. This context condition results into a large increase of generative power of both the sequential and parallel context-independent grammars, represented by context-free grammars and E0L grammars, respectively. In fact, even if W contains strings consisting of no more than two symbols, the resulting power of these grammars is equal to that of Turing machines.

3.1 Sequential Grammars over Word Monoids

Definition 7. A *context-free grammar over word monoid*, a *wm*-grammar for short (see [103], [111]), is a pair

$$(G, W),$$

where

$$G = (V, T, P, S)$$

is a context-free grammar, and W, called the *set of generators*, is a finite language over V. (G, W) is of *degree i*, where i is a natural number, if $y \in W$ implies $|y| \leq i$. (G, W) is said to be *propagating* if $A \to x \in P$ implies $x \neq \varepsilon$.

Roughly speaking, such a production $A \to x$ of a *wm*-grammar can be applied to a word w only when w is in W^*.

Formally, the direct derivation $\Rightarrow_{(G,W)}$ on W^* is defined as follows: if $p = A \to y \in P$, $xAz, xyz \in W^*$ for some $x, z \in V^*$, then xAz *directly derives* xyz,

$$xAz \Rightarrow_{(G,W)} xyz \ [p]$$

in symbols. In the standard manner, we denote the k-fold product of $\Rightarrow_{(G,W)}$ (for some $k \geq 0$) by $\Rightarrow_{(G,W)}^k$, the transitive closure of $\Rightarrow_{(G,W)}$ by $\Rightarrow_{(G,W)}^+$, and the reflexive and transitive closure of $\Rightarrow_{(G,W)}$ by $\Rightarrow^*_{(G,W)}$. The language of (G,W), symbolically denoted by $L(G,W)$, is defined as

$$L(G,W) = \{w \in T^* : \; S \Rightarrow^*_{(G,W)} w\}.$$

We denote by **WM** the family of languages generated by wm-grammars. The family of languages generated by wm-grammars of degree i is denoted by **WM**(i). The families of propagating wm-grammars of degree i and propagating wm-grammars of any degree are denoted by **prop-WM**(i) and **prop-WM**, respectively.

Let us examine the generative capacity of (propagating) wm-grammars.

Theorem 4. prop-WM$(0) =$ **WM**$(0) = \emptyset$, **prop-WM**$(1) =$ **WM**$(1) =$ **CF**.

Proof. Follows immediately from the definitions.   ∎

Next, we prove that (i) a language is context-sensitive if and only if it is generated by a propagating wm-grammar (of degree 2) and (ii) a language is recursively enumerable if and only if it is generated by a wm-grammar (of degree 2).

Theorem 5. prop-WM$(2) =$ **CS**.

Proof. It is straightforward to prove that **prop-WM**$(2) \subseteq$ **CS**; hence it suffices to prove the converse inclusion.

Let L be a context-sensitive language. Without loss of generality we can assume that L is generated by a context-sensitive grammar

$$G = (N_{CF} \cup N_{CS} \cup T, T, P, S)$$

of the form described in Lemma 4. Let

$$V = N_{CS} \cup N_{CF} \cup T.$$

The propagating wm-grammar (G',W) of degree 2 is defined as follows:

$$G' = (V', T, P', S),$$

where

$$
\begin{aligned}
V' &= V \cup Q, \\
Q &= \{\langle A,B,C \rangle : \; AB \rightarrow AC \in P, \; A,C \in N_{CF}, \; B \in N_{CS}\}.
\end{aligned}
$$

Clearly, without loss of generality, we can assume that $Q \cap V = \emptyset$. The set of productions P' is defined in the following way:

1. if $A \rightarrow x \in P$, $A \in N_{CF}$, $x \in N_{CS} \cup T \cup N_{CF}^2$, then add $A \rightarrow x$ to P';

2. if $AB \rightarrow AC \in P$, $A, C \in N_{CF}$, $B \in N_{CS}$, then add $B \rightarrow \langle A,B,C \rangle$ and $\langle A,B,C \rangle \rightarrow C$ to P'.

The set of generators W is defined as follows:

$$W = \{A\langle A, B, C\rangle : \langle A, B, C\rangle \in Q, \ A \in N_{CF}\} \cup V.$$

Obviously (G', W) is a propagating wm-grammar of degree 2. Next, let h be a finite substitution from $(V')^*$ into V^* defined as:

1. for all $D \in V$, $h(D) = D$;

2. for all $\langle X, D, Z\rangle \in Q$, $h(\langle X, D, Z\rangle) = D$.

Let h^{-1} be the inverse of h. To show that $L(G) = L(G', W)$, we first prove that

$$S \Rightarrow_G^m w \quad \text{if and only if} \quad S \Rightarrow_{(G'W)}^n v,$$

where $v \in W^* \cap h^{-1}(w)$, $w \in V^+$, for some $m, n \geq 0$.

Only if: This is established by induction on the length m of derivations in G.

Basis: Let $m = 0$. The only w is S because $S \Rightarrow_G^0 S$. Clearly, $S \Rightarrow_{(G',W)}^0 S$ and $S \in h^{-1}(S)$.

Induction Hypothesis: Let us suppose that our claim holds for all derivations of length at most m, for some $m \geq 0$.

Induction Step: Consider a derivation

$$S \Rightarrow_G^{m+1} x,$$

where $x \in V^+$. Since $m + 1 \geq 1$, there is some $y \in V^+$ and $p \in P$ such that

$$S \Rightarrow_G^m y \Rightarrow_G x \ [p],$$

and by the induction hypothesis, there is also a derivation

$$S \Rightarrow_{(G',W)}^n y''$$

for some $y'' \in W^* \cap h^{-1}(y)$, $n \geq 0$.

(i) Let us assume that $p = D \to y_2$, $D \in N_{CF}$, $y_2 \in N_{CS} \cup T \cup N_{CF}^2$, $y = y_1 D y_3$, $y_1, y_3 \in V^*$, and $x = y_1 y_2 y_3$. Since from the definition of h^{-1} it is clear that $h^{-1}(Z) = \{Z\}$ for all $Z \in N_{CF}$, we can write $y'' = z_1 D z_3$, where $z_1 \in h^{-1}(y_1)$ and $z_3 \in h^{-1}(y_3)$. It is clear that $D \to y_2 \in P'$ (see the definition of P').

Let $z_3 \notin Q(V')^*$. Then,

$$S \Rightarrow_{(G',W)}^n z_1 D z_3 \Rightarrow_{(G',W)} z_1 y_2 z_3,$$

and clearly, $z_1 y_2 z_3 \in h^{-1}(y_1 y_2 y_3) \cap W^*$.

Let $z_3 \in Q(V')^*$; that is, $z_3 = Yr$ for some $Y \in Q$, $r \in (V')^*$. Thus, $Dh(Y) \to DC \in P$ (for some $C \in N_{CF}$), $y_3 = h(Y)s$, where $r \in h^{-1}(s)$ and $s \in V^*$. Hence, we have $h(Y) \to Y \in P'$ (see (2) in the definition of P'). Observe that $h(Y) \to Y$ is the only production in P' that has Y appearing on its right-hand side. Also it is clear thar r is not in $Q(V')^*$ (see the definition of W). Thus, $\{z_1 Dh(Y)r, z_1 y_2 h(Y)r\} \subseteq W^*$, and since

$$S \Rightarrow^n_{(G',W)} z_1 DYr,$$

there must be also the following derivation in (G', W):

$$S \Rightarrow^{n-1}_{(G',W)} z_1 Dh(Y)r \Rightarrow_{(G',W)} z_1 DYr \; [h(Y) \to Y].$$

So we get

$$S \Rightarrow^{n-1}_{(G',W)} z_1 Dh(Y)r \Rightarrow_{(G',W)} z_1 y_2 h(Y)r \; [D \to y_2]$$

such that $z_1 y_2 h(Y)r$ is in $h^{-1}(x) \cap W^*$.

(ii) Let $p = AB \to AC$, $A, C \in N_{CF}$, $B \in N_{CS}$, $y = y_1 AB y_2$, $y_1, y_2 \in V^*$, $x = y_1 AC y_2$, $y'' = z_1 AY z_2$, $z_i \in h^{-1}(y_i)$, $i \in \{1, 2\}$, and $Y \in h^{-1}(B)$. Clearly, $\{B \to \langle A, B, C \rangle, \langle A, B, C \rangle \to C\} \subseteq P'$ and $A\langle A, B, C \rangle \in W$.

Let $Y = B$. Since $B \in N_{CS}$, $z_2 \notin Q(V')^*$, and so $z_1 A\langle A, B, C \rangle z_2 \in W^*$ (see the definition of W). Thus,

$$
\begin{aligned}
S \quad &\Rightarrow^n_{(G',W)} \quad z_1 AB z_2 \\
&\Rightarrow_{(G',W)} \quad z_1 A\langle A, B, C \rangle z_2 \quad [B \to \langle A, B, C \rangle] \\
&\Rightarrow_{(G',W)} \quad z_1 AC z_2 \quad\quad\quad [\langle A, B, C \rangle \to C]
\end{aligned}
$$

and $z_1 AC z_2 \in h^{-1}(x) \cap W^*$.

Let $Y \in Q$. Clearly, $h(Y) = B$ and by the definitions of Q and P', we have $B \to Y \in P'$. Thus, we can express the derivation

$$S \Rightarrow^n_{(G',W)} z_1 AY z_2$$

in the form

$$S \Rightarrow^{n-1}_{(G',W)} z_1 AB z_2 \Rightarrow_{(G',W)} z_1 AY z_2 \; [B \to Y].$$

Since $z_1 A\langle A, B, C \rangle z_2 \in W^*$, we get

$$
\begin{aligned}
S \quad &\Rightarrow^{n-1}_{(G',W)} \quad z_1 AB z_2 \\
&\Rightarrow_{(G',W)} \quad z_1 A\langle A, B, C \rangle z_2 \\
&\Rightarrow_{(G',W)} \quad z_1 AC z_2,
\end{aligned}
$$

where $z_1 AC z_2 \in h^{-1}(x) \cap W^*$.

If: This is also established by induction, but in this case on $n \geq 0$.

Basis: For $n = 0$ the only v is S because $S \Rightarrow^0_{(G',W)} S$. Since $S \in h^{-1}(S)$, we have $w = S$. Clearly, $S \Rightarrow^0_G S$.

Induction Hypothesis: Let us assume the claim holds for all derivations of length at most n, for some $n \geq 0$.

Induction Step: Consider a derivation

$$S \Rightarrow^{n+1}_{(G',W)} u,$$

where $u \in h^{-1}(x) \cap W^*$ and $x \in V^+$. Since $n + 1 \geq 1$, there is some $p \in P'$, $y \in V^+$, and $v \in h^{-1}(y) \cap W^*$ such that

$$S \Rightarrow^n_{(G',W)} v \Rightarrow_{(G',W)} u \; [p],$$

and by the induction hypothesis,

$$S \Rightarrow^*_G y.$$

Let $v = r'Ds'$, $y = rBs$, $r' \in h^{-1}(r)$, $s' \in h^{-1}(s)$, $r, s \in V^*$, $D \in h^{-1}(B)$, $u = r'z's'$, and $p = D \to z' \in P'$. Moreover, let us consider the following three cases:

(i) Let $h(z') = B$, (see (2)). Then, $u = r'z's' \in h^{-1}(rBs)$; that is, $x = rBs$. By the induction hypothesis we have

$$S \Rightarrow^*_G rBs.$$

(ii) Let $z' \in T \cup N_{CS} \cup N^2_{CF}$. Then, there is a production $B \to z' \in P$. Since $z' \in h^{-1}(z')$, we have $x = rz's$. Clearly,

$$S \Rightarrow^*_G rBs \Rightarrow_G rz's \; [B \to z'].$$

(iii) Let $z' = C \in N_{CF}$, $D = \langle A, B, C \rangle \in Q$. By the definition of W, we have $r' = t'A$, $r = tA$, where $t' \in h^{-1}(t)$, $t \in V^*$, and so $x = tACs$. By the definition of Q, there is a production $AB \to AC \in P$. Thus,

$$S \Rightarrow^*_G tABs \Rightarrow_G tACs \; [AB \to AC].$$

By the inspection of P', we have considered all possible derivations of the form

$$S \Rightarrow^n_{(G',W)} v \Rightarrow_{(G',W)} u$$

in (G', W). Thus, by the principle of induction, we have established that

$$S \Rightarrow^n_{(G',W)} u$$

for some $n \geq 0$ and $u \in W^*$ implies

$$S \Rightarrow_G^* x,$$

where $x \in V^*$ and $u \in h^{-1}(x)$. Hence,

$$S \Rightarrow_G^m w \quad \text{if and only if} \quad S \Rightarrow_{(G',W)}^n v,$$

where $v \in W^* \cap h^{-1}(w)$ and $w \in V^*$, for some $m, n \geq 0$.

The proof of the equivalence of G and (G', W) can easily be derived from the above: by the definition of h^{-1}, we have $h^{-1}(a) = \{a\}$ for all $a \in T$. Thus, by the statement above and by the definition of W, we have for any $x \in T^*$,

$$S \Rightarrow_G^* x \quad \text{if and only if} \quad S \Rightarrow_{(G',W)}^* x;$$

that is, $L(G) = L(G', W)$. Thus, **prop-WM**$(2) = $**CS**, which proves the theorem. ∎

Observe that the form of the *wm*-grammar in the proof of Theorem 5 implies the following corollary:

Corollary 1. *Let L be a context-sensitive language over an alphabet T. Then, L can be generated by a propagating* wm-*grammar (G, W) of degree 2, where $G = (V, T, P, S)$ satisfies*

(i) $T \subseteq W$ and $(W - V) \subseteq (V - T)^2$;

(ii) *if $A \rightarrow x$ and $|x| > 1$, then $x \in (V - T)^2$.*

Next, we study the *wm*-grammars of degree 2 with erasing productions. We prove that these grammars generate precisely **RE**.

Theorem 6. **WM**$(2) = $ **RE**.

Proof. Clearly, we have **WM**$(2) \subseteq$ **RE**; hence it suffices to show **RE** $\subseteq$ **WM**(2). The containment **RE** $\subseteq$ **WM**(2) can be proved by the techniques given in the proof of Theorem 5 because every language $L \in$ **RE** can be generated by a grammar $G = (V, T, P, S)$ of the form of Lemma 5. The details are left to the reader. ∎

Since the form of the resulting *wm*-grammar in the proof of Theorem 6 is analogous to the *wm*-grammar in the proof of Theorem 5 (except that the former may contain some erasing productions), we have:

Corollary 2. *Let L be a recursively enumerable language over an alphabet T, Then, L can be generated by a* wm-*grammar (G, W) of degree 2, where $G = (V, T, P, S)$ such that*

(i) $T \subseteq W$ and $(W - V) \subseteq (V - T)^2$;

(ii) *if $A \rightarrow x$ and $|x| > 1$, then $x \in (V - T)^2$.*

Summing up Theorems 4, 5, and 6, we obtain the following corollary:

Corollary 3.
$$\textbf{prop-WM}(1) = \textbf{WM}(1) = \textbf{CF}$$
$$\subset$$
$$\textbf{prop-WM}(2) = \textbf{prop-WM} = \textbf{CS}$$
$$\subset$$
$$\textbf{WM}(2) = \textbf{WM} = \textbf{RE}.$$

So far we have demonstrated that propagating *wm*-grammars of degree 2 and *wm*-grammars of degree 2 characterize **CS** and **RE**, respectively. Next, we show that the characterization of **RE** can be further improved in such a way that even some reduced versions of *wm*-grammars suffice to generate all the family of recursively enumerable languages. More specifically, we can simultaneously reduce the number of nonterminals and the number of words of length two occurring in the set of generators without any decrease of the generative power (see [111]).

Theorem 7. *Every $L \in \textbf{RE}$ can be defined by a 10-nonterminal context-free grammar over a word monoid generated by an alphabet and six words of length two.*

Proof. Let $L \in \textbf{RE}$. By Geffert (see [69]), $L = L(G)$, where G is a phrase-structure grammar of the form

$$G = (V, T, P \cup \{AB \to \varepsilon, CD \to \varepsilon\}, S)$$

such that P contains only context-free productions and

$$V - T = \{S, A, B, C, D\}.$$

Let us define a *wm*-grammar (G', W) of degree 2, where

$$G' = (V', T, P', S)$$

and

$$
\begin{aligned}
V' \;=\; & \{S, A, B, C, D, \langle AB \rangle, \langle CD \rangle, \langle left \rangle, \langle right \rangle, \langle empty \rangle\} \cup T, \\
P' \;=\; & P \cup \{B \to \langle AB \rangle, \langle AB \rangle \to \langle right \rangle, \\
& D \to \langle CD \rangle, \langle CD \rangle \to \langle right \rangle, \\
& A \to \langle left \rangle, C \to \langle left \rangle, \\
& \langle left \rangle \to \langle empty \rangle, \langle right \rangle \to \langle empty \rangle, \langle empty \rangle \to \varepsilon\}.
\end{aligned}
$$

The set of generators is defined as

$$
\begin{aligned}
W = \{ & A\langle AB \rangle, C\langle CD \rangle, \langle left \rangle \langle AB \rangle, \langle left \rangle \langle CD \rangle, \\
& \langle left \rangle \langle right \rangle, \langle empty \rangle \langle right \rangle, \langle empty \rangle\} \cup T \cup \{S, A, B, C, D\}.
\end{aligned}
$$

Clearly, (G', W) is a *wm*-grammar with the required properties. To establish $L(G) \subseteq L(G', W)$, we first prove the following claim:

Claim 1. $S \Rightarrow_G^m w$ *implies* $S \Rightarrow_{(G',W)}^* w$, *where* $w \in V^*$ *for some* $m \geq 0$.

Proof. This is established by induction on m.

Basis: Let $m = 0$. The only w is S because $S \Rightarrow_G^0 S$. Clearly, $S \Rightarrow_{(G',W)}^0 S$.

Induction Hypothesis: Suppose that our claim holds for all derivations of length m or less, for some $m \geq 0$.

Induction Step: Consider a derivation of the form

$$S \Rightarrow_G^{m+1} w$$

with $w \in V^*$. As $m + 1 \geq 1$, there exists $y \in W^+$ and $p \in P$ such that

$$S \Rightarrow_G^m y \Rightarrow_G w \ [p];$$

by the induction hypothesis, there also exists a derivation

$$S \Rightarrow_{(G',W)}^n y.$$

Observe that $y \in W^*$ because $V \subseteq W$. The production p has one of these three forms:

(i) p is a context-free production in P,

(ii) p has the form $AB \rightarrow \varepsilon$,

(iii) p has the form $CD \rightarrow \varepsilon$.

Next, we consider these three possibilites.

(i) Let us assume that $p = E \rightarrow y_2$, $y = y_1 E y_3$, $E \in \{S, A, B, C, D\}$, $y_1, y_3 \in V^*$, and $w = y_1 y_2 y_3$. By the construction of P', $E \rightarrow y_2 \in P'$. Thus,

$$S \Rightarrow_{(G',W)}^n y_1 E y_3 \Rightarrow_{(G',W)} y_1 y_2 y_3 \ [E \rightarrow y_2].$$

(ii) Let $p = AB \rightarrow \varepsilon$, $y = y_1 A B y_2$, $y_1, y_2 \in V^*$, $w = y_1 y_2$. At this point, we construct the following derivation in (G', W):

$$
\begin{array}{lll}
S & \Rightarrow_{(G',W)}^n & y_1 A B y_2 \\
& \Rightarrow_{(G',W)} & y_1 A \langle AB \rangle y_2 & [B \rightarrow \langle AB \rangle] \\
& \Rightarrow_{(G',W)} & y_1 \langle left \rangle \langle AB \rangle y_2 & [A \rightarrow \langle left \rangle] \\
& \Rightarrow_{(G',W)} & y_1 \langle left \rangle \langle right \rangle y_2 & [\langle AB \rangle \rightarrow \langle right \rangle] \\
& \Rightarrow_{(G',W)} & y_1 \langle empty \rangle \langle right \rangle y_2 & [\langle left \rangle \rightarrow \langle empty \rangle] \\
& \Rightarrow_{(G',W)} & y_1 \langle empty \rangle \langle empty \rangle y_2 & [\langle right \rangle \rightarrow \langle empty \rangle] \\
& \Rightarrow_{(G',W)} & y_1 \langle empty \rangle y_2 & [\langle empty \rangle \rightarrow \varepsilon] \\
& \Rightarrow_{(G',W)} & y_1 y_2 & [\langle empty \rangle \rightarrow \varepsilon].
\end{array}
$$

(iii) Let $p = CD \rightarrow \varepsilon$, $y = y_1 CD y_2$, $y_1, y_2 \in V^*$, $w = y_1 y_2$. By analogy with (ii), we can prove that

$$S \Rightarrow^*_{(G',W)} y_1 y_2.$$

Thus, Claim 1 now follows by the principle of induction. $\square$

Next, we sketch how to verify $L(G', W) \subseteq L(G)$. First, we make two observations, which follow from the definition of W.

Observation 1. Let

$$
\begin{aligned}
S \quad &\Rightarrow^*_{(G',W)} \quad y_1 AB y_2 \\
&\Rightarrow_{(G',W)} \quad y_1 A \langle AB \rangle y_2 \quad [B \rightarrow \langle AB \rangle] \\
&\Rightarrow^*_{(G',W)} \quad w,
\end{aligned}
$$

where $w \in T^*$. Then, during the derivation

$$y_1 A \langle AB \rangle y_2 \Rightarrow^*_{(G',W)} w,$$

the following six derivation steps necessarily occur:

1. A is rewritten according to $A \rightarrow \langle left \rangle$, so $\langle left \rangle \langle AB \rangle$ is produced.

2. $\langle AB \rangle$ is rewritten according to $\langle AB \rangle \rightarrow \langle right \rangle$, so $\langle left \rangle \langle right \rangle$ is produced.

3. $\langle left \rangle$ is rewritten according to $\langle left \rangle \rightarrow \langle empty \rangle$, so $\langle empty \rangle \langle right \rangle$ is produced.

4. $\langle right \rangle$ is rewritten according to $\langle right \rangle \rightarrow \langle empty \rangle$, so $\langle empty \rangle \langle empty \rangle$ is produced.

5. One $\langle empty \rangle$ in $\langle empty \rangle \langle empty \rangle$ is erased according to $\langle empty \rangle \rightarrow \varepsilon$.

6. The other $\langle empty \rangle$ is erased according to $\langle empty \rangle \rightarrow \varepsilon$.

Observation 2. Let

$$
\begin{aligned}
S \quad &\Rightarrow^*_{(G',W)} \quad y_1 CD y_2 \\
&\Rightarrow_{(G',W)} \quad y_1 C \langle CD \rangle y_2 \quad [D \rightarrow \langle CD \rangle] \\
&\Rightarrow^*_{(G',W)} \quad w,
\end{aligned}
$$

where $w \in T^*$. Then, during the derivation

$$y_1 C \langle CD \rangle y_2 \Rightarrow^*_{(G',W)} w,$$

the following six derivation steps necessarily occur:

1. C is rewritten according to $C \rightarrow \langle left \rangle$, so $\langle left \rangle \langle CD \rangle$ is produced.

2. $\langle CD \rangle$ is rewritten according to $\langle CD \rangle \rightarrow \langle right \rangle$, so $\langle left \rangle \langle right \rangle$ is produced.

3. $\langle left \rangle$ is rewritten according to $\langle left \rangle \to \langle empty \rangle$, so $\langle empty \rangle \langle right \rangle$ is produced.

4. $\langle right \rangle$ is rewritten according to $\langle right \rangle \to \langle empty \rangle$, so $\langle empty \rangle \langle empty \rangle$ is produced.

5. One $\langle empty \rangle$ in $\langle empty \rangle \langle empty \rangle$ is erased according to $\langle empty \rangle \to \varepsilon$.

6. The other $\langle empty \rangle$ is erased according to $\langle empty \rangle \to \varepsilon$.

Considering Observations 1 and 2, we can easily prove the following claim:

Claim 2. $S \Rightarrow^m_{(G',W)} w$ *implies* $S \Rightarrow^*_G w$, *where* $w \in T^*$, *for some* $m \geq 0$.

Proof. This proof is left to the reader. $\square$

By Claim 1, $L(G) \subseteq L(G', W)$. From Claim 2, we get $L(G', W) \subseteq L(G)$. Therefore, $L(G) = L(G', W)$, and Theorem 7 holds.   ∎

Recall that for ordinary context-free grammars (which coincide with the *wm-grammars* of degree 1 in terms of the present chapter), Gruska [77] proved that for every natural number $n \geq 1$, the context-free grammars with $n+1$ nonterminals are more powerful that the context-free grammars with n nonterminals. Consequently, if we reduce the number of nonterminals in context-free grammars over letter monoids, then we also reduce the power of these grammars. On the other hand, by Theorem 7, context-free grammars defined over word monoids keep their power even if we reduce their number of nonterminals to 10.

3.2   Parallel Grammars over Word Monoids

Definition 8. An *E0L grammar on word monoid*, a *WME0L grammar* for short, is a pair

$$(G, W),$$

where

$$G = (V, T, P, S)$$

is an E0L grammar. The set of generators W is a finite language over V. By analogy with *wm-grammars*, (G, W) has *degree i*, where i is a natural number, if every $y \in W$ satisfies $|y| \leq i$. If $A \to x \in P$ implies $x \neq \varepsilon$, (G, W) is said to be propagating. Let $x, y \in W^*$ such that $x = a_1 a_2 \ldots a_n$, $y = y_1 y_2 \ldots y_n$, $a_i \in V$, $y_i \in V^*$, $1 \leq i \leq n$, $n \geq 0$. If $a_i \to y_i \in P$ for all $i = 1 \ldots n$, then x *directly derives* y according to productions $a_1 \to y_1$, $a_2 \to y_2$, ..., $a_n \to y_n$,

$$x \Rightarrow_{(G,W)} y \; [a_1 \to y_1, \ldots, a_n \to y_n]$$

in symbols. As usual, the list of applied productions is omitted when no confusion arises. In the standard way, $\Rightarrow^k_{(G,W)}$, $\Rightarrow^+_{(G,W)}$, and $\Rightarrow^*_{(G,W)}$ denote the k-fold product of $\Rightarrow_{(G,W)}$, $k \geq 0$, the transitive closure of $\Rightarrow_{(G,W)}$, and the transitive and reflexive closure of $\Rightarrow_{(G,W)}$, respectively. The language of (G, W), denoted by $L(G, W)$, is defined in the following way:

$$L(G, W) = \{w \in T^* : \; S \Rightarrow^*_{(G,W)} w\}.$$

By **WME0L**(i), **WMEP0L**(i), **WME0L**, and **WMEP0L**, we denote the families of languages generated by WME0L grammars of degree i, propagating WME0L grammars of degree i, WME0L grammars, and propagating WME0L grammars, respectively.

Note that WME0L grammars of degree 2 are called *symbiotic E0L grammars* in [105]. The families of languages generated by symbiotic E0L grammars and propagating symbiotic E0L grammars are denoted by **SE0L** and **SEP0L**; that is, **SE0L** = **WME0L**(2) and **SEP0L** = **WME0L**(2).

Let us investigate the generative power of WME0L grammars. Clearly,

$$\mathbf{WMEP0L}(0) = \mathbf{WME0L}(0) = \emptyset.$$

Recall that for ordinary E0L languages, **EP0L** = **E0L** (see Theorem 2.4 in [157]). Therefore, the following theorem follows immediately from the definitions:

Theorem 8. WMEP0L(1) = **WME0L**(1) = **EP0L** = **E0L**.

Next, let us investigate WME0L grammars of degree 2 (symbiotic E0L grammars). In Theorems 9 and 10, we demonstrate that these grammars have remarkably higher generative capacity than WME0L grammars of degree 1. More specifically, propagating WME0L grammars of degree 2 generate precisely the family of context-sensitive languages and WME0L grammars of degree 2 generate all the family of recursively enumerable languages.

Theorem 9. WMEP0L(2) = **CS**.

Proof. It is straightforward to prove that **WMEP0L**(2) $\subseteq$ **CS**; hence it suffices to prove the converse inclusion. Let L be a context-sensitive language generated by a context-sensitive grammar

$$G = (N_{CF} \cup N_{CS} \cup T, T, P, S)$$

of the form described in Lemma 4. Let

$$V = N_{CF} \cup N_{CS} \cup T$$

and

$$V' = V \cup Q,$$

where

$$Q = \{\langle A, B, C \rangle : \; AB \to AC \in P, \; A, C \in N_{CF}, \; B \in N_{CS}\}.$$

Clearly, without loss of generality, we can assume that $Q \cap V = \emptyset$.

The WMEP0L grammar of degree 2, (G', W), is defined as follows:

$$G' = (V', T, P', S),$$

where P' is constructed as

1. for all $A \in V'$, add $A \to A$ to P';

2. if $A \to x \in P$, $A \in N_{CF}$, $x \in N_{CS} \cup T \cup N_{CF}^2$, then add $A \to x$ to P';

3. if $AB \to AC \in P$, $A, C \in N_{CF}$, $B \in N_{CS}$, then add $B \to \langle A, B, C \rangle$ and $\langle A, B, C \rangle \to C$ to P'.

The set of generators, $W \subseteq (V \cup V^2)$, is defined in the following way:

$$W = \{A\langle A, B, C\rangle : \langle A, B, C\rangle \in Q, \ A \in N_{CF}\} \cup V.$$

Obviously, (G', W) is a WMEP0L grammar of degree 2. Let us introduce a substitution from $(V')^*$ into V^* as

1. for all $D \in V$, $h(D) = D$,

2. for all $\langle X, D, Z \rangle \in Q$, $h(\langle X, D, Z \rangle) = D$.

Let h^{-1} be the inverse of h. To demonstrate that $L(G) = L(G', W)$, we first prove two claims:

Claim 3. *If $S \Rightarrow_G^m w$, $w \in V^+$, for some $m \geq 0$, then $S \Rightarrow_{(G', W)}^* v$, where $v \in h^{-1}(w)$.*

Proof. This is established by induction on the length m of derivations in G.

Basis: Let $m = 0$. The only w is S because $S \Rightarrow_G^0 S$. Since $S \in W^*$, $S \Rightarrow_{(G', W)}^0 S$ and by the definition of h^{-1}, $S \in h^{-1}(S)$.

Induction Hypothesis: Let us suppose that our claim holds for all derivations of length at most m, for some $m \geq 0$.

Induction Step: Consider a derivation

$$S \Rightarrow_G^{m+1} x,$$

$x \in V^*$. Since $m + 1 \geq 1$, there is some $y \in V^+$ and $p \in P$ such that

$$S \Rightarrow_G^m y \Rightarrow_G x \ [p]$$

and, by the induction hypothesis, there is also a derivation

$$S \Rightarrow_{(G', W)}^n y'$$

for some $y' \in h^{-1}(y)$, $n \geq 0$. By definition, $y' \in W^*$.

(i) Let us first assume that $p = D \to y_2 \in P$, $D \in N_{CF}$, $y_2 \in N_{CS} \cup T \cup N_{CF}^2$, $y = y_1 D y_3$, and $x = y_1 y_2 y_3$, $y_1 = a_1 \ldots a_i$, $y_3 = b_1 \ldots b_j$, where $a_k, b_l \in V$, $1 \leq k \leq i, 1 \leq l \leq j$, for some $i, j \geq 0$ ($i = 0$ implies $y_1 = \varepsilon$ and $j = 0$ implies $y_3 = \varepsilon$). Since from the definition of h^{-1} it is clear that $h^{-1}(Z) = \{Z\}$ for all $Z \in N_{CF}$, we can write $y' = z_1 D z_3$, where $z_1 \in h^{-1}(y_1)$ and $z_3 \in h^{-1}(y_3)$, that is to say, $z_1 = c_1 \ldots c_i$, $z_3 = d_1 \ldots d_j$, where $c_k \in h^{-1}(a_k)$, $d_l \in h^{-1}(b_l)$, for $1 \le k \le i$, $1 \le l \le j$. It is clear that $D \to y_2 \in P'$.

Let $d_1 \notin Q$. Then, it is easy to see that $z_1 y_2 z_3 \in W^*$, and so

$$z_1 D z_3 \Rightarrow_{(G',W)} z_1 y_2 z_3 \ [c_1 \to c_1, \ldots, c_i \to c_i, D \to y_2, d_1 \to d_1, \ldots, d_j \to d_j].$$

Therefore,

$$S \Rightarrow^n_{(G',W)} z_1 D z_3 \Rightarrow_{(G',W)} z_1 y_2 z_3$$

and $z_1 y_2 z_3 \in h^{-1}(y_1 y_2 y_3)$.

Let $d_1 \in Q$. That is, $D h(d_1) \to DC \in P$ (for some $C \in N_{CF}$); see the definition of h. Hence, we have $h(d_1) \to d_1 \in P'$; see (3) (observe that this production is the only production in P' that has d_1 appearing on its right-hand side). It is clear, by the definition of W, that $d_2 \notin Q$. Thus,

$$\{z_1 D h(d_1) d_2 \ldots d_j, z_1 y_2 h(d_1) d_2 \ldots d_j\} \subseteq W^*.$$

Since

$$S \Rightarrow^n_{(G',W)} z_1 D d_1 \ldots d_j,$$

there must exist the following derivation in (G', W):

$$
\begin{aligned}
S \quad &\Rightarrow^{n-1}_{(G',W)} \quad z_1 D h(d_1) d_2 \ldots d_j \\
&\Rightarrow_{(G',W)} \quad z_1 D d_1 d_2 \ldots d_j \ [c_1 \to c_1, \ldots, c_i \to c_i, D \to D, \\
&\qquad\qquad h(d_1) \to d_1, d_2 \to d_2, \ldots, d_j \to d_j].
\end{aligned}
$$

So we get

$$
\begin{aligned}
S \quad &\Rightarrow^{n-1}_{(G',W)} \quad z_1 D h(d_1) d_2 \ldots d_j \\
&\Rightarrow_{(G',W)} \quad z_1 y_2 h(d_1) d_2 \ldots d_j \ [c_1 \to c_1, \ldots, c_i \to c_i, D \to y_2, \\
&\qquad\qquad h(d_1) \to h(d_1), d_2 \to d_2, \ldots, d_j \to d_j]
\end{aligned}
$$

such that $z_1 y_2 h(d_1) d_2 \ldots d_j$ is in $h^{-1}(x)$.

(ii) Let $p = AB \to AC \in P$, $A, C \in N_{CF}$, $B \in N_{CS}$, $y = y_1 A B y_2$, $y_1, y_2 \in V^*$, $x = y_1 A C y_2$, $y' = z_1 A Y z_2$, $z_i \in h^{-1}(y_i)$, $i \in \{1, 2\}$, $Y \in h^{-1}(B)$, and $y_1 = a_1 \ldots a_i$, $y_3 = b_1 \ldots b_j$, $a_k, b_l \in V$, $1 \le k \le i$, $1 \le l \le j$, for some $i, j \ge 0$. Let $z_1 = c_1 \ldots c_i$, $z_3 = d_1 \ldots d_j$, $c_k \in h^{-1}(a_k)$, $d_l \in h^{-1}(b_l)$, $1 \le k \le i$, $1 \le l \le j$. Clearly, $\{B \to \langle A, B, C \rangle, \langle A, B, C \rangle \to C\} \subseteq P'$, and $A \langle A, B, C \rangle \in W$, see the definition of W.

Let $Y = B$. Since $y' \in W^*$ and $B \in N_{CS}$, we have $d_1 \notin Q$. Consequently, $z_1 A \langle A, B, C \rangle z_2$ and $z_1 A C z_2$ are in W^* by the definition of W. Thus,

$$
\begin{aligned}
S \quad &\Rightarrow^n_{(G',W)} \quad z_1 A B z_2 \\
&\Rightarrow_{(G',W)} \quad z_1 A \langle A, B, C \rangle z_2 \quad [\pi_1] \\
&\Rightarrow_{(G',W)} \quad z_1 A C z_2 \quad [\pi_2],
\end{aligned}
$$

where

$$\pi_1 = c_1 \to c_1, \ldots, c_i \to c_i, A \to A, B \to \langle A, B, C \rangle, d_1 \to d_1, \ldots, d_j \to d_j,$$

$$\pi_2 = c_1 \to c_1, \ldots, c_i \to c_i, A \to A, \langle A, B, C \rangle \to C, d_1 \to d_1, \ldots, d_j \to d_j,$$

and $z_1 A C z_2 \in h^{-1}(x)$.

Let $Y \in Q$. Clearly, $h(Y)$ must be equal to B. By (3) and the definition of Q, we have $B \to Y \in P'$. Clearly, $z_1 A C z_2$ is in W^* for $d_1 \notin Q$ as we have already shown. Thus, since

$$S \Rightarrow^n_{(G',W)} z_1 A Y z_2,$$

the word $z_1 A Y z_2$ can be derived in (G', W) as follows:

$$
\begin{aligned}
S \quad &\Rightarrow^{n-1}_{(G',W)} \quad z_1 A B z_2 \\
&\Rightarrow_{(G',W)} \quad z_1 A Y z_2 \quad [\pi],
\end{aligned}
$$

where

$$\pi = c_1 \to c_1, \ldots, c_i \to c_i, A \to A, B \to Y, d_1 \to d_1, \ldots, d_j \to d_j.$$

Since $z_1 A \langle A, B, C \rangle z_2$ and $z_1 A C z_2$ belong to W^*, we get

$$
\begin{aligned}
S \quad &\Rightarrow^{n-1}_{(G',W)} \quad z_1 A B z_2 \\
&\Rightarrow_{(G',W)} \quad z_1 A \langle A, B, C \rangle z_2 \quad [\pi_1] \\
&\Rightarrow_{(G',W)} \quad z_1 A C z_2 \quad [\pi_2],
\end{aligned}
$$

where

$$\pi_1 = c_1 \to c_1, \ldots, c_i \to c_i, A \to A, B \to \langle A, B, C \rangle, d_1 \to d_1, \ldots, d_j \to d_j,$$

$$\pi_2 = c_1 \to c_1, \ldots, c_i \to c_i, A \to A, \langle A, B, C \rangle \to C, d_1 \to d_1, \ldots, d_j \to d_j,$$

and $z_1 A C z_2 \in h^{-1}(x)$.

Cases (i) and (ii) cover all possible rewriting of y in G. Thus, the claim now follows from the principle of induction. $\qquad\square$

Claim 4. *Let* $S \Rightarrow^*_{(G',W)} v$, $v \in W^*$, $v = rDs$, *and* $p = D \to z \in P$. *Then,* $h(v) \Rightarrow^i_G h(r)h(z)h(s)$ *for some* $i = 0, 1$.

Proof. To verify this claim, consider the following three cases:

(i) Let $h(z) = h(D)$. Then,

$$h(v) \Rightarrow^0_G h(r)h(z)(s).$$

(ii) Let $z \in T \cup N_{CS} \cup N_{CF}^2$, $D \in N_{CF}$. Then, there is a production $B \to z \in P$, and by the definition of h, we have $B \to z = h(B) \to h(z)$. Thus,

$$h(r)h(D)h(s) \Rightarrow_G h(r)h(z)h(s) \; [h(B) \to h(z)].$$

(iii) Let $z = C \in N_{CF}$ and $D = \langle A, B, C \rangle$ for some $\langle A, B, C \rangle \in Q$; see (3). By the definition of W, we have $r = tA$, where $t \in W^*$, and so $v = tACs$. By the definition of Q, there is a production $AB \to AC \in P$. Thus,

$$tABs \Rightarrow_G tACs \; [AB \to AC],$$

where $tABs = h(tA)h(\langle A, B, C \rangle)h(s)$ and $tACs = h(tA)h(C)h(s)$.

By inspection of P', cases (i) through (iii) cover all possible types of productions in P', which proves the claim. ☐

Claim 5. *If $S \Rightarrow_{(G',W)}^n u$, $u \in W^*$, for some $n \geq 0$, then $S \Rightarrow_G^* h(u)$.*

Proof.

Basis: For $n = 0$, the only u is S because $S \Rightarrow_{(G',W)}^0 S$. Since $S = h(S)$ we have $S \Rightarrow_G^0 S$ in G.

Induction Hypothesis: Let us assume that the claim holds for all derivations of length at most n, for some $n \geq 0$.

Induction Step: Consider a derivation

$$S \Rightarrow_{(G',W)}^{n+1} u,$$

where $u \in W^*$. Since $n + 1 \geq 1$, there is some $v \in W^*$ such that

$$S \Rightarrow_{(G',W)}^n v \Rightarrow_{(G',W)} u,$$

and by the induction hypothesis

$$S \Rightarrow_G^* h(v).$$

Return to the proof of Claim 4. It should be clear that by using (i) through (iii) from Claim 5, we can construct a derivation

$$h(v) \Rightarrow_G^i h(u),$$

for some $i \in \{0, \ldots, |u|\}$, in the following way: first rewrite all occurrences of symbols corresponding to the case (iii) and then all occurrences of symbols corresponding to (ii); the technical details are left to the reader.

  Thus,

$$S \Rightarrow_G^* h(v) \Rightarrow_G^i h(u)$$

in G. Hence, by the principle of induction, we have established Claim 5. ☐

Next, the proof of the equivalence of G and (G', W) can be derived from Claims 3 and 5: By the definition of h^{-1}, we have $h^{-1}(a) = \{a\}$ for all $a \in T$. Thus, by Claim 3, we have for any $x \in T^*$,

$$S \Rightarrow_G^* x \quad \text{implies} \quad S \Rightarrow_{(G',W)}^* x;$$

that is, $L(G) \subseteq L(G', W)$.

Conversely, since $T^* \subseteq W^*$, we get, by the definition of h and Claim 5, for any $x \in T^*$,

$$S \Rightarrow_{(G',W)}^* x \quad \text{implies} \quad S \Rightarrow_G^* x;$$

that is, $L(G', W) \subseteq L(G)$. As a result, $L(G) = L(G', W)$ and so **WMEP0L**$(2) =$ **CS** $=$ **SEP0L**, which proves the theorem. ∎

Observe that Theorem 9 and the definitions yield the following normal form:

Corollary 4. *Let L be a context-sensitive language over an alphabet T. Then, L can be generated by an WMEP0L grammar (G, W) of degree 2, $G = (V, T, P, S)$, where W is over an alphabet V such that $T \subseteq W$, $(W - V) \subseteq (V - T)^2$, and if $A \rightarrow x$ and $|x| > 1$, then $x \in (V - T)^2$.*

Let us turn the investigation to WME0L grammars of degree 2 with erasing productions.

Theorem 10. WME0L$(2) = $ **RE.**

Proof. Clearly, **WME0L**$(2) \subseteq $ **RE**, hence it suffices to show **RE** $\subseteq $ **WME0L**(2).

Each language $L \in $ **RE** can be generated by a phrase-structure grammar G having the form of Lemma 5. Thus, the containment **RE** $\subseteq $ **WME0L**(2) can be proved by analogy with the techniques used in the proof of Theorem 9. The details are left to the reader. ∎

Since the forms of the resulting WME0L(2) grammar in the proofs of Theorem 9 and Theorem 10 are analogous, we obtain the following corollary as an analogy to Corollary 4:

Corollary 5. *Let L be a recursively enumerable language over an alphabet T. Then, L can be generated by an WME0L grammar (G, W) of degree 2, $G = (V, T, P, S)$, where W is over an alphabet V such that $T \subseteq W$, $(W - V) \subseteq (V - T)^2$, and if $A \rightarrow x$ and $|x| > 1$, then $x \in (V - T)^2$.*

Summing up Theorems 8, 9 and 10, we obtain the following corollary:

Corollary 6.

$$\textbf{CF}$$
$$\subset$$
$$\textbf{WMEP0L}(1) = \textbf{WME0L}(1) = \textbf{EP0L} = \textbf{E0L}$$
$$\subset$$
$$\textbf{WMEP0L}(2) = \textbf{CS}$$
$$\subset$$
$$\textbf{WME0L}(2) = \textbf{RE}.$$

Open Problems.   In this chapter, we have discussed grammars with derivations over the word monoids rather than the letter monoids. From a broader algebraic perspective, we could consider many other modifications of the derivation domains. Specifically, what is the generative power of context-free grammars whose derivations are defined over free groups?

Chapter 4

Context Conditions Placed on the Use of Productions

In this chapter, we discuss grammars with context conditions represented by strings associated with productions. We distinguish between two types of these conditions—*forbidding conditions* and *permitting conditions*. A production is applicable to a sentential form if each of its permitting conditions occurs in the sentential form and any of its forbidding conditions does not. In Section 4.1, we study sequential grammars with context conditions, originally introduced by van der Walt [175] in 1970. Then, in Section 4.2, we introduce and discuss parallel versions of these grammars. In both sections, we demonstrate that this concept of context conditions attached to grammatical productions significantly increase the grammatical generative power. Furthermore, in some grammars, we explain how to reduce the number of conditional productions, the length of context conditions, and the number of nonterminals.

4.1 Sequential Conditional Grammars

Informally, a sequential conditional grammar is an ordinary context-free grammar in which the application of productions is regulated by the permitting and forbidding context conditions. In every derivation step, such a grammar can rewrite only one nonterminal symbol in the given sentential form; that is, it works purely sequentially. Making use of this basic principle, the formal language theory has introduced a large number of variants of these grammars. In order to unify the notations and definitions, we start with the basic definition of a context-conditional grammar in Section 4.1.1. Then, in Sections 4.1.2 through 4.1.5, we investigate some special cases of the context-conditional grammars.

4.1.1 Context-Conditional Grammars

Definition 9. A *context-conditional grammar* is a quadruple,

$$G = (V, T, P, S),$$

where V, T, and S are the total alphabet, the terminal alphabet ($T \subset V$), and the axiom ($S \in V - T$), respectively. P is a finite set of productions of the form

$(A \rightarrow x, Per, For)$, where $A \in V - T$, $x \in V^*$, and finite sets $Per, For \subseteq V^+$. If $Per \neq \emptyset$ or $For \neq \emptyset$, the production is said to be *conditional*; otherwise, it is called *context-free*. G has *degree* (r, s), where r and s are natural numbers, if for every $(A \rightarrow x, Per, For) \in P$, $\max(Per) \leq r$ and $\max(For) \leq s$. If $(A \rightarrow x, Per, For) \in P$ implies $x \neq \varepsilon$, G is said to be *propagating*. Let $u, v \in V^*$ and $(A \rightarrow x, Per, For) \in P$. Then, u *directly derives* v according to $(A \rightarrow x, Per, For)$ in G, denoted by

$$u \Rightarrow_G v \; [(A \rightarrow x, Per, For)],$$

provided that for some $u_1, u_2 \in V^*$, the following conditions hold:

(a) $u = u_1 A u_2$,

(b) $v = u_1 x u_2$,

(c) $Per \subseteq \mathrm{sub}(u)$,

(d) $For \cap \mathrm{sub}(u) = \emptyset$.

When no confusion exists, we simply write $u \Rightarrow_G v$ instead of $u \Rightarrow_G v \; [(A \rightarrow x, Per, For)]$. By analogy with context-free grammars, we extend $\Rightarrow_G$ to $\Rightarrow_G^k$ (where $k \geq 0$), $\Rightarrow_G^+$, and $\Rightarrow_G^*$. The language of G, denoted by $L(G)$, is defined as

$$L(G) = \{w \in T^* : \; S \Rightarrow_G^* w\}.$$

The families of languages generated by context-conditional grammars and propagating context-conditional grammars of degree (r, s) are denoted by $\mathbf{CG}(r, s)$ and $\mathbf{prop\text{-}CG}(r, s)$, respectively. Furthermore, we define

$$\mathbf{CG} = \bigcup_{r=0}^{\infty} \bigcup_{s=0}^{\infty} \mathbf{CG}(r, s)$$

and

$$\mathbf{prop\text{-}CG} = \bigcup_{r=0}^{\infty} \bigcup_{s=0}^{\infty} \mathbf{prop\text{-}CG}(r, s).$$

Next, we establish several theorems dealing with the generative power of context-conditional grammars. Let us note, however, that a number of specializations of these grammars will be defined and investigated in Sections 4.1.2 through 4.1.5. Therefore, only the results concerning the general versions of context-conditional grammars are presented here.

Theorem 11. prop-CG$(0, 0)$ = CG$(0, 0)$ = CF

Proof. This theorem follows immediately from the definition. Clearly, context-conditional grammars of degree $(0, 0)$ are ordinary context-free grammars. ∎

Lemma 6. prop-CG $\subseteq$ CS.

Proof. Let $r = s = 0$. Then, **prop-CG**$(0,0) = $ **CF** $\subset$ **CS**. The rest of the proof establishes the inclusion for degrees (r, s) such that $r + s > 0$.

Consider a propagating context-conditional grammar

$$G = (V, T, P, S)$$

of degree (r, s), $r + s > 0$, for some $r, s \geq 0$. Let k be the greater number of r and s. Set

$$M = \{x \in V^+ : |x| \leq k\}.$$

Next, define

$$\mathrm{cf}(P) = \{A \to x : (A \to x, Per, For) \in P, \; A \in (V - T), \; x \in V^+\}.$$

Then, set

$$
\begin{aligned}
N_F &= \{\langle X, x \rangle : X \subseteq M, \; x \in M \cup \{\varepsilon\}\}, \\
N_T &= \{\lfloor X \rfloor : X \subseteq M\}, \\
N_B &= \{\lceil p \rceil : p \in \mathrm{cf}(P)\} \cup \{\lceil \emptyset \rceil\}, \\
V' &= V \cup N_F \cup N_T \cup N_B \cup \{\triangleright, \triangleleft, \$, S', \#\}, \\
T' &= T \cup \{\#\}.
\end{aligned}
$$

Construct the context-sensitive grammar

$$G' = (V', T', P', S')$$

with the finite set of productions P' defined as follows:

1. Add $S' \to \triangleright \langle \emptyset, \varepsilon \rangle S \triangleleft$ to P'.

2. For all $X \subseteq M$, $x \in (V^k \cup \{\varepsilon\})$ and $y \in V^k$, add the next production to P':

$$\langle X, x \rangle y \to y \langle X \cup \mathrm{sub}(xy, k), y \rangle.$$

3. For all $X \subseteq M$, $x \in (V^k \cup \{\varepsilon\})$ and $y \in V^+$, $|y| \leq k$, add the next production to P':

$$\langle X, x \rangle y \triangleleft \to y \lfloor X \cup \mathrm{sub}(xy, k) \rfloor \triangleleft.$$

4. For all $X \subseteq M$ and every $p = A \to x \in \mathrm{cf}(P)$ such that there exists $(A \to x, Per, For) \in P$ satisfying $Per \subseteq X$ and $For \cap X = \emptyset$, add the next production to P':

$$\lfloor X \rfloor \triangleleft \to \lceil p \rceil \triangleleft.$$

5. For every $p \in \mathrm{cf}(P)$ and $a \in V$, add the next production to P':

$$a \lceil p \rceil \to \lceil p \rceil a.$$

6. For every $p = A \to x \in \mathrm{cf}(P)$, $A \in (V - T)$, $x \in V^+$, add the next production to P':

$$A \lceil p \rceil \to \lceil \emptyset \rceil x.$$

7. For every $a \in V$, add the following production to P':

$$a\lceil \emptyset \rceil \rightarrow \lceil \emptyset \rceil a.$$

8. Add $\triangleright\lceil \emptyset \rceil \rightarrow \triangleright\langle \emptyset, \varepsilon \rangle$ to P'.

9. Add $\triangleright\langle \emptyset, \varepsilon \rangle \rightarrow \#\$$, $\$\triangleleft \rightarrow \#\#$, and $\$a \rightarrow a\$$, for all $a \in T$, to P'.

Claim 6. *Every successful derivation in G' has the form*

$$
\begin{aligned}
S' &\Rightarrow_{G'} \triangleright\langle \emptyset, \varepsilon \rangle S\triangleleft \\
&\Rightarrow_{G'}^{+} \triangleright\langle \emptyset, \varepsilon \rangle x\triangleleft \\
&\Rightarrow_{G'} \#\$x\triangleleft \\
&\Rightarrow_{G'}^{|x|} \#x\$\triangleleft \\
&\Rightarrow_{G'} \#x\#\#
\end{aligned}
$$

such that $x \in T^{+}$, and during

$$\triangleright\langle \emptyset, \varepsilon \rangle S\triangleleft \Rightarrow_{G'}^{+} \triangleright\langle \emptyset, \varepsilon \rangle x\triangleleft,$$

every sentential form w satisfies $w \in \{\triangleright\}H^{+}\{\triangleleft\}$, where $H \subseteq V'-\{\triangleright, \triangleleft, \#, \$, S'\}$.

Proof. Observe that the only production that rewrites S' is $S' \rightarrow \triangleright\langle \emptyset, \varepsilon \rangle S\triangleleft$; thus,

$$S' \Rightarrow_{G'} \triangleright\langle \emptyset, \varepsilon \rangle S\triangleleft.$$

After that, every sentential form that occurs in

$$\triangleright\langle \emptyset, \varepsilon \rangle S\triangleleft \Rightarrow_{G'}^{+} \triangleright\langle \emptyset, \varepsilon \rangle x\triangleleft$$

can be rewritten by using any of the productions (2) through (8) from the construction of P'. By inspection of these productions, it is obvious that the edge symbols $\triangleright$ and $\triangleleft$ remain unchanged and no other occurrences of them appear inside the sentential form. Moreover, there is no production generating a symbol from $\{\#, \$, S'\}$. Therefore, all these sentential forms belong to $\{\triangleright\}H^{+}\{\triangleleft\}$.

Next, let us explain how G' generates a word from $L(G')$. Only $\triangleright\langle \emptyset, \varepsilon \rangle \rightarrow \#\$$ can rewrite $\triangleright$ to a symbol from T (see (9) in the definition of P'). According to the left-hand side of this production, we obtain

$$S' \Rightarrow_{G'} \triangleright\langle \emptyset, \varepsilon \rangle S\triangleleft \Rightarrow_{G'}^{*} \triangleright\langle \emptyset, \varepsilon \rangle x\triangleleft \Rightarrow_{G'} \#\$x\triangleleft,$$

where $x \in H^{+}$. To rewrite $\triangleleft$, G' uses $\$\triangleleft \rightarrow \#\#$. Thus, G' needs $\$$ as the left neighbor of $\triangleleft$. Suppose that $x = a_1 a_2 \ldots a_q$, where $q = |x|$ and $a_i \in T$, for all $i \in \{1, \ldots, q\}$. Since for every $a \in T$ there is $\$a \rightarrow a\$ \in P'$ (see (9)), we can construct

$$
\begin{aligned}
\#\$a_1 a_2 \ldots a_n\triangleleft &\Rightarrow_{G'} \#a_1\$a_2 \ldots a_n\triangleleft \\
&\Rightarrow_{G'} \#a_1 a_2\$ \ldots a_n\triangleleft \\
&\Rightarrow_{G'}^{|x|-2} \#a_1 a_2 \ldots a_n\$\triangleleft.
\end{aligned}
$$

Notice that this derivation can be constructed only for x that belong to T^+. Then, $\$ \lhd$ is rewritten to $\#\#$. As a result,

$$S' \Rightarrow_{G'} \vartriangleright\langle\emptyset,\varepsilon\rangle S\lhd \Rightarrow_{G'}^{+} \vartriangleright\langle\emptyset,\varepsilon\rangle x\lhd \Rightarrow_{G'} \#\$x\lhd \Rightarrow_{G'}^{|x|} \#x\$\lhd \Rightarrow_{G'} \#x\#\#$$

with the required properties. Thus, the claim holds. $\qquad\square$

The following claim demonstrates how G' simulates a direct derivation from G—the heart of the construction.

Let $x \Rightarrow_{G'}^{\oplus} y$ denote the derivation $x \Rightarrow_{G'}^{+} y$ such that $x = \vartriangleright\langle\emptyset,\varepsilon\rangle u\lhd$, $y = \vartriangleright\langle\emptyset,\varepsilon\rangle v\lhd$, $u,v \in V^+$, and there is no other occurrence of a string of the form $\vartriangleright\langle\emptyset,\varepsilon\rangle z\lhd$, $z \in V^*$, during $x \Rightarrow_{G'}^{+} y$.

Claim 7. *For every $u,v \in V^*$, it holds that*

$$\vartriangleright\langle\emptyset,\varepsilon\rangle u\lhd \Rightarrow_{G'}^{\oplus} \vartriangleright\langle\emptyset,\varepsilon\rangle v\lhd \quad \text{if and only if} \quad u \Rightarrow_G v.$$

Proof.

Only if: Let us show how G' rewrites $\vartriangleright\langle\emptyset,\varepsilon\rangle u\lhd$ to $\vartriangleright\langle\emptyset,\varepsilon\rangle v\lhd$. The simulation consists of two phases.

During the first, forward phase, G' scans u to get all nonempty substrings of length k or less. By repeatedly using productions $\langle X,x\rangle y \to y\langle X \cup \mathrm{sub}(xy,k), y\rangle$, $X \subseteq M$, $x \in (V^k \cup \{\varepsilon\})$, $y \in V^k$ (see (2) in the definition of P'), the occurrence of a symbol with form $\langle X,x\rangle$ is moved toward the end of the sentential form. Simultaneously, the substrings of u are collected in X. The forward phase is finished by $\langle X,x\rangle y\lhd \to y\lfloor X \cup \mathrm{sub}(xy,k)\rfloor\lhd$, $x \in (V^k \cup \{\varepsilon\})$, $y \in V^+$, $|y| \le k$ (see (3)); this production reaches the end of u and completes $X = \mathrm{sub}(u,k)$. Formally,

$$\vartriangleright\langle\emptyset,\varepsilon\rangle u\lhd \Rightarrow_{G'}^{+} \vartriangleright u\lfloor X\rfloor\lhd$$

such that $X = \mathrm{sub}(u,k)$.

The second, backward phase simulates the application of a conditional production. Assume that $u = u_1 A u_2$, $u_1, u_2 \in V^*$, $A \in (V - T)$, and there exists a production $A \to x \in \mathrm{cf}(P)$ such that $(A \to x, Per, For) \in P$ for some $Per, For \subseteq M$, where $Per \subseteq X$, $For \cap X = \emptyset$. Let $u_1 x u_2 = v$. Then, G' derives

$$\vartriangleright u\lfloor X\rfloor\lhd \Rightarrow_{G'}^{+} \vartriangleright\langle\emptyset,\varepsilon\rangle v\lhd$$

by performing the following five steps:

(i) $\lfloor X\rfloor$ is changed to $\lceil p\rceil$, where $p = A \to x$ satisfies the conditions above (see (4) in the definition of P').

(ii) $\vartriangleright u_1 A u_2\lceil p\rceil\lhd$ is rewritten to $\vartriangleright u_1 A\lceil p\rceil u_2\lhd$ by using the productions of the form $a\lceil p\rceil \to \lceil p\rceil a$, $a \in V$ (see (5)).

(iii) $\vartriangleright u_1 A\lceil p\rceil u_2\lhd$ is rewritten to $\vartriangleright u_1\lceil\emptyset\rceil x u_2\lhd$ by using $A\lceil p\rceil \to \lceil\emptyset\rceil x$ (see (6)).

(iv) $\triangleright u_1\lceil\emptyset\rceil xu_2\triangleleft$ is rewritten to $\triangleright\lceil\emptyset\rceil u_1xu_2\triangleleft$ by using the productions of the form $a\lceil\emptyset\rceil \to \lceil\emptyset\rceil a$, $a \in V$ (see (7)).

(v) Finally, $\triangleright\lceil\emptyset\rceil$ is rewritten to $\triangleright\langle\emptyset,\varepsilon\rangle$ by $\triangleright\lceil\emptyset\rceil \to \triangleright\langle\emptyset,\varepsilon\rangle$.

As a result, we obtain

$$\triangleright\langle\emptyset,\varepsilon\rangle u\triangleleft \;\Rightarrow^+_{G'}\; \triangleright u\lfloor X\rfloor\triangleleft \;\Rightarrow_{G'}\; \triangleright u\lceil p\rceil\triangleleft$$
$$\Rightarrow^{\lceil u\rceil}_{G'}\; \triangleright\lceil\emptyset\rceil v\triangleleft \;\Rightarrow_{G'}\; \triangleright\langle\emptyset,\varepsilon\rangle v\triangleleft.$$

Observe that this is the only way of deriving

$$\triangleright\langle\emptyset,\varepsilon\rangle u\triangleleft \;\Rightarrow^\oplus_{G'}\; \triangleright\langle\emptyset,\varepsilon\rangle v\triangleleft.$$

Let us show that $u \Rightarrow_G v$. Indeed, the application of $A\lceil p\rceil \to \lceil\emptyset\rceil x$ implies that there exists $(A \to x, Per, For) \in P$, where $Per \subseteq \mathrm{sub}(u,k)$ and $For \cap \mathrm{sub}(u,k) = \emptyset$. Hence, there exists a derivation

$$u \Rightarrow_G v\ [p],$$

where $u = u_1 A u_2$, $v = u_1 x u_2$ and $p = (A \to x, Per, For) \in P$.

If: The converse implication is similar to the only-if part, so we leave it to the reader. $\qquad\square$

Claim 8. $S' \Rightarrow^+_{G'} \triangleright\langle\emptyset,\varepsilon\rangle x\triangleleft$ *if and only if* $S \Rightarrow^*_G x$, *for all* $x \in V^+$.

Proof.

Only if: The only-if part is proved by induction on the ith occurrence of the sentential form w satisfying $w = \triangleright\langle\emptyset,\varepsilon\rangle u\triangleleft$, $u \in V^+$, during the derivation in G'.

Basis: Let $i = 1$. Then, $S' \Rightarrow_{G'} \triangleright\langle\emptyset,\varepsilon\rangle S\triangleleft$ and $S \Rightarrow^0_G S$.

Induction Hypothesis: Suppose that the claim holds for all $i \leq h$, for some $h \geq 1$.

Induction Step: Let $i = h + 1$. Since $h + 1 \geq 2$, we can express

$$S' \Rightarrow^+_{G'} \triangleright\langle\emptyset,\varepsilon\rangle x_i\triangleleft$$

as

$$S' \Rightarrow^+_{G'} \triangleright\langle\emptyset,\varepsilon\rangle x_{i-1}\triangleleft \Rightarrow^\oplus_{G'} \triangleright\langle\emptyset,\varepsilon\rangle x_i\triangleleft,$$

where $x_{i-1}, x_i \in V^+$. By the induction hypothesis,

$$S \Rightarrow^*_G x_{i-1}.$$

Claim 7 says that

$$\triangleright\langle\emptyset,\varepsilon\rangle x_{i-1}\triangleleft \Rightarrow^\oplus_{G'} \triangleright\langle\emptyset,\varepsilon\rangle x_i\triangleleft \quad \text{if and only if} \quad x_{i-1} \Rightarrow_G x_i.$$

Hence,

$$S \Rightarrow^*_G x_{i-1} \Rightarrow_G x_i,$$

and the only-if part holds.

If: By induction on n, we prove that

$$S \Rightarrow_G^n x \quad \text{implies} \quad S' \Rightarrow_{G'}^+ \vartriangleright \langle \emptyset, \varepsilon \rangle x \vartriangleleft$$

for all $n \geq 0$, $x \in V^+$.

Basis: For $n = 0$, $S \Rightarrow_G^0 S$ and $S' \Rightarrow_{G'} \vartriangleright \langle \emptyset, \varepsilon \rangle S \vartriangleleft$.

Induction Hypothesis: Assume that the claim holds for all n or less, for some $n \geq 0$.

Induction Step: Let

$$S \Rightarrow_G^{n+1} x,$$

$x \in V^+$. Because $n + 1 \geq 1$, there exists $y \in V^+$ such that

$$S \Rightarrow_G^n y \Rightarrow_G x,$$

and by the induction hypothesis, there is also a derivation

$$S' \Rightarrow_{G'}^+ \vartriangleright \langle \emptyset, \varepsilon \rangle y \vartriangleleft.$$

From Claim 7 we have

$$\vartriangleright \langle \emptyset, \varepsilon \rangle y \vartriangleleft \Rightarrow_{G'}^{\oplus} \vartriangleright \langle \emptyset, \varepsilon \rangle x \vartriangleleft.$$

Therefore,

$$S' \Rightarrow_{G'}^+ \vartriangleright \langle \emptyset, \varepsilon \rangle x \vartriangleleft,$$

and the converse implication holds as well. $\square$

From Claims 6 and 8 we see that any successful derivation in G' is of the form

$$S' \Rightarrow_{G'}^+ \vartriangleright \langle \emptyset, \varepsilon \rangle x \vartriangleleft \Rightarrow_{G'}^+ \# x \# \#$$

such that

$$S \Rightarrow_G^* x, \; x \in T^+.$$

Therefore, we have for each $x \in T^+$,.

$$S' \Rightarrow_{G'}^+ \# x \# \# \quad \text{if and only if} \quad S \Rightarrow_G^* x.$$

Define the homomorphism h over $(T \cup \{\#\})^*$ as $h(\#) = \varepsilon$ and $h(a) = a$ for all $a \in T$. Observe that h is 4-linear erasing with respect to $L(G')$ (see page 98 in [161]). Furthermore, notice that $h(L(G')) = L(G)$. Because **CS** is closed under linear erasing (see Theorem 10.4 on page 98 in [161]), $L \in$ **CS**. Thus, Lemma 6 holds. $\square$

Theorem 12. prop-CG = CS.

Proof. By Lemma 6, we have **prop-CG** $\subseteq$ **CS**. **CS** $\subseteq$ **prop-CG** holds true as well. In fact, later in this book, we introduce several special cases of propagating context-conditional grammars and prove that even these grammars generate **CS** (see Theorems 26 and 28). As a result, **prop-CG** = **CS**.   ∎

Lemma 7. CG $\subseteq$ RE.

Proof. This lemma follows from Church's thesis. To obtain an algorithm converting any context-conditional grammar to an equivalent phrase-structure grammar, use the technique presented in Lemma 6.   □

Theorem 13. CG = RE.

Proof. By Lemma 7, **CG** $\subseteq$ **RE**. Later on we define some special cases of context-conditional grammars and demonstrate that they characterize **RE** (e.g., see Theorems 19, 27, and 29). Thus, **RE** $\subseteq$ **CG** too.   ∎

4.1.2   Random-Context Grammars

This section discusses three special cases of context-conditional grammars whose conditions are nonterminal symbols, so their degree is not greater than $(1,1)$. Specifically, *random-context grammars*, also known as *permitting grammars*, are of degree $(1,0)$. *Forbidding grammars* are of degree $(0,1)$. Finally, *random-context grammars with appearance checking* are of degree $(1,1)$.

Definition 10. Let $G = (V,T,P,S)$ be a context-conditional grammar. G is called a *random-context grammar with appearance checking* provided that every $(A \rightarrow x, Per, For) \in P$ satisfies $Per \subseteq N$ and $For \subseteq N$.

Definition 11. Let $G = (V,T,P,S)$ be a random-context grammar with appearance checking. G is called a *random-context grammar* (an *rc-grammar* for short) or *permitting grammar* provided that every $(A \rightarrow x, Per, For) \in P$ satisfies $For = \emptyset$.

Definition 12. Let $G = (V,T,P,S)$ be a random-context grammar with appearance checking. G is called a *forbidding grammar* provided that every $(A \rightarrow x, Per, For) \in P$ satisfies $Per = \emptyset$.

The following convention simplifies productions in permitting grammars and forbidding grammars, respectively:

Convention 1. Let $G = (V,T,P,S)$ be a permitting grammar, and let $p = (A \rightarrow x, Per, For) \in P$. Since by the definition $For = \emptyset$, we usually omit the empty set of forbidding conditions. That is, we write $(A \rightarrow x, Per)$ when no confusion arises.
    Let $G = (V,T,P,S)$ be a forbidding grammar, and let $p = (A \rightarrow x, Per, For) \in P$. Analogously, we write $(A \rightarrow x, For)$ instead of $(A \rightarrow x, Per, For)$ because $Per = \emptyset$ for all $p \in P$.

The families of languages defined by random-context grammars, random-context grammars with appearance checking, and forbidding grammars are denoted by **RC**, **RC(ac)**, and **F**, respectively. To indicate that only propagating grammars are considered, we use the prefix **prop-**. That is, **prop-RC**, **prop-RC(ac)**, and **prop-F** denote the families of languages defined by propagating random-context grammars, propagating random-context grammars with appearance checking, and propagating forbidding grammars, respectively.

Example 1 ([43]). Let

$$G = (\{S, A, B, C, D, A', B', C', a, b, c\}, \{a, b, c\}, P, S)$$

be a permitting grammar, where P is defined as follows:

$$P = \{(S \rightarrow ABC, \emptyset),$$
$$(A \rightarrow aA', \{B\}),$$
$$(B \rightarrow bB', \{C\}),$$
$$(C \rightarrow cC', \{A'\}),$$
$$(A' \rightarrow A, \{B'\}),$$
$$(B' \rightarrow B, \{C'\}),$$
$$(C' \rightarrow C, \{A\}),$$
$$(A \rightarrow a, \{B\}),$$
$$(B \rightarrow b, \{C\}),$$
$$(C \rightarrow c, \emptyset)\}.$$

Consider the word $aabbcc$. G generates this word in the following way:

$$S \Rightarrow ABC \Rightarrow aA'BC \Rightarrow aA'bB'C \Rightarrow aA'bB'cC' \Rightarrow$$
$$aAbB'cC' \Rightarrow aAbBcC' \Rightarrow aAbBcC \Rightarrow$$
$$aabBcC \Rightarrow aabbcC \Rightarrow aabbcc.$$

Observe that G is a propagating rc-grammar and $L(G) = \{a^n b^n c^n : n \geq 1\}$. Recall that $\{a^n b^n c^n : n \geq 1\}$ is a non-context-free language.

Example 2 ([43]). Let

$$G = (\{S, A, B, D, a\}, \{a\}, P, S)$$

be an rc-grammar with appearance checking. The set of productions P is defined as follows:

$$P = \{(S \rightarrow AA, \emptyset, \{B, D\}),$$
$$(A \rightarrow B, \emptyset, \{S, D\}),$$
$$(B \rightarrow S, \emptyset, \{A, D\}),$$
$$(A \rightarrow D, \emptyset, \{S, B\}),$$
$$(D \rightarrow a, \emptyset, \{S, A, B\})\}.$$

Notice that G is a propagating forbidding grammar. For $aaaaaaaa$, G makes the following derivation:

$$S \Rightarrow AA \Rightarrow AB \Rightarrow BB \Rightarrow BS \Rightarrow SS \Rightarrow AAS \Rightarrow AAAA \Rightarrow BAAA \Rightarrow$$
$$BABA \Rightarrow BBBA \Rightarrow BBBB \Rightarrow SBBB \Rightarrow SSBB \Rightarrow SSSB \Rightarrow$$
$$SSSS \Rightarrow AASSS \Rightarrow^3 AAAAAAAA \Rightarrow^8 DDDDDDDD \Rightarrow^8 aaaaaaaa.$$

Clearly, G generates the non-context-free language $L(G) = \{a^{2^n} : n \geq 1\}$.

The generative power of random-context grammars is intensively studied in [43] and [148], which present the next two theorems.

Theorem 14. CF $\subset$ prop-RC $\subseteq$ prop-RC(ac) $\subset$ CS.

Proof. **CF $\subset$ prop-RC** follows from Example 1. By the definition of rc-grammars and rc-grammars with appearance checking, we have **prop-RC $\subseteq$ prop-RC(ac)**. **prop-RC(ac) $\subset$ CS** follows from Theorems 1.2.4 and 1.4.5 in [43]. ∎

Theorem 15. prop-RC $\subseteq$ RC $\subset$ RC(ac) = RE.

Proof. **prop-RC $\subseteq$ RC** follows immediately from the definitions. By Theorem 1.2.5 in [43], **RC(ac) = RE**. Furthermore, from Theorem 2.7 in Chapter 3 of Volume 2 of [157], it follows that **RC $\subset$ RC(ac)**; thus, the theorem holds. ∎

Lemma 8. ET0L $\subset$ prop-F.

Proof (see [148]). Let $L \in$ **ET0L**, $L = L(G)$ for some ET0L grammar,

$$G = (V, T, P_1, \ldots, P_t, S).$$

Without loss of generality we can assume that G is propagating. Now we introduce the alphabets

$$\begin{aligned}
V^{(i)} &= \{a^{(i)} : a \in V\}, \ 1 \leq i \leq t, \\
V' &= \{a' : a \in V\}, \\
V'' &= \{a'' : a \in V\}, \\
\bar{V} &= \{\bar{a} : a \in T\}.
\end{aligned}$$

For $w \in V^*$, by $w^{(i)}$, w', w'', and $\bar{w}$ we denote the words obtained from w by replacing each occurrence of a symbol $a \in V$ by $a^{(i)}$, a', a'', and $\bar{a}$, respectively. Let P' be the set of all random-context productions defined as

1. for every $a \in V$, add $(a' \rightarrow a'', \emptyset, \bar{V} \cup V^{(1)} \cup V^{(2)} \cup \ldots \cup V^{(t)})$ to P';

2. for every $a \in V$ for all $1 \leq i \leq t$, add $(a'' \rightarrow a^{(i)}, \emptyset, \bar{V} \cup V' \cup V^{(1)} \cup V^{(2)} \cup \ldots \cup V^{(i-1)} \cup V^{(i+1)} \cup \ldots \cup V^{(t)})$ to P';

3. for all $i \in \{1, \ldots, t\}$ for every $a \rightarrow u \in P_i$, add $(a^{(i)} \rightarrow u', \emptyset, V'' \cup \bar{V})$ to P';

4. for all $a \in T$, add $(a' \rightarrow \bar{a}, \emptyset, V'' \cup V^{(1)} \cup V^{(2)} \cup \ldots \cup V^{(t)})$ to P';

5. for all $a \in T$, add $(\bar{a} \rightarrow a, \emptyset, V' \cup V'' \cup V^{(1)} \cup V^{(2)} \cup \ldots \cup V^{(t)})$ to P'.

Then, define the random-context grammar

$$G' = (V' \cup V'' \cup \bar{V} \cup V^{(1)} \cup V^{(2)} \cup \ldots \cup V^{(t)}, T, P', S'),$$

which has only forbidding context conditions.

Let x' be a string over V'. To x' we can apply only productions whose left-hand side is in V'.

(i) We use $a' \to a''$ for some $a' \in V'$. Now the obtained sentential form contains symbols of V' and V''. Hence we can use only productions of type (1). Continuing in this way we get $x' \Rightarrow^*_{G'} x''$. By analogous arguments we now have to rewrite all symbols of x'' by productions of (2) with the same index (i). Thus, we obtain $x^{(i)}$. Now to each symbol $a^{(i)}$ of $x^{(i)}$ we apply a production $a^{(i)} \to u'$, where $a \to u \in P_i$. Since again all symbols of $x^{(i)}$ have to be replaced before starting with productions of another type, we simulate a derivation step in G and get z', where $x \Rightarrow_G z$ in G. Therefore, starting with a production of (1), we simulate a derivation step in G, and conversely, each derivation step in G can be simulated in this way.

(ii) We apply to x' a production $a' \to \bar{a}$. Next, each a' of T' occurring in x' has to be substituted by $\bar{a}$ and then by a using the productions of (5). Therefore, we obtain a terminal word only if $x' \in (T')^*$.

By these considerations the successful derivations in G' are of the form

$$
\begin{aligned}
S' &\Rightarrow_{G'} S'' \Rightarrow_{G'} S^{(i_0)} \\
&\Rightarrow_{G'} z_1' \Rightarrow^*_{G'} z_1'' \Rightarrow^*_{G'} z_1^{(i_1)} \\
&\quad\vdots \\
&\Rightarrow^*_{G'} z_n' \Rightarrow^*_{G'} z_n'' \Rightarrow^*_{G'} z_n^{(i_n)} \\
&\Rightarrow^*_{G'} z_{n+1} \Rightarrow^*_{G'} \bar{z}_{n+1} \Rightarrow^*_{G'} z_{n+1}
\end{aligned}
$$

and such a derivation exists if and only if

$$
S \Rightarrow_G z_1 \Rightarrow_G z_2 \Rightarrow_G \cdots \Rightarrow_G z_n \Rightarrow_G z_{n+1}
$$

is a successful derivation in G. In conclusion, $L(G) = L(G')$.

In order to finish the proof, it suffices to find a language that is not in **ETOL** and can be generated by a forbidding grammar. A language of this kind is

$$
L = \{b(ba^m)^n \; : \; m \geq n \geq 0\},
$$

which can be generated by the grammar

$$
G = (\{S, A, A', B, B', B'', C, D, E\}, \{a, b\}, P, s)
$$

with P consisting of the following productions:

$$
\begin{aligned}
&(S \to SA, \emptyset, \emptyset), \\
&(S \to C, \emptyset, \emptyset), \\
&(C \to D, \emptyset, \{S, A', B', B'', D, E\}), \\
&(B \to B'a, \emptyset, \{S, C, E\}), \\
&(A \to B''a, \emptyset, \{S, C, E, B''\}), \\
&(A \to A'a, \emptyset, \{S, C, E\}),
\end{aligned}
$$

$$(D \rightarrow C, \emptyset, \{A, B\}),$$
$$(B' \rightarrow B, \emptyset, \{D\}),$$
$$(B'' \rightarrow B, \emptyset, \{D\}),$$
$$(A' \rightarrow A, \emptyset, \{D\}),$$
$$(D \rightarrow E, \emptyset, \{S, A, A', B', B'', C, E\}),$$
$$(B \rightarrow b, \emptyset, \{S, A, A', B', B'', C, D\}),$$
$$(E \rightarrow b, \emptyset, \{S, A, A', B, B', B'', C, D\}).$$

First, we have the derivation

$$S \Rightarrow_G^* SA^n \Rightarrow_G CA^n \Rightarrow_G DA^n,$$

and then we have to replace all occurrences of A. If we want to replace an A by a terminal word in some steps, it is necessary to use $A \rightarrow B''a$. However, this can be done at most once in a phase that replaces all A. Therefore, $m \geq n$. □

Theorem 16. $\mathbf{CF} \subset \mathbf{ET0L} \subset \mathbf{prop\text{-}F} \subseteq \mathbf{F} \subset \mathbf{CS}$.

Proof. According to Example 2, we already have $\mathbf{CF} \subset \mathbf{prop\text{-}F}$. By [155] and Lemma 8, $\mathbf{CF} \subset \mathbf{ET0L} \subset \mathbf{prop\text{-}F}$. Moreover, in [148], Penttonen proved that $\mathbf{prop\text{-}F} \subseteq \mathbf{F} \subset \mathbf{CS}$. Therefore, the theorem holds. ■

The following corollary summarizes the relationships of language families generated by random-context grammars:

Corollary 7.
$$\mathbf{CF} \subset \mathbf{prop\text{-}RC} \subseteq \mathbf{prop\text{-}RC(ac)} \subset \mathbf{CS},$$

$$\mathbf{prop\text{-}RC} \subseteq \mathbf{RC} \subset \mathbf{RC(ac)} = \mathbf{RE},$$

$$\mathbf{CF} \subset \mathbf{ET0L} \subset \mathbf{prop\text{-}F} \subseteq \mathbf{F} \subset \mathbf{CS},$$

Open Problem. Consider the inclusions that are not proper in Corollary 7. Which of them are, in fact, identities?

4.1.3 Generalized Forbidding Grammars

Generalized forbidding grammars introduced by Meduna in [104] represent a generalized variant of forbidding grammars (see Section 4.1.2) in which forbidding context conditions are formed by finite languages.

Definition 13. Let $G = (V, T, P, S)$ be a context-conditional grammar. If every $(A \rightarrow x, Per, For)$ satisfies $Per = \emptyset$, then G is said to be a *generalized forbidding grammar* (a *gf*-grammar for short).

The following convention simplifies the notation of *gf*-grammars:

Convention 2. Let $G = (V, T, P, S)$ be a *gf*-grammar of degree (r, s). Since every $(A \to x, Per, For) \in P$ implies $Per = \emptyset$, we omit the empty set of permitting conditions. That is, we write $(A \to x, For)$ instead of $(A \to x, Per, For)$. For simplicity, we also say that G's degree is s instead of (r, s).

The families generated by *gf*-grammars and propagating *gf*-grammars of degree s are denoted by $\mathbf{GF}(s)$ and $\mathbf{prop\text{-}GF}(s)$, respectively. Furthermore,

$$\mathbf{GF} = \bigcup_{s=0}^{\infty} \mathbf{GF}(s)$$

and

$$\mathbf{prop\text{-}GF} = \bigcup_{s=0}^{\infty} \mathbf{prop\text{-}GF}(s).$$

By analogy with Theorem 11, it is easy to see that *gf*-grammars of degree 0 are ordinary context-free grammars:

Theorem 17. $\mathbf{prop\text{-}GF}(0) = \mathbf{GF}(0) = \mathbf{CF}$.

Futhermore, *gf*-grammars of degree 1 are as powerful as forbidding grammars:

Theorem 18. $\mathbf{GF}(1) = \mathbf{F}$.

Proof. This simple proof is left to the reader.   ∎

Theorem 19. $\mathbf{GF}(2) = \mathbf{RE}$.

Proof. It is straightforward to prove that $\mathbf{GF}(2) \subseteq \mathbf{RE}$; hence it suffices to prove the converse inclusion.

Let L be a recursively enumerable language. Without loss of generality we can assume that L is generated by a phrase-structure grammar,

$$G = (V, T, P, S),$$

of the Penttonen normal form (see Lemma 3) and let $N = V - T$.

Let @, \$, S' be new symbols and m be the cardinality of $V \cup \{@\}$. Clearly, $m \geq 1$. Furthermore, let f be an arbitrary fixed bijection from $V \cup \{@\}$ onto $\{1, \ldots, m\}$ and f^{-1} be the inverse of f.

The *gf*-grammar,

$$G' = (V' \cup \{@, \$, S'\}, T, P', S'),$$

of degree 2 is defined as follows:

$$
\begin{aligned}
V' &= W \cup V, \text{ where} \\
W &= \{[AB \to AC, j] : AB \to AC \in P, \ A, B, C \in N, 1 \leq j \leq m+1\},
\end{aligned}
$$

W, $\{@, \$, S'\}$, and V are pairwise disjoint alphabets. The set of productions P' is defined in the following way:

1. Add $(S' \rightarrow @S, \emptyset)$ to P'.

2. If $A \rightarrow x \in P$, $A \in N$, $x \in \{\varepsilon\} \cup T \cup N^2$, then add $(A \rightarrow x, \{\$\})$ to P'.

3. If $AB \rightarrow AC \in P$, $A, B, C \in N$, then:

   (a) add $(B \rightarrow \$[AB \rightarrow AC, 1], \{\$\})$ to P';

   (b) for all $j = 1, \ldots, m$, $f(A) \neq j$, add $([AB \rightarrow AC, j] \rightarrow [AB \rightarrow AC, j + 1], \{f^{-1}(j)\$\})$ to P';

   (c) add $([AB \rightarrow AC, f(A)] \rightarrow [AB \rightarrow AC, f(A) + 1], \emptyset)$ and $([AB \rightarrow AC, m + 1] \rightarrow C, \emptyset)$ to P'.

4. Add the following two productions $(@ \rightarrow \varepsilon, N \cup W \cup \{\$\})$ and $(\$ \rightarrow \varepsilon, W)$ to P'.

Basic Idea. Basically, the application of $AB \rightarrow AC$ in G is simulated in G' as follows: An occurrence of B is rewritten with $\$[AB \rightarrow AC, 1]$. Then, the left adjoining symbol of $\$$ is checked not to be any symbol from $(V \cup \{@\})$ except A. After this, the right adjoining symbol of $\$$ is $[AB \rightarrow AC, m + 1]$. This symbol is rewritten with C. Formal proof is given below.

Immediately from the definition of P' it follows:

$$S' \Rightarrow_{G'}^{+} x,$$

where $x \in (V' \cup \{@, S'\})^*$, implies

(I) $S' \notin \mathrm{sub}(x)$;

(II) $\#_{(\mathrm{sub}(\{\$\}W)-\{\varepsilon\})} x \leq 1$ such that if $\#_W x = 1$, then $\#_{\{\$\}W} x = 1$;

(III) if $x \notin T^*$, then the left-most symbol of x is $@$.

Next, we define a finite letter-to-letters substitution g from V^* into $(V')^*$ such that for all $B \in V$,

$$g(B) = \{B\} \cup \{[AB \rightarrow AC, j] \in W : AB \rightarrow AC \in P, A, C \in N, j = 1, \ldots, m+1\}.$$

Let g^{-1} be the inverse of g.

To show that $L(G) = L(G')$, we first prove that

$$S \Rightarrow_G^n x \quad \text{if and only if} \quad S \Rightarrow_{G'}^{n'} x',$$

where $x' = @v'Xw'$, $X \in \{\$, \varepsilon\}$, $v'w' \in g(x)$, $x \in V^*$, for some $n \geq 0$, $n' \geq 1$.

Only if: This is established by induction on the length n of derivations; that is, we have to demonstrate that $S \Rightarrow_G^n x$, $x \in V^*$, $n \geq 0$, implies $S \Rightarrow_{G'}^{+} x'$ for some x' such that $x' = @v'Xw'$, $X \in \{\$, \varepsilon\}$, $v'w' \in g(x)$.

Basis: Let $n = 0$. The only x is S because $S \Rightarrow_G^0 S$. Clearly, $S' \Rightarrow_{G'} @S$ and $S \in g(S)$.

Induction Hypothesis: Suppose that our claim holds for all derivations of length at most n, for some $n \geq 0$.

Induction Step: Let us consider a derivation

$$S \Rightarrow_G^{n+1} x,$$

$x \in V^*$. Since $n + 1 \geq 1$, there is some $y \in V^+$ and $p \in P$ such that

$$S \Rightarrow_G^n y \Rightarrow_G x \; [p],$$

and by the induction hypothesis, there is also a derivation

$$S \Rightarrow_{G'}^{n'} y',$$

for some $n' \geq 1$, such that $y' = @r'Ys'$, $Y \in \{\$, \varepsilon\}$, and $r's' \in g(y)$.

(i) Let us assume that $p = D \to y_2 \in P$, $D \in N$, $y_2 \in \{\varepsilon\} \cup T \cup N^2$, $y = y_1 D y_3$, $y_1, y_3 \in V^*$, $x = y_1 y_2 y_3$. From (2) it is clear that $(D \to y_2, \{\$\}) \in P'$.

  (a) Let $\$ \notin \text{alph}(y')$. Then, we have $y' = @r's' = @y_1 D y_3$,

  $$S' \Rightarrow_{G'}^{n'} @y_1 D y_3 \Rightarrow_{G'} @y_1 y_2 y_3 \; [(D \to y_2, \{\$\})],$$

  and $y_1 y_2 y_3 \in g(y_1 y_2 y_3) = g(x)$.

  (b) Let $Y = \$ \in \text{sub}(y')$ and $W \cap \text{sub}(y') = \emptyset$. Then, there is the following derivation in G':

  $$S' \Rightarrow_{G'}^{n'} @r'\$s' \Rightarrow_{G'} @r's' \; [(\$ \to \varepsilon, W)].$$

  By analogy with (a) above, we have $@r's' = @y_1 D y_2$ and so

  $$S' \Rightarrow_{G'}^{n'+1} @y_1 D y_3 \Rightarrow_{G'} @y_1 y_2 y_3 \; [(D \to y_2, \{\$\})],$$

  where $y_1 y_2 y_3 \in g(x)$.

  (c) Let $\$[AB \to AC, i] \in \text{sub}(y')$ for some $i \in \{1, \ldots, m+1\}$, $AB \to AC \in P$, $A, B, C \in N$. Thus, $y' = @r'\$[AB \to AC, i]t'$, where $s' = [AB \to AC, i]t'$. By inspection of the productions (see (3)) it can be seen (and the reader should be able to produce a formal proof) that we can express the derivation

  $$S' \Rightarrow_{G'}^* y'$$

  in the following form:

$$
\begin{aligned}
S' \quad & \Rightarrow_{G'}^* \quad @r'Bt' \\
& \Rightarrow_{G'} \quad @r'\$[AB \to AC, 1]t' \; [(B \to \$[AB \to AC, 1], \{\$\})] \\
& \Rightarrow_{G'}^{i-1} \quad @r'\$[AB \to AC, i]t'.
\end{aligned}
$$

Clearly, $r'Bt' \in g(y)$ and $\$ \notin sub(r'Bt')$. Thus, $r'Bt' = y_1 D y_3$, and there is a derivation

$$S' \Rightarrow^*_{G'} @y_1 D y_3 \Rightarrow_{G'} @y_1 y_2 y_3 \ [(D \to y_2, \{\$\})]$$

and $y_1 y_2 y_3 \in g(x)$.

(ii) Let $p = AB \to AC \in P$, $A, B, C \in N$, $y = y_1 A B y_2$, $y_1, y_2 \in V^*$, $x = y_1 A C y_2$.

   (a) Let $\$ \notin sub(y')$. Thus, $r's' = y_1 A B y_2$. By inspection of the productions introduced in (3) (technical details are left to the reader), there is the following derivation in G':

$$
\begin{aligned}
S' \quad &\Rightarrow^{n'}_{G'} \quad y_1 A B y_2 \\
&\Rightarrow_{G'} \quad @y_1 A \$[AB \to AC, 1] y_2 \\
&\qquad [(B \to \$[AB \to AC, 1], \{\$\})] \\
&\Rightarrow_{G'} \quad @y_1 A \$[AB \to AC, 2] y_2 \\
&\qquad [([AB \to AC, 1] \to [AB \to AC, 2], \{f^{-1}(1)\$\})] \\
&\ \ \vdots \\
&\Rightarrow_{G'} \quad @y_1 A \$[AB \to AC, f(A)] y_2 \\
&\qquad [([AB \to AC, f(A) - 1] \to [AB \to AC, f(A)], \\
&\qquad\quad \{f^{-1}(f(A) - 1)\$\})] \\
&\Rightarrow_{G'} \quad @y_1 A \$[AB \to AC, f(A) + 1] y_2 \\
&\qquad [([AB \to AC, f(A)] \to [AB \to AC, f(A) + 1], \emptyset)] \\
&\ \ \vdots \\
&\Rightarrow_{G'} \quad @y_1 A \$[AB \to AC, m + 1] y_2 \\
&\qquad [([AB \to AC, m] \to [AB \to AC, m + 1], \{f^{-1}(m)\$\})] \\
&\Rightarrow_{G'} \quad @y_1 A \$ C y_2 \\
&\qquad [([AB \to AC, m + 1] \to C, \emptyset)]
\end{aligned}
$$

such that $y_1 A C y_2 \in g(y_1 A C y_2) = g(x)$.

   (b) Let $\$ \in sub(y')$, $sub(y') \cap W = \emptyset$. Using an analogue from (i.b), the derivation

$$S' \Rightarrow^*_{G'} @r's',$$

where $@r's' = @y_1 A B y_2$, can be constructed in G'. Then, by analogy with (ii.a), one can construct the derivation

$$S' \Rightarrow^*_{G'} @y_1 A B y_2 \Rightarrow^*_{G'} @y_1 A \$ C y_2$$

such that $y_1 A C y_2 \in g(x)$.

   (c) Let $\#_{(\{\$\}W - \{\varepsilon\})} y' = 1$. By analogy with (i.c), one can construct the derivation

$$S' \Rightarrow^*_{G'} @y_1 A B y_2.$$

Next, using an analogue from (ii.a), the derivation

$$S' \Rightarrow^*_{G'} @y_1 A B y_2 \Rightarrow^*_{G'} @y_1 A \$ C y_2$$

can be constructed in G' such that $y_1 A C y_2 \in g(x)$.

In (i) and (ii) above we have considered all possible forms of p. In cases (a), (b), (c) of (i) and (ii), we have considered all possible forms of y'. In any of these cases we have constructed the desired derivation of the form

$$S' \Rightarrow^+_{G'} x'$$

such that $x' = @r'Xs'$, $X \in \{\$, \varepsilon\}$, $r's' \in g(x)$. So, we have established the only-if part of our claim by the principle of induction.

If: This is also demonstrated by induction but in this case on n'. We have to demonstrate that if $S' \Rightarrow^{n'}_{G'} x'$, $x' = @r'Xs'$, $X \in \{\$, \varepsilon\}$, $r's' \in g(x)$, $x \in V^*$, for some $n' \geq 1$, then $S \Rightarrow^*_G x$.

Basis: For $n' = 1$ the only x' is $@S$ since $S' \Rightarrow_{G'} @S$. Because $S \in g(S)$, we have $x = S$. Clearly, $S \Rightarrow^0_G S$.

Induction Hypothesis: Assume that the claim holds for all derivations of length at most n' for some $n' \geq 1$. Let us show that it is also true for $n' + 1$.

Induction Step: Consider a derivation

$$S' \Rightarrow^{n'+1}_{G'} x',$$

$x' = @r'Xs'$, $X \in \{\$, \varepsilon\}$, $r's' \in g(x)$, $x \in V^*$. Since $n' + 1 \geq 2$, we have

$$S' \Rightarrow^{n'}_{G'} y' \Rightarrow_{G'} x' \; [p']$$

for some $p' = (Z' \to w', For) \in P'$, $y' = @q'Yt'$, $Y \in \{\$, \varepsilon\}$, $q't' \in g(y)$, $y \in V^*$, and by the induction hypothesis,

$$S \Rightarrow^*_G y.$$

Suppose:

(i) $Z' \in N$, $w' \in \{\varepsilon\} \cup T \cup N^2$. Inspecting P' (see (2)) we have $For = \{\$\}$ and $Z' \to w' \in P$. Thus, $\$ \notin sub(y')$ and so $q't' = y$. Hence, there is the following derivation

$$S \Rightarrow^*_G y \Rightarrow_G x \; [Z' \to w'].$$

(ii) $g^{-1}(Z') = g^{-1}(w')$. But then $y = x$, and by the induction hypothesis, we have the derivation

$$S \Rightarrow^*_G y.$$

(iii) $p' = (B \rightarrow \$[AB \rightarrow AC, 1], \{\$\})$; that is, $Z' = B$, $w' = \$[AB \rightarrow AC, 1]$, $For = \{\$\}$ and so $w' \in \{\$\}g(Z')$, $Y = \varepsilon$, $X = \$$. By analogy with (ii) we get

$$S \Rightarrow_G^* y$$

and $y = x$.

(iv) $Z' = Y = \$$; that is, $p' = (\$ \rightarrow \varepsilon, W)$. Then, $X = \varepsilon$, $r's' = q't' \in g(y)$, and

$$S \Rightarrow_G^* y.$$

(v) $p' = ([AB \rightarrow AC, m + 1] \rightarrow C, \emptyset)$; that is, $Z' = [AB \rightarrow AC, m + 1]$, $w' = C$, $For = \emptyset$. From (3) it follows that there is a production of the form $AB \rightarrow AC \in P$. Moreover, on inspecting (3), it is not too difficult to see (technical details are left to the reader) that $Y = \$$, $r' = q'$, $t' = [AB \rightarrow AC, m + 1]o'$, $s' = Co'$, and the derivation

$$S' \Rightarrow_{G'}^{n'} y' \Rightarrow_{G'} x' \ [p']$$

can be expressed in the form

$$
\begin{aligned}
S' \quad &\Rightarrow_{G'}^* \quad @q'Bo' \\
&\Rightarrow_{G'} \quad @q'\$[AB \rightarrow AC, 1]o' \qquad [(B \rightarrow \$[AB \rightarrow AC, 1], \{\$\})] \\
&\Rightarrow_{G'}^{m+1} \quad @q'\$[AB \rightarrow AC, m + 1]o' \quad [h] \\
&\Rightarrow_{G'} \quad @q'\$Co' \qquad\qquad\qquad\quad [([AB \rightarrow AC, m + 1] \rightarrow C, \emptyset)],
\end{aligned}
$$

where

$$
\begin{aligned}
h &= h_1([AB \rightarrow AC, f(A)] \rightarrow [AB \rightarrow AC, f(A) + 1], \emptyset)h_2, \\
h_1 &= ([AB \rightarrow AC, 1] \rightarrow [AB \rightarrow AC, 2], \{f^{-1}(1)\$\}) \\
&\quad ([AB \rightarrow AC, 2] \rightarrow [AB \rightarrow AC, 3], \{f^{-1}(2)\$\}) \\
&\qquad\qquad \vdots \\
&\quad ([AB \rightarrow AC, f(A) - 1] \rightarrow [AB \rightarrow AC, f(A)], \{f^{-1}(f(A) - 1)\$\}),
\end{aligned}
$$

where $f(A) = 1$ implies $h_1 = \varepsilon$,

$$
\begin{aligned}
h_2 &= ([AB \rightarrow AC, f(A) + 1] \rightarrow [AB \rightarrow AC, f(A) + 2], \{f^{-1}(f(A) + 1)\$\}) \\
&\qquad\qquad \vdots \\
&\quad ([AB \rightarrow AC, m] \rightarrow [AB \rightarrow AC, m + 1], \{f^{-1}(m)\$\}),
\end{aligned}
$$

where $f(A) = m$ implies $h_2 = \varepsilon$; that is, the right-most symbol of $q' = r'$ must be A.

Since $q't' \in g(y)$, we have $y = q'Bo'$. Because the right-most symbol of q' is A and $AB \rightarrow AC \in P$, we get

$$S \Rightarrow_G^* q'Bo' \Rightarrow_G q'Co' \ [AB \rightarrow AC],$$

where $q'Co' = x$.

Now, regarding (i) through (v) and inspecting P', we have considered all possible derivations of the form

$$S' \Rightarrow_{G'}^{n'} y' \Rightarrow_{G'} x',$$

and thus we have established that

$$S \Rightarrow_G^* x \quad \text{if and only if} \quad S' \Rightarrow_{G'}^+ x',$$

where $x' = @r'Xs'$, $r's' \in g(x)$, $X \in \{\$, \varepsilon\}$, $x \in V^*$, by the principle of induction.

The proof of the equivalence of G and G' can easily be derived from above. By the definition of g, we have $g(a) = \{a\}$ for all $a \in T$. Thus, we have for any $x \in T^*$,

$$S \Rightarrow_G^* x \quad \text{if and only if} \quad S' \Rightarrow_{G'}^* @rXs,$$

where $X \in \{\$, \varepsilon\}$, $rs = x$. If $X = \varepsilon$, then

$$@x \Rightarrow_{G'} x \; [(@ \to \varepsilon, N \cup W \cup \{\$\})].$$

If $X = \$$, then

$$@r\$s \Rightarrow_{G'} @x \; [(\$ \to \varepsilon, W)] \Rightarrow_{G'} x \; [(@ \to \varepsilon, N \cup W \cup \{\$\})].$$

Hence,

$$S \Rightarrow_G^+ x \quad \text{if and only if} \quad S' \Rightarrow_{G'}^+ x$$

for all $x \in T^*$, and so $L(G) = L(G')$. Thus, $\mathbf{RE} = \mathbf{GF}(2)$. ∎

Theorem 20. $\mathbf{GF}(2) = \mathbf{GF} = \mathbf{RE}$.

Proof. It follows immediately from the definitions and Theorem 19. ∎

Note that in G' in the proof of Theorem 19 only certain types of productions are used, establishing the following normal form:

Corollary 8. *Every recursively enumerable language L over some alphabet T can be generated by a gf-grammar $G = (V, T, P \cup \{p_1, p_2\}, S)$ of degree 2 such that*

(i) $(A \to x, For) \in P$ implies $|x| = 2$ and the cardinality of For is at most 1;

(ii) $p_i = (A_i \to \varepsilon, For_i)$, $i = 1, 2$, where $For_i \subseteq V$; that is, $\max(For_i) \leq 1$.

In fact, the corollary above represents one of the reduced forms of *gf*-grammars of degree 2. Perhaps most important, it reduces the cardinality of the sets of forbidding conditions so that if a production contains a condition of length two, this condition is the only context condition attached to the production. Next, we study another reduced form of *gf*-grammars of degree 2. We show that we can simultaneously reduce the number of conditional productions and the number of nonterminals in *gf*-grammars of degree 2 without any decrease of their generative power (see [136]).

Theorem 21. *Every recursively enumerable language can be defined by a generalized forbidding grammar of degree 2 with no more than 13 forbidding productions and 15 nonterminals.*

Proof. Let L be a recursively enumerable language. By Geffert [69], without loss of generality we can assume that L is generated by a grammar G of the form

$$G = (V, T, P \cup \{AB \to \varepsilon, CD \to \varepsilon\}, S)$$

such that P contains only context-free productions and

$$V - T = \{S, A, B, C, D\}.$$

We construct a *gf*-grammar G' of degree 2 as follows:

$$\begin{aligned}
&G' = (V', T, P', S'), \quad \text{where} \\
&V' = V \cup W, \\
&W = \{S', @, \widetilde{A}, \widetilde{B}, \langle \varepsilon_A \rangle, \$, \widetilde{C}, \widetilde{D}, \langle \varepsilon_C \rangle, \#\}, \ V \cap W = \emptyset.
\end{aligned}$$

Let

$$N' = (V' - T) - \{S', @\}.$$

Informally, N' denotes the set of all nonterminals in G' except S' and $@$. Then, the set of productions P' is defined in the following way:

1. If $H \to y \in P$, $H \in V - T$, $y \in V^*$, then add $(H \to y, \emptyset)$ to P'.

2. Add $(S' \to @S@, \emptyset)$ and $(@ \to \varepsilon, N')$ to P'.

3. Add
$$\begin{aligned}
&(A \to \widetilde{A}, \{\widetilde{A}\}), \\
&(B \to \widetilde{B}, \{\widetilde{B}\}), \\
&(\widetilde{A} \to \langle \varepsilon_A \rangle, \{\widetilde{A}a : \ a \in V' - \{\widetilde{B}\}\}), \\
&(\widetilde{B} \to \$, \{a\widetilde{B} : \ a \in V' - \{\langle \varepsilon_A \rangle\}\}), \\
&(\langle \varepsilon_A \rangle \to \varepsilon, \{\widetilde{B}\}), \\
&(\$ \to \varepsilon, \{\langle \varepsilon_A \rangle\})
\end{aligned}$$
   to P'.

4. Add
$$\begin{aligned}
&(C \to \widetilde{C}, \{\widetilde{C}\}), \\
&(D \to \widetilde{D}, \{\widetilde{D}\}), \\
&(\widetilde{C} \to \langle \varepsilon_C \rangle, \{\widetilde{C}a : \ a \in V' - \{\widetilde{D}\}\}), \\
&(\widetilde{D} \to \#, \{a\widetilde{D} : \ a \in V' - \{\langle \varepsilon_C \rangle\}\}), \\
&(\langle \varepsilon_C \rangle \to \varepsilon, \{\widetilde{D}\}), \\
&(\# \to \varepsilon, \{\langle \varepsilon_C \rangle\})
\end{aligned}$$
   to P'.

Next, we prove that $L(G') = L(G)$.

Basic Idea. Notice that G' has degree 2 and contains only 13 forbidding productions and 15 nonterminals. The productions of (3) simulate the application of $AB \to \varepsilon$ in G' and the productions of (4) simulate the application of $CD \to \varepsilon$ in G'.

Let us describe the simulation of $AB \to \varepsilon$. First, one occurrence of A and one occurrence of B are rewritten with $\widetilde{A}$ and $\widetilde{B}$, respectively (no sentential form contains more than one occurrence of $\widetilde{A}$ or $\widetilde{B}$). The right neighbor of $\widetilde{A}$ is checked to be $\widetilde{B}$ and $\widetilde{A}$ is rewritten with $\langle \varepsilon_A \rangle$. Then, analogously, the left neighbor of $\widetilde{B}$ is checked to be $\langle \varepsilon_A \rangle$ and $\widetilde{B}$ is rewritten with \$. Finally, $\langle \varepsilon_A \rangle$ and \$ are erased. The simulation of $CD \to \varepsilon$ is analogical.

To establish $L(G) = L(G')$, we first prove the following claims:

Claim 9. $S' \Rightarrow_{G'}^+ w'$ *implies that w' has one of the following two forms:*

(I) $w' = @x'@$, $x' \in (N' \cup T)^*$, $\mathrm{alph}(x') \cap N' \neq \emptyset$;

(II) $w' = Xx'Y$, $x' \in T^*$, $X, Y \in \{@, \varepsilon\}$.

Proof. Axiom S' is always rewritten with $@S@$. After this initial step, $@$ can be erased in a sentential form provided that any nonterminal occurring in the sentential form belongs to $\{@, S'\}$ (see N' and (2) in the definition of P'). In addition, notice that only productions of (2) contain $@$ and S'. Thus, any sentential form containing some nonterminals from N' is of the form (I).

Case (II) covers sentential forms containing no nonterminal from N'. At this point, $@$ can be erased, and we obtain a word from $L(G')$. □

Claim 10. $S' \Rightarrow_{G'}^* w'$ *implies* $\#_{\widetilde{X}} w' \leq 1$ *for all* $\widetilde{X} \in \{\widetilde{A}, \widetilde{B}, \widetilde{C}, \widetilde{D}\}$ *and some* $w' \in (V')^*$.

Proof. By inspection of productions in P', the only production that can generate $\widetilde{X}$ is of the form $(X \to \widetilde{X}, \{\widetilde{X}\})$. This production can be applied only when no $\widetilde{X}$ occurs in the rewritten sentential form. Thus, it is impossible to derive w' from S' such that $\#_{\widetilde{X}} w' \geq 2$. □

Informally, next claim says that every occurrence of $\langle \varepsilon_A \rangle$ in derivations from S' is always followed either by $\widetilde{B}$ or \$, and every occurrence of $\langle \varepsilon_C \rangle$ is always followed either by $\widetilde{D}$ or \#.

Claim 11. *It holds that*

(I) $S' \Rightarrow_{G'}^* y_1' \langle \varepsilon_A \rangle y_2'$ *implies* $y_2' \in (V')^+$ *and* $\mathrm{first}(y_2') \in \{\widetilde{B}, \$\}$ *for any* $y_1' \in (V')^*$;

(II) $S' \Rightarrow_{G'}^* y_1' \langle \varepsilon_C \rangle y_2'$ *implies* $y_2' \in (V')^+$ *and* $\mathrm{first}(y_2') \in \{\widetilde{D}, \#\}$ *for any* $y_1' \in (V')^*$.

Proof. We establish the proof by examination of all possible forms of derivations that may occur when deriving a sentential form containing $\langle \varepsilon_A \rangle$ or $\langle \varepsilon_C \rangle$.

(I) By the definition of P', the only production that can generate $\langle\varepsilon_A\rangle$ is $p = (\widetilde{A} \to \langle\varepsilon_A\rangle, \{\widetilde{A}a : a \in V' - \{\widetilde{B}\}\})$. The production can be used provided that $\widetilde{A}$ occurs in a sentential form. It also holds that $\widetilde{A}$ has always a right neighbor (as follows from Claim 9), and according to the set of forbidding conditions in p, the only allowed right neighbor of $\widetilde{A}$ is $\widetilde{B}$. Furthermore, by Claim 10, no other occurrence of $\widetilde{A}$ or $\widetilde{B}$ can appear in the given sentential form. Consequently, we obtain a derivation

$$S' \Rightarrow^*_{G'} u'_1 \widetilde{A}\widetilde{B}u'_2 \Rightarrow_{G'} u'_1 \langle\varepsilon_A\rangle\widetilde{B}u'_2 \ [p]$$

for some $u'_1, u'_2 \in (V')^*$, $\widetilde{A}, \widetilde{B} \notin \mathrm{sub}(u'_1 u'_2)$. Obviously, $\langle\varepsilon_A\rangle$ is always followed by $\widetilde{B}$ in $u'_1 \langle\varepsilon_A\rangle\widetilde{B}u'_2$.

Next, we discuss how G' can rewrite the subword $\langle\varepsilon_A\rangle\widetilde{B}$ in $u'_1 \langle\varepsilon_A\rangle\widetilde{B}u'_2$. There are only two productions having the nonterminals $\langle\varepsilon_A\rangle$ or $\widetilde{B}$ on their left-hand side, $p_1 = (\widetilde{B} \to \$, \{a\widetilde{B} : a \in V' - \{\langle\varepsilon_A\rangle\}\})$ and $p_2 = (\langle\varepsilon_A\rangle \to \varepsilon, \{\widetilde{B}\})$. G' cannot use p_2 to erase $\langle\varepsilon_A\rangle$ in $u'_1 \langle\varepsilon_A\rangle\widetilde{B}u'_2$ because p_2 forbids an occurrence of $\widetilde{B}$ in the rewritten string. But we can use p_1 to rewrite $\widetilde{B}$ with $\$$ because its set of forbidding conditions defines that the left neighbor of $\widetilde{B}$ must be just $\langle\varepsilon_A\rangle$. Hence, we obtain a derivation of the form

$$\begin{aligned}
S' \quad &\Rightarrow^*_{G'} \quad u'_1 \widetilde{A}\widetilde{B}u'_2 \quad &&\Rightarrow_{G'} \quad u'_1 \langle\varepsilon_A\rangle\widetilde{B}u'_2 \quad &&[p]\\
&\Rightarrow^*_{G'} \quad v'_1 \langle\varepsilon_A\rangle\widetilde{B}v'_2 \quad &&\Rightarrow_{G'} \quad v'_1 \langle\varepsilon_A\rangle\$v'_2 \quad &&[p_1].
\end{aligned}$$

Notice that during this derivation, G' may rewrite u'_1 and u'_2 with some v'_1 and v'_2, respectively ($v'_1, v'_2 \in (V')^*$); however, $\langle\varepsilon_A\rangle\widetilde{B}$ remains unchanged after this rewriting.

In this derivation we obtained the second symbol $\$$, which can appear as the right neighbor of $\langle\varepsilon_A\rangle$. It suffices to show that there is no other symbol that can appear immediately after $\langle\varepsilon_A\rangle$. By inspection of P', only $(\$ \to \varepsilon, \{\langle\varepsilon_A\rangle\})$ can rewrite $\$$. However, this production cannot be applied when $\langle\varepsilon_A\rangle$ occurs in the given sentential form. In other words, the occurrence of $\$$ in the subword $\langle\varepsilon_A\rangle\$$ cannot be rewritten before $\langle\varepsilon_A\rangle$ is erased by p_2. Hence, $\langle\varepsilon_A\rangle$ is always followed either by $\widetilde{B}$ or $\$$, and thus the first part of Claim 11 holds.

(II) By inspection of productions simulating $AB \to \varepsilon$ and $CD \to \varepsilon$ in G' (see (3) and (4) in the definition of P'), these two sets of productions work analogously. Thus, part (II) of Claim 11 can be proved by analogy with part (I).

$\square$

Let us return to the main part of the proof. Let g be a finite substitution from $(N' \cup T)^*$ to V^* defined as follows:

1. For all $X \in V : g(X) = \{X\}$.

2. $g(\widetilde{A}) = \{A\}$, $g(\widetilde{B}) = \{B\}$, $g(\langle\varepsilon_A\rangle) = \{A\}$, $g(\$) = \{B, AB\}$.

3. $g(\widetilde{C}) = \{C\}$, $g(\widetilde{D}) = \{D\}$, $g(\langle \varepsilon_C \rangle) = \{C\}$, $g(\#) = \{C, CD\}$.

Having this substitution, we can now prove the following claim:

Claim 12. $S \Rightarrow_G^* x$ if and only if $S' \Rightarrow_{G'}^+ @x'@$ for some $x \in g(x')$, $x \in V^*$, $x' \in (N' \cup T)^*$.

Proof. The claim is proved by induction on the length of derivations.

Only if: We show that

$$S \Rightarrow_G^m x \quad \text{implies} \quad S' \Rightarrow_{G'}^+ @x@,$$

where $m \geq 0$, $x \in V^*$; clearly $x \in g(x)$. This is established by induction on m.

Basis: Let $m = 0$. That is, $S \Rightarrow_G^0 S$. Clearly, $S' \Rightarrow_{G'} @S@$.

Induction Hypothesis: Suppose that the claim holds for all derivations of length m or less, for some $m \geq 0$.

Induction Step: Let us consider a derivation

$$S \Rightarrow_G^{m+1} x, \ x \in V^*.$$

Since $m + 1 \geq 1$, there is some $y \in V^+$ and $p \in P \cup \{AB \to \varepsilon, CD \to \varepsilon\}$ such that

$$S \Rightarrow_G^m y \Rightarrow_G x \ [p].$$

By the induction hypothesis, there is a derivation

$$S' \Rightarrow_{G'}^+ @y@.$$

There are three cases that cover all possible forms of p:

(i) $p = H \to y_2 \in P$, $H \in V - T$, $y_2 \in V^*$. Then, $y = y_1 H y_3$ and $x = y_1 y_2 y_3$, $y_1, y_3 \in V^*$. Because we have $(H \to y_2, \emptyset) \in P'$,

$$S' \Rightarrow_{G'}^+ @y_1 H y_3@ \Rightarrow_{G'} @y_1 y_2 y_3@ \ [(H \to y_2, \emptyset)]$$

and $y_1 y_2 y_3 = x$.

(ii) $p = AB \to \varepsilon$. Then, $y = y_1 AB y_3$ and $x = y_1 y_3$, $y_1, y_3 \in V^*$. In this case, there is the following derivation:

$$
\begin{array}{lll}
S' & \Rightarrow_{G'}^+ & @y_1 AB y_3@ \\
   & \Rightarrow_{G'} & @y_1 \widetilde{A} B y_3@ & [(A \to \widetilde{A}, \{\widetilde{A}\})] \\
   & \Rightarrow_{G'} & @y_1 \widetilde{A} \widetilde{B} y_3@ & [(B \to \widetilde{B}, \{\widetilde{B}\})] \\
   & \Rightarrow_{G'} & @y_1 \langle \varepsilon_A \rangle \widetilde{B} y_3@ & [(\widetilde{A} \to \langle \varepsilon_A \rangle, \{\widetilde{A} a : \ a \in V' - \{\widetilde{B}\}\})] \\
   & \Rightarrow_{G'} & @y_1 \langle \varepsilon_A \rangle \$ y_3@ & [(\widetilde{B} \to \$, \{a \widetilde{B} : \ a \in V' - \{\langle \varepsilon_A \rangle\}\})] \\
   & \Rightarrow_{G'} & @y_1 \$ y_3@ & [(\langle \varepsilon_A \rangle \to \varepsilon, \{\widetilde{B}\})] \\
   & \Rightarrow_{G'} & @y_1 y_3@ & [(\$ \to \varepsilon, \{\langle \varepsilon_A \rangle\})].
\end{array}
$$

(iii) $p = CD \to \varepsilon$. Then, $y = y_1 CD y_3$ and $x = y_1 y_3$, $y_1, y_3 \in V^*$. In this case, there exists the following derivation:

$$
\begin{aligned}
S' &\Rightarrow_{G'}^{+} & @y_1 CD y_3 @ & \\
&\Rightarrow_{G'} & @y_1 \widetilde{C} D y_3 @ & \quad [(C \to \widetilde{C}, \{\widetilde{C}\})] \\
&\Rightarrow_{G'} & @y_1 \widetilde{C} \widetilde{D} y_3 @ & \quad [(D \to \widetilde{D}, \{\widetilde{D}\})] \\
&\Rightarrow_{G'} & @y_1 \langle \varepsilon_C \rangle \widetilde{D} y_3 @ & \quad [(\widetilde{C} \to \langle \varepsilon_C \rangle, \{\widetilde{C} a : a \in V' - \{\widetilde{D}\}\})] \\
&\Rightarrow_{G'} & @y_1 \langle \varepsilon_C \rangle \# y_3 @ & \quad [(\widetilde{D} \to \#, \{a\widetilde{D} : a \in V' - \{\langle \varepsilon_C \rangle\}\})] \\
&\Rightarrow_{G'} & @y_1 \# y_3 @ & \quad [(\langle \varepsilon_C \rangle \to \varepsilon, \{\widetilde{D}\})] \\
&\Rightarrow_{G'} & @y_1 y_3 @ & \quad [(\# \to \varepsilon, \{\langle \varepsilon_C \rangle\})].
\end{aligned}
$$

If: By induction on the length n of derivations in G', we prove that

$$ S' \Rightarrow_{G'}^{n} @x'@ \quad \text{implies} \quad S \Rightarrow_{G}^{*} x $$

for some $x \in g(x')$, $x \in V^*$, $x' \in (N' \cup T)^*$, $n \geq 1$.

Basis: Let $n = 1$. According to the definition of P', the only production rewriting S' is $(S' \to @S@, \emptyset)$, and thus $S' \Rightarrow_{G'} @S@$. It is obvious that $S \Rightarrow_{G}^{0} S$ and $S \in g(S)$.

Induction Hypothesis: Assume that the claim holds for all derivations of length n or less, for some $n \geq 1$.

Induction Step: Consider a derivation

$$ S' \Rightarrow_{G'}^{n+1} @x'@, \; x' \in (N' \cup T)^*. $$

Since $n + 1 \geq 2$, there is some $y' \in (N' \cup T)^+$ and $p' \in P'$ such that

$$ S' \Rightarrow_{G'}^{n} @y'@ \Rightarrow_{G'} @x'@ \; [p'], $$

and by the induction hypothesis, there is also a derivation

$$ S \Rightarrow_{G}^{*} y $$

such that $y \in g(y')$.

By inspection of P', the following cases (i) through (xiii) cover all possible forms of p':

(i) $p' = (H \to y_2, \emptyset) \in P'$, $H \in V - T$, $y_2 \in V^*$. Then, $y' = y_1' H y_3'$, $x' = y_1' y_2 y_3'$, $y_1', y_3' \in (N' \cup T)^*$, and y has the form $y = y_1 Z y_3$, where $y_1 \in g(y_1')$, $y_3 \in g(y_3')$, and $Z \in g(H)$. Because for all $X \in V - T$: $g(X) = \{X\}$, the only Z is H; thus, $y = y_1 H y_3$. By the definition of P' (see (1)), there exists a production $p = H \to y_2$ in P, and we can construct the derivation

$$ S \Rightarrow_{G}^{*} y_1 H y_3 \Rightarrow_{G} y_1 y_2 y_3 \; [p] $$

such that $y_1 y_2 y_3 = x$, $x \in g(x')$.

(ii) $p' = (A \to \widetilde{A}, \{\widetilde{A}\})$. Then, $y' = y_1' A y_3'$, $x' = y_1' \widetilde{A} y_3'$, $y_1', y_3' \in (N' \cup T)^*$ and $y = y_1 Z y_3$, where $y_1 \in g(y_1')$, $y_3 \in g(y_3')$ and $Z \in g(A)$. Because $g(A) = \{A\}$, the only Z is A, so we can express $y = y_1 A y_3$. Having the derivation $S \Rightarrow_G^* y$ such that $y \in g(y')$, it is easy to see that also $y \in g(x')$ because $A \in g(\widetilde{A})$.

(iii) $p' = (B \to \widetilde{B}, \{\widetilde{B}\})$. By analogy with (ii), $y' = y_1' B y_3'$, $x' = y_1' \widetilde{B} y_3'$, $y = y_1 B y_3$, where $y_1', y_3' \in (N' \cup T)^*$, $y_1 \in g(y_1')$, $y_3 \in g(y_3')$; thus, $y \in g(x')$ because $B \in g(\widetilde{B})$.

(iv) $p' = (\widetilde{A} \to \langle \varepsilon_A \rangle, \{\widetilde{A}a : a \in V' - \{\widetilde{B}\}\})$. In this case, it holds that:

    (a) application of p' implies $\widetilde{A} \in \mathrm{alph}(y')$, and moreover, by Claim 10, $\#_{\widetilde{A}} y' \le 1$;

    (b) $\widetilde{A}$ has always a right neighbor in $@y'@$;

    (c) according to the set of forbidding conditions in p', the only allowed right neighbor of $\widetilde{A}$ is $\widetilde{B}$.

Hence, y' must be of the form $y' = y_1' \widetilde{A} \widetilde{B} y_3'$, where $y_1', y_3' \in (N' \cup T)^*$ and $\widetilde{A} \notin \mathrm{sub}(y_1' y_3')$. Then, $x' = y_1' \langle \varepsilon_A \rangle \widetilde{B} y_3'$ and y is of the form $y = y_1 Z y_3$, where $y_1 \in g(y_1')$, $y_3 \in g(y_3')$ and $Z \in g(\widetilde{A}\widetilde{B})$. Because $g(\widetilde{A}\widetilde{B}) = \{AB\}$, the only Z is AB; thus, we obtain $y = y_1 A B y_3$. By the induction hypothesis, we have a derivation $S \Rightarrow_G^* y$ such that $y \in g(y')$. According to the definition of g, $y \in g(x')$ as well because $A \in g(\langle \varepsilon_A \rangle)$ and $B \in g(\widetilde{B})$.

(v) $p' = (\widetilde{B} \to \$, \{a\widetilde{B} : a \in V' - \{\langle \varepsilon_A \rangle\}\})$. Then, it holds that:

    (a) $\widetilde{B} \in \mathrm{alph}(y')$ and, by Claim 10, $\#_{\widetilde{B}} y' \le 1$;

    (b) $\widetilde{B}$ has always a left neighbor in $@y'@$;

    (c) by the set of forbidding conditions in p', the only allowed left neighbor of $\widetilde{B}$ is $\langle \varepsilon_A \rangle$.

Therefore, we can express $y' = y_1' \langle \varepsilon_A \rangle \widetilde{B} y_3'$, where $y_1', y_3' \in (N' \cup T)^*$ and $\widetilde{B} \notin \mathrm{sub}(y_1' y_3')$. Then, $x' = y_1' \langle \varepsilon_A \rangle \$ y_3'$ and $y = y_1 Z y_3$, where $y_1 \in g(y_1')$, $y_3 \in g(y_3')$, and $Z \in g(\langle \varepsilon_A \rangle \widetilde{B})$. By the definition of g, $g(\langle \varepsilon_A \rangle \widetilde{B}) = \{AB\}$, so $Z = AB$ and $y = y_1 A B y_3$. By the induction hypothesis, we have a derivation $S \Rightarrow_G^* y$ such that $y \in g(y')$. Because $A \in g(\langle \varepsilon_A \rangle)$ and $B \in g(\$)$, $y \in g(x')$ as well.

(vi) $p' = (\langle \varepsilon_A \rangle \to \varepsilon, \{\widetilde{B}\})$. An application of $(\langle \varepsilon_A \rangle \to \varepsilon, \{\widetilde{B}\})$ implies that $\langle \varepsilon_A \rangle$ occurs in y'. Claim 11 says that $\langle \varepsilon_A \rangle$ has either $\widetilde{B}$ or $\$$ as its right neighbor. Since the forbidding condition of p' forbids an occurrence of $\widetilde{B}$ in y', the right neighbor of $\langle \varepsilon_A \rangle$ must be $\$$. As a result, we obtain $y' = y_1' \langle \varepsilon_A \rangle \$ y_3'$, where $y_1', y_3' \in (N' \cup T)^*$. Then, $x' = y_1' \$ y_3'$, and y is of the form $y = y_1 Z y_3$, where $y_1 \in g(y_1')$, $y_3 \in g(y_3')$, and $Z \in g(\langle \varepsilon_A \rangle \$)$. By the definition of g, $g(\langle \varepsilon_A \rangle \$) = \{AB, AAB\}$. If $Z = AB$, $y = y_1 A B y_3$. Having the derivation $S \Rightarrow_G^* y$, it holds that $y \in g(x')$ because $AB \in g(\$)$.

(vii) $p' = (\$ \rightarrow \varepsilon, \{\langle \varepsilon_A \rangle\})$. Then, $y' = y_1'\$y_3'$ and $x' = y_1'y_3'$, where $y_1', y_3' \in (N' \cup T)^*$. Express $y = y_1 Z y_3$ so that $y_1 \in g(y_1')$, $y_3 \in g(y_3')$, and $Z \in g(\$)$, where $g(\$) = \{B, AB\}$. Let $Z = AB$. Then, $y = y_1 A B y_3$, and there exists the derivation

$$S \Rightarrow_G^* y_1 A B y_3 \Rightarrow_G y_1 y_3 \ [AB \rightarrow \varepsilon],$$

where $y_1 y_3 = x$, $x \in g(x')$.

In cases (ii) through (vii) we discussed all six productions simulating the application of $AB \rightarrow \varepsilon$ in G' (see (3) in the definition of P'). Cases (viii) through (xiii) should cover the productions simulating the application of $CD \rightarrow \varepsilon$ in G' (see (4)). However, by inspection of these two sets of productions, it is easy to see that they work analogously. Therefore, we leave this part of the proof to the reader.

We have completed the proof and established Claim 12 by the principle of induction. $\qquad \square$

Observe that $L(G) = L(G')$ can be easily derived from the above claim. According to the definition of g, we have $g(a) = \{a\}$ for all $a \in T$. Thus, from Claim 12, we have for any $x \in T^*$:

$$S \Rightarrow_G^* x \quad \text{if and only if} \quad S' \Rightarrow_{G'}^+ @x@.$$

Since

$$@x@ \Rightarrow_{G'}^2 x \ [(@ \rightarrow \varepsilon, N')(@ \rightarrow \varepsilon, N')],$$

we obtain for any $x \in T^*$:

$$S \Rightarrow_G^* x \quad \text{if and only if} \quad S' \Rightarrow_{G'}^+ x.$$

Consequently, $L(G) = L(G')$, so the theorem holds. $\qquad \blacksquare$

4.1.4 Semi-conditional Grammars

A semi-conditional grammar is a context-conditional grammar in which the cardinality of any context-conditional set is no more than one. These grammars were introduced and studied by Paun in [146].

Definition 14. Let $G = (V, T, P, S)$ be a context-conditional grammar. G is called a *semi-conditional grammar* (an *sc*-grammar for short) provided that every $(A \rightarrow x, Per, For) \in P$ satisfies $|Per| \leq 1$ and $|For| \leq 1$.

Convention 3. Let $G = (V, T, P, S)$ be a semi-conditional grammar, and let $(A \rightarrow x, Per, For) \in P$. In each $(A \rightarrow x, Per, For) \in P$ we omit braces, and instead of $\emptyset$, we write 0. For instance, we write $(A \rightarrow x, BC, 0)$ instead of $(A \rightarrow x, \{BC\}, \emptyset)$.

The families of languages generated by *sc*-grammars and propagating *sc*-grammars of degree (r, s) are denoted by **SC**(r, s) and **prop-SC**(r, s), respectively. The families of languages generated by sc-grammars and propagating sc-grammars of any degree are defined as

$$\mathbf{SC} = \bigcup_{r=0}^{\infty} \bigcup_{s=0}^{\infty} \mathbf{SC}(r, s)$$

and

$$\mathbf{prop\text{-}SC} = \bigcup_{r=0}^{\infty} \bigcup_{s=0}^{\infty} \mathbf{prop\text{-}SC}(r, s).$$

First, we give examples of sc-grammars with degrees $(1,0)$, $(0,1)$, and $(1,1)$.

Example 3 ([146]). Let us consider an sc-grammar

$$G = (\{S, A, B, A', B', a, b\}, \{a, b\}, P, S),$$

where

$$\begin{aligned}
P = \{&(S \to AB, 0, 0), (A \to A'A', B, 0),\\
&(B \to bB', 0, 0), (A' \to A, B', 0),\\
&(B' \to B, 0, 0), (B \to b, 0, 0),\\
&(A' \to a, 0, 0), (A \to a, 0, 0)\}.
\end{aligned}$$

Observe that A can be replaced by $A'A'$ only if B occurs in the rewritten string, and A' can be replaced by A only if B' occurs in the rewritten string. If there is an occurrence of B, the number of occurrences of A and A' can be doubled. However, the application of $(B \to bB', 0, 0)$ implies an introduction of one occurrence of b. As a result,

$$L(G) = \{a^n b^m : m \geq 1, \ 1 \leq n \leq 2^m\},$$

which is not a context-free language.

Example 4 ([146]). Let

$$G = (\{S, A, B, A', A'', B', a, b, c\}, \{a, b, c\}, P, S),$$

where

$$\begin{aligned}
P = \{&(S \to AB, 0, 0), (A \to A', 0, B'),\\
&(A' \to A''A'', 0, c), (A'' \to A, 0, B),\\
&(B \to bB', 0, 0), (B' \to B, 0, 0),\\
&(B \to c, 0, 0), (A \to a, 0, 0),\\
&(A'' \to a, 0, 0)\}.
\end{aligned}$$

In this case, we get a non-context-free language

$$L(G) = \{a^n b^m c : m \geq 0, \ 1 \leq n \leq 2^{m+1}\}.$$

Example 5. Let

$$G = (\{S, P, Q, R, X, Y, Z, a, b, c, d, e, f\}, \{a, b, c, d, e, f\}, P, S)$$

be an *sc*-grammar, where the set of productions is defined as follows:

$$P = \{(S \rightarrow PQR, 0, 0),$$
$$(P \rightarrow aXb, Q, Z),$$
$$(Q \rightarrow cYd, X, Z),$$
$$(R \rightarrow eZf, X, Q),$$
$$(X \rightarrow P, Z, Q),$$
$$(Y \rightarrow Q, P, R),$$
$$(Z \rightarrow R, P, Y),$$
$$(P \rightarrow \varepsilon, Q, Z),$$
$$(Q \rightarrow \varepsilon, R, P),$$
$$(R \rightarrow \varepsilon, 0, Y)\}.$$

Note that this grammar is an *sc*-grammar of degree $(1,1)$. Consider $aabbccddeeff$. For this word, G makes the following derivation:

$$S \Rightarrow PQR \Rightarrow aXbQR \Rightarrow aXbcYdR \Rightarrow aXbcYdeZf \Rightarrow$$
$$aPbcYdeZf \Rightarrow aPbcQdeZf \Rightarrow aPbcQdeRf \Rightarrow$$
$$aaXbbcQdeRf \Rightarrow aaXbbccYddeRf \Rightarrow aaXbbccYddeeZff \Rightarrow$$
$$aaPbbccYddeeZff \Rightarrow aaPbbccQddeeZff \Rightarrow aaPbbccQddeeRff \Rightarrow$$
$$aabbccQddeeRff \Rightarrow aabbccddeeRff \Rightarrow aabbccddeeff.$$

Clearly, G generates the following language:

$$L(G) = \{a^n b^n c^n d^n e^n f^n : n \geq 0\}.$$

As is obvious, this language is non-context-free.

The following theorems deal with the generative power of semi-conditional grammars.

Theorem 22. prop-SC$(0,0)$ = SC$(0,0)$ = CF.

Proof. Follows trivially from the definitions. ∎

Theorem 23. CF $\subset$ prop-SC$(1,0)$, CF $\subset$ prop-SC$(0,1)$.

Proof. In Examples 3 and 4, we show propagating *sc*-grammars of degrees $(1,0)$ and $(0,1)$ that generate non-context-free languages. Therefore, the theorem holds. ∎

Theorem 24. prop-SC$(1,1)$ $\subset$ CS.

Proof. Consider a propagating *sc*-grammar of degree $(1,1)$,

$$G = (V, T, P, S).$$

If $(A \rightarrow x, A, \beta) \in P$, then the permitting condition A does not impose any restriction. Hence, we can replace this production by $(A \rightarrow x, 0, \beta)$. If $(A \rightarrow$

$x, \alpha, A) \in P$, then this production cannot ever by applied; thus, we can remove it from P. Let $T' = \{a' : a \in T\}$ and $V' = V \cup T' \cup \{S', X, Y\}$. Define a homomorphism τ from V^* to $((V - T) \cup (T'))^*$ as $\tau(a) = a'$ for all $a \in T$ and $\tau(A) = A$ for every $A \in V - T$. Furthermore, introduce a mapping ω from $V \cup \{0\}$ to $2^{((V-T)\cup T')}$ as $g(0) = \emptyset$, $g(a) = \{a'\}$ for all $a \in T$, and $g(A) = \{A\}$ for all $A \in V - T$. Next, construct a propagating random context grammar with appearance checking

$$G' = (V', T \cup \{c\}, P', S'),$$

where

$$
\begin{aligned}
P' = \{ &(S' \to SX, \emptyset, \emptyset), (X \to Y, 0, 0), (Y \to c, 0, 0)\} \cup \\
&\{(A \to \tau(x), \omega(\alpha) \cup \{X\}, \omega(\beta)) : (A \to x, \alpha, \beta) \in P\} \cup \\
&\{(a' \to a, \{Y\}, \emptyset) : a \in T\}.
\end{aligned}
$$

It is obvious that $L(G') = L(G)\{c\}$. Therefore, $L(G)\{c\} \in$ **prop-RC(ac)**. Because **prop-RC(ac)** is closed under restricted homomorphisms (see [43], page 48), and by Theorem 14 it holds that **prop-RC(ac)** $\subset$ **CS**, we obtain **prop-SC**$(1, 1) \subset$ **CS**. ∎

The following corollary summarizes the generative power of propagating *sc*-grammars of degrees $(1, 0)$, $(0, 1)$, and $(1, 1)$; that is, propagating *sc*-grammars containing only symbols as their context conditions.

Corollary 9.

$$\mathbf{CF} \subset \mathbf{prop\text{-}SC}(0, 1) \subseteq \mathbf{prop\text{-}SC}(1, 1).$$
$$\mathbf{CF} \subset \mathbf{prop\text{-}SC}(1, 0) \subseteq \mathbf{prop\text{-}SC}(1, 1).$$
$$\mathbf{prop\text{-}SC}(1, 1) \subseteq \mathbf{prop\text{-}RC}(\mathbf{ac}) \subset \mathbf{CS}.$$

The next theorem says that propagating *sc*-grammars of degrees $(1, 2)$, $(2, 1)$ and propagating *sc*-grammars of any degree generate exactly the family of context-sensitive languages. Furthermore, if we allow erasing productions, these grammars generate even the family of recursively enumerable languages. Note that in the next section, we prove a stronger result in terms of a special variant of *sc*-grammars—simple semi-conditional grammars. Therefore, we omit the proof here; for a rigorous proof, see Theorems 28 and 29 in Section 4.1.5.

Theorem 25.

$$\mathbf{CF}$$
$$\subset$$
$$\mathbf{prop\text{-}SC}(2, 1) = \mathbf{prop\text{-}SC}(1, 2) = \mathbf{prop\text{-}SC} = \mathbf{CS}$$
$$\subset$$
$$\mathbf{SC}(2, 1) = \mathbf{SC}(1, 2) = \mathbf{SC} = \mathbf{RE}.$$

4.1.5   Simple Semi-conditional Grammars

Simple semi-conditional grammars, a special case of semi-conditional grammars, were introduced by Meduna and Gopalaratnam in 1994 (see [129]). Informally, a simple semi-conditional grammar is defined as an *sc*-grammar in which every production has no more than one condition.

Definition 15. Let $G = (V, T, P, S)$ be a semi-conditional grammar. G is a *simple semi-conditional grammar* (an *ssc*-grammar for short) if $(A \to x, \alpha, \beta) \in P$ implies $0 \in \{\alpha, \beta\}$.

The families of languages generated by *ssc*-grammars and propagating *ssc*-grammars of degree (r, s) are denoted by $\mathbf{SSC}(r, s)$ and $\mathbf{prop\text{-}SSC}(r, s)$, respectively. Furthermore,

$$\mathbf{SSC} = \bigcup_{r=0}^{\infty} \bigcup_{s=0}^{\infty} \mathbf{SSC}(r, s)$$

and

$$\mathbf{prop\text{-}SSC} = \bigcup_{r=0}^{\infty} \bigcup_{s=0}^{\infty} \mathbf{prop\text{-}SSC}(r, s).$$

The following proposition provides an alternative definition based on context-conditional grammars.

Proposition 1. Let $G = (V, T, P, S)$ be a context-conditional grammar. G is a simple semi-conditional grammar if and only if every $(A \to x, Per, For) \in P$ satisfies $|Per| + |For| \le 1$.

Example 6. Let
$$G = (\{S, A, X, C, Y, a, b\}, \{a, b\}, P, S)$$

be an *ssc*-grammar, where

$$\begin{aligned}
P = \{&(S \to AC, 0, 0), \\
&(A \to aXb, Y, 0), \\
&(C \to Y, A, 0), \\
&(Y \to Cc, 0, A), \\
&(A \to ab, Y, 0), \\
&(Y \to c, 0, A), \\
&(X \to A, C, 0)\}.
\end{aligned}$$

Notice that G is propagating, and it has degree $(1, 1)$. Consider *aabbcc*. G derives this word as follows:

$$S \Rightarrow AC \Rightarrow AY \Rightarrow aXbY \Rightarrow aXbCc \Rightarrow$$
$$aAbCc \Rightarrow aAbYc \Rightarrow aabbYc \Rightarrow aabbcc$$

Obviously,

$$L(G) = \{a^n b^n c^n : n \ge 1\}.$$

Example 7. Let
$$G = (\{S, A, B, X, Y, a\}, \{a\}, P, S)$$
be an *ssc*-grammar, where P is defined as follows:

$$P = \{(S \rightarrow a, 0, 0),$$
$$(S \rightarrow X, 0, 0),$$
$$(X \rightarrow YB, 0, A),$$
$$(X \rightarrow aB, 0, A),$$
$$(Y \rightarrow XA, 0, B),$$
$$(Y \rightarrow aA, 0, B),$$
$$(A \rightarrow BB, XA, 0),$$
$$(B \rightarrow AA, YB, 0),$$
$$(B \rightarrow a, a, 0)\}.$$

G is a propagating *ssc*-grammar of degree $(2, 1)$. Consider the word $aaaaaaaa$. G derives this word as follows:

$$S \Rightarrow X \Rightarrow YB \Rightarrow YAA \Rightarrow XAAA \Rightarrow XBBAA \Rightarrow XBBABB \Rightarrow$$
$$XBBBBBB \Rightarrow aBBBBBBB \Rightarrow aBBaBBBB \Rightarrow^6 aaaaaaaa.$$

It is obvious that G generates the following language:

$$L(G) = \{a^{2^n} : n \geq 0\}.$$

Recall that $\{a^{2^n} : n \geq 0\}$ is not a context-free language.

Theorem 26. prop-SSC$(2, 1) = $ CS.

Proof. Because **prop-SSC$(2, 1) \subseteq$ prop-CG** and by Lemma 6 **prop-CG $\subseteq$ CS**, it suffices to prove the converse inclusion.

Let $G = (V, T, P, S)$ be a context-sensitive grammar in Penttonen normal form (see Lemma 2). We construct an *ssc*-grammar,

$$G' = (V \cup W, T, P', S),$$

that generates $L(G)$. Let

$$W = \{\widetilde{B} : AB \rightarrow AC \in P, \ A, B, C \in V - T\}.$$

Define P' in the following way:

1. If $A \rightarrow x \in P$, $A \in V - T$, $x \in T \cup (V - T)^2$, then add $(A \rightarrow x, 0, 0)$ to P'.

2. If $AB \rightarrow AC \in P$, $A, B, C \in V - T$, then add $(B \rightarrow \widetilde{B}, 0, \widetilde{B})$, $(\widetilde{B} \rightarrow C, A\widetilde{B}, 0)$, $(\widetilde{B} \rightarrow B, 0, 0)$ to P'.

Notice that G' is a propagating *ssc*-grammar of degree $(2, 1)$. Moreover, from (2), we have for any $\widetilde{B} \in W$,

$$S \Rightarrow^*_{G'} w \quad \text{implies} \quad \#_{\widetilde{B}} w \leq 1$$

for all $w \in (V')^*$, because the only production that can generate $\widetilde{B}$ is of the form $(B \to \widetilde{B}, 0, \widetilde{B})$.

Let g be a finite substitution from V^* into $(V \cup W)^*$ defined as follows: for all $D \in V$,

1. if $\widetilde{D} \in W$, then $g(D) = \{D, \widetilde{D}\}$;

2. if $\widetilde{D} \notin W$, then $g(D) = \{D\}$.

Claim 13. *For any $x \in V^+$, $m, n \geq 0$, $S \Rightarrow^m_G x$ if and only if $S \Rightarrow^n_{G'} x'$ with $x' \in g(x)$.*

Proof.

Only if: This is proved by induction on m, $m \geq 0$.

Basis: Let $m = 0$. The only x is S as $S \Rightarrow^0_G S$. Clearly, $S \Rightarrow^n_{G'} S$ for $n = 0$ and $S \in g(S)$.

Induction Hypothesis: Assume that the claim holds for all derivations of length m or less, for some $m \geq 0$.

Induction Step: Consider a derivation

$$S \Rightarrow^{m+1}_G x,$$

where $x \in V^+$. Because $m + 1 \geq 1$, there is some $y \in V^*$ and $p \in P$ such that

$$S \Rightarrow^m_G y \Rightarrow_{G'} x \; [p].$$

By the induction hypothesis,
$$S \Rightarrow^n_{G'} y'$$

for some $y' \in g(y)$ and $n \geq 0$. Next, we distinguish between two cases: case (i) considers p with one nonterminal on its left-hand side, and case (ii) considers p with two nonterminals on its left-hand side.

(i) Let $p = D \to y_2 \in P$, $D \in V - T$, $y_2 \in T \cup (V - T)^2$, $y = y_1 D y_3$, $y_1, y_3 \in V^*$, $x = y_1 y_2 y_3$, $y' = y'_1 X y'_3$, $y'_1 \in g(y_1)$, $y'_3 \in g(y_3)$, and $X \in g(D)$. By (1) in the definition of P', $(D \to y_2, 0, 0) \in P$. If $X = D$, then

$$S \Rightarrow^n_{G'} y'_1 D y'_3 \Rightarrow_{G'} y'_1 y_2 y'_3 \; [(D \to y_2, 0, 0)].$$

Because $y'_1 \in g(y_1)$, $y'_3 \in g(y_3)$, and $y_2 \in g(y_2)$, we obtain $y'_1 y_2 y'_3 \in g(y_1 y_2 y_3) = g(x)$. If $X = \widetilde{D}$, we have $(X \to D, 0, 0)$ in P', so

$$S \Rightarrow^n_{G'} y'_1 X y'_3 \Rightarrow_{G'} y'_1 D y'_3 \Rightarrow_{G'} y'_1 y_2 y'_3 \; [(X \to D, 0, 0)(D \to y_2, 0, 0)],$$

and $y'_1 y_2 y'_3 \in g(x)$.

(ii) Let $p = AB \to AC \in P$, $A, B, C \in V - T$, $y = y_1 AB y_2$, $y_1, y_2 \in V^*$, $x = y_1 AC y_2$, $y' = y_1' XY y_2'$, $y_1' \in g(y_1)$, $y_2' \in g(y_2)$, $X \in g(A)$, and $Y \in g(B)$. Recall that for any $\tilde{B}$, $\#_{\tilde{B}} y' \leq 1$ and $(\tilde{B} \to B, 0, 0) \in P'$. Then,

$$y' \Rightarrow^i_{G'} y_1' AB y_2'$$

for some $i \in \{0, 1, 2\}$. At this point, we have

$$
\begin{aligned}
S \quad &\Rightarrow^*_{G'} \quad y_1' AB y_2' \\
&\Rightarrow_{G'} \quad y_1' A\tilde{B} y_2' \quad [(B \to \tilde{B}, 0, \tilde{B})] \\
&\Rightarrow_{G'} \quad y_1' AC y_2' \quad [(\tilde{B} \to C, A\tilde{B}, 0)],
\end{aligned}
$$

where $y_1' AC y_2' \in g(x)$.

If: This is established by induction on $n \geq 0$; in other words, we demonstrate that if $S \Rightarrow^n_{G'} x'$ with $x' \in g(x)$ for some $x \in V^+$, then $S \Rightarrow^*_G x$.

Basis: For $n = 0$, x' surely equals S as $S \Rightarrow^0_{G'} S$. Because $S \in g(S)$, we have $x = S$. Clearly, $S \Rightarrow^0_G S$.

Induction Hypothesis: Assume that the claim holds for all derivations of length n of less, for some $n \geq 0$.

Induction Step: Consider a derivation,

$$S \Rightarrow^{n+1}_{G'} x',$$

$x' \in g(x)$, $x \in V^+$. As $n + 1 \geq 1$, there exists some $y \in V^+$ such that

$$S \Rightarrow^n_{G'} y' \Rightarrow_{G'} x' \ [p],$$

$y' \in g(y)$. By the induction hypothesis,

$$S \Rightarrow^*_G y.$$

Let $y' = y_1' B' y_2'$, $y = y_1 B y_2$, $y_1' \in g(y_1)$, $y_2' \in g(y_2)$, $y_1, y_2 \in V^*$, $B' \in g(B)$, $B \in V - T$, $x' = y_1' z' y_2'$, and $p = (B' \to z', \alpha, \beta) \in P'$. The following three cases cover all possible forms of the derivation step $y' \Rightarrow_{G'} x' \ [p]$.

(i) $z' \in g(B)$. Then,

$$S \Rightarrow^*_G y_1 B y_2,$$

where $y_1' z' y_2' \in g(y_1 B y_2)$; that is, $x' \in g(y_1 B y_2)$.

(ii) $B' = B \in V - T$, $z' \in T \cup (V - T)^2$, $\alpha = \beta = 0$. Then, there exists a production, $B \to z' \in P$, so

$$S \Rightarrow^*_G y_1 B y_2 \Rightarrow_G y_1 z' y_2 \ [B \to z'].$$

Since $z' \in g(z')$, we have $x = y_1 z' y_2$ such that $x' \in g(x)$.

(iii) $B' = \widetilde{B}$, $z' = C$, $\alpha = A\widetilde{B}$, $\beta = 0$, $A, B, C \in V - T$. Then, there exists a production of the form $AB \to AC \in P$. Since $\#_Z y' \leq 1$, $Z = \widetilde{B}$, and $A\widetilde{B} \in \mathrm{sub}(y')$, we have $y_1' = u'A$, $y_1 = uA$, $u' \in g(u)$ for some $u \in V^*$. Thus,

$$S \Rightarrow_G^* uABy_2 \Rightarrow_G uACy_2 \; [AB \to AC],$$

where $uACy_2 = y_1 C y_2$. Because $C \in g(C)$, we get $x = y_1 C y_2$ such that $x' \in g(x)$.

As cases (i) through (iii) cover all possible forms of a derivation step in G', we have completed the induction step and established Claim 13 by the principle of induction.   □

The statement of Theorem 26 follows immediately from Claim 13. Because for all $a \in T$, $g(a) = \{a\}$, we have for every $w \in T^+$,

$$S \Rightarrow_G^* w \quad \text{if and only if} \quad S \Rightarrow_{G'}^* w.$$

Therefore, $L(G) = L(G')$, so the theorem holds.   ■

Corollary 10. prop-SSC$(2, 1)$ = prop-SSC = prop-SC$(2, 1)$ = prop-SC = CS.

Proof. It follows from Theorem 26 and the definitions of propagating *ssc*-grammars.   □

Next, we turn our investigation to the *ssc*-grammars of degree $(2, 1)$ with erasing productions. We prove that these grammars generate precisely the family of recursively enumerable languages.

Theorem 27. SSC$(2, 1)$ = RE.

Proof. Clearly, **SSC**$(2, 1) \subseteq$ **RE**; hence it suffices to show that **RE** $\subseteq$ **SSC**$(2, 1)$. Every recursively enumerable language, $L \in$ **RE**, can be generated by a phrase-structure grammar G in Penttonen normal form (see Lemma 3). That is, G's productions are of the form $AB \to AC$ or $A \to x$, where $A, B, C \in V - T$, $x \in \{\varepsilon\} \cup T \cup (V - T)^2$. Thus, the inclusion **RE** $\in$ **SSC**$(2, 1)$ can be proved by analogy with the proof of Theorem 26. The details are left to the reader.   ■

Corollary 11. SSC$(2, 1)$ = SSC = SC$(2, 1)$ = SC = RE.

To demonstrate that propagating *ssc*-grammars of degree $(1, 2)$ characterize **CS**, we first establish a normal form for context-sensitive grammars.

Lemma 9. *Every $L \in$ CS can be generated by a context-sensitive grammar,*

$$G = (\{S\} \cup N_{CF} \cup N_{CS} \cup T, T, P, S),$$

where $\{S\}$, N_{CF}, N_{CS}, and T are pairwise disjoint alphabets, and every production in P is either of the form $S \to aD$ or $AB \to AC$ or $A \to x$, where $a \in T$, $D \in N_{CF} \cup \{\varepsilon\}$, $B \in N_{CS}$, $A, C \in N_{CF}$, $x \in N_{CS} \cup T \cup (\bigcup_{i=1}^{2} N_{CF}^i)$.

Proof. Let L be a context-sensitive language over an alphabet, T. Without loss of generality, we can express L as $L = L_1 \cup L_2$, where $L_1 \subseteq T$ and $L_2 \subseteq TT^+$. Thus, by analogy with the proofs of Theorems 1 and 2 in [146], L_2 can be represented as $L_2 = \bigcup_{a \in T} aL_a$, where each L_a is a context-sensitive language. Let L_a be generated by a context-sensitive grammar,

$$G_a = (N_{CF_a} \cup N_{CS_a} \cup T, T, P_a, S_a),$$

of the form of Lemma 4. Clearly, we can assume that for all as, the nonterminal alphabets N_{CF_a} and N_{CS_a} are pairwise disjoint. Let S be a new start symbol. Consider the context-sensitive grammar

$$G = (\{S\} \cup N_{CF} \cup N_{CS} \cup T, T, P, S)$$

defined as

$$
\begin{aligned}
N_{CF} &= \bigcup_{a \in T} N_{CF_a}, \\
N_{CS} &= \bigcup_{a \in T} N_{CS_a}, \\
P &= \bigcup_{a \in T} P_a \cup \{S \to aS_a : a \in T\} \cup \{S \to a : a \in L_1\}.
\end{aligned}
$$

Obviously, G satisfies the required form, and we have

$$L(G) = L_1 \cup \left(\bigcup_{a \in T} aL(G_a)\right) = L_1 \cup \left(\bigcup_{a \in T} aL_a\right) = L_1 \cup L_2 = L.$$

Consequently, the lemma holds. $\qquad\square$

We are now ready to characterize **CS** by propagating *ssc*-grammars of degree $(1,2)$.

Theorem 28. CS = prop-SSC$(1, 2)$.

Proof. By Lemma 6, **prop-SSC**$(1, 2) \subseteq$ **prop-CG** $\subseteq$ **CS**; thus, it suffices to prove the converse inclusion.

Let L be a context-sensitive language. Without loss of generality, we can assume that L is generated by a context-sensitive grammar,

$$G = (\{S\} \cup N_{CF} \cup N_{CS} \cup T, T, P, S)$$

of the form of Lemma 9. Set

$$V = \{S\} \cup N_{CF} \cup NCS \cup T.$$

Let q be the cardinality of V; $q \geq 1$. Furthermore, let f be an arbitrary fixed bijection from V onto $\{1, \ldots, q\}$, and let f^{-1} be the inverse of f. Let

$$\widetilde{G} = (\widetilde{V}, T, \widetilde{P}, S)$$

be a propagating *ssc*-grammar of degree $(1, 2)$, in which

$$\widetilde{V} = \left(\bigcup_{i=1}^{4} W_i\right) \cup V,$$

where

$$W_1 = \{\langle a, AB \to AC, j\rangle : a \in T, \ AB \to AC \in P, \ 1 \le j \le 5\},$$
$$W_2 = \{[a, AB \to AC, j] : a \in T, \ AB \to AC \in P, \ 1 \le j \le q+3\},$$
$$W_3 = \{\widehat{B}, B', B'' : B \in N_{CS}\},$$
$$W_4 = \{\bar{a} : a \in T\}.$$

$\widetilde{P}$ is defined as follows:

1. If $S \to aA \in P$, $a \in T$, $A \in (N_{CF} \cup \{\varepsilon\})$, then add $(S \to \bar{a}A, 0, 0)$ to $\widetilde{P}$.

2. If $a \in T$, $A \to x \in P$, $A \in N_{CF}$, $x \in (V - \{S\}) \cup (N_{CF})^2$, then add $(A \to x, \bar{a}, 0)$ to $\widetilde{P}$.

3. If $a \in T$, $AB \to AC \in P$, $A, C \in N_{CF}$, $B \in N_{CS}$, then add the following productions to P' (an informal explanation of these productions can be found below):

   (a) $(\bar{a} \to \langle a, AB \to AC, 1\rangle, 0, 0)$.

   (b) $(B \to B', \langle a, AB \to AC, 1\rangle, 0)$.

   (c) $(B \to \widehat{B}, \langle a, AB \to AC, 1\rangle, 0)$.

   (d) $(\langle a, AB \to AC, 1\rangle \to \langle a, AB \to AC, 2\rangle, 0, B)$.

   (e) $(\widehat{B} \to B'', 0, B'')$.

   (f) $(\langle a, AB \to AC, 2\rangle \to \langle a, AB \to AC, 3\rangle, 0, \widehat{B})$.

   (g) $(B'' \to [a, AB \to AC, 1], \langle a, AB \to AC, 3\rangle, 0)$.

   (h) $([a, AB \to AC, j] \to [a, AB \to AC, j+1], 0, f^{-1}(j)[a, AB \to AC, j])$, for all $j = 1 \ldots q$, $f(A) \ne j$.

   (i) $([a, AB \to AC, f(A)] \to [a, AB \to AC, f(A)+1], 0, 0)$.

   (j) $([a, AB \to AC, q+1] \to [a, AB \to AC, q+2], 0, B'[a, AB \to AC, q+1])$.

   (k) $([a, AB \to AC, q+2] \to [a, AB \to AC, q+3], 0, \langle a, AB \to AC, 3\rangle[a, AB \to AC, q+2])$.

   (l) $(\langle a, AB \to AC, 3\rangle \to \langle a, AB \to AC, 4\rangle, [a, AB \to AC, q+3], 0)$.

   (m) $(B' \to B, \langle a, AB \to AC, 4\rangle, 0)$.

   (n) $(\langle a, AB \to AC, 4\rangle \to \langle a, AB \to AC, 5\rangle, 0, B')$.

   (o) $([a, AB \to AC, q+3] \to C, \langle a, AB \to AC, 5\rangle, 0)$.

   (p) $(\langle a, AB \to AC, 5\rangle \to \bar{a}, 0, [a, AB \to AC, q+3])$.

4. If $a \in T$, then add $(\bar{a} \to a, 0, 0)$ to $\widetilde{P}$.

Basic Idea. Let us informally explain the basic idea behind (3)—the heart of all the construction. The productions introduced in (3) simulate the application of productions of the form $AB \to AC$ in G as follows: an occurrence of B is chosen, and its left neighbor is checked not to belong to $\widetilde{V} - \{A\}$. At this point, the left neighbor necessarily equals A, so B is rewritten with C.

Formally, we define a finite letter-to-letters substitution g from V^* into $\widetilde{V}^*$ as follows:

(a) If $D \in V$, then add D to $g(D)$.

(b) If $\langle a, AB \to AC, j \rangle \in W_1$, $a \in T$, $AB \to AC \in P$, $B \in N_{CS}$, $A, C \in N_{CF}$, $j \in \{1, \ldots, 5\}$, then add $\langle a, AB \to AC, j \rangle$ to $g(a)$.

(c) If $[a, AB \to AC, j] \in W_2$, $a \in T$, $AB \to AC \in P$, $B \in N_{CS}$, $A, C \in N_{CF}$, $j \in \{1, \ldots, q+3\}$, then add $[a, AB \to AC, j]$ to $g(B)$.

(d) If $\{\widehat{B}, B', B''\} \subseteq W_3$, $B \in N_{CS}$, then include $\{\widehat{B}, B', B''\}$ to $g(B)$.

(e) If $\bar{a} \in W_4$, $a \in T$, then add $\bar{a}$ to $g(a)$.

Let g^{-1} be the inverse of g. To show that $L(G) = L(\widetilde{G})$, we first prove three claims.

Claim 14. $S \Rightarrow_G^+ x$, $x \in V^*$, implies $x \in T(V - \{S\})^*$.

Proof. Observe that the start symbol, S, does not appear on the right side of any production and that $S \to x \in P$ implies $x \in T \cup T(V - \{S\})$. Hence, the claim holds. □

Claim 15. *If $S \Rightarrow_{\widetilde{G}}^+ x$, $x \in \widetilde{V}^*$, then x has one of the following seven forms:*

 (i) $x = ay$, *where $a \in T$, $y \in (V - \{S\})^*$.*

 (ii) $x = \bar{a}y$, *where $\bar{a} \in W_4$, $y \in (V - \{S\})^*$.*

 (iii) $x = \langle a, AB \to AC, 1 \rangle y$, *where $\langle a, AB \to AC, 1 \rangle \in W_1$, $y \in ((V - \{S\}) \cup \{B', \widehat{B}, B''\})^*$, $\#_{B''} y \leq 1$.*

 (iv) $x = \langle a, AB \to AC, 2 \rangle y$, *where $\langle a, AB \to AC, 2 \rangle \in W_1$, $y \in ((V - \{S, B\}) \cup \{B', \widehat{B}, B''\})^*$, $\#_{B'} y \leq 1$.*

 (v) $x = \langle a, AB \to AC, 3 \rangle y$, *where $\langle a, AB \to AC, 3 \rangle \in W_1$, $y \in ((V - \{S, B\}) \cup \{B'\})^*(\{[a, AB \to AC, j] : 1 \leq j \leq q+3\} \cup \{\varepsilon, B''\})((V - \{S, B\}) \cup \{B'\})^*$.*

 (vi) $x = \langle a, AB \to AC, 4 \rangle y$, *where $\langle a, AB \to AC, 4 \rangle \in W_1$, $y \in ((V - \{S\}) \cup \{B'\})^*[a, AB \to AC, q+3]((V - \{S\}) \cup \{B'\})^*$.*

 (vii) $x = \langle a, AB \to AC, 5 \rangle y$, *where $\langle a, AB \to AC, 5 \rangle \in W_1$, $y \in (V - \{S\})^*\{[a, AB \to AC, q+3], \varepsilon\}(V - \{S\})^*$.*

Proof. The claim is proved by induction on the length of derivations.

Basis: Consider $S \Rightarrow_{\widetilde{G}} x$, $x \in \widetilde{V}^*$. By inspection of the productions, we have

$$S \Rightarrow_{\widetilde{G}} \bar{a}A \; [(S \to \bar{a}A, 0, 0)]$$

for some $\bar{a} \in W_4$, $A \in (\{\varepsilon\} \cup N_{CF})$. Therefore, $x = \bar{a}$ or $x = \bar{a}A$; in either case, x is a word of the required form.

Induction Hypothesis: Assume that the claim holds for all derivations of length at most n, for some $n \geq 1$.

Induction Step: Consider a derivation of the form

$$S \Rightarrow_{\widetilde{G}}^{n+1} x,$$

where $x \in \widetilde{V}^*$. Since $n \geq 1$, we have $n + 1 \geq 2$. Thus, there is some z of the required form, $z \in \widetilde{V}^*$, such that

$$S \Rightarrow_{\widetilde{G}}^{n} z \Rightarrow_{\widetilde{G}} x \; [p]$$

for some $p \in \widetilde{P}$.

Let us first prove by contradiction that the first symbol of z does not belong to T. Assume that the first symbol of z belongs to T. As z is of the required form, we have $z = ay$ for some $a \in (V - \{S\})^*$. By inspection of $\widetilde{P}$, there is no $p \in \widetilde{P}$ such that $ay \Rightarrow_{\widetilde{G}} x \; [p]$, where $x \in \widetilde{V}^*$. We have thus obtained a contradiction, so the first symbol of z is not in T.

Because the first symbol of z does not belong to T, z cannot have form (i); as a result, z has one of forms (ii) through (vii). The following cases (I) through (VI) demonstrate that if z has one of these six forms, then x has one of the required forms, too.

(I) Assume that z is of form (ii); that is, $z = \bar{a}y$, $\bar{a} \in W_4$, and $y \in (V - \{S\})^*$. By inspection of the productions in $\widetilde{P}$, we see that p has one of the following forms (a), (b), and (c):

   (a) $p = (A \to u, \bar{a}, 0)$, where $A \in N_{CF}$ and $u \in (V - \{S\}) \cup N_{CF}^2$;
   (b) $p = (\bar{a} \to \langle a, AB \to AC, 1 \rangle, 0, 0)$, where $\langle a, AB \to AC, 1 \rangle \in W_1$;
   (c) $p = (\bar{a} \to a, 0, 0)$, where $a \in T$.

   Note that productions of forms (a), (b), and (c) are introduced in construction steps 2, 3, and 4, respectively. If p has form (a), then x has form (ii). If p has form (b), then x has form (iii). Finally, if p has form (c), then x has form (i). In any of these three cases, we obtain x that has one of the required forms.

(II) Assume that z has form (iii); that is, $z = \langle a, AB \to AC, 1 \rangle y$ for some $\langle a, AB \to AC, 1 \rangle \in W_1$, $y \in ((V - \{S\}) \cup \{B', \widehat{B}, B''\})^*$, and $\#_{B''} y \leq 1$. By the inspection of $\widetilde{P}$, we see that z can be rewritten by productions of these four forms:

(a) $(B \to B', \langle a, AB \to AC, 1 \rangle, 0)$.

(b) $(B \to \widehat{B}, \langle a, AB \to AC, 1 \rangle, 0)$.

(c) $(\widehat{B} \to B'', 0, B'')$ if $B'' \notin \text{alph}(y)$; that is, $\#_{B''} y = 0$.

(d) $(\langle a, AB \to AC, 1 \rangle \to \langle a, AB \to AC, 2 \rangle, 0, B)$ if $B \notin \text{alph}(y)$; that is, $\#_B y = 0$;

Clearly, in cases (a) and (b), we obtain x of form (iii). If $z \Rightarrow_{\widetilde{G}} x \ [p]$, where p is of form (c), then $\#_{B''} x = 1$, so we get x of form (iii). Finally, if we use the production of form (d), then we obtain x of form (iv) because $\#_B z = 0$.

(III) Assume that z is of form (iv); that is, $z = \langle a, AB \to AC, 2 \rangle y$, where $\langle a, AB \to AC, 2 \rangle \in W_1$, $y \in ((V - \{S, B\}) \cup \{B', \widehat{B}, B''\})^*$, and $\#_{B''} y \leq 1$. By inspection of $\widetilde{P}$, we see that the following two productions can be used to rewrite z:

(a) $(\widehat{B} \to B'', 0, B'')$ if $B'' \notin \text{alph}(y)$.

(b) $(\langle a, AB \to AC, 2 \rangle \to \langle a, AB \to AC, 3 \rangle, 0, \widehat{B})$ if $\widehat{B} \notin \text{alph}(y)$.

In case (a), we get x of form (iv). In case (b), we have $\#_{\widehat{B}} y = 0$, so $\#_{\widehat{B}} x = 0$. Moreover, notice that $\#_{B''} x \leq 1$ in this case. Indeed, the symbol B'' can be generated only if there is no occurrence of B'' in a given rewritten word, so no more than one occurrence of B'' appears in any sentential form. As a result, we have $\#_{B''} \langle a, AB \to AC, 3 \rangle y \leq 1$; that is, $\#_{B''} x \leq 1$. In other words, we get x of form (v).

(IV) Assume that z is of form (v); that is, $z = \langle a, AB \to AC, 3 \rangle y$ for some $\langle a, AB \to AC, 3 \rangle \in W_1$, $y \in ((V - \{S, B\}) \cup \{B'\})^*(\{[a, AB \to AC, j] : 1 \leq j \leq q + 3\} \cup \{B'', \varepsilon\})((V - \{S, B\}) \cup \{B'\})^*$. Assume that $y = y_1 Y y_2$ with $y_1, y_2 \in ((V - \{S, B\}) \cup \{B'\})^*$. If $Y = \varepsilon$, then we can use no production from $\widetilde{P}$ to rewrite z. Because $z \Rightarrow_{\widetilde{G}} x$, we have $Y \neq \varepsilon$. The following cases (a) through (f) cover all possible forms of Y.

(a) Assume $Y = B''$. By inspection of $\widetilde{P}$, we see that the only production that can rewrite z has the form

$$(B'' \to [a, AB \to AC, 1], \langle a, AB \to AC, 3 \rangle, 0).$$

In this case, we get x of form (v).

(b) Assume $Y = [a, AB \to AC, j]w$, $j \in \{1, \ldots, q\}$, and $f(A) \neq j$. Then, z can be rewritten only according to the production

$$([a, AB \to AC, j] \to [a, AB \to AC, j + 1], 0, f^{-1}(j)[a, AB \to AC, j]),$$

which can be used unless the right-most symbol of $\langle a, AB \to AC, 3 \rangle y_1$ is $f^{-1}(j)$. Clearly, in this case we again get x of form (v).

(c) Assume $Y = [a, AB \rightarrow AC, j]$, $j \in \{1, \ldots, q\}$, $f(A) = j$. This case forms an analogy to case (b), except that the production of the form

$$([a, AB \rightarrow AC, f(A)] \rightarrow [a, AB \rightarrow AC, f(A) + 1], 0, 0)$$

is now used.

(d) Assume $Y = [a, AB \rightarrow AC, q + 1]$. This case forms an analogy to case (b); the only change is the application of the production

$$([a, AB \rightarrow AC, q+1] \rightarrow [a, AB \rightarrow AC, q+2], 0, B'[a, AB \rightarrow AC, q+1]).$$

(e) Assume $Y = [a, AB \rightarrow AC, q + 2]$. This case forms an analogy to case (b) except that the production

$$([a, AB \rightarrow AC, q + 2] \rightarrow [a, AB \rightarrow AC, q + 3], 0,$$
$$\langle a, AB \rightarrow AC, 3\rangle[a, AB \rightarrow AC, q + 2])$$

is used.

(f) Assume $Y = [a, AB \rightarrow AC, q + 3]$. By inspection of $\widetilde{P}$, we see that the only production that can rewrite z is

$$(\langle a, AB \rightarrow AC, 3\rangle \rightarrow \langle a, AB \rightarrow AC, 4\rangle, [a, AB \rightarrow AC, q + 3], 0).$$

If this production is used, we get x of form (vi).

(V) Assume that z is of form (vi); that is, $z = \langle a, AB \rightarrow AC, 4\rangle y$, where $\langle a, AB \rightarrow AC, 4\rangle \in W_1$ and $y \in ((V - \{S\}) \cup \{B'\})^*[a, AB \rightarrow AC, q + 3]((V - \{S\}) \cup \{B'\})^*$. By inspection of $\widetilde{P}$, these two productions can rewrite z:

(a) $(B' \rightarrow B, \langle a, AB \rightarrow AC, 4\rangle, 0)$.

(b) $(\langle a, AB \rightarrow AC, 4\rangle \rightarrow \langle a, AB \rightarrow AC, 5\rangle, 0, B')$ if $B' \notin \mathrm{alph}(y)$.

Clearly, in case (a), we get x of form (vi). In case (b), we get x of form (vii) because $\#_{B'}y = 0$, so $y \in (V - \{S\})^*\{[a, AB \rightarrow AC, q + 3], \varepsilon\}(V - \{S\})^*$.

(VI) Assume that z is of form (vii); that is, $z = \langle a, AB \rightarrow AC, 5\rangle y$, where $\langle a, AB \rightarrow AC, 5\rangle \in W_1$ and $y \in (V - \{S\})^*\{[a, AB \rightarrow AC, q + 3], \varepsilon\}(V - \{S\})^*$. By inspection of $\widetilde{P}$, one of the following two productions can be used to rewrite z:

(a) $([a, AB \rightarrow AC, q + 3] \rightarrow C, \langle a, AB \rightarrow AC, 5\rangle, 0)$.

(b) $(\langle a, AB \rightarrow AC, 5\rangle \rightarrow \bar{a}, 0, [a, AB \rightarrow AC, q + 3])$ if $[a, AB \rightarrow AC, q+3] \notin \mathrm{alph}(z)$.

In case (a), we get x of form (vii). Case (b) implies $\#_{[a, AB \rightarrow AC, q+3]}y = 0$; thus, x is of form (ii).

This completes the induction step and establishes Claim 15.   □

Claim 16. *It holds that*

$$S \Rightarrow_G^m w \quad \text{if and only if} \quad S \Rightarrow_{\widetilde{G}}^n v$$

where $v \in g(w)$ and $w \in V^+$, for some $m, n \geq 0$.

Proof.

Only if: The only-if part is established by induction on m; that is, we have to demonstrate that

$$S \Rightarrow_G^m w \quad \text{implies} \quad S \Rightarrow_{\widetilde{G}}^* v$$

for some $v \in g(w)$ and $w \in V^+$.

Basis: Let $m = 0$. The only w is S because $S \Rightarrow_G^0 S$. Clearly, $S \Rightarrow_{\widetilde{G}}^0 S$, and $S \in g(S)$.

Induction Hypothesis: Suppose that our claim holds form all derivations of length m or less, for some $m \geq 0$.

Induction Step: Let us consider a derivation,

$$S \Rightarrow_G^{m+1} x,$$

where $x \in V^+$. Because $m + 1 \geq 1$, there are $y \in V^+$ and $p \in P$ such that

$$S \Rightarrow_G^m y \Rightarrow_G x \; [p],$$

and by the induction hypothesis, there is also a derivation

$$S \Rightarrow_{\widetilde{G}}^n \widetilde{y}$$

for some $\widetilde{y} \in g(y)$. The following cases (i) through (iii) cover all possible forms of p:

(i) Let $p = S \rightarrow aA \in P$ for some $a \in T$, $A \in N_{CF} \cup \{\varepsilon\}$. Then, by Claim 14, $m = 0$, so $y = S$ and $x = aA$. By (1) in the construction of $\widetilde{G}$, $(S \rightarrow \bar{a}A, 0, 0) \in \widetilde{P}$. Hence,

$$S \Rightarrow_{\widetilde{G}} \widetilde{a}A,$$

where $\widetilde{a}A \in g(aA)$.

(ii) Let us assume that $p = D \rightarrow y_2 \in P$, $D \in N_{CF}$, $y_2 \in (V - \{S\}) \cup N_{CF}^2$, $y = y_1 D y_3$, $y_1, y_3 \in V^*$, and $x = y_1 y_2 y_3$. From the definition of g, it is clear that $g(Z) = \{Z\}$ for all $Z \in N_{CF}$; therefore, we can express $\widetilde{y} = z_1 D z_3$, where $z_1 \in g(y_1)$ and $z_3 \in g(y_3)$. Without loss of generality, we can also assume that $y_1 = au$, $a \in T$, $u \in (V - \{S\})^*$ (see Claim 14), so $z_1 = a''u''$, $a'' \in g(a)$, and $u'' \in g(u)$. Moreover, by (2) in the construction, we have $(D \rightarrow y_2, \bar{a}, 0) \in \widetilde{P}$. The following cases (a) through (e) cover all possible forms of a''.

(a) Let $a'' = \bar{a}$ (see (ii) in Claim 15). Then, we have

$$S \Rightarrow^n_{\widetilde{G}} \bar{a}u''Dz_3 \Rightarrow_{\widetilde{G}} \bar{a}u''y_2z_3 \; [(D \to y_2, \bar{a}, 0)],$$

and $\bar{a}u''y_2z_3 = z_1y_2z_3 \in g(y_1y_2y_3) = g(x)$.

(b) Let $a'' = a$ (see (i) in Claim 15). By (4) in the construction of $\widetilde{G}$, we can express the derivation

$$S \Rightarrow^n_{\widetilde{G}} au''Dz_3$$

as

$$S \Rightarrow^{n-1}_{\widetilde{G}} \bar{a}u''Dz_3 \Rightarrow_{\widetilde{G}} au''Dz_3 \; [(\bar{a} \to a, 0, 0)];$$

thus, there exists the derivation

$$S \Rightarrow^{n-1}_{\widetilde{G}} \bar{a}u''Dz_3 \Rightarrow_{\widetilde{G}} \bar{a}u''y_2z_3 \; [(D \to y_2, \bar{a}, 0)]$$

with $\bar{a}u''y_2z_3 \in g(x)$.

(c) Let $a'' = \langle a, AB \to AC, 5 \rangle$ for some $AB \to AC \in P$ (see (vii) in Claim 15), and let $u''Dz_3 \in (V - \{S\})^*$; that is, $[a, AB \to AC, q+3] \notin \mathrm{alph}(u''Dz_3)$. Then, there exists the derivation

$$\begin{aligned}
S \;\; &\Rightarrow^n_{\widetilde{G}} \;\; \langle a, AB \to AC, 5 \rangle u''Dz_3 \\
&\Rightarrow_{\widetilde{G}} \;\; \bar{a}u''Dz_3 \; [(\langle a, AB \to AC, 5 \rangle \to \bar{a}, 0, [a, AB \to AC, q+3])] \\
&\Rightarrow_{\widetilde{G}} \;\; \bar{a}u''y_2z_3 \; [(D \to y_2, \bar{a}, 0)],
\end{aligned}$$

and $\bar{a}u''y_2z_3 \in g(x)$.

(d) Let $a'' = \langle a, AB \to AC, 5 \rangle$ (see (vii) in Claim 15). Let $[a, AB \to AC, q+3] \in \mathrm{alph}(u''Dz_3)$. Without loss of generality, we can assume that $\widetilde{y} = \langle a, AB \to AC, 5 \rangle u''Do''[a, AB \to AC, q+3]t''$, where $o''[a, AB \to AC, q+3]t'' = z_3$, $oBt = y_3$, $o'' \in g(t)$, $o, t \in (V - \{S\})^*$. By inspection of $\widetilde{P}$ (see (3) in the construction of $\widetilde{G}$), we can express the derivation

$$S \Rightarrow^n_{\widetilde{G}} \widetilde{y}$$

as

$$\begin{aligned}
S \Rightarrow^*_{\widetilde{G}} \quad & \bar{a}u''Do''Bt'' \\
\Rightarrow_{\widetilde{G}} \quad & \langle a, AB \to AC, 1 \rangle u''Do''Bt'' \\
& [(\bar{a} \to \langle a, AB \to AC, 1 \rangle, 0, 0)] \\
\Rightarrow^{1+|m_1m_2|}_{\widetilde{G}} \quad & \langle a, AB \to AC, 1 \rangle u'Do'\widehat{B}t' \\
& [m_1(B \to \widehat{B}, \langle a, AB \to AC, 1 \rangle, 0)m_2] \\
\Rightarrow_{\widetilde{G}} \quad & \langle a, AB \to AC, 2 \rangle u'Do'\widehat{B}t' \\
& [(\langle a, AB \to AC, 1 \rangle \to \langle a, AB \to AC, 2 \rangle, 0, B)]
\end{aligned}$$

$$\Rightarrow_{\widetilde{G}} \quad \langle a, AB \to AC, 2 \rangle u' Do' B'' t'$$
$$[\widehat{B} \to B'', 0, B'']$$

$$\Rightarrow_{\widetilde{G}} \quad \langle a, AB \to AC, 3 \rangle u' Do' B'' t'$$
$$[(\langle a, AB \to AC, 2 \rangle \to \langle a, AB \to AC, 3 \rangle, 0, \widehat{B})]$$

$$\Rightarrow_{\widetilde{G}} \quad \langle a, AB \to AC, 3 \rangle u' Do' [a, AB \to AC, 1] t'$$
$$[(B'' \to [a, AB \to AC, 1], \langle a, AB \to AC, 3 \rangle, 0)]$$

$$\Rightarrow_{\widetilde{G}}^{q+2} \quad \langle a, AB \to AC, 3 \rangle u' Do' [a, AB \to AC, q+3] t'$$
$$[\omega]$$

$$\Rightarrow_{\widetilde{G}} \quad \langle a, AB \to AC, 4 \rangle u' Do' [a, AB \to AC, q+3] t'$$
$$[(\langle a, AB \to AC, 3 \rangle \to \langle a, AB \to AC, 4 \rangle,$$
$$[a, AB \to AC, q+3], 0)]$$

$$\Rightarrow_{\widetilde{G}}^{|m_3|} \quad \langle a, AB \to AC, 4 \rangle u'' Do'' [a, AB \to AC, q+3] t''$$
$$[m_3]$$

$$\Rightarrow_{\widetilde{G}} \quad \langle a, AB \to AC, 5 \rangle u'' Do'' [a, AB \to AC, q+3] t''$$
$$[(\langle a, AB \to AC, 4 \rangle \to \langle a, AB \to AC, 5 \rangle, 0, B')],$$

where $m_1, m_2 \in \{(B \to B', \langle a, AB \to AC, 1 \rangle, 0)\}^*$, $m_3 \in \{(B' \to B, \langle a, AB \to AC, 4 \rangle, 0)\}^*$, $|m_3| = |m_1 m_2|$, $\omega = ([a, AB \to AC, 1] \to [a, AB \to AC, 2], 0, f^{-1}(1)[a, AB \to AC, 1]) \dots ([a, AB \to AC, f(A) - 1] \to [a, AB \to AC, f(A)], 0, f^{-1}(f(A) - 1)[a, AB \to AC, f(A) - 1])([a, AB \to AC, f(A)] \to [a, AB \to AC, f(A) + 1], 0, 0)([a, AB \to AC, f(A) + 1] \to [a, AB \to AC, f(A) + 2], 0, f^{-1}(f(A) + 1)[a, AB \to AC, f(A) + 1]) \dots ([a, AB \to AC, q] \to [a, AB \to AC, q + 1], 0, f^{-1}(q)[a, AB \to AC, q])([a, AB \to AC, q + 1] \to [a, AB \to AC, q + 2], 0, B'[a, AB \to AC, q + 1])([a, AB \to AC, q + 2] \to [a, AB \to AC, q + 3]), 0, \langle a, AB \to AC, 3 \rangle [a, AB \to AC, q + 2])$, $u' \in ((\text{alph}(u'') - \{B\}) \cup \{B'\})^*$, $g^{-1}(u') = u$, $o' \in ((\text{alph}(o'') - \{B\}) \cup \{B''\})^*$, $g^{-1}(o') = g^{-1}(o'') = o$, $t' \in ((\text{alph}(t'') - \{B\}) \cup \{B'\})^*$, $g^{-1}(t') = g^{-1}(t'') = t$.

Clearly, $\bar{a} u'' Do'' Bt'' \in g(auDoBt) = g(auDy_3) = g(y)$. Thus, there exists the derivation

$$S \Rightarrow_{\widetilde{G}}^* \bar{a} u'' Do'' Bt'' \Rightarrow_{\widetilde{G}} \bar{a} u'' y_2 o'' Bt'' \ [(D \to y_2, \bar{a}, 0)],$$

where $z_1 y_2 z_3 = \bar{a} u'' y_2 o'' Bt'' \in g(auy_2 oBt) = g(y_1 y_2 y_3) = g(x)$.

(e) Let $a'' = \langle a, AB \to AC, i \rangle$ for some $AB \to AC \in P$ and $i \in \{1, \dots, 4\}$ (see (iii) – (vi) in Claim 15). By analogy with (d), we can construct the derivation

$$S \Rightarrow_{\widetilde{G}}^* \bar{a} u'' Do'' Bt'' \Rightarrow_{\widetilde{G}} \bar{a} u'' y_2 o'' Bt'' \ [(D \to y_2, \bar{a}, 0)]$$

such that $\bar{a} u'' y_2 o'' Bt'' \in g(y_1 y_2 y_3) = g(x)$ (the details are left to the reader).

(iii) Let $p = AB \to AC \in P$, $A, C \in N_{CF}$, $B \in N_{CS}$, $y = y_1 AB y_3$, $y_1, y_3 \in V^*$, $x = y_1 AC y_3$, $\widetilde{y} = z_1 AY z_3$, $Y \in g(B)$, $z_i \in g(y_i)$ where $i \in \{1, 3\}$. Moreover, let $y_1 = au$ (see Claim 14), $z_1 = a'' u''$, $a'' \in g(a)$, $u'' \in g(u)$. The following cases (a) through (e) cover all possible forms of a'':

(a) Let $a'' = \bar{a}$. Then, by Claim 15, $Y = B$. By (3) in the construction of $\widetilde{G}$, there exists the following derivation:

$$
\begin{aligned}
S &\Rightarrow_{\widetilde{G}}^{n} &&\bar{a} u'' AB z_3 \\
&\Rightarrow_{\widetilde{G}} &&\langle a, AB \to AC, 1 \rangle u'' AB z_3 \\
& && [(\bar{a} \to \langle a, AB \to AC, 1 \rangle, 0, 0)] \\
&\Rightarrow_{\widetilde{G}}^{1+|m_1|} &&\langle a, AB \to AC, 1 \rangle u' A \widehat{B} u_3 \\
& && [m_1 (B \to \widehat{B}, \langle a, AB \to AC, 1 \rangle, 0)] \\
&\Rightarrow_{\widetilde{G}} &&\langle a, AB \to AC, 2 \rangle u' A \widehat{B} u_3 \\
& && [(\langle a, AB \to AC, 1 \rangle \to \langle a, AB \to AC, 2 \rangle, 0, B)] \\
&\Rightarrow_{\widetilde{G}} &&\langle a, AB \to AC, 2 \rangle u' A B'' u_3 \\
& && [(\widehat{B} \to B'', 0, B'')] \\
&\Rightarrow_{\widetilde{G}} &&\langle a, AB \to AC, 3 \rangle u' A B'' u_3 \\
& && [(\langle a, AB \to AC, 2 \rangle \to \langle a, AB \to AC, 3 \rangle, 0, \widehat{B})] \\
&\Rightarrow_{\widetilde{G}} &&\langle a, AB \to AC, 3 \rangle u' A [a, AB \to AC, 1] u_3 \\
& && [(B'' \to [a, AB \to AC, 1], \langle a, AB \to AC, 3 \rangle, 0)] \\
&\Rightarrow_{\widetilde{G}}^{q+2} &&\langle a, AB \to AC, 3 \rangle u' A [a, AB \to AC, q+3] u_3 \\
& && [\omega] \\
&\Rightarrow_{\widetilde{G}} &&\langle a, AB \to AC, 4 \rangle u' A [a, AB \to AC, q+3] u_3 \\
& && [(\langle a, AB \to AC, 3 \rangle \to \langle a, AB \to AC, 4 \rangle, \\
& && \quad [a, AB \to AC, q+3], 0)] \\
&\Rightarrow_{\widetilde{G}}^{|m_2|} &&\langle a, AB \to AC, 4 \rangle u'' A [a, AB \to AC, q+3] z_3 \\
& && [m_2] \\
&\Rightarrow_{\widetilde{G}} &&\langle a, AB \to AC, 5 \rangle u'' A [a, AB \to AC, q+3] z_3 \\
& && [(\langle a, AB \to AC, 4 \rangle \to \langle a, AB \to AC, 5 \rangle, 0, B')] \\
&\Rightarrow_{\widetilde{G}} &&\langle a, AB \to AC, 5 \rangle u'' AC z_3 \\
& && [([a, AB \to AC, q+3] \to C, \langle a, AB \to AC, 5 \rangle, 0)],
\end{aligned}
$$

where $m_1 \in \{(B \to B', \langle a, AB \to AC, 1 \rangle, 0)\}^*$, $m_2 \in \{(B' \to B, \langle a, AB \to AC, 4 \rangle, 0)\}^*$, $|m_1| = |m_2|$, $\omega = ([a, AB \to AC, 1] \to [a, AB \to AC, 2], 0, f^{-1}(1)[a, AB \to AC, 1]) \ldots ([a, AB \to AC, f(A) - 1] \to [a, AB \to AC, f(A)], 0, f^{-1}(f(A) - 1)[a, AB \to AC, f(A) - 1])([a, AB \to AC, f(A)] \to [a, AB \to AC, f(A) + 1], 0, 0)([a, AB \to AC, f(A) + 1] \to$

$[a, AB \rightarrow AC, f(A)+2], 0, f^{-1}(f(A)+1)[a, AB \rightarrow AC, f(A)+1]) \ldots ([a, AB \rightarrow AC, q] \rightarrow [a, AB \rightarrow AC, q + 1], 0, f^{-1}(q)[a, AB \rightarrow AC, q])([a, AB \rightarrow AC, q + 1] \rightarrow [a, AB \rightarrow AC, q + 2], 0, B'[a, AB \rightarrow AC, q + 1])([a, AB \rightarrow AC, q + 2] \rightarrow [a, AB \rightarrow AC, q + 3]), 0, \langle a, AB \rightarrow AC, 3 \rangle[a, AB \rightarrow AC, q+2]), u_3 \in ((\text{alph}(z_3) - \{B\}) \cup \{B'\})^*, g^{-1}(u_3) = g^{-1}(z_3) = y_3, u' \in ((\text{alph}(u'') - \{B\}) \cup \{B'\})^*, g^{-1}(u') = g^{-1}(u'') = u.$ It is clear that $\langle a, AB \rightarrow AC, 5 \rangle \in g(a)$; thus, $\langle a, AB \rightarrow AC, 5 \rangle u'' AC z_3 \in g(auACy_3) = g(x)$.

(b) Let $a'' = a$. Then, by Claim 15, $Y = B$. By analogy with (ii.b) and (iii.a) in the proof of this claim (see above), we obtain

$$S \Rightarrow_{\widetilde{G}}^{n-1} \bar{a}u'' ABz_3 \Rightarrow_{\widetilde{G}}^* \langle a, AB \rightarrow AC, 5 \rangle u'' AC z_3,$$

so $\langle a, AB \rightarrow AC, 5 \rangle u'' AC z_3 \in g(x)$.

(c) Let $a'' = \langle a, AB \rightarrow AC, 5 \rangle$ for some $AB \rightarrow AC \in P$ (see (vii) in Claim 15), and let $u'' AY z_3 \in (V - \{S\})^*$. At this point, $Y = B$. By analogy with (ii.c) and (iii.a) in the proof of this claim (see above), we can construct

$$S \Rightarrow_{\widetilde{G}}^{n+1} \bar{a}u'' ABz_3 \Rightarrow_{\widetilde{G}}^* \langle a, AB \rightarrow AC, 5 \rangle u'' AC z_3,$$

so $\langle a, AB \rightarrow AC, 5 \rangle u'' AC z_3 \in g(x)$.

(d) Let $a'' = \langle a, AB \rightarrow AC, 5 \rangle$ for some $AB \rightarrow AC \in P$ (see (vii) in Claim 15), and let $[a, AB \rightarrow AC, q + 3] \in \text{alph}(u'' AY z_3)$. By analogy with (ii.d) and (iii.a) in the proof of this claim (see above), we can construct

$$S \Rightarrow_{\widetilde{G}}^* \bar{a}u'' ABz_3,$$

and then

$$S \Rightarrow_{\widetilde{G}}^* \bar{a}u'' ABz_3 \Rightarrow_{\widetilde{G}}^* \langle a, AB \rightarrow AC, 5 \rangle u'' AC z_3$$

so that $\langle a, AB \rightarrow AC, 5 \rangle u'' AC z_3 \in g(auACy_3) = g(x)$.

(e) Let $a'' = \langle a, AB \rightarrow AC, i \rangle$ for some $AB \rightarrow AC \in P$, $i \in \{1, \ldots, 4\}$, see (III) – (IV) in Claim 15. By analogy with (ii.e) and (iii.d) in the proof of this claim, we can construct

$$S \Rightarrow_{\widetilde{G}}^* \bar{a}u'' AC z_3,$$

where $\bar{a}u'' AC z_3 \in g(x)$.

If: By induction on n, we next prove that if $S \Rightarrow_{\widetilde{G}}^n v$ with $v \in g(w)$ and $w \in V^*$ for some $n \geq 0$, then $S \Rightarrow_G^* w$.

Basis: For $n = 0$, the only v is S as $S \Rightarrow_{\widetilde{G}}^0 S$. Because $\{S\} = g(S)$, we have $w = S$. Clearly, $S \Rightarrow_G^0 S$.

Induction Hypothesis: Assume that the claim holds for all derivations of length n or less, for some $n \geq 0$. Let us show that it is also true for $n + 1$.

Induction Step: For $n + 1 = 1$, there only exists a direct derivation of the form

$$S \Rightarrow_{\widetilde{G}} \bar{a}A \ [(S \to \bar{a}A, 0, 0)],$$

where $A \in N_{CF} \cup \{\varepsilon\}$, $a \in T$, and $\bar{a}A \in g(aA)$. By (1), we have in P a production of the form $S \to aA$, and thus a direct derivation $S \Rightarrow_G aA$.

Suppose $n + 1 \geq 2$ (i.e., $n \geq 1$). Consider a derivation

$$S \Rightarrow_G^{n+1} x',$$

where $x' \in g(x)$, $x \in V^*$. Because $n + 1 \geq 2$, there exist $\bar{a} \in W_4$, $A \in N_{CF}$, and $y \in V^+$ such that

$$S \Rightarrow_{\widetilde{G}} \bar{a}A \Rightarrow_{\widetilde{G}}^{n-1} y' \Rightarrow_{\widetilde{G}} x' \ [p],$$

where $p \in \widetilde{P}$, $y' \in g(y)$, and by the induction hypothesis,

$$S \Rightarrow_G^* y.$$

Let us assume that $y' = z_1 Z z_2$, $y = y_1 D y_2$, $z_j \in g(y_j)$, $y_j \in (V - \{S\})^*$, $j = 1, 2$, $Z \in g(D)$, $D \in V - \{S\}$, $p = (Z \to u', \alpha, \beta) \in P'$, $\alpha = 0$ or $\beta = 0$, $x' = z_1 u' z_2$, $u' \in g(u)$ for some $u \in V^*$; that is, $x' \in g(y_1 u y_2)$. The following cases (i) through (iii) cover all possible forms of

$$y' \Rightarrow_{\widetilde{G}} x' \ [p].$$

(i) Let $Z \in N_{CF}$. By inspection of $\widetilde{P}$, we see that $Z = D$, $p = (D \to u', \bar{a}, 0) \in \widetilde{P}$, $D \to u \in P$ and $u = u'$. Thus,

$$S \Rightarrow_G^* y_1 B y_2 \Rightarrow_G y_1 u y_2 \ [B \to u].$$

(ii) Let $u = D$. Then, by induction hypothesis, we have the derivation

$$S \Rightarrow_G^* y_1 D y_2$$

and $y_1 D y_2 = y_1 u y_2$ in G.

(iii) Let $p = ([a, AB \to AC, q + 3] \to C, \langle a, AB \to AC, 5 \rangle, 0)$, $Z = [a, AB \to AC, q + 3]$. Thus, $u' = C$ and $D = B \in N_{CS}$. By case (VI) in Claim 15 and the form of p, we have $z_1 = \langle a, AB \to AC, 5 \rangle t$ and $y_1 = ao$, where $t \in g(o)$, $\langle a, AB \to AC, 5 \rangle \in g(a)$, $o \in (V - \{S\})^*$, and $a \in T$. From (3) in the construction of $\widetilde{G}$, it follows that there exists a production of the form $AB \to AC \in P$. Moreover, (3) and Claim 15 imply that the derivation

$$S \Rightarrow_{\widetilde{G}} \bar{a}A \Rightarrow_{\widetilde{G}}^{n-1} y' \Rightarrow_{\widetilde{G}} x' \ [p]$$

can be expressed in the form

$$
\begin{aligned}
S \quad &\Rightarrow_{\widetilde{G}} && \bar{a}A \\
&\Rightarrow^{*}_{\widetilde{G}} && \bar{a}tBz_2 \\
&\Rightarrow_{\widetilde{G}} && \langle a, AB \to AC, 1\rangle vtBz_2 \\
& && \quad [(\bar{a} \to \langle a, AB \to AC, 1\rangle, 0, 0)] \\
&\Rightarrow^{|\omega'|}_{\widetilde{G}} && \langle a, AB \to AC, 1\rangle v\widehat{B}w_2 \\
& && \quad [\omega'] \\
&\Rightarrow_{\widetilde{G}} && \langle a, AB \to AC, 1\rangle vB''w_2 \\
& && \quad [(\widehat{B} \to B'', 0, B'')] \\
&\Rightarrow_{\widetilde{G}} && \langle a, AB \to AC, 2\rangle vB''w_2 \\
& && \quad [(\langle a, AB \to AC, 1\rangle \to \langle a, AB \to AC, 2\rangle, 0, B)] \\
&\Rightarrow_{\widetilde{G}} && \langle a, AB \to AC, 3\rangle vB''w_2 \\
& && \quad [(\langle a, AB \to AC, 2\rangle \to \langle a, AB \to AC, 3\rangle, 0, \widehat{B})] \\
&\Rightarrow_{\widetilde{G}} && \langle a, AB \to AC, 3\rangle v[a, AB \to AC, 1]w_2 \\
& && \quad [(B'' \to [a, AB \to AC, 1], \langle a, AB \to AC, 3\rangle, 0)] \\
&\Rightarrow^{|\omega|}_{\widetilde{G}} && \langle a, AB \to AC, 3\rangle v[a, AB \to AC, q+3]w_2 \\
& && \quad [\omega] \\
&\Rightarrow_{\widetilde{G}} && \langle a, AB \to AC, 4\rangle v[a, AB \to AC, q+3]w_2 \\
& && \quad [(\langle a, AB \to AC, 3\rangle \to \langle a, AB \to AC, 4\rangle, \\
& && \quad\quad [a, AB \to AC, q+3], 0)] \\
&\Rightarrow^{|\omega'|-1}_{\widetilde{G}} && \langle a, AB \to AC, 4\rangle t[a, AB \to AC, q+3]z_2 \\
& && \quad [\omega''] \\
&\Rightarrow_{\widetilde{G}} && \langle a, AB \to AC, 5\rangle t[a, AB \to AC, q+3]z_2 \\
& && \quad [(\langle a, AB \to AC, 4\rangle \to \langle a, AB \to AC, 5\rangle, 0, B')] \\
&\Rightarrow_{\widetilde{G}} && \langle a, AB \to AC, 5\rangle tCz_2 \\
& && \quad [([a, AB \to AC, q+3] \to C, \langle a, AB \to AC, 5\rangle, 0)],
\end{aligned}
$$

where $\omega' \in \{(B \to B', \langle a, AB \to AC, 1\rangle, 0)\}^* \{(B \to \widehat{B}, \langle a, AB \to AC, 1\rangle, 0)\}$ $\{(B \to B', \langle a, AB \to AC, 1\rangle, 0)\}^*$, $g(B) \cap \operatorname{alph}(vw_2) \subseteq \{B'\}$, $g^{-1}(v) = g^{-1}(t)$, $g^{-1}(w_2) = g^{-1}(z_2)$, $\omega = \omega_1([a, AB \to AC, f(A)] \to [a, AB \to AC, f(A)+1], 0, 0)\omega_2([a, AB \to AC, q+1] \to [a, AB \to AC, q+2], 0, B'[a, AB \to AC, q+1])([a, AB \to AC, q+2] \to [a, AB \to AC, q+3], 0, \langle a, AB \to AC, 3\rangle[a, AB \to AC, q+2])$, $\omega_1 = ([a, AB \to AC, 1] \to [a, AB \to AC, 2], 0, f^{-1}(1)[a, AB \to AC, 1]) \ldots ([a, AB \to AC, f(A)-1] \to [a, AB \to AC, f(A)], 0, f^{-1}(f(A)-1)[a, AB \to AC, f(A)-1])$, where $f(A)$ implies $q_1 = \varepsilon$, $\omega_2 = ([a, AB \to AC, f(A)+1] \to [a, AB \to AC, f(A)+2], 0, f^{-1}(f(A)+1)[a, AB \to AC, f(A)+1]) \ldots ([a, AB \to AC, q] \to [a, AB \to AC, q+1], 0, f^{-1}(q)[a, AB \to AC, q])$, where $f(A) = q$ implies $q_2 = \varepsilon$, $\omega'' \in \{(B' \to B, \langle a, AB \to AC, 4\rangle, 0)\}^*$.

The derivation above implies that the right-most symbol of t must be A. As $t \in g(o)$, the right-most symbol of o must be A as well. That is, $t = s'A$, $o = sA$ and $s' \in g(s)$ for some $s \in (V - \{S\})^*$. By the induction hypothesis, there exists a derivation

$$S \Rightarrow_G^* asABy_2.$$

Because $AB \rightarrow AC \in P$, we get

$$S \Rightarrow_G^* asABy_2 \Rightarrow_G asACy_2 \; [AB \rightarrow AC],$$

where $asACy_2 = y_1uy_2$.

By (i), (ii), and (iii) and inspection of $\widetilde{P}$, we see that we have considered all possible derivations of the form

$$S \Rightarrow_{\widetilde{G}}^{n+1} x',$$

so we have established Claim 16 by the principle of induction. $\quad\square$

The equivalence of G and $\widetilde{G}$ can be easily derived from Claim 16. By the definition of g, we have $g(a) = \{a\}$ for all $a \in T$. Thus, by Claim 16, we have for all $x \in T^*$,

$$S \Rightarrow_G^* x \quad \text{if and only if} \quad S \Rightarrow_{\widetilde{G}}^* x.$$

Consequently, $L(G) = L(\widetilde{G})$, and the theorem holds. $\quad\blacksquare$

Corollary 12. prop-SSC$(1,2)$ = prop-SSC = prop-SC$(1,2)$ = prop-SC = CS.

We now turn to the investigation of *ssc*-grammars of degree $(1,2)$ with erasing productions.

Theorem 29. SSC$(1,2)$ = RE.

Proof. Clearly, we have **SSC$(1,2)$ $\subseteq$ RE**. Thus, it suffices to show that **RE $\subseteq$ SSC$(1,2)$**. Every language $L \in$ **RE** can be generated by a grammar $G = (V, T, P, S)$ in which each production is of the form $AB \rightarrow AC$ or $A \rightarrow x$, where $A, B, C \in V - T$, $x \in \{\varepsilon\} \cup T \cup (V - T)^2$ (see Lemma 3). Thus, the inclusion can be established by analogy with the proof of Theorem 28 (the details are left to the reader). $\quad\blacksquare$

Corollary 13. SSC$(1,2)$ = SSC = SC$(1,2)$ = SC = RE.

Corollaries 10, 11, 12, and 13 imply the following relationships of language families generated by simple semi-conditional grammars:

Corollary 14.

$$\textbf{CF}$$
$$\subset$$
$$\textbf{prop-SSC} = \textbf{prop-SSC}(2,1) = \textbf{prop-SSC}(1,2)$$
$$= \textbf{prop-SC} = \textbf{prop-SC}(2,1) = \textbf{prop-SC}(1,2) = \textbf{CS}$$
$$\subset$$
$$\textbf{SSC} = \textbf{SSC}(2,1) = \textbf{SSC}(1,2) = \textbf{SC} = \textbf{SC}(2,1) = \textbf{SC}(1,2) = \textbf{RE}.$$

Next, we turn or attention to reduced versions of *ssc*-grammars. More specifically, we demonstrate that there exist several normal forms of *ssc*-grammars with a limited number of conditional productions and nonterminals.

Theorem 30 ([135]). *Every recursively enumerable language can be defined by a simple semi-conditional grammar of degree $(2,1)$ with no more than 12 conditional productions and 13 nonterminals.*

Proof. Let L be a recursively enumerable language. By Geffert [69], we can assume that L is generated by a grammar G of the form

$$G = (V, T, P \cup \{AB \rightarrow \varepsilon, CD \rightarrow \varepsilon\}, S)$$

such that P contains only context-free productions and

$$V - T = \{S, A, B, C, D\}.$$

Construct an *ssc*-grammar G' of degree $(2,1)$,

$$G' = (V', T, P', S),$$

where

$$V' = V \cup W,$$
$$W = \{\widetilde{A}, \widetilde{B}, \langle \varepsilon_A \rangle, \$, \widetilde{C}, \widetilde{D}, \langle \varepsilon_C \rangle, \# \}, \ V \cap W = \emptyset.$$

The set of productions P' is defined in the following way:

1. If $H \rightarrow y \in P$, $H \in V - T$, $y \in V^*$, then add $(H \rightarrow y, 0, 0)$ to P'.

2. Add the following six productions to P':

$$(A \rightarrow \widetilde{A}, 0, \widetilde{A}),$$
$$(B \rightarrow \widetilde{B}, 0, \widetilde{B}),$$
$$(\widetilde{A} \rightarrow \langle \varepsilon_A \rangle, \widetilde{A}\widetilde{B}, 0),$$
$$(\widetilde{B} \rightarrow \$, \langle \varepsilon_A \rangle \widetilde{B}, 0),$$
$$(\langle \varepsilon_A \rangle \rightarrow \varepsilon, 0, \widetilde{B}),$$
$$(\$ \rightarrow \varepsilon, 0, \langle \varepsilon_A \rangle).$$

3. Add the following six productions to P':

$$(C \rightarrow \widetilde{C}, 0, \widetilde{C}),$$
$$(D \rightarrow \widetilde{D}, 0, \widetilde{D}),$$
$$(\widetilde{C} \rightarrow \langle \varepsilon_C \rangle, \widetilde{C}\widetilde{D}, 0),$$
$$(\widetilde{D} \rightarrow \#, \langle \varepsilon_C \rangle \widetilde{D}, 0),$$
$$(\langle \varepsilon_C \rangle \rightarrow \varepsilon, 0, \widetilde{D}),$$
$$(\# \rightarrow \varepsilon, 0, \langle \varepsilon_C \rangle).$$

Basic Idea. Notice that G' has degree $(2,1)$ and contains only 12 conditional productions and 13 nonterminals. The productions of (2) simulate the application of $AB \to \varepsilon$ in G' and the productions of (3) simulate the application of $CD \to \varepsilon$ in G'.

Let us describe the simulation of $AB \to \varepsilon$. First, one occurrence of A and one occurrence of B are rewritten to $\widetilde{A}$ and $\widetilde{B}$, respectively (no more than one $\widetilde{A}$ and one $\widetilde{B}$ appear in any sentential form). The right neighbor of $\widetilde{A}$ is checked to be $\widetilde{B}$ and $\widetilde{A}$ is rewritten to $\langle \varepsilon_A \rangle$. Then, analogously, the left neighbor of $\widetilde{B}$ is checked to be $\langle \varepsilon_A \rangle$ and $\widetilde{B}$ is rewritten to \$. Finally, $\langle \varepsilon_A \rangle$ and \$ are erased. The simulation of $CD \to \varepsilon$ is analogous.

To establish $L(G) = L(G')$, we first prove the following two claims.

Claim 17. $S \Rightarrow^*_{G'} x'$ implies $\#_{\widetilde{X}} x' \leq 1$ for all $\widetilde{X} \in \{\widetilde{A}, \widetilde{B}, \widetilde{C}, \widetilde{D}\}$ and some $x' \in (V')^*$.

Proof. By inspection of productions in P', the only production that can generate $\widetilde{X}$ is of the form $(X \to \widetilde{X}, 0, \widetilde{X})$. This production can be applied only when no $\widetilde{X}$ occurs in the rewritten sentential form. Thus, it is not possible to derive x' from S such that $\#_{\widetilde{X}} x' \geq 2$. $\square$

Informally, the next claim says that every occurrence of $\langle \varepsilon_A \rangle$ in derivations from S is always followed either by $\widetilde{B}$ or \$, and every occurrence of $\langle \varepsilon_C \rangle$ is always followed either by $\widetilde{D}$ or #.

Claim 18. *It holds that*

(I) $S \Rightarrow^*_{G'} y'_1 \langle \varepsilon_A \rangle y'_2$ implies $y'_2 \in (V')^+$ and $\mathrm{first}(y'_2) \in \{\widetilde{B}, \$\}$ for any $y'_1 \in (V')^*$;

(II) $S \Rightarrow^*_{G'} y'_1 \langle \varepsilon_C \rangle y'_2$ implies $y'_2 \in (V')^+$ and $\mathrm{first}(y'_2) \in \{\widetilde{D}, \#\}$ for any $y'_1 \in (V')^*$.

Proof. We establish the proof by the examination of all possible forms of derivations that may occur when deriving a sentential form containing $\langle \varepsilon_A \rangle$ or $\langle \varepsilon_C \rangle$.

(I) By the definition of P', the only production that can generate $\langle \varepsilon_A \rangle$ is $p = (\widetilde{A} \to \langle \varepsilon_A \rangle, \widetilde{A}\widetilde{B}, 0)$. This production has the permitting condition $\widetilde{A}\widetilde{B}$, so it can be used provided that $\widetilde{A}\widetilde{B}$ occurs in a sentential form. Furthermore, by Claim 17, no other occurrence of $\widetilde{A}$ or $\widetilde{B}$ can appear in the given sentential form. Consequently, we obtain a derivation

$$S \Rightarrow^*_{G'} u'_1 \widetilde{A} \widetilde{B} u'_2 \Rightarrow_{G'} u'_1 \langle \varepsilon_A \rangle \widetilde{B} u'_2 \; [p]$$

for some $u'_1, u'_2 \in (V')^*$, $\widetilde{A}, \widetilde{B} \notin \mathrm{sub}(u'_1 u'_2)$, which represents the only way how to get $\langle \varepsilon_A \rangle$. Obviously, $\langle \varepsilon_A \rangle$ is always followed by $\widetilde{B}$ in $u'_1 \langle \varepsilon_A \rangle \widetilde{B} u'_2$.

Next, we discuss how G' can rewrite the subword $\langle \varepsilon_A \rangle \widetilde{B}$ in $u'_1 \langle \varepsilon_A \rangle \widetilde{B} u'_2$. There are only two productions having the nonterminals $\langle \varepsilon_A \rangle$ or $\widetilde{B}$ on their left-hand side, $p_1 = (\widetilde{B} \to \$, \langle \varepsilon_A \rangle \widetilde{B}, 0)$ and $p_2 = (\langle \varepsilon_A \rangle \to \varepsilon, 0, \widetilde{B})$. G' cannot use p_2 to erase $\langle \varepsilon_A \rangle$ in $u'_1 \langle \varepsilon_A \rangle \widetilde{B} u'_2$ because p_2 forbids an occurrence of $\widetilde{B}$ in the rewritten string. Production p_1 has also a context condition, but $\langle \varepsilon_A \rangle \widetilde{B} \in \mathrm{sub}(u'_1 \langle \varepsilon_A \rangle \widetilde{B} u'_2)$, and thus p_1 can be used to rewrite $\widetilde{B}$ with $\$$. Hence, we obtain a derivation of the form

$$
\begin{aligned}
S \quad &\Rightarrow^*_{G'} u'_1 \widetilde{A} \widetilde{B} u'_2 \quad &&\Rightarrow_{G'} u'_1 \langle \varepsilon_A \rangle \widetilde{B} u'_2 \quad [p] \\
&\Rightarrow^*_{G'} v'_1 \langle \varepsilon_A \rangle \widetilde{B} v'_2 \quad &&\Rightarrow_{G'} v'_1 \langle \varepsilon_A \rangle \$ v'_2 \quad [p_1].
\end{aligned}
$$

Notice that during this derivation, G' may rewrite u'_1 and u'_2 to some v'_1 and v'_2, respectively $(v'_1, v'_2 \in (V')^*)$; however, $\langle \varepsilon_A \rangle \widetilde{B}$ remains unchanged after this rewriting.

In this derivation we obtained the second symbol $\$$, that can appear as the right neighbor of $\langle \varepsilon_A \rangle$. It suffices to show that there is no other symbol that can appear immediately after $\langle \varepsilon_A \rangle$. By inspection of P', only $(\$ \to \varepsilon, 0, \langle \varepsilon_A \rangle)$ can rewrite $\$$. However, this production cannot be applied when $\langle \varepsilon_A \rangle$ occurs in the given sentential form. In other words, the occurrence of $\$$ in the subword $\langle \varepsilon_A \rangle \$$ cannot be rewritten before $\langle \varepsilon_A \rangle$ is erased by the production p_2. Hence, $\langle \varepsilon_A \rangle$ is always followed by either $\widetilde{B}$ or $\$$, and thus the first part of Claim 18 holds.

(II) By inspection of productions simulating $AB \to \varepsilon$ and $CD \to \varepsilon$ in G' (see (2) and (3) in the definition of P'), these two sets of productions work analogously. Thus, part (II) of Claim 18 can be proved by analogy with part (I).

$\square$

Let us return to the main part of the proof. Let g be a finite substitution from $(V')^*$ to V^* defined as follows:

1. For all $X \in V$: $g(X) = \{X\}$.

2. $g(\widetilde{A}) = \{A\}$, $g(\widetilde{B}) = \{B\}$, $g(\langle \varepsilon_A \rangle) = \{A\}$, $g(\$) = \{B, AB\}$.

3. $g(\widetilde{C}) = \{C\}$, $g(\widetilde{D}) = \{D\}$, $g(\langle \varepsilon_C \rangle) = \{C\}$, $g(\#) = \{C, CD\}$.

Having this substitution, we can now prove the following claim:

Claim 19. $S \Rightarrow^*_G x$ if and only if $S \Rightarrow^*_{G'} x'$ for some $x \in g(x')$, $x \in V^*$, $x' \in (V')^*$.

Proof. The claim is proved by induction on the length of derivations.

Only if: We show that

$$
S \Rightarrow^m_G x \quad \text{implies} \quad S \Rightarrow^*_{G'} x,
$$

where $m \geq 0$, $x \in V^*$; clearly $x \in g(x)$. This is established by induction on m.

Basis: Let $m = 0$. That is, $S \Rightarrow_G^0 S$. Clearly, $S \Rightarrow_{G'}^0 S$.

Induction Hypothesis: Suppose that the claim holds for all derivations of length m or less, for some $m \geq 0$.

Induction Step: Let us consider a derivation

$$S \Rightarrow_G^{m+1} x, \; x \in V^*.$$

Since $m + 1 \geq 1$, there is some $y \in V^+$ and $p \in P \cup \{AB \to \varepsilon, CD \to \varepsilon\}$ such that

$$S \Rightarrow_G^m y \Rightarrow_G x \; [p].$$

By the induction hypothesis, there is a derivation

$$S \Rightarrow_{G'}^* y.$$

The following three cases cover all possible forms of p:

(i) $p = H \to y_2 \in P$, $H \in V - T$, $y_2 \in V^*$. Then, $y = y_1 H y_3$ and $x = y_1 y_2 y_3$, $y_1, y_3 \in V^*$. Because we have $(H \to y_2, 0, 0) \in P'$,

$$S \Rightarrow_{G'}^* y_1 H y_3 \Rightarrow_{G'} y_1 y_2 y_3 \; [(H \to y_2, 0, 0)]$$

and $y_1 y_2 y_3 = x$.

(ii) $p = AB \to \varepsilon$. Then, $y = y_1 A B y_3$ and $x = y_1 y_3$, $y_1, y_3 \in V^*$. In this case, there is the derivation

$$
\begin{aligned}
S \quad &\Rightarrow_{G'}^* \quad y_1 A B y_3 \\
&\Rightarrow_{G'} \quad y_1 \widetilde{A} B y_3 && [(A \to \widetilde{A}, 0, \widetilde{A})] \\
&\Rightarrow_{G'} \quad y_1 \widetilde{A} \widetilde{B} y_3 && [(B \to \widetilde{B}, 0, \widetilde{B})] \\
&\Rightarrow_{G'} \quad y_1 \langle \varepsilon_A \rangle \widetilde{B} y_3 && [(\widetilde{A} \to \langle \varepsilon_A \rangle, \widetilde{A}\widetilde{B}, 0)] \\
&\Rightarrow_{G'} \quad y_1 \langle \varepsilon_A \rangle \$ y_3 && [(\widetilde{B} \to \$, \langle \varepsilon_A \rangle \widetilde{B}, 0)] \\
&\Rightarrow_{G'} \quad y_1 \$ y_3 && [(\langle \varepsilon_A \rangle \to \varepsilon, 0, \widetilde{B})] \\
&\Rightarrow_{G'} \quad y_1 y_3 && [(\$ \to \varepsilon, 0, \langle \varepsilon_A \rangle)].
\end{aligned}
$$

(iii) $p = CD \to \varepsilon$. Then, $y = y_1 C D y_3$ and $x = y_1 y_3$, $y_1, y_3 \in V^*$. By analogy with (ii), there exists the derivation

$$
\begin{aligned}
S \quad &\Rightarrow_{G'}^* \quad y_1 C D y_3 \\
&\Rightarrow_{G'} \quad y_1 \widetilde{C} D y_3 && [(C \to \widetilde{C}, 0, \widetilde{C})] \\
&\Rightarrow_{G'} \quad y_1 \widetilde{C} \widetilde{D} y_3 && [(D \to \widetilde{D}, 0, \widetilde{D})] \\
&\Rightarrow_{G'} \quad y_1 \langle \varepsilon_C \rangle \widetilde{D} y_3 && [(\widetilde{C} \to \langle \varepsilon_C \rangle, \widetilde{C}\widetilde{D}, 0)] \\
&\Rightarrow_{G'} \quad y_1 \langle \varepsilon_C \rangle \# y_3 && [(\widetilde{D} \to \#, \langle \varepsilon_C \rangle \widetilde{D}, 0)] \\
&\Rightarrow_{G'} \quad y_1 \# y_3 && [(\langle \varepsilon_C \rangle \to \varepsilon, 0, \widetilde{D})] \\
&\Rightarrow_{G'} \quad y_1 y_3 && [(\# \to \varepsilon, 0, \langle \varepsilon_C \rangle)].
\end{aligned}
$$

If: By induction on the length n of derivations in G', we prove that

$$S \Rightarrow_{G'}^n x' \quad \text{implies} \quad S \Rightarrow_G^* x$$

for some $x \in g(x')$, $x \in V^*$, $x' \in (V')^*$.

Basis: Let $n = 0$. That is, $S \Rightarrow_{G'}^0 S$. It is obvious that $S \Rightarrow_G^0 S$ and $S \in g(S)$.

Induction Hypothesis: Assume that the claim holds for all derivations of length n or less, for some $n \geq 0$.

Induction Step: Consider a derivation

$$S \Rightarrow_{G'}^{n+1} x', \ x' \in (V')^*.$$

Since $n + 1 \geq 1$, there is some $y' \in (V')^+$ and $p' \in P'$ such that

$$S \Rightarrow_{G'}^n y' \Rightarrow_{G'} x' \ [p'],$$

and by the induction hypothesis, there is also a derivation

$$S \Rightarrow_G^* y$$

such that $y \in g(y')$.

By inspection of P', the following cases (i) through (xiii) cover all possible forms of p':

(i) $p' = (H \to y_2, 0, 0) \in P'$, $H \in V - T$, $y_2 \in V^*$. Then, $y' = y_1' H y_3'$, $x' = y_1' y_2 y_3'$, $y_1', y_3' \in (V')^*$ and y has the form $y = y_1 Z y_3$, where $y_1 \in g(y_1')$, $y_3 \in g(y_3')$ and $Z \in g(H)$. Because for all $X \in V - T$: $g(X) = \{X\}$, the only Z is H, and thus $y = y_1 H y_3$. By the definition of P' (see (1)), there exists a production $p = H \to y_2$ in P, and we can construct the derivation

$$S \Rightarrow_G^* y_1 H y_3 \Rightarrow_G y_1 y_2 y_3 \ [p]$$

such that $y_1 y_2 y_3 = x$, $x \in g(x')$.

(ii) $p' = (A \to \widetilde{A}, 0, \widetilde{A})$. Then, $y' = y_1' A y_3'$, $x' = y_1' \widetilde{A} y_3'$, $y_1', y_3' \in (V')^*$, and $y = y_1 Z y_3$, where $y_1 \in g(y_1')$, $y_3 \in g(y_3')$ and $Z \in g(A)$. Because $g(A) = \{A\}$, the only Z is A, so we can express $y = y_1 A y_3$. Having the derivation $S \Rightarrow_G^* y$ such that $y \in g(y')$, it is easy to see that also $y \in g(x')$ because $A \in g(\widetilde{A})$.

(iii) $p' = (B \to \widetilde{B}, 0, \widetilde{B})$. By analogy with (ii), $y' = y_1' B y_3'$, $x' = y_1' \widetilde{B} y_3'$, $y = y_1 B y_3$, where $y_1', y_3' \in (V')^*$, $y_1 \in g(y_1')$, $y_3 \in g(y_3')$, and thus $y \in g(x')$ because $B \in g(\widetilde{B})$.

(iv) $p' = (\widetilde{A} \to \langle \varepsilon_A \rangle, \widetilde{A}\widetilde{B}, 0)$. By the permitting condition of this production, $\widetilde{A}\widetilde{B}$ surely occurs in y'. By Claim 17, no more than one $\widetilde{A}$ can occur in y'. Therefore, y' must be of the form $y' = y_1' \widetilde{A}\widetilde{B} y_3'$, where $y_1', y_3' \in (V')^*$ and

$\widetilde{A} \notin \mathrm{sub}(y_1' y_3')$. Then, $x' = y_1' \langle \varepsilon_A \rangle \widetilde{B} y_3'$ and y is of the form $y = y_1 Z y_3$, where $y_1 \in g(y_1')$, $y_3 \in g(y_3')$ and $Z \in g(\widetilde{A}\widetilde{B})$. Because $g(\widetilde{A}\widetilde{B}) = \{AB\}$, the only Z is AB; thus, we obtain $y = y_1 A B y_3$. By the induction hypothesis, we have a derivation $S \Rightarrow_G^* y$ such that $y \in g(y')$. According to the definition of g, $y \in g(x')$ as well because $A \in g(\langle \varepsilon_A \rangle)$ and $B \in g(\widetilde{B})$.

(v) $p' = (\widetilde{B} \to \$, \langle \varepsilon_A \rangle \widetilde{B}, 0)$. This production can be applied provided that $\langle \varepsilon_A \rangle \widetilde{B} \in \mathrm{sub}(y')$. Moreover, by Claim 17, $\#_{\widetilde{B}} y' \leq 1$. Hence, we can express $y' = y_1' \langle \varepsilon_A \rangle \widetilde{B} y_3'$, where $y_1', y_3' \in (V')^*$ and $\widetilde{B} \notin \mathrm{sub}(y_1' y_3')$. Then, $x' = y_1' \langle \varepsilon_A \rangle \$ y_3'$ and $y = y_1 Z y_3$, where $y_1 \in g(y_1')$, $y_3 \in g(y_3')$ and $Z \in g(\langle \varepsilon_A \rangle \widetilde{B})$. By the definition of g, $g(\langle \varepsilon_A \rangle \widetilde{B}) = \{AB\}$, so $Z = AB$ and $y = y_1 A B y_3$. By the induction hypothesis, we have a derivation $S \Rightarrow_G^* y$ such that $y \in g(y')$. Because $A \in g(\langle \varepsilon_A \rangle)$ and $B \in g(\$)$, $y \in g(x')$ as well.

(vi) $p' = (\langle \varepsilon_A \rangle \to \varepsilon, 0, \widetilde{B})$. Application of $(\langle \varepsilon_A \rangle \to \varepsilon, 0, \widetilde{B})$ implies that $\langle \varepsilon_A \rangle$ occurs in y'. Claim 18 says that $\langle \varepsilon_A \rangle$ has either $\widetilde{B}$ or $\$$ as its right neighbor. Since the forbidding condition of p' forbids an occurrence of $\widetilde{B}$ in y', the right neighbor of $\langle \varepsilon_A \rangle$ must be $\$$. As a result, we obtain $y' = y_1' \langle \varepsilon_A \rangle \$ y_3'$ where $y_1', y_3' \in (V')^*$. Then, $x' = y_1' \$ y_3'$ and y is of the form $y = y_1 Z y_3$, where $y_1 \in g(y_1')$, $y_3 \in g(y_3')$ and $Z \in g(\langle \varepsilon_A \rangle \$)$. By the definition of g, $g(\langle \varepsilon_A \rangle \$) = \{AB, AAB\}$. If $Z = AB$, $y = y_1 A B y_3$. Having the derivation $S \Rightarrow_G^* y$, it holds that $y \in g(x')$ because $AB \in g(\$)$.

(vii) $p' = (\$ \to \varepsilon, 0, \langle \varepsilon_A \rangle)$. Then, $y' = y_1' \$ y_3'$ and $x' = y_1' y_3'$, where $y_1', y_3' \in (V')^*$. Express $y = y_1 Z y_3$ so that $y_1 \in g(y_1')$, $y_3 \in g(y_3')$ and $Z \in g(\$)$, where $g(\$) = \{B, AB\}$. Let $Z = AB$. Then, $y = y_1 A B y_3$, and there exists the derivation

$$S \Rightarrow_G^* y_1 A B y_3 \Rightarrow_G y_1 y_3 \; [AB \to \varepsilon],$$

where $y_1 y_3 = x$, $x \in g(x')$.

In cases (ii) through (vii) we discussed all six productions simulating the application of $AB \to \varepsilon$ in G' (see (2) in the definition of P'). Cases (viii) through (xiii) should cover productions simulating the application of $CD \to \varepsilon$ in G' (see (3)). However, by inspection of these two sets of productions, it is easy to see that they work analogously. Therefore, we leave this part of the proof to the reader.

We have completed the proof and established Claim 19 by the principle of induction. $\qquad \square$

Observe that $L(G) = L(G')$ follows from Claim 19. Indeed, according to the definition of g, we have $g(a) = \{a\}$ for all $a \in T$. Thus, from Claim 19, we have for any $x \in T^*$:

$$S \Rightarrow_G^* x \quad \text{if and only if} \quad S \Rightarrow_{G'}^* x.$$

Consequently, $L(G) = L(G')$, and the theorem holds. $\qquad \blacksquare$

Let us note that very recently Vaszil has improved Theorem 30 by demonstrating that even 10 conditional productions and 12 nonterminals suffice to generate every recursively enumerable language (see [174]):

Theorem 31. *Every recursively enumerable language can be generated by a simple semi-conditional grammar of degree $(2, 1)$ having no more than 10 conditional productions and 12 nonterminals.*

Continuing with the investigation of reduced *ssc*-grammars, Vaszil also proved that if we allow permitting conditions of length three—that is, *ssc*-grammars of degree $(3, 1)$—the number of conditional productions and nonterminals can be further decreased.

Theorem 32. *Every recursively enumerable language can be generated by a simple semi-conditional grammar of degree $(3, 1)$ with no more than 8 conditional productions and 11 nonterminals.*

Proof. Let L by a recursively enumerable language. Without any loss of generality, we can assume that L is generated by a phrase-structure grammar

$$G = (V, T, P \cup \{ABC \to \varepsilon\}, S),$$

where

$$V - T = \{S, S', A, B, C\}$$

and P contains only context-free productions of the forms $S \to zSx$, $z \in \{A, B\}^*$, $x \in T$, $S \to S'$, $S' \to uS'v$, $u \in \{A, B\}^*$, $v \in \{B, C\}^*$, $S' \to \varepsilon$ (see [68]). Every successful derivation in G consists of the following two phases:

1. $S \Rightarrow_G^* z_n \dots z_1 S x_1 \dots x_n \Rightarrow_G z_n \dots z_1 S' x_1 \dots x_n$, $z_i \in \{A, B\}^*$, $1 \le i \le n$.

2. $z_n \dots z_1 S' x_1 \dots x_n \Rightarrow_G^* z_n \dots z_1 u_m \dots u_1 S' v_1 \dots v_m x_1 \dots x_n \Rightarrow_G z_n \dots z_1 u_m \dots u_1 v_1 \dots v_m x_1 \dots x_n$, where $u_j \in \{A, B\}^*$, $v_j \in \{B, C\}^*$, $1 \le j \le m$, and the terminal word $x_1 \dots x_n$ is generated by G if and only if by using the erasing production $ABC \to \varepsilon$, the substring $z_n \dots z_1 u_m \dots u_1 v_1 \dots v_m$ can be deleted.

Next, we introduce the *ssc*-grammar

$$G' = (V', T, P', S)$$

of degree $(3, 1)$, where

$$V' = \{S, S', A, A', A'', B, B', B'', C, C', C''\} \cup T$$

and P' constructed as

1. for every $H \to y \in P$, add $(H \to y, 0, 0)$ to P';

2. for every $X \in \{A, B, C\}$, add $(X \to X', 0, X')$ to P';

3. add the following six productions to P':

$$(C' \to C'', A'B'C', 0),$$
$$(A' \to A'', A'B'C'', 0),$$
$$(B' \to B'', A''B'C'', 0),$$
$$(A'' \to \varepsilon, 0, C''),$$
$$(C'' \to \varepsilon, 0, B'),$$
$$(B'' \to \varepsilon, 0, 0).$$

Observe that G' satisfies all the requirements of this theorem; that is, it contains only 8 conditional productions and 11 nonterminals. G' reproduces the first two phases of generating a terminal word in G by using the productions of the form $(H \to y, 0, 0) \in P'$. The third phase, during which $ABC \to \varepsilon$ is applied, is simulated by the additional productions. Examine these productions to see that all words generated by G can also be generated by G'. Indeed, for every derivation step

$$y_1 ABC y_2 \Rightarrow_G y_1 y_2 \ [ABC \to \varepsilon]$$

in G, $y_1, y_2 \in V^*$, there exists the following derivation in G':

$$
\begin{array}{lll}
y_1 ABC y_2 & \Rightarrow_{G'} \ y_1 A'BC y_2 & [(A \to A', 0, A')] \\
& \Rightarrow_{G'} \ y_1 A'B'C y_2 & [(B \to B', 0, B')] \\
& \Rightarrow_{G'} \ y_1 A'B'C' y_2 & [(C \to C', 0, C')] \\
& \Rightarrow_{G'} \ y_1 A'B'C'' y_2 & [(C' \to C'', A'B'C', 0)] \\
& \Rightarrow_{G'} \ y_1 A''B'C'' y_2 & [(A' \to A'', A'B'C'', 0)] \\
& \Rightarrow_{G'} \ y_1 A''B''C'' y_2 & [(B' \to B'', A''B'C'', 0)] \\
& \Rightarrow_{G'} \ y_1 A''B'' y_2 & [(C'' \to \varepsilon, 0, B')] \\
& \Rightarrow_{G'} \ y_1 B'' y_2 & [(A'' \to \varepsilon, 0, C'')] \\
& \Rightarrow_{G'} \ y_1 y_2 & [(B'' \to \varepsilon, 0, 0)]
\end{array}
$$

As a result, $L(G) \subseteq L(G')$. In the following we show that G' does not generate words that cannot be generated by G; thus, $L(G') - L(G) = \emptyset$, so $L(G') = L(G)$.

Let us study how G' can generate a terminal word. All derivations start from S. While the sentential form contains S or S', its form is zSw or $zuS'vw$, $z, u, v \in \{A, B, C, A', B', C'\}^*$, $w \in T^*$, where if $g(X') = X$ for $X \in \{A, B, C\}$ and $g(X) = X$ for all other symbols of V, then $g(zSw)$ or $g(zuS'vw)$ are valid sentential forms of G. Furthermore, zu contains at most one occurrence of A', v contains at most one occurrence of C', and zuv contains at most one occurrence of B' (see (2) in the construction of P'). After $(S' \to \varepsilon, 0, 0)$ is used, we get a sentential form $zuvw$ with z, u, v, and w as above such that

$$S \Rightarrow_G^* g(zuvw).$$

Next, we demonstrate that

$$zuv \Rightarrow_{G'}^* \varepsilon \quad \text{implies} \quad g(zuv) \Rightarrow_G^* \varepsilon.$$

More specifically, we investigate all possible derivations rewriting a sentential form containing a single occurrence of each of the letters A', B', and C'.

Consider a sentential form $zuvw$, where $z, u, v \in \{A, B, C, A', B', C'\}^*$, $w \in T^*$, and $\#_{A'}zu = \#_{B'}zuv = \#_{C'}v = 1$. By the definition of productions rewriting A', B', and C' (see (3) in the construction of P'), we see that these three symbols must form a substring $A'B'C'$; otherwise, no next derivation step can be made. That is, $zuvw = z\bar{u}A'B'C'\bar{v}w$ for some $\bar{u}, \bar{v} \in \{A, B, C\}^*$. Next, observe that the only applicable production is $(C' \rightarrow C'', A'B'C', 0)$. Thus, we get

$$z\bar{u}A'B'C'\bar{v}w \Rightarrow_{G'} z\bar{u}A'B'C''\bar{v}w.$$

This sentential form can be rewritten in two ways. First, we can rewrite A' to A'' by $(A' \rightarrow A'', A'B'C'', 0)$. Second, we can replace another occurrence of C with C'. Let us investigate the derivation

$$z\bar{u}A'B'C''\bar{v}w \Rightarrow_{G'} z\bar{u}A''B'C''\bar{v}w \;\; [(A' \rightarrow A'', A'B'C'', 0)].$$

As before, we can either rewrite another occurrence of A to A', or rewrite an occurrence of C to C', or rewrite B' to B'' by using $(B' \rightarrow B'', A''B'C'', 0)$. Taking into account all possible combinations of the above-described steps, we see that after the first application of $(B' \rightarrow B'', A''B'C'', 0)$ the whole derivation is of the form:

$$z\bar{u}A'B'C'\bar{v}w \Rightarrow^+_{G'} zu_1Xu_2A''B''C''v_1Yv_2w,$$

where $X \in \{A', \varepsilon\}$, $Y \in \{C', \varepsilon\}$, $u_1g(X)u_2 = \bar{u}$, and $v_1g(Y)v_2 = \bar{v}$. Let $zu_1Xu_2 = x$ and $v_1Yv_2 = y$. The next derivation step can be made in four ways. By an application of $(B \rightarrow B', 0, B')$, we can rewrite an occurrence of B in x or y. In both cases, this derivation is blocked in the next step. The remaining two derivations are

$$xA''B''C''yw \Rightarrow_{G'} xA''C''yw \;\; [(B'' \rightarrow \varepsilon, 0, 0)]$$

and

$$xA''B''C''yw \Rightarrow_{G'} xA''B''yw \;\; [(C'' \rightarrow \varepsilon, 0, B')].$$

Let us examine how G' can rewrite $xA''C''yw$. The following three cases cover all possible steps:

(i) $xA''C''yw \Rightarrow_{G'} x_1B'x_2A''C''yw \;\; [(B \rightarrow B', 0, B')]$, where $x_1Bx_2 = x$, and the derivation is blocked.

(ii) $xA''C''yw \Rightarrow_{G'} xA''C''y_1B'y_2w \;\; [(B \rightarrow B', 0, B')]$, where $y_1By_2 = y$. As before, no next derivation step can be made.

(iii) $xA''C''yw \Rightarrow_{G'} xA''yw \;\; [(C'' \rightarrow \varepsilon, 0, B')]$. Then, all the following derivations

$$xA''yw \Rightarrow_{G'} xyw,$$

$$xA''yw \Rightarrow_{G'} x_1B'x_2A''yw \Rightarrow_{G'} x_1B'x_2yw,$$

where $x_1 B x_2 = x$, and

$$xA''yw \Rightarrow_{G'} xA''y_1 B'y_2 w \Rightarrow_{G'} xy_1 B'y_2 w,$$

where $y_1 B y_2 = y$, produce a sentential form in which the substring $A''B''C''$ is erased. This sentential form contains at most one occurrence of A', B', and C'.

Return to

$$xA''B''C''yw \Rightarrow_{G'} xA''B''yw.$$

Observe that by analogy with case (iii), any rewriting of $xA''B''yw$ removes the substring $A''B''$, and produces a sentential form containing at most one occurrence of A', B', and C'.

To summarize the considerations above, the reader can see that as long as there exists an occurrence of A'', B'', or C'' in the sentential form, only the erasing productions or $(B \rightarrow B', 0, B')$ can be applied. The derivation either enters a sentential form that blocks the derivation or the substring $A'B'C'$ is completely erased, and new occurrences of A, B, and C can then be changed to A', B', and C'. That is,

$$z\bar{u}A'B'C'\bar{v}w \Rightarrow_{G'}^{+} xyw \quad \text{implies} \quad g(z\bar{u}A'B'C'\bar{v}w) \Rightarrow_{G} g(xyw),$$

where $z, \bar{u}, \bar{v} \in \{A, B, C\}^*$, $x, y \in \{A, B, C, A', B', C'\}^*$, $w \in T^*$, and $z\bar{u} = g(x)$, $\bar{v}w = g(yw)$. In other words, the productions constructed in (2) and (3) correctly simulate the application of the only non-context-free production $ABC \rightarrow \varepsilon$. Recall that $g(a) = a$ for all $a \in T$. Hence, $g(xyw) = g(xy)w$. Thus, $L(G') - L(G) = \emptyset$.

Having $L(G) \subseteq L(G')$ and $L(G') - L(G) = \emptyset$, we get $L(G) = L(G')$, and the theorem holds. ∎

Open Problems. Let us state several open problems regarding *ssc*-grammars. In Theorems 26, 27, 28, and 29, we proved that *ssc*-grammars of degrees $(1, 2)$ and $(2, 1)$ generate the family of recursively enumerable languages, and propagating *ssc*-grammars of degrees $(1, 2)$ and $(2, 1)$ generate the family of context-sensitive languages. However, we discussed no *ssc*-grammars of degree $(1, 1)$. According to Penttonen (see Theorem 24), propagating *sc*-grammars of degree $(1, 1)$ generate a proper subfamily of context-sensitive languages. That is, **prop-SSC**$(1, 1) \subseteq$ **prop-SC**$(1, 1) \subset$ **CS**. Are propagating *ssc*-grammars of degree $(1, 1)$ as powerful as propagating *sc*-grammars of degree $(1, 1)$? Furthermore, consider *ssc*-grammars of degree $(1, 1)$ with erasing productions. Are they more powerful than propagating *ssc*-grammars of degree $(1, 1)$? Do they generate the family of all context-sensitive languages or, even more, the family of recursively enumerable languages?

In Theorems 30 through 32, several reduced normal forms of these grammars were presented. These normal forms give rise to the following questions. Can any of the results be further improved with respect to the number of conditional productions or nonterminals? Are there analogical reduced forms of *ssc*-grammars with degrees $(2, 1)$ and $(3, 1)$? Moreover, reconsider these results in terms of propagating *ssc*-grammars. Is it possible to achieve analogical results if we disallow erasing productions?

4.2 Parallel Conditional Grammars

In this section, we study parallel grammars with permitting and forbidding context conditions. As ET0L grammars represent a very important type of parallel grammars in modern theoretical computer science (see [149], [150], [155], [156], [166]), we base our discussion on these grammars extended by context conditions. By analogy with sequential context-conditional grammars, we first define context-conditional ET0L grammars as ET0L grammars with finite sets of permitting and forbidding conditions. Then, we investigate the generative power of their two specific cases—forbidding ET0L grammars and simple semi-conditional ET0L grammars.

4.2.1 Context-Conditional ET0L Grammars

Definition 16. A *context-conditional ET0L grammar* (a *CET0L grammar* for short) is defined as a $t+3$-tuple,

$$G = (V, T, P_1, \ldots, P_t, S),$$

where V, T, and S are the total alphabet, the terminal alphabet $(T \subset V)$, and the axiom $(S \in V - T)$, respectively. Every P_i, $1 \leq i \leq t$, for some $t \geq 1$, is a finite set of productions of the form

$$(a \rightarrow x, Per, For)$$

with $a \in V$, $x \in V^*$, and $Per, For \subseteq V^+$ are finite languages. A CET0L grammar without erasing productions is said to be *propagating* (a *CEPT0L grammar* for short). G has *degree* (r, s), where r and s are natural numbers, if for every $i = 1, \ldots, t$ and $(a \rightarrow x, Per, For) \in P_i$, $\max(Per) \leq r$ and $\max(For) \leq s$ (see Section 2.1 for the definition of max). Let $u, v \in V^*$, $u = a_1 a_2 \ldots a_q$, $v = v_1 v_2 \ldots v_q$, $q = |u|$, $a_j \in V$, $v_j \in V^*$, and $p_1, p_2, \ldots, p_q$ is a sequence of productions $p_j = (a_j \rightarrow v_j, Per_j, For_j) \in P_i$ for all $j = 1, \ldots, q$ and some $i \in \{1, \ldots, t\}$. If for every p_j, $Per_j \subseteq \mathrm{sub}(u)$ and $For_j \cap \mathrm{sub}(u) = \emptyset$, then u *directly derives* v according to $p_1, p_2, \ldots, p_q$ in G, denoted by

$$u \Rightarrow_G v \ [p_1, p_2, \ldots, p_q].$$

The language of G is defined as

$$L(G) = \{x \in T^* : S \Rightarrow_G^* x\}.$$

If $t = 1$, then G is called a *context-conditional E0L* grammar (a *CE0L grammar* for short). If G is a propagating CE0L grammar, then G is said to be a CEP0L grammar. The families of languages defined by CEPT0L, CET0L, CEP0L, and CE0L grammars of degree (r, s) are denoted by $\mathbf{CEPT0L}(r, s)$, $\mathbf{CET0L}(r, s)$, $\mathbf{CEP0L}(r, s)$, and $\mathbf{CE0L}(r, s)$, respectively. Set

$$\mathbf{CEPT0L} = \bigcup_{r=0}^{\infty} \bigcup_{s=0}^{\infty} \mathbf{CEPT0L}(r, s), \quad \mathbf{CET0L} = \bigcup_{r=0}^{\infty} \bigcup_{s=0}^{\infty} \mathbf{CET0L}(r, s),$$

$$\mathbf{CEP0L} = \bigcup_{r=0}^{\infty} \bigcup_{s=0}^{\infty} \mathbf{CEP0L}(r, s), \quad \mathbf{CE0L} = \bigcup_{r=0}^{\infty} \bigcup_{s=0}^{\infty} \mathbf{CE0L}(r, s).$$

The following lemmas and theorems establish several general results concering the generative power of context-conditional ET0L grammars:

Lemma 10. $\mathbf{CEP0L} \subseteq \mathbf{CEPT0L} \subseteq \mathbf{CET0L}, \mathbf{CEP0L} \subseteq \mathbf{CE0L} \subseteq \mathbf{CET0L}$. *For any $r, s \geq 0$, $\mathbf{CEP0L}(r, s) \subseteq \mathbf{CEPT0L}(r, s) \subseteq \mathbf{CET0L}(r, s)$, $\mathbf{CEP0L}(r, s) \subseteq \mathbf{CE0L}(r, s) \subseteq \mathbf{CET0L}(r, s)$.*

Proof. Follows trivially from the definitions. $\qquad\square$

Theorem 33.

$$\mathbf{CF}$$
$$\subset$$
$$\mathbf{CE0L}(0, 0) = \mathbf{CEP0L}(0, 0) = \mathbf{E0L} = \mathbf{EP0L}$$
$$\subset$$
$$\mathbf{CET0L}(0, 0) = \mathbf{CEPT0L}(0, 0) = \mathbf{ET0L} = \mathbf{EPT0L}$$
$$\subset$$
$$\mathbf{CS}$$

Proof. Clearly, CEP0L and CE0L grammars of degree $(0, 0)$ are ordinary EP0L and E0L grammars, respectively. Analogously, CEPT0L and CET0L grammars of degree $(0, 0)$ are EPT0L and ET0L grammars, respectively. Because $\mathbf{CF} \subset \mathbf{E0L} = \mathbf{EP0L} \subset \mathbf{ET0L} = \mathbf{EPT0L} \subset \mathbf{CS}$ (see Theorem 2), we get $\mathbf{CF} \subset \mathbf{CE0L}(0, 0) = \mathbf{CEP0L}(0, 0) = \mathbf{E0L} \subset \mathbf{CET0L}(0, 0) = \mathbf{CEPT0L}(0, 0) = \mathbf{ET0L} \subset \mathbf{CS}$; therefore, the theorem holds. $\qquad\blacksquare$

Lemma 11. $\mathbf{CEPT0L}(r, s) \subseteq \mathbf{CS}$, *for any $r \geq 0$, $s \geq 0$.*

Proof. For $r = 0$ and $s = 0$, we have

$$\mathbf{CEPT0L}(0, 0) = \mathbf{EPT0L} \subset \mathbf{CS}.$$

The following proof demonstrates that the inclusion holds for any r and s such that $r + s \geq 1$.

Let L be a language generated by a CEPT0L grammar,

$$G = (V, T, P_1, \ldots, P_t, S),$$

of degree (r, s), for some $r, s \geq 0$, $r + s \geq 1$, $t \geq 1$. Let k be the greater number of r and s. Let

$$M = \{x \in V^+ : |x| \leq k\}.$$

For every P_i, $1 \leq i \leq t$, set

$$\mathrm{cf}(P_i) = \{a \to z : (a \to z, Per, For) \in P_i, \ a \in V, \ z \in V^+\}.$$

Then, set

$$
\begin{aligned}
N_F &= \{\langle X, x \rangle : X \subseteq M, \ x \in M \cup \{\varepsilon\}\}, \\
N_T &= \{\lfloor X \rfloor : X \subseteq M\}, \\
N_B &= \{\lceil Q \rceil : Q \subseteq \mathrm{cf}(P_i), \ 1 \leq i \leq t\}, \\
V' &= V \cup N_F \cup N_T \cup N_B \cup \{\triangleright, \triangleleft, \$, S', \#\}, \\
T' &= T \cup \{\#\}.
\end{aligned}
$$

Construct the context-sensitive grammar

$$G' = (V', T', P', S')$$

with the finite set of productions P' defined as follows:

1. Add $S' \to \triangleright \langle \emptyset, \varepsilon \rangle S \triangleleft$ to P'.

2. For all $X \subseteq M$, $x \in (V^k \cup \{\varepsilon\})$ and $y \in V^k$, add the next production to P':

$$\langle X, x \rangle y \to y \langle X \cup \mathrm{sub}(xy, k), y \rangle.$$

3. For all $X \subseteq M$, $x \in (V^k \cup \{\varepsilon\})$ and $y \in V^+$, $|y| \leq k$, add the next production to P':

$$\langle X, x \rangle y \triangleleft \to y \lfloor X \cup \mathrm{sub}(xy, k) \rfloor \triangleleft.$$

4. For all $X \subseteq M$ and $Q \subseteq \mathrm{cf}(P_i)$, where $i \in \{1, \ldots, t\}$, such that for every $a \to z \in Q$, there exists $(a \to z, Per, For) \in P_i$ satisfying $Per \subseteq X$ and $For \cap X = \emptyset$, add the next production to P':

$$\lfloor X \rfloor \triangleleft \to \lceil Q \rceil \triangleleft.$$

5. For every $Q \subseteq \mathrm{cf}(P_i)$ for some $i \in \{1, \ldots, t\}$, $a \in V$ and $z \in V^+$ such that $a \to z \in Q$, add the next production to P':

$$a \lceil Q \rceil \to \lceil Q \rceil z.$$

6. For all $Q \subseteq \mathrm{cf}(P_i)$ for some $i = \{1, \ldots, t\}$, add the next production to P':

$$\triangleright \lceil Q \rceil \to \triangleright \langle \emptyset, \varepsilon \rangle.$$

7. Add $\triangleright \langle \emptyset, \varepsilon \rangle \to \#\$$, $\$\triangleleft \to \#\#$, and $\$a \to a\$$, for all $a \in T$, to P'.

Claim 20. *Every successful derivation in G' has the form*

$$S' \Rightarrow_{G'} \quad \triangleright\langle\emptyset,\varepsilon\rangle S\triangleleft$$
$$\Rightarrow_{G'}^{+} \quad \triangleright\langle\emptyset,\varepsilon\rangle x\triangleleft$$
$$\Rightarrow_{G'} \quad \#\$x\triangleleft$$
$$\Rightarrow_{G'}^{|x|} \quad \#x\$\triangleleft$$
$$\Rightarrow_{G'} \quad \#x\#\#$$

such that $x \in T^{+}$ and during $\triangleright\langle\emptyset,\varepsilon\rangle S\triangleleft \Rightarrow_{G'}^{+} \triangleright\langle\emptyset,\varepsilon\rangle x\triangleleft$, every sentential form w satisfies $w \in \{\triangleright\}H^{+}\{\triangleleft\}$, where $H \subseteq V' - \{\triangleright, \triangleleft, \#, \$, S'\}$.

Proof. Observe that the only production that can rewrite the axiom is $S' \rightarrow \triangleright\langle\emptyset,\varepsilon\rangle S\triangleleft$; thus,

$$S' \Rightarrow_{G'} \triangleright\langle\emptyset,\varepsilon\rangle S\triangleleft.$$

After that, every sentential form that occurs in

$$\triangleright\langle\emptyset,\varepsilon\rangle S\triangleleft \Rightarrow_{G'}^{+} \triangleright\langle\emptyset,\varepsilon\rangle x\triangleleft$$

can be rewritten by using any of the productions (2) through (6) from the construction of P'. By inspection of these productions, it is obvious that the edge symbols $\triangleright$ and $\triangleleft$ remain unchanged and no other occurrences of them appear inside the sentential form. Moreover, there is no production generating a symbol from $\{\#, \$, S'\}$. Therefore, all these sentential forms belong to $\{\triangleright\}H^{+}\{\triangleleft\}$.

Next, let us explain how G' generates a word from $L(G')$. Only $\triangleright\langle\emptyset,\varepsilon\rangle \rightarrow \#\$$ can rewrite $\triangleright$ to a symbol from T (see (7) in the definition of P'). According to the left-hand side of this production, we obtain

$$S' \Rightarrow_{G'} \triangleright\langle\emptyset,\varepsilon\rangle S\triangleleft \Rightarrow_{G'}^{*} \triangleright\langle\emptyset,\varepsilon\rangle x\triangleleft \Rightarrow_{G'} \#\$x\triangleleft,$$

where $x \in H^{+}$. To rewrite $\triangleleft$, G' uses $\$\triangleleft \rightarrow \#\#$. Thus, G' needs $\$$ as the left neighbor of $\triangleleft$. Suppose that $x = a_1 a_2 \ldots a_q$, where $q = |x|$ and $a_i \in T$, for all $i \in \{1,\ldots,q\}$. Since for every $a \in T$ there is $\$a \rightarrow a\$ \in P'$ (see (7)), we can construct

$$\#\$a_1 a_2 \ldots a_n\triangleleft \Rightarrow_{G'} \quad \#a_1\$a_2 \ldots a_n\triangleleft$$
$$\Rightarrow_{G'} \quad \#a_1 a_2\$ \ldots a_n\triangleleft$$
$$\Rightarrow_{G'}^{|x|-2} \quad \#a_1 a_2 \ldots a_n\$\triangleleft.$$

Notice that this derivation can be constructed only for x that belong to T^{+}. Then, $\$\triangleleft$ is rewritten to $\#\#$. As a result,

$$S' \Rightarrow_{G'} \triangleright\langle\emptyset,\varepsilon\rangle S\triangleleft \Rightarrow_{G'}^{+} \triangleright\langle\emptyset,\varepsilon\rangle x\triangleleft \Rightarrow_{G'} \#\$x\triangleleft \Rightarrow_{G'}^{|x|} \#x\$\triangleleft \Rightarrow_{G'} \#x\#\#$$

with the required properties. Thus, the claim holds. $\square$

The following claim demonstrates how G' simulates a direct derivation from G—the heart of the construction.

Let $x \Rightarrow_{G'}^{\oplus} y$ denote the derivation $x \Rightarrow_{G'}^{+} y$ such that $x = \triangleright\langle\emptyset,\varepsilon\rangle u\triangleleft$, $y = \triangleright\langle\emptyset,\varepsilon\rangle v\triangleleft$, $u,v \in V^{+}$, and there is no other occurrence of a string of the form $\triangleright\langle\emptyset,\varepsilon\rangle z\triangleleft$, $z \in V^{*}$, during $x \Rightarrow_{G'}^{+} y$.

Claim 21. *For every $u, v \in V^*$,*

$$\triangleright\langle\emptyset, \varepsilon\rangle u \triangleleft \Rightarrow_{G'}^{\oplus} \triangleright\langle\emptyset, \varepsilon\rangle v \triangleleft \quad \text{if and only if} \quad u \Rightarrow_G v.$$

Proof.

Only if: Let us show how G' rewrites $\triangleright\langle\emptyset, \varepsilon\rangle u \triangleleft$ to $\triangleright\langle\emptyset, \varepsilon\rangle v \triangleleft$. The simulation consists of two phases.

During the first, forward phase, G' scans u to get all nonempty substrings of length k or less. By repeatedly using productions

$$\langle X, x\rangle y \rightarrow y\langle X \cup \mathrm{sub}(xy, k), y\rangle,$$

where $X \subseteq M$, $x \in (V^k \cup \{\varepsilon\})$, $y \in V^k$ (see (2) in the definition of P'), the occurrence of a symbol with form $\langle X, x\rangle$ is moved toward the end of the sentential form. Simultaneously, the substrings of u are collected in X. The forward phase is finished by

$$\langle X, x\rangle y \triangleleft \rightarrow y\lfloor X \cup \mathrm{sub}(xy, k)\rfloor \triangleleft,$$

where $x \in (V^k \cup \{\varepsilon\})$, $y \in V^+$, $|y| \leq k$ (see (3)); the production reaches the end of u and completes $X = \mathrm{sub}(u, k)$. Formally,

$$\triangleright\langle\emptyset, \varepsilon\rangle u \triangleleft \Rightarrow_{G'}^{+} \triangleright u\lfloor X\rfloor \triangleleft$$

such that $X = \mathrm{sub}(u, k)$. Then, $\lfloor X\rfloor$ is changed to $\lceil Q\rceil$, where

$$Q = \{a \rightarrow z : (a \rightarrow z, Per, For) \in P_i, \ a \in V, \ z \in V^+,$$
$$Per, For \subseteq M, \ Per \subseteq X, \ For \cap X = \emptyset\},$$

for some $i \in \{1, \ldots, t\}$, by

$$\lfloor X\rfloor \triangleleft \rightarrow \lceil Q\rceil \triangleleft$$

(see (4)). In other words, G' selects a subset of productions from P_i that could be used to rewrite u in G.

The second, backward phase simulates rewriting of all symbols in u in parallel. Since

$$a\lceil Q\rceil \rightarrow \lceil Q\rceil z \in P'$$

for all $a \rightarrow z \in Q$, $a \in V$, $z \in V^+$ (see (5)),

$$\triangleright u\lceil Q\rceil \triangleleft \Rightarrow_{G'}^{|u|} \triangleright\lceil Q\rceil v \triangleleft$$

such that $\lceil Q\rceil$ moves left and every symbol $a \in V$ in u is rewritten to some z provided that $a \rightarrow z \in Q$. Finally, $\lceil Q\rceil$ is rewritten to $\langle\emptyset, \varepsilon\rangle$ by

$$\triangleright\lceil Q\rceil \rightarrow \triangleright\langle\emptyset, \varepsilon\rangle.$$

As a result, we obtain

$$\triangleright\langle\emptyset, \varepsilon\rangle u \triangleleft \Rightarrow_{G'}^{+} \triangleright u\lfloor X\rfloor \triangleleft \Rightarrow_{G'} \triangleright u\lceil Q\rceil \triangleleft$$
$$\Rightarrow_{G'}^{|u|} \triangleright\lceil Q\rceil v \triangleleft \Rightarrow_{G'} \triangleright\langle\emptyset, \varepsilon\rangle v \triangleleft.$$

Observe that this is the only way of deriving

$$\rhd\langle\emptyset,\varepsilon\rangle u\lhd \Rightarrow_{G'}^{\oplus} \rhd\langle\emptyset,\varepsilon\rangle v\lhd.$$

Let us show that $u \Rightarrow_G v$. Indeed, because we have $(a \to z, Per, For) \in P_i$ for every $a\lceil Q\rceil \to \lceil Q\rceil z \in P$ used in the backward phase, where $Per \subseteq \mathrm{sub}(u, k)$ and $For \cap \mathrm{sub}(u, k) = \emptyset$ (see the construction of Q), there exists a derivation

$$u \Rightarrow_G v\ [p_1 \dots p_q],$$

where $|u| = q$, and $p_j = (a \to z, Per, For) \in P_i$ such that $a\lceil Q\rceil \to \lceil Q\rceil z$ has been applied in the $(q - j + 1)$-th derivation step in

$$\rhd u\lceil Q\rceil\lhd \Rightarrow_{G'}^{|u|} \rhd\lceil Q\rceil v\lhd,$$

where $a \in V$, $z \in V^+$, $1 \le j \le q$.

If: The converse implication is similar to the only-if part, so we leave it to the reader. $\qquad\square$

Claim 22. $S' \Rightarrow_{G'}^{+} \rhd\langle\emptyset,\varepsilon\rangle x\lhd$ *if and only if* $S \Rightarrow_G^* x$, *for all* $x \in V^+$.

Proof.

Only if: The only-if part is proved by induction on the ith occurrence of the sentential form w satisfying $w = \rhd\langle\emptyset,\varepsilon\rangle u\lhd$, $u \in V^+$, during the derivation in G'.

Basis: Let $i = 1$. Then, $S' \Rightarrow_{G'} \rhd\langle\emptyset,\varepsilon\rangle S\lhd$ and $S \Rightarrow_G^0 S$.

Induction Hypothesis: Suppose that the claim holds for all $i \le h$, for some $h \ge 1$.

Induction Step: Let $i = h + 1$. Since $h + 1 \ge 2$, we can express

$$S' \Rightarrow_{G'}^{+} \rhd\langle\emptyset,\varepsilon\rangle x_i\lhd$$

as

$$S' \Rightarrow_{G'}^{+} \rhd\langle\emptyset,\varepsilon\rangle x_{i-1}\lhd \Rightarrow_{G'}^{\oplus} \rhd\langle\emptyset,\varepsilon\rangle x_i\lhd,$$

where $x_{i-1}, x_i \in V^+$. By the induction hypothesis,

$$S \Rightarrow_G^* x_{i-1}.$$

Claim 21 says that

$$\rhd\langle\emptyset,\varepsilon\rangle x_{i-1}\lhd \Rightarrow_{G'}^{\oplus} \rhd\langle\emptyset,\varepsilon\rangle x_i\lhd \quad \text{if and only if} \quad x_{i-1} \Rightarrow_G x_i.$$

Hence,

$$S \Rightarrow_G^* x_{i-1} \Rightarrow_G x_i$$

and the only-if part holds.

If: By induction on n, we prove that

$$S \Rightarrow_G^n x \quad \text{implies} \quad S' \Rightarrow_{G'}^+ \triangleright \langle \emptyset, \varepsilon \rangle x \triangleleft$$

for all $n \geq 0$, $x \in V^+$.

Basis: For $n = 0$, $S \Rightarrow_G^0 S$ and $S' \Rightarrow_{G'} \triangleright \langle \emptyset, \varepsilon \rangle S \triangleleft$.

Induction Hypothesis: Assume that the claim holds for all n or less, for some $n \geq 0$.

Induction Step: Let

$$S \Rightarrow_G^{n+1} x, \ x \in V^+.$$

Because $n + 1 \geq 1$, there exists $y \in V^+$ such that

$$S \Rightarrow_G^n y \Rightarrow_G x,$$

and by the induction hypothesis, there is also a derivation

$$S' \Rightarrow_{G'}^+ \triangleright \langle \emptyset, \varepsilon \rangle y \triangleleft.$$

From Claim 21, we have

$$\triangleright \langle \emptyset, \varepsilon \rangle y \triangleleft \Rightarrow_{G'}^\oplus \triangleright \langle \emptyset, \varepsilon \rangle x \triangleleft.$$

Therefore,

$$S' \Rightarrow_{G'}^+ \triangleright \langle \emptyset, \varepsilon \rangle y \triangleleft \Rightarrow_{G'}^\oplus \triangleright \langle \emptyset, \varepsilon \rangle x \triangleleft,$$

and the converse implication holds as well. □

From Claims 20 and 22, we see that any successful derivation in G' is of the form

$$S' \Rightarrow_{G'}^+ \triangleright \langle \emptyset, \varepsilon \rangle x \triangleleft \Rightarrow_{G'}^+ \#x\#\#$$

such that

$$S \Rightarrow_G^* x, \ x \in T^+.$$

Therefore, we have for each $x \in T^+$,

$$S' \Rightarrow_{G'}^+ \#x\#\# \quad \text{if and only if} \quad S \Rightarrow_G^* x.$$

Define the homomorphism h over $(T \cup \{\#\})^*$ as $h(\#) = \varepsilon$ and $h(a) = a$ for all $a \in T$. Observe that h is 4-linear erasing with respect to $L(G')$ (see page 98 in [161]). Furthermore, notice that $h(L(G')) = L(G)$. Because **CS** is closed under linear erasing (see Theorem 10.4 on page 98 in [161]), $L \in$ **CS**. Thus, Lemma 11 holds. □

Theorem 34. CEPT0L = CS.

Proof. By Lemma 11, **CEPT0L** $\subseteq$ **CS**. Later in this chapter we define two special cases of CEPT0L grammars and prove that they generate all the family of context-sensitive languages (see Theorems 38 and 41). Therefore, **CS** $\subseteq$ **CEPT0L**, and hence **CEPT0L** = **CS**.   ∎

Lemma 12. CET0L $\subseteq$ **RE**.

Proof. This lemma follows from Church's thesis. To obtain an algorithm converting any CET0L grammar to an equivalent phrase-structure grammar, use the technique presented in Lemma 11.   □

Theorem 35. CET0L = RE.

Proof. By Lemma 12, **CET0L** $\subseteq$ **RE**. In Sections 4.2.2 and 4.2.3, we introduce two special cases of CET0L grammars and demonstrate that even these grammars generate **RE** (see Theorems 39 and 40) and therefore **RE** $\subseteq$ **CET0L**. As a result, **CET0L = RE**.   ∎

4.2.2   Forbidding ET0L Grammars

In this section, we discuss forbidding ET0L grammars (see [137]). First, we define forbidding ET0L grammars. Then, we establish their generative power.

Definition 17. Let $G = (V, T, P_1, \ldots, P_t, S)$ be a CET0L grammar. If every $p = (a \rightarrow x, Per, For) \in P_i$, where $i = 1, \ldots, t$, satisfies $Per = \emptyset$, then G is said to be *forbidding ET0L grammar* (an *FET0L grammar* for short). If G is a propagating FET0L grammar, then G is said to be an *FEPT0L grammar*. If $t = 1$, G is called an *FE0L grammar*. If G is a propagating FE0L grammar, G is called an *FEP0L grammar*.

Convention 4. Let $G = (V, T, P_1, \ldots, P_t, S)$ be an FET0L grammar of degree (r, s). Clearly, $(a \rightarrow x, Per, For) \in P_i$ implies $Per = \emptyset$ for all $i = 1, \ldots, t$. By analogy with sequential forbidding grammars, we thus omit the empty set in the productions. For simplicity, we also say that G's degree is s instead of (r, s).

The families of languages generated by FE0L grammars, FEP0L grammars, FET0L grammars, and FEPT0L grammars of degree s are denoted by $\mathbf{FE0L}(s)$, $\mathbf{FEP0L}(s)$, $\mathbf{FET0L}(s)$, and $\mathbf{FEPT0L}(s)$, respectively. Moreover,

$$\mathbf{FEPT0L} = \bigcup_{s=0}^{\infty} \mathbf{FEPT0L}(s), \qquad \mathbf{FET0L} = \bigcup_{s=0}^{\infty} \mathbf{FET0L}(s),$$

$$\mathbf{FEP0L} = \bigcup_{s=0}^{\infty} \mathbf{FEP0L}(s), \qquad \mathbf{FE0L} = \bigcup_{s=0}^{\infty} \mathbf{FE0L}(s).$$

Example 8. Let
$$G = (\{S, A, B, C, a, \bar{a}, b\}, \{a, b\}, P, S)$$

be an FEP0L grammar, where

$$P = \{(S \to ABA, \emptyset),$$
$$(A \to aA, \{\bar{a}\}),$$
$$(B \to bB, \emptyset),$$
$$(A \to \bar{a}, \{\bar{a}\}),$$
$$(\bar{a} \to a, \emptyset),$$
$$(B \to C, \emptyset),$$
$$(C \to bC, \{A\}),$$
$$(C \to b, \{A\}),$$
$$(a \to a, \emptyset),$$
$$(b \to b, \emptyset)\}.$$

Obviously, G is an FEP0L grammar of degree 1. Observe that for every word from $L(G)$, there exists a derivation of the form

$$
\begin{aligned}
S \quad &\Rightarrow_G \quad ABA \\
&\Rightarrow_G \quad aAbBaA \\
&\Rightarrow_G^+ \quad a^{m-1}Ab^{m-1}Ba^{m-1}A \\
&\Rightarrow_G \quad a^{m-1}\bar{a}b^{m-1}Ca^{m-1}\bar{a} \\
&\Rightarrow_G \quad a^m b^m C a^m \\
&\Rightarrow_G^+ \quad a^m b^{n-1} C a^m \\
&\Rightarrow_G \quad a^m b^n a^m,
\end{aligned}
$$

with $1 \leq m \leq n$. Hence,

$$L(G) = \{a^m b^n a^m : \ 1 \leq m \leq n\}.$$

Note that $L(G) \notin$ **E0L** (see page 268 in Volume 1 of [157]); however, $L(G) \in$ **FEP0L**(1). As a result, FEP0L grammars (of degree 1) are more powerful than ordinary E0L grammars.

Next, we investigate the generative power of FET0L grammars of all degrees.

Theorem 36. FEPT0L$(0) =$ **EPT0L, FET0L**$(0) =$ **ET0L, FEP0L**$(0) =$ **EP0L,** *and* **FE0L**$(0) =$ **E0L.**

Proof. It follows from the definition of FET0L grammars.   □

Lemmas 13, 14, 15, and 16 inspect the generative power of forbidding ET0L grammars of degree 1. As a conclusion, in Theorem 37, we demonstrate that both FEPT0L(1) and FET0L(1) grammars generate precisely the family of ET0L languages.

Lemma 13. EPT0L $\subseteq$ **FEP0L**(1).

Proof. Let

$$G = (V, T, P_1, \ldots, P_t, S)$$

be an EPT0L grammar, where $t \geq 1$. Set

$$W = \{\langle a, i \rangle : a \in V, \ i = 1, \ldots, t\}$$

and

$$F(i) = \{\langle a, j \rangle \in W : j \neq i\}.$$

Then, construct an FEP0L grammar of degree 1,

$$G' = (V', T, P', S),$$

where

$$V' = V \cup W, \ (V \cap W = \emptyset),$$

and the set of productions P' is defined as follows:

1. For each $a \in V$ and $i = 1, \ldots, t$, add $(a \to \langle a, i \rangle, \emptyset)$ to P'.

2. If $a \to z \in P_i$ for some $i \in \{1, \ldots, t\}$, $a \in V$, $z \in V^+$, add $(\langle a, i \rangle \to z, F(i))$ to P'.

Let us demonstrate that $L(G) = L(G')$.

Claim 23. *For each derivation* $S \Rightarrow_{G'}^n x$, $n \geq 0$,

 (I) *if* $n = 2k + 1$ *for some* $k \geq 0$, $x \in W^+$;

(II) *if* $n = 2k$ *for some* $k \geq 0$, $x \in V^+$.

Proof. The claim follows from the definition of P'. Indeed, every production in P' is either of the form $(a \to \langle a, i \rangle, \emptyset)$ or $(\langle a, i \rangle \to z, F(i))$, where $a \in V$, $\langle a, i \rangle \in W$, $z \in V^+$, $i \in \{1, \ldots, t\}$. Since $S \in V$,

$$S \Rightarrow_{G'}^{2k+1} x \quad \text{implies} \quad x \in W^+$$

and

$$S \Rightarrow_{G'}^{2k} x \quad \text{implies} \quad x \in V^+;$$

thus, the claim holds. $\square$

Define the finite substitution g from V^* to $(V')^*$ such that for every $a \in V$,

$$g(a) = \{a\} \cup \{\langle a, i \rangle \in W : i = 1, \ldots, t\}.$$

Claim 24. $S \Rightarrow_G^* x$ *if and only if* $S \Rightarrow_{G'}^* x'$ *for some* $x' \in g(x)$, $x \in V^+$, $x' \in (V')^+$.

Proof.

Only If: By induction on $n \geq 0$, we show that for all $x \in V^+$,

$$S \Rightarrow_G^n x \quad \text{implies} \quad S \Rightarrow_{G'}^{2n} x.$$

Basis: Let $n = 0$. Then, the only x is S; therefore, $S \Rightarrow^0_G S$ and also $S \Rightarrow^0_{G'} S$.

Induction Hypothesis: Suppose that

$$S \Rightarrow^n_G x \quad \text{implies} \quad S \Rightarrow^{2n}_{G'} x$$

for all derivations of length n or less, for some $n \geq 0$.

Induction Step: Consider $S \Rightarrow^{n+1}_G x$. Because $n + 1 \geq 1$, we can express

$$S \Rightarrow^{n+1}_G x$$

as

$$S \Rightarrow^n_G y \Rightarrow_G x \; [p_1, p_2, \ldots, p_q]$$

such that $y \in V^+$, $q = |y|$, and $p_j \in P_i$ for all $j = 1, \ldots, q$ and some $i \in \{1, \ldots, t\}$. By the induction hypothesis,

$$S \Rightarrow^{2n}_{G'} y.$$

Suppose that $y = a_1 a_2 \ldots a_q$, $a_j \in V$. Let G' make the derivation

$$
\begin{aligned}
S \quad &\Rightarrow^{2n}_{G'} \quad a_1 a_2 \ldots a_q \\
&\Rightarrow_{G'} \quad \langle a_1, i \rangle \langle a_2, i \rangle \ldots \langle a_q, i \rangle \quad [p'_1, p'_2, \ldots, p'_q] \\
&\Rightarrow_{G'} \quad z_1 z_2 \ldots z_q \quad [p''_1, p''_2, \ldots, p''_q],
\end{aligned}
$$

where $p'_j = (a_j \to \langle a_j, i \rangle, \emptyset)$ and $p''_j = (\langle a_j, i \rangle \to z_j, F(i))$ such that $p_j = a_j \to z_j$, $z_j \in V^+$, for all $j = 1, \ldots, q$. Then, $z_1 z_2 \ldots z_q = x$, and therefore

$$S \Rightarrow^{2(n+1)}_{G'} x.$$

If: The converse implication is established by induction on the length of derivations in G'. We prove that

$$S \Rightarrow^n_{G'} x' \quad \text{implies} \quad S \Rightarrow^*_G x$$

for some $x' \in g(x)$, $n \geq 0$.

Basis: For $n = 0$, $S \Rightarrow^0_{G'} S$ and $S \Rightarrow^0_G S$; clearly, $S \in g(S)$.

Induction Hypothesis: Assume that there exists a natural number m such that the claim holds for every $0 \leq n \leq m$.

Induction Step: Let

$$S \Rightarrow^{m+1}_{G'} x'.$$

Express this derivation as

$$S \Rightarrow^m_{G'} y' \Rightarrow_{G'} x' \; [p'_1, p'_2, \ldots, p'_q],$$

where $y' \in (V')^+$, $q = |y'|$, and $p'_1, p'_2, \ldots, p'_q$ is a sequence of productions from P'. By the induction hypothesis,

$$S \Rightarrow^*_G y,$$

where $y \in V^+$, $y' \in g(y)$. Claim 23 says that there exist the following two cases:

(i) Let $m = 2k$ for some $k \geq 0$. Then, $y' \in V^+$, $x' \in W^+$, and every production

$$p'_j = (a_j \to \langle a_j, i \rangle, \emptyset),$$

where $a_j \in V$, $\langle a_j, i \rangle \in W$, $i \in \{1, \ldots, t\}$. In this case, $\langle a_j, i \rangle \in g(a_j)$ for every a_j and any i (see the definition of g); hence, $x' \in g(y)$ as well.

(ii) Let $m = 2k + 1$. Then, $y' \in W^+$, $x' \in V^+$, and each p'_j is of the form

$$p'_j = (\langle a_j, i \rangle \to z_j, F(i)),$$

where $\langle a_j, i \rangle \in W$, $z_j \in V^+$. Moreover, according to the forbidding conditions of p'_j, all $\langle a_j, i \rangle$ in y' have the same i. Thus, $y' = \langle a_1, i \rangle \langle a_2, i \rangle \ldots \langle a_q, i \rangle$ for some $i \in \{1, \ldots, t\}$, $y = g^{-1}(y') = a_1 a_2 \ldots a_q$, and $x' = z_1 z_2 \ldots z_q$. By the definition of P',

$$(\langle a_j, i \rangle \to z_j, F(i)) \in P' \quad \text{implies} \quad a_j \to z_j \in P_i.$$

Therefore,

$$S \Rightarrow^*_G a_1 a_2 \ldots a_q \Rightarrow_G z_1 z_2 \ldots z_q \, [p_1, p_2, \ldots, p_q],$$

where $p_j = a_j \to z_j \in P_i$ such that $p'_j = (\langle a_j, i \rangle \to z_j, F(i))$. Obviously, $z_1 z_2 \ldots z_q = x = x'$.

This completes the induction and establishes Claim 24.   □

By Claim 24, for any $x \in T^+$,

$$S \Rightarrow^*_G x \quad \text{if and only if} \quad S \Rightarrow^*_{G'} x$$

Therefore, $L(G) = L(G')$, so the lemma holds.   □

In order to simplify the notation in the following lemma, for a set of productions

$$P \subseteq \{(a \to z, F) : a \in V, \ z \in V^*, \ F \subseteq V\},$$

define

$$\text{left}(P) = \{a : (a \to z, F) \in P\}.$$

Informally, $\text{left}(P)$ denotes the set of left-hand sides of all productions in P.

Lemma 14. FEPT0L$(1) \subseteq$ EPT0L.

Proof. Let

$$G = (V, T, P_1, \ldots, P_t, S)$$

be an FEPT0L grammar of degree 1, $t \geq 1$. Let Q be the set of all subsets $O \subseteq P_i$, $1 \leq i \leq t$, such that every $(a \to z, F) \in O$, $a \in V$, $z \in V^+$, $F \subseteq V$, satisfies $F \cap \text{left}(O) = \emptyset$. Create a new set Q' so that for each $O \in Q$, add

$$\{a \to z : (a \to z, F) \in O\}$$

to Q'. Express

$$Q' = \{Q'_1, \ldots, Q'_m\},$$

where m is the cardinality of Q'. Then, construct the EPT0L grammar

$$G' = (V, T, Q'_1, \ldots, Q'_m, S).$$

Basic Idea. To see the basic idea behind the construction of G', consider a pair of productions $p_1 = (a_1 \to z_1, F_1)$ and $p_2 = (a_2 \to z_2, F_2)$ from P_i, for some $i \in \{1, \ldots, t\}$. During a single derivation step, p_1 and p_2 can concurrently rewrite a_1 and a_2 provided that $a_2 \notin F_1$ and $a_1 \notin F_2$, respectively. Consider any $O \subseteq P_i$ containing no pair of productions $(a_1 \to z_1, F_1)$ and $(a_2 \to z_2, F_2)$ such that $a_1 \in F_2$ or $a_2 \in F_1$. Observe that for any derivation step based on O, no production from O is blocked by its forbidding conditions; thus, the conditions can be omitted. Formal proof is given next.

Claim 25. *$S \Rightarrow_G^n x$ if and only if $S \Rightarrow_{G'}^n x$, $x \in V^*$, $n \geq 0$.*

Proof. The claim is proved by induction on the length of derivations.

Only If: By induction on n, $n \geq 0$, we prove that

$$S \Rightarrow_G^n x \quad \text{implies} \quad S \Rightarrow_{G'}^n x$$

for all $x \in V^*$.

Basis: Let $n = 0$. Then, $S \Rightarrow_G^0 S$ and $S \Rightarrow_{G'}^0 S$.

Induction Hypothesis: Suppose that the claim holds for all derivations of length n or less, for some $n \geq 0$.

Induction Step: Consider a derivation

$$S \Rightarrow_G^{n+1} x.$$

Because $n + 1 \geq 1$, there exists $y \in V^+$, $q = |y|$, and a sequence $p_1, \ldots, p_q$, where $p_j \in P_i$ for all $j = 1, \ldots, q$ and some $i \in \{1, \ldots, t\}$, such that

$$S \Rightarrow_G^n y \Rightarrow_G x \ [p_1, \ldots, p_q].$$

By the induction hypothesis,

$$S \Rightarrow_{G'}^{n} y.$$

Let

$$O = \{p_j : 1 \leq j \leq q\}.$$

Observe that

$$y \Rightarrow_G x \; [p_1, \ldots, p_q]$$

implies $\mathrm{alph}(y) = \mathrm{left}(O)$. Moreover, every $p_j = (a \rightarrow z, F) \in O$, $a \in V$, $z \in V^+$, $F \subseteq V$, satisfies $F \cap \mathrm{alph}(y) = \emptyset$. Hence, $(a \rightarrow z, F) \in O$ implies $F \cap \mathrm{left}(O) = \emptyset$. Inspect the definition of G' to see that there exists

$$Q'_r = \{a \rightarrow z : \; (a \rightarrow z, F) \in O\}$$

for some r, $1 \leq r \leq m$. Therefore,

$$S \Rightarrow_{G'}^{n} y \Rightarrow_{G'} x \; [p'_1, \ldots, p'_q],$$

where $p'_j = a \rightarrow z \in Q'_r$ such that $p_j = (a \rightarrow z, F) \in O$, for all $j = 1, \ldots, q$.

If: The if-part demonstrates for every $n \geq 0$,

$$S \Rightarrow_{G'}^{n} x \;\; \text{implies} \;\; S \Rightarrow_{G}^{n} x,$$

where $x \in V^*$.

Basis: Suppose that $n = 0$. Then, $S \Rightarrow_{G'}^{0} S$ and $S \Rightarrow_{G}^{0} S$.

Induction Hypothesis: Assume that the claim holds for all derivations of length n or less, for some $n \geq 0$.

Induction Step: Let

$$S \Rightarrow_{G'}^{n+1} x.$$

As $n + 1 \geq 1$, there exists a derivation

$$S \Rightarrow_{G'}^{n} y \Rightarrow_{G'} x \; [p'_1, \ldots, p'_q]$$

such that $y \in V^+$, $q = |y|$, each $p'_i \in Q'_r$ for some $r \in \{1, \ldots, m\}$, and by the induction hypothesis,

$$S \Rightarrow_{G}^{n} y.$$

Then, by the definition of Q'_r, there exists P_i and $O \subseteq P_i$ such that every $(a \rightarrow z, F) \in O$, $a \in V$, $z \in V^+$, $F \subseteq V$, satisfies $a \rightarrow z \in Q'_r$ and $F \cap \mathrm{left}(O) = \emptyset$. Since $\mathrm{alph}(y) \subseteq \mathrm{left}(O)$, $(a \rightarrow z, F) \in O$ implies $F \cap \mathrm{alph}(y) = \emptyset$. Hence,

$$S \Rightarrow_{G}^{n} y \Rightarrow_G x \; [p_1, \ldots, p_q],$$

where $p_j = (a \rightarrow z, F) \in O$ for all $j = 1, \ldots, q$. $\qquad\qquad$ $\square$

From the claim above,

$$S \Rightarrow_G^* x \quad \text{if and only if} \quad S \Rightarrow_{G'}^* x$$

for all $x \in T^*$. Consequently, $L(G) = L(G')$. $\qquad \square$

The following two lemmas can be proved by analogy with Lemmas 13 and 14. The details are left to the reader.

Lemma 15. ET0L $\subseteq$ FE0L(1).

Lemma 16. FET0L(1) $\subseteq$ ET0L.

Theorem 37. FEP0L(1) = FEPT0L(1) = FE0L(1) = FET0L(1) = ET0L = EPT0L.

Proof. By Lemmas 13 and 14, we have **EPT0L $\subseteq$ FEP0L(1)** and **FEPT0L(1) $\subseteq$ EPT0L**, respectively. Since **FEP0L(1) $\subseteq$ FEPT0L(1)**, we get **FEP0L(1) = FEPT0L(1) = EPT0L**. Analogously, from Lemmas 15 and 16, **FE0L(1) = FET0L(1) = ET0L**. However, **EPT0L = ET0L** (see Theorem V.1.6 on page 239 in [155]). Therefore,

FEP0L(1) = FEPT0L(1) = FE0L(1) = FET0L(1) = EPT0L = ET0L;

thus, the theorem holds. $\qquad \square$

Next, we investigate the generative power of FEPT0L grammars of degree 2. The following lemma establishes a normal form for context-sensitive grammars so that the grammars satisfying this form generate only sentential forms containing no nonterminal from N_{CS} as the left-most symbol of the string. We make use of this normal form in Lemma 18.

Lemma 17. *Every context-sensitive language, $L \in$ **CS**, can be generated by a context-sensitive grammar, $G = (N_1 \cup N_{CF} \cup N_{CS} \cup T, T, P, S_1)$, where N_1, N_{CF}, N_{CS}, and T are pairwise disjoint alphabets, $S_1 \in N_1$, and every production in P has one of the following forms:*

(i) $AB \to AC$, where $A \in (N_1 \cup N_{CF})$, $B \in N_{CS}$, $C \in N_{CF}$.

(ii) $A \to B$, where $A \in N_{CF}$, $B \in N_{CS}$.

(iii) $A \to a$, where $A \in (N_1 \cup N_{CF})$, $a \in T$.

(iv) $A \to C$, where $A, C \in N_{CF}$.

(v) $A_1 \to C_1$, where $A_1, C_1 \in N_1$.

(vi) $A \to DE$, where $A, D, E \in N_{CF}$.

(vii) $A_1 \to D_1 E$, where $A_1, D_1 \in N_1$, $E \in N_{CF}$.

Proof. Let

$$G' = (N_{CF} \cup N_{CS} \cup T, T, P', S)$$

be a context-sensitive grammar of the form defined in Lemma 4. From this grammar, we construct a grammar

$$G = (N_1 \cup N_{CF} \cup N_{CS} \cup T, T, P, S_1),$$

where

$$
\begin{aligned}
N_1 &= \{X_1 : X \in N_{CF}\}, \\
P &= P' \cup \{A_1 B \to A_1 C : AB \to AC \in P', A, C \in N_{CF}, B \in N_{CS}, A_1 \in N_1\} \\
&\quad \cup \{A_1 \to a : A \to a \in P', A \in N_{CF}, A_1 \in N_1, a \in T\} \\
&\quad \cup \{A_1 \to C_1 : A \to C \in P', A, C \in N_{CF}, A_1, C_1 \in N_1\} \\
&\quad \cup \{A_1 \to D_1 E : A \to DE \in P', A, D, E \in N_{CF}, A_1, D_1 \in N_1\}.
\end{aligned}
$$

Basic Idea. G works by analogy with G' except that in G every sentential form starts with a symbol from $N_1 \cup T$ followed by symbols that are not in N_1. Notice, however, that by $AB \to AC$, G' can never rewrite the left-most symbol of any sentential form. Based on these observations, it is rather easy to see that $L(G) = L(G')$; a formal proof of this identity is left to the reader. As G is of the required form, Lemma 17 holds.   □

Lemma 18. CS $\subseteq$ FEP0L(2).

Proof. Let L be a context-sensitive language generated by a grammar

$$G = (N_1 \cup N_{CF} \cup N_{CS} \cup T, T, P, S_1)$$

of the form of Lemma 17. Let

$$
\begin{aligned}
V &= N_1 \cup N_{CF} \cup N_{CS} \cup T, \\
P_{CS} &= \{AB \to AC : AB \to AC \in P, A \in (N_1 \cup N_{CF}), B \in N_{CS}, C \in N_{CF}\}, \\
P_{CF} &= P - P_{CS}.
\end{aligned}
$$

Informally, P_{CS} and P_{CF} are the sets of context-sensitive and context-free productions in P, respectively, and V denotes the total alphabet of G.

Let f be an arbitrary bijection from V to $\{1, \ldots, m\}$, where m is the cardinality of V, and let f^{-1} be the inverse of f.

Construct an FEP0L grammar of degree 2,

$$G' = (V', T, P', S_1),$$

with V' defined as

$$
\begin{aligned}
W_0 &= \{\langle A, B, C \rangle : AB \to AC \in P_{CS}\}, \\
W_S &= \{\langle A, B, C, j \rangle : AB \to AC \in P_{CS}, 1 \le j \le m + 1\}, \\
W &= W_0 \cup W_S, \\
V' &= V \cup W,
\end{aligned}
$$

where V, W_0, and W_S are pairwise disjoint alphabets. The set of productions P' is defined as follows:

1. For every $X \in V$, add $(X \rightarrow X, \emptyset)$ to P'.

2. For every $A \rightarrow u \in P_{CF}$, add $(A \rightarrow u, W)$ to P'.

3. For every $AB \rightarrow AC \in P_{CS}$, add the following productions to P':

   (a) $(B \rightarrow \langle A, B, C \rangle, W)$;

   (b) $(\langle A, B, C \rangle \rightarrow \langle A, B, C, 1 \rangle, W - \{\langle A, B, C \rangle\})$;

   (c) $(\langle A, B, C, j \rangle \rightarrow \langle A, B, C, j+1 \rangle, \{f^{-1}(j)\langle A, B, C, j \rangle\})$ for all $1 \leq j \leq m$ such that $f(A) \neq j$;

   (d) $(\langle A, B, C, f(A) \rangle \rightarrow \langle A, B, C, f(A)+1 \rangle, \emptyset)$;

   (e) $(\langle A, B, C, m+1 \rangle \rightarrow C, \{\langle A, B, C, m+1 \rangle^2\})$.

Basic Idea. Let us informally explain how G' simulates the non-context-free productions of the form $AB \rightarrow AC$ (see productions of (3) in the construction of P'). First, chosen occurrences of B are rewritten with $\langle A, B, C \rangle$ by $(B \rightarrow \langle A, B, C \rangle, W)$. The forbidding condition of this production guarantees that there is no simulation already in process. After that, left neighbors of all occurrences of $\langle A, B, C \rangle$ are checked not to be any symbols from $V - \{A\}$. In more detail, G' rewrites $\langle A, B, C \rangle$ with $\langle A, B, C, i \rangle$ for $i = 1$. Then, in every $\langle A, B, C, i \rangle$, G' increments i by one as long as i is less or equal to the cardinality of V; simultaneously, it verifies that the left neighbor of every $\langle A, B, C, i \rangle$ differs from the symbol that f maps to i except for the case when $f(A) = i$. Finally, G' checks that there are no two adjoining symbols $\langle A, B, C, m+1 \rangle$. At this point, the left neighbors of $\langle A, B, C, m+1 \rangle$ are necessarily equal to A, so every occurrence of $\langle A, B, C, m+1 \rangle$ is rewritten to C.

Observe that the other symbols remain unchanged during the simulation. Indeed, by the forbidding conditions, the only productions that can rewrite symbols $X \notin W$ are of the form $(X \rightarrow X, \emptyset)$. Moreover, the forbidding condition of $(\langle A, B, C \rangle \rightarrow \langle A, B, C, 1 \rangle, W - \{\langle A, B, C \rangle\})$ implies that it is not possible to simulate two different non-context-free productions at the same time.

To establish the identity of languages generated by G and G', we first prove Claims 26 through 30.

Claim 26. $S_1 \Rightarrow_{G'}^n x'$ implies first$(x') \in (N_1 \cup T)$ for every $n \geq 0$, $x' \in (V')^*$.

Proof. The claim is proved by induction on n.

Basis: Let $n = 0$. Then, $S_1 \Rightarrow_{G'}^0 S_1$ and $S_1 \in N_1$.

Induction Hypothesis: Assume that the claim holds for all derivations of length n or less, for some $n \geq 0$.

Induction Step: Consider a derivation

$$S_1 \Rightarrow_{G'}^{n+1} x',$$

where $x' \in (V')^*$. Because $n + 1 \geq 1$, there is a derivation

$$S_1 \Rightarrow_{G'}^n y' \Rightarrow_{G'} x' \; [p_1, \ldots, p_q],$$

$y' \in (V')^*$, $q = |y'|$, and by the induction hypothesis, $\mathrm{first}(y') \in (N_1 \cup T)$. Inspect P' to see that the production p_1 that rewrites the left-most symbol of y' is one of the following forms: $(A_1 \rightarrow A_1, \emptyset)$, $(a \rightarrow a, \emptyset)$, $(A_1 \rightarrow a, W)$, $(A_1 \rightarrow C_1, W)$, or $(A_1 \rightarrow D_1 E, W)$, where $A_1, C_1, D_1 \in N_1$, $a \in T$, $E \in N_{CF}$ (see (1) and (2) in the definition of P' and Lemma 17). It is obvious that the left-most symbols of the right-hand sides of these productions belong to $(N_1 \cup T)$. Hence,

$$\mathrm{first}(x') \in (N_1 \cup T),$$

so the claim holds.   □

Claim 27. $S_1 \Rightarrow_{G'}^n y_1' X y_3'$, $X \in W_S$, implies $y_1' \in (V')^+$ for any $y_3' \in (V')^*$.

Proof. Informally, the claim says that every occurrence of a symbol from W_S has always a left neighbor. Clearly, this claim follows from the statement of Claim 26. Since $W_S \cap (N_1 \cup T) = \emptyset$, X cannot be the left-most symbol in a sentential form and the claim holds.   □

Claim 28. $S_1 \Rightarrow_{G'}^n x'$, $n \geq 0$, implies that x' has one of the following three forms:

(I) $x' \in V^*$.

(II) $x' \in (V \cup W_0)^*$ and $\#_{W_0} x' > 0$.

(III) $x' \in (V \cup \{\langle A, B, C, j \rangle\})^*$, $\#_{\{\langle A,B,C,j\rangle\}} x' > 0$, and $\{f^{-1}(k)\langle A, B, C, j \rangle : 1 \leq k < j, k \neq f(A)\} \cap \mathrm{sub}(x') = \emptyset$, where $\langle A, B, C, j \rangle \in W_S$, $A \in (N_1 \cup N_{CF})$, $B \in N_{CS}$, $C \in N_{CF}$, $1 \leq j \leq m + 1$.

Proof. We prove the claim by the induction on $n \geq 0$.

Basis: Let $n = 0$. Clearly, $S_1 \Rightarrow_{G'}^0 S_1$ and S_1 is of type (I).

Induction Hypothesis: Suppose that the claim holds for all derivations of length n or less, for some $n \geq 0$.

Induction Step: Let us consider any derivation of the form

$$S_1 \Rightarrow_{G'}^{n+1} x'.$$

Because $n + 1 \geq 1$, there exists $y' \in (V')^*$ and a sequence of productions $p_1, \ldots, p_q$, where $p_i \in P'$, $1 \leq i \leq q$, $q = |y'|$, such that

$$S_1 \Rightarrow_{G'}^n y' \Rightarrow_{G'} x' \; [p_1, \ldots, p_q].$$

Let $y' = a_1 a_2 \ldots a_q$, $a_i \in V'$.

By the induction hypothesis, y' can only be of forms (I) through (III). Thus, the following three cases cover all possible forms of y':

(i) Let $y' \in V^*$ (form (I)). In this case, every production p_i can be either of the form $(a_i \to a_i, \emptyset)$, $a_i \in V$, or $(a_i \to u, W)$ such that $a_i \to u \in P_{CF}$, or $(a_i \to \langle A, a_i, C \rangle, W)$, $a_i \in N_{CS}$, $\langle A, a_i, C \rangle \in W_0$ (see the definition of P').

Suppose that for every $i \in \{1, \ldots, q\}$, p_i has one of the first two listed forms. According to the right-hand sides of these productions, we obtain $x' \in V^*$; that is, x' is of form (I).

If there exists i such that $p_i = (a_i \to \langle A, a_i, C \rangle, W)$ for some $A \in (N_1 \cup N_{CF})$, $a_i \in N_{CS}$, $C \in N_{CF}$, $\langle A, a_i, C \rangle \in W_0$, we get $x' \in (V \cup W_0)^*$ with $\#_{W_0} x' > 0$. Thus, x' belongs to (II).

(ii) Let $y' \in (V \cup W_0)^*$ and $\#_{W_0} y' > 0$ (form (II)). At this point, p_i is either $(a_i \to a_i, \emptyset)$ (rewriting $a_i \in V$ to itself) or $(\langle A, B, C \rangle \to \langle A, B, C, 1 \rangle, W - \{\langle A, B, C \rangle\})$ rewriting $a_i = \langle A, B, C \rangle \in W_0$ to $\langle A, B, C, 1 \rangle \in W_S$, where $A \in (N_1 \cup N_{CF})$, $B \in N_{CS}$, $C \in N_{CF}$. Since $\#_{W_0} y' > 0$, there exists at least one i such that $a_i = \langle A, B, C \rangle \in W_0$. The corresponding production p_i can be used provided that $\#_{(W - \{\langle A, B, C \rangle\})} y' = 0$. Therefore, $y' \in (V \cup \{\langle A, B, C \rangle\})^*$, and hence $x' \in (V \cup \{\langle A, B, C, 1 \rangle\})^*$, $\#_{\{\langle A, B, C, 1 \rangle\}} x' > 0$; that is, x' is of type (III).

(iii) Assume that $y' \in (V \cup \{\langle A, B, C, j \rangle\})^*$, $\#_{\{\langle A, B, C, j \rangle\}} y' > 0$, and

$$\mathrm{sub}(y') \cap \{f^{-1}(k)\langle A, B, C, j \rangle : 1 \leq k < j, k \neq f(A)\} = \emptyset,$$

where $\langle A, B, C, j \rangle \in W_S$, $A \in (N_1 \cup N_{CF})$, $B \in N_{CS}$, $C \in N_{CF}$, $1 \leq j \leq m + 1$ (form (III)). By inspection of P', we see that the following four forms of productions can be used to rewrite y' to x':

(a) $(a_i \to a_i, \emptyset)$, $a_i \in V$.

(b) $(\langle A, B, C, j \rangle \to \langle A, B, C, j + 1 \rangle, \{f^{-1}(j)\langle A, B, C, j \rangle\})$, $1 \leq j \leq m$, $j \neq f(A)$.

(c) $(\langle A, B, C, f(A) \rangle \to \langle A, B, C, f(A) + 1 \rangle, \emptyset)$.

(d) $(\langle A, B, C, m + 1 \rangle \to C, \{\langle A, B, C, m + 1 \rangle^2\})$.

Let $1 \leq j \leq m$, $j \neq f(A)$. Then, symbols from V are rewritten to themselves (case (a)) and every occurrence of $\langle A, B, C, j \rangle$ is rewritten to $\langle A, B, C, j + 1 \rangle$ by (b). Clearly, we obtain $x' \in (V \cup \{\langle A, B, C, j + 1 \rangle\})^*$ such that $\#_{\{\langle A, B, C, j + 1 \rangle\}} x' > 0$. Furthermore, (b) can be used only when $f^{-1}(j)\langle A, B, C, j \rangle \notin \mathrm{sub}(y')$. As

$$\mathrm{sub}(y') \cap \{f^{-1}(k)\langle A, B, C, j \rangle : 1 \leq k < j, \ k \neq f(A)\} = \emptyset,$$

it holds that

$$\mathrm{sub}(y') \cap \{f^{-1}(k)\langle A, B, \dot{C}, j \rangle : 1 \leq k \leq j, \ k \neq f(A)\} = \emptyset.$$

Since every occurrence of $\langle A, B, C, j \rangle$ is rewritten to $\langle A, B, C, j+1 \rangle$ and other symbols are unchanged,

$$\text{sub}(x') \cap \{f^{-1}(k)\langle A, B, C, j+1 \rangle : \ 1 \leq k < j+1, \ k \neq f(A)\} = \emptyset;$$

therefore, x' is of form (III).

Assume that $j = f(A)$. Then, all occurrences of $\langle A, B, C, j \rangle$ are rewritten to $\langle A, B, C, j+1 \rangle$ by (c), and symbols from V are rewritten to themselves. As before, we obtain $x' \in (V \cup \{\langle A, B, C, j+1 \rangle\})^*$ and $\#_{\{\langle A,B,C,j+1 \rangle\}} x' > 0$. Moreover, because

$$\text{sub}(y') \cap \{f^{-1}(k)\langle A, B, C, j \rangle : \ 1 \leq k < j, \ k \neq f(A)\} = \emptyset$$

and j is just $f(A)$,

$$\text{sub}(x') \cap \{f^{-1}(k)\langle A, B, C, j+1 \rangle : \ 1 \leq k < j+1, \ k \neq f(A)\} = \emptyset$$

and x' belongs to (III) as well.

Finally, let $j = m + 1$. Then, every occurrence of $\langle A, B, C, j \rangle$ is rewritten to C (case (d)), and therefore $x' \in V^*$; that is, x' has form (I).

In (i), (ii), and (iii) we have considered all derivations that rewrite y' to x', and in each of these cases we have shown that x' has one of the requested forms. Therefore, Claim 28 holds.   □

To prove the following claims, we need a finite letter-to-letters substitution g from V^* into $(V')^*$ defined as

$$g(X) \ = \ \{X\} \cup \{\langle A, X, C \rangle : \ \langle A, X, C \rangle \in W_0\} \\ \cup \{\langle A, X, C, j \rangle : \ \langle A, X, C, j \rangle \in W_S, 1 \leq j \leq m + 1\}$$

for all $X \in V$, $A \in (N_1 \cup N_{CF})$, $C \in N_{CF}$. Let g^{-1} be the inverse of g.

Claim 29. *Let $y' = a_1 a_2 \ldots a_q$, $a_i \in V'$, $q = |y'|$, and $g^{-1}(a_i) \Rightarrow_G^{h_i} g^{-1}(u_i)$ for all $i \in \{1, \ldots, q\}$ and some $h_i \in \{0, 1\}$, $u_i \in (V')^+$. Then, $g^{-1}(y') \Rightarrow_G^r g^{-1}(x')$ such that $x' = u_1 u_2 \ldots u_q$, $r = \sum_{i=1}^q h_i$, $r \leq q$.*

Proof. First, consider a derivation

$$g^{-1}(X) \Rightarrow_G^h g^{-1}(u),$$

$X \in V'$, $u \in (V')^+$, $h \in \{0, 1\}$. If $h = 0$, then $g^{-1}(X) = g^{-1}(u)$. Let $h = 1$. Then, there surely exists a production $p = g^{-1}(X) \to g^{-1}(u) \in P$ such that

$$g^{-1}(X) \Rightarrow_G g^{-1}(u) \ [p].$$

Return to the statement of this claim. We can construct a derivation

$$
\begin{aligned}
g^{-1}(a_1)g^{-1}(a_2)\ldots g^{-1}(a_q) &\Rightarrow_G^{h_1} g^{-1}(u_1)g^{-1}(a_2)\ldots g^{-1}(a_q) \\
&\Rightarrow_G^{h_2} g^{-1}(u_1)g^{-1}(u_2)\ldots g^{-1}(a_q) \\
&\vdots \\
&\Rightarrow_G^{h_q} g^{-1}(u_1)g^{-1}(u_2)\ldots g^{-1}(u_q),
\end{aligned}
$$

where $g^{-1}(y') = g^{-1}(a_1)\ldots g^{-1}(a_q)$ and $g^{-1}(u_1)\ldots g^{-1}(u_q) = g^{-1}(u_1\ldots u_q) = g^{-1}(x')$. In such a derivation, each $g^{-1}(a_i)$ is either left unchanged (if $h_i = 0$) or rewritten to $g^{-1}(u_i)$ by the corresponding production $g^{-1}(a_i) \to g^{-1}(u_i)$. Obviously, the length of this derivation is $\sum_{i=1}^{q} h_i$. $\qquad\square$

Claim 30. $S_1 \Rightarrow_G^* x$ *if and only if* $S_1 \Rightarrow_{G'}^* x'$, *where* $x \in V^*$, $x' \in (V')^*$, $x' \in g(x)$.

Proof.

Only if: The only-if part is established by induction on the length of derivations in G. That is, we show that

$$
S_1 \Rightarrow_G^n x \quad \text{implies} \quad S_1 \Rightarrow_{G'}^* x,
$$

where $x \in V^*$, for $n \geq 0$.

Basis: Let $n = 0$. Then, $S_1 \Rightarrow_G^0 S_1$ and $S_1 \Rightarrow_{G'}^0 S_1$ as well.

Induction Hypothesis: Assume that the claim holds for all derivations of length n or less, for some $n \geq 0$.

Induction Step: Consider a derivation

$$
S_1 \Rightarrow_G^{n+1} x.
$$

Because $n + 1 > 0$, there exists $y \in V^*$ and $p \in P$ such that

$$
S_1 \Rightarrow_G^n y \Rightarrow_G x \ [p],
$$

and by the induction hypothesis, there is also a derivation

$$
S_1 \Rightarrow_{G'}^* y.
$$

Let $y = a_1 a_2 \ldots a_q$, $a_i \in V$, $1 \leq i \leq q$, $q = |y|$. The following cases (i) and (ii) cover all possible forms of p:

(i) $p = A \to u \in P_{CF}$, $A \in (N_1 \cup N_{CF})$, $u \in V^*$. Then, $y = y_1 A y_3$ and $x = y_1 u y_3$, $y_1, y_3 \in V^*$. Let $s = |y_1| + 1$. Since we have $(A \to u, W) \in P'$, we can construct a derivation

$$
S_1 \Rightarrow_{G'}^* y \Rightarrow_{G'} x \ [p_1, \ldots, p_q]
$$

such that $p_s = (A \to u, W)$ and $p_i = (a_i \to a_i, \emptyset)$ for all $i \in \{1, \ldots, q\}$, $i \neq s$.

(ii) $p = AB \to AC \in P_{CS}$, $A \in (N_1 \cup N_{CF})$, $B \in N_{CS}$, $C \in N_{CF}$. Then, $y = y_1 ABy_3$ and $x = y_1 ACy_3$, $y_1, y_3 \in V^*$. Let $s = |y_1| + 2$. In this case, there is the following derivation:

$$S_1 \Rightarrow^*_{G'} y_1 ABy_3$$
$$\Rightarrow_{G'} y_1 A\langle A, B, C\rangle y_3 \qquad [p_s = (B \to \langle A, B, C\rangle, W)]$$
$$\Rightarrow_{G'} y_1 A\langle A, B, C, 1\rangle y_3 \qquad [p_s = (\langle A, B, C\rangle \to \langle A, B, C, 1\rangle,$$
$$W - \{\langle A, B, C\rangle\})]$$
$$\Rightarrow_{G'} y_1 A\langle A, B, C, 2\rangle y_3 \qquad [p_s = (\langle A, B, C, 1\rangle \to \langle A, B, C, 2\rangle,$$
$$\{f^{-1}(1)\langle A, B, C, j\rangle\})]$$

$$\vdots$$

$$\Rightarrow_{G'} y_1 A\langle A, B, C, f(A)\rangle y_3 \qquad [p_s = (\langle A, B, C, f(A) - 1\rangle \to$$
$$\langle A, B, C, f(A)\rangle, \{f^{-1}(f(A) - 1)$$
$$\langle A, B, C, f(A) - 1\rangle\})]$$
$$\Rightarrow_{G'} y_1 A\langle A, B, C, f(A) + 1\rangle y_3 \quad [p_s = (\langle A, B, C, f(A)\rangle \to$$
$$\langle A, B, C, f(A) + 1\rangle, \emptyset)]$$
$$\Rightarrow_{G'} y_1 A\langle A, B, C, f(A) + 2\rangle y_3 \quad [p_s = (\langle A, B, C, f(A) + 1\rangle \to$$
$$\langle A, B, C, f(A) + 2\rangle, \{f^{-1}(f(A) + 1)$$
$$\langle A, B, C, f(A) + 1\rangle\})]$$

$$\vdots$$

$$\Rightarrow_{G'} y_1 A\langle A, B, C, m + 1\rangle y_3 \qquad [p_s = (\langle A, B, C, m\rangle \to \langle A, B, C, m + 1\rangle,$$
$$\{f^{-1}(m)\langle A, B, C, m\rangle\})]$$
$$\Rightarrow_{G'} y_1 ACy_3 \qquad [p_s = (\langle A, B, C, m + 1\rangle \to C,$$
$$\{\langle A, B, C, m + 1\rangle^2\})]$$

such that $p_i = (a_i \to a_i, \emptyset)$ for all $i \in \{1, \ldots, q\}$, $i \neq s$.

If: By induction on n, we prove that

$$S_1 \Rightarrow^n_{G'} x' \quad \text{implies} \quad S_1 \Rightarrow^*_G x,$$

where $x' \in (V')^*$, $x \in V^*$ and $x' \in g(x)$.

Basis: Let $n = 0$. The only x' is S_1 because $S_1 \Rightarrow^0_{G'} S_1$. Obviously, $S_1 \Rightarrow^0_G S_1$ and $S_1 \in g(S_1)$.

Induction Hypothesis: Suppose that the claim holds for any derivation of length n or less, for some $n \geq 0$.

Induction Step: Consider a derivation of the form

$$S_1 \Rightarrow^{n+1}_{G'} x'.$$

Since $n + 1 \geq 1$, there exists $y' \in (V')^*$ and a sequence of productions $p_1, \ldots, p_q$ from P', $q = |x'|$, such that

$$S_1 \Rightarrow^n_{G'} y' \Rightarrow_{G'} x' [p_1, \ldots, p_q].$$

Let $y' = a_1 a_2 \ldots a_q$, $a_i \in V'$, $1 \le i \le q$. By the induction hypothesis, we have

$$S_1 \Rightarrow^*_G y,$$

where $y \in V^*$, such that $y' \in g(y)$.

From Claim 28, y' can have one of the following forms:

(i) Let $y' \in (V')^*$ (see (I) in Claim 28). Inspect P' to see that there are three forms of productions rewriting symbols a_i in y':

  (a) $p_i = (a_i \to a_i, \emptyset) \in P'$, $a_i \in V$. In this case,

  $$g^{-1}(a_i) \Rightarrow^0_G g^{-1}(a_i).$$

  (b) $p_i = (a_i \to u_i, W) \in P'$ such that $a_i \to u_i \in P_{CF}$. Because $a_i = g^{-1}(a_i)$, $u_i = g^{-1}(u_i)$ and $a_i \to u_i \in P$,

  $$g^{-1}(a_i) \Rightarrow_G g^{-1}(u_i) \ [a_i \to u_i].$$

  (c) $p_i = (a_i \to \langle A, a_i, C \rangle, W) \in P'$, $a_i \in N_{CS}$, $A \in (N_1 \cup N_{CF})$, $C \in N_{CF}$. Since $g^{-1}(a_i) = g^{-1}(\langle A, a_i, C \rangle)$, we have

  $$g^{-1}(a_i) \Rightarrow^0_G g^{-1}(\langle A, a_i, C \rangle).$$

We see that for all a_i, there exists a derivation

$$g^{-1}(a_i) \Rightarrow^{h_i}_G g^{-1}(z_i)$$

for some $h_i \in \{0, 1\}$, where $z_i \in (V')^+$, $x' = z_1 z_2 \ldots z_q$. Therefore, by Claim 29, we can construct

$$S_1 \Rightarrow^*_G y \Rightarrow^r_G x,$$

where $0 \le r \le q$, $x = g^{-1}(x')$.

(ii) Let $y' \in (V \cup W_0)^*$ and $\#_{W_0} y' > 0$ (see (II)). At this point, the following two forms of productions can be used to rewrite a_i in y':

  (a) $p_i = (a_i \to a_i, \emptyset) \in P'$, $a_i \in V$. As in case (i.a),

  $$g^{-1}(a_i) \Rightarrow^0_G g^{-1}(a_i).$$

  (b) $p_i = (\langle A, B, C \rangle \to \langle A, B, C, 1 \rangle, W - \{\langle A, B, C \rangle\})$, $a_i = \langle A, B, C \rangle \in W_0$, $A \in (N_1 \cup N_{CF})$, $B \in N_{CS}$, $C \in N_{CF}$. Because $g^{-1}(\langle A, B, C \rangle) = g^{-1}(\langle A, B, C, 1 \rangle)$,

  $$g^{-1}(\langle A, B, C \rangle) \Rightarrow^0_G g^{-1}(\langle A, B, C, 1 \rangle).$$

Thus, there exists a derivation

$$S_1 \Rightarrow_G^* y \Rightarrow_G^0 x,$$

where $x = g^{-1}(x')$.

(iii) Let $y' \in (V \cup \{\langle A, B, C, j \rangle\})^*$, $\#_{\{\langle A,B,C,j \rangle\}} y' > 0$, and

$$\text{sub}(y') \cap \{f^{-1}(k)\langle A, B, C, j \rangle : 1 \leq k < j, \ k \neq f(A)\} = \emptyset,$$

where $\langle A, B, C, j \rangle \in W_S$, $A \in (N_1 \cup N_{CF})$, $B \in N_{CS}$, $C \in N_{CF}$, $1 \leq j \leq m+1$ (see (III)). By inspection of P', the following four forms of productions can be used to rewrite y' to x':

(a) $p_i = (a_i \to a_i, \emptyset)$, $a_i \in V$.

(b) $p_i = (\langle A, B, C, j \rangle \to \langle A, B, C, j+1 \rangle, \{f^{-1}(j)\langle A, B, C, j \rangle\})$, $1 \leq j \leq m$, $j \neq f(A)$.

(c) $p_i = (\langle A, B, C, f(A) \rangle \to \langle A, B, C, f(A)+1 \rangle, \emptyset)$.

(d) $p_i = (\langle A, B, C, m+1 \rangle \to C, \{\langle A, B, C, m+1 \rangle^2\})$.

Let $1 \leq j \leq m$. G' can rewrite such y' using only the productions (a) through (c). Because $g^{-1}(\langle A, B, C, j \rangle) = g^{-1}(\langle A, B, C, j+1 \rangle)$ and $g^{-1}(a_i) = g^{-1}(a_i)$, by analogy with (ii), we obtain a derivation

$$S_1 \Rightarrow_G^* y \Rightarrow_G^0 x$$

such that $x = g^{-1}(x')$.

Let $j = m + 1$. In this case, only the productions (a) and (d) can be used. Since $\#_{\{\langle A,B,C,j \rangle\}} y' > 0$, there is at least one occurrence of $\langle A, B, C, m+1 \rangle$ in y', and by the forbidding condition of the production (c), $\langle A, B, C, m+1 \rangle^2 \notin \text{sub}(y')$. Observe that for $j = m+1$,

$$\{f^{-1}(k)\langle A, B, C, m+1 \rangle : 1 \leq k < j, \ k \neq f(A)\}$$
$$= \{X\langle A, B, C, m+1 \rangle : X \in V, \ X \neq A\},$$

and thus

$$\text{sub}(y') \cap \{X\langle A, B, C, m+1 \rangle : X \in V, \ X \neq A\} = \emptyset.$$

According to Claim 27, $\langle A, B, C, m+1 \rangle$ has always a left neighbor in y'. As a result, the left neighbor of every occurrence of $\langle A, B, C, m+1 \rangle$ is A. Therefore, we can express:

$$y' = y_1 A\langle A, B, C, m+1 \rangle y_2 A\langle A, B, C, m+1 \rangle y_3 \ldots y_r A\langle A, B, C, m+1 \rangle y_{r+1},$$
$$y = g^{-1}(y_1) AB g^{-1}(y_2) AB g^{-1}(y_3) \ldots g^{-1}(y_r) AB g^{-1}(y_{r+1}),$$
$$x' = y_1 AC y_2 AC y_3 \ldots y_r AC y_{r+1},$$

where $r \geq 1$, $y_s \in V^*$, $1 \leq s \leq r + 1$. Since we have $p = AB \to AC \in P$, there is a derivation:

$$
\begin{aligned}
S_1 &\Rightarrow^*_G g^{-1}(y_1)ABg^{-1}(y_2)ABg^{-1}(y_3)\ldots g^{-1}(y_r)ABg^{-1}(y_{r+1}) \\
&\Rightarrow_G g^{-1}(y_1)ACg^{-1}(y_2)ABg^{-1}(y_3)\ldots g^{-1}(y_r)ABg^{-1}(y_{r+1}) \quad [p] \\
&\Rightarrow_G g^{-1}(y_1)ACg^{-1}(y_2)ACg^{-1}(y_3)\ldots g^{-1}(y_r)ABg^{-1}(y_{r+1}) \quad [p] \\
&\;\vdots \\
&\Rightarrow_G g^{-1}(y_1)ACg^{-1}(y_2)ACg^{-1}(y_3)\ldots g^{-1}(y_r)ACg^{-1}(y_{r+1}) \quad [p],
\end{aligned}
$$

where $g^{-1}(y_1)ACg^{-1}(y_2)ACg^{-1}(y_3)\ldots g^{-1}(y_r)ACg^{-1}(y_{r+1}) = g^{-1}(x') = x$.

Because cases (i), (ii), and (iii) cover all possible forms of y', we have completed the induction and established Claim 30. $\qquad\square$

The equivalence of G and G' follows from Claim 30. Indeed, observe that by the definition of g, we have $g(a) = \{a\}$ for all $a \in T$. Therefore, by Claim 30, we have for any $x \in T^*$,

$$S_1 \Rightarrow^*_G x \quad \text{if and only if} \quad S_1 \Rightarrow^*_{G'} x.$$

Thus, $L(G) = L(G')$, and the lemma holds. $\qquad\square$

Theorem 38. $\mathbf{CS} = \mathbf{FEP0L}(2) = \mathbf{FEPT0L}(2) = \mathbf{FEP0L} = \mathbf{FEPT0L}$.

Proof. By Lemma 18, $\mathbf{CS} \subseteq \mathbf{FEP0L}(2) \subseteq \mathbf{FEPT0L}(2) \subseteq \mathbf{FEPT0L}$. From Lemma 11 and the definition of FET0L grammars, it follows that $\mathbf{FEPT0L}(s) \subseteq \mathbf{FEPT0L} \subseteq \mathbf{CEPT0L} \subseteq \mathbf{CS}$ for any $s \geq 0$. Moreover, $\mathbf{FEP0L}(s) \subseteq \mathbf{FEP0L} \subseteq \mathbf{FEPT0L}$. Thus, $\mathbf{CS} = \mathbf{FEP0L}(2) = \mathbf{FEPT0L}(2) = \mathbf{FEP0L} = \mathbf{FEPT0L}$, and the theorem holds. $\qquad\square$

Return to the proof of Lemma 18. Observe that the productions of the FEP0L grammar G' are of restricted forms. This observation gives rise to the next corollary.

Corollary 15. *Every context-sensitive language can be generated by an FEP0L grammar $G = (V, T, P, S)$ of degree 2 such that every production from P has one of the following forms:*

(i) $(a \to a, \emptyset)$, $a \in V$.

(ii) $(X \to x, F)$, $X \in V - T$, $|x| \in \{1, 2\}$, $\max(F) = 1$.

(iii) $(X \to Y, \{z\})$, $X, Y \in V - T$, $z \in V^2$.

Next, we demonstrate that the family of recursively enumerable languages is generated by the forbidding E0L grammars of degree 2.

Lemma 19. $\mathbf{RE} \subseteq \mathbf{FE0L}(2)$.

Proof. Let L be a recursively enumerable language generated by a phrase structure grammar

$$G = (V, T, P, S)$$

having the form defined in Lemma 5, where

$$
\begin{aligned}
V &= N_{CF} \cup N_{CS} \cup T, \\
P_{CS} &= \{AB \to AC \in P : A, C \in N_{CF}, B \in N_{CS}\}, \\
P_{CF} &= P - P_{CS}.
\end{aligned}
$$

Let \$ be a new symbol and m be the cardinality of $V \cup \{\$\}$. Furthermore, let f be an arbitrary bijection from $V \cup \{\$\}$ onto $\{1, \ldots, m\}$, and let f^{-1} be the inverse of f.

Then, we define an FE0L grammar

$$G' = (V', T, P', S')$$

of degree 2 as follows:

$$
\begin{aligned}
W_0 &= \{\langle A, B, C\rangle : AB \to AC \in P\}, \\
W_S &= \{\langle A, B, C, j\rangle : AB \to AC \in P, 1 \le j \le m\}, \\
W &= W_0 \cup W_S, \\
V' &= V \cup W \cup \{S', \$\},
\end{aligned}
$$

where $A, C \in N_{CF}, B \in N_{CS}$, and V, W_0, W_S, and $\{S', \$\}$ are pairwise disjoint alphabets. The set of productions P' is defined in the following way:

1. Add $(S' \to \$S, \emptyset)$, $(\$ \to \$, \emptyset)$ and $(\$ \to \varepsilon, V' - T - \{\$\})$ to P'.

2. For all $X \in V$, add $(X \to X, \emptyset)$ to P'.

3. For all $A \to u \in P_{CF}$, $A \in N_{CF}$, $u \in \{\varepsilon\} \cup N_{CS} \cup T \cup (\bigcup_{i=1}^{2} N_{CF}^{i})$, add $(A \to u, W)$ to P'.

4. If $AB \to AC \in P_{CS}$, $A, C \in N_{CF}, B \in N_{CS}$, then add the following productions to P':

   (a) $(B \to \langle A, B, C\rangle, W)$.

   (b) $(\langle A, B, C\rangle \to \langle A, B, C, 1\rangle, W - \{\langle A, B, C\rangle\})$.

   (c) $(\langle A, B, C, j\rangle \to \langle A, B, C, j + 1\rangle, \{f^{-1}(j)\langle A, B, C, j\rangle\})$ for all $1 \le j \le m$ such that $f(A) \ne j$.

   (d) $(\langle A, B, C, f(A)\rangle \to \langle A, B, C, f(A) + 1\rangle, \emptyset)$.

   (e) $(\langle A, B, C, m + 1\rangle \to C, \{\langle A, B, C, m + 1\rangle^2\})$.

Basic Idea. Let us only sketch the proof that $L(G) = L(G')$. The construction above resembles the construction in Lemma 18 very much. Indeed, to simulate the non-context-free productions $AB \to AC$ in FE0L grammars, we use the same technique as in FEP0L grammars from Lemma 18. We only need to guarantee that no sentential form begins with a symbol from N_{CS}. This is solved by an auxiliary nonterminal $ in the definition of G'. The symbol is always generated in the first derivation step by $(S' \to \$S, \emptyset)$ (see (1) in the definition of P'). After that, it appears as the left-most symbol of all sentential forms containing some nonterminals. The only production that can erase it is $(\$ \to \varepsilon, V' - T - \{\$\})$.

Therefore, by analogy with the technique used in Lemma 18, we can establish

$$S \Rightarrow_G^* x \quad \text{if and only if} \quad S' \Rightarrow_{G'}^+ \$x'$$

such that $x \in V^*$, $x' \in (V' - \{S', \$\})^*$, $x' \in g(x)$, where g is a finite substitution from V^* into $(V' - \{S', \$\})^*$ defined as

$$g(X) = \{X\} \cup \{\langle A, X, C\rangle : \langle A, X, C\rangle \in W_0\} \\ \cup \{\langle A, X, C, j\rangle : \langle A, X, C, j\rangle \in W_S, 1 \le j \le m+1\}$$

for all $X \in V$, $A, C \in N_{CF}$. The details are left to the reader.

As in Lemma 18, we have $g(a) = \{a\}$ for all $a \in T$; hence, for all $x \in T^*$,

$$S \Rightarrow_G^* x \quad \text{if and only if} \quad S' \Rightarrow_{G'}^+ \$x.$$

Since

$$\$x \Rightarrow_{G'} x \ [(\$ \to \varepsilon, V' - T - \{\$\})],$$

we obtain

$$S \Rightarrow_G^* x \quad \text{if and only if} \quad S' \Rightarrow_{G'}^+ x.$$

Consequently, $L(G) = L(G')$; thus, **RE** $\subseteq$ **FE0L**(2). $\qquad\square$

Theorem 39. **RE** = **FE0L**(2) = **FET0L**(2) = **FE0L** = **FET0L**.

Proof. By Lemma 19, we have **RE** $\subseteq$ **FE0L**(2) $\subseteq$ **FET0L**(2) $\subseteq$ **FET0L**. From Lemma 12, it follows that **FET0L**$(s) \subseteq$ **FET0L** $\subseteq$ **CET0L** $\subseteq$ **RE**, for any $s \ge 0$. Therefore, **RE** = **FE0L**(2) = **FET0L**(2) = **FE0L** = **FET0L**, so the theorem holds. $\qquad\square$

By analogy with Corollary 15, we obtain the following normal form:

Corollary 16. *Every recursively enumerable language can be generated by an FE0L grammar $G = (V, T, P, S)$ of degree 2 such that every production from P has one of the following forms:*

(i) $(a \to a, \emptyset)$, $a \in V$.

(ii) $(X \to x, F)$, $X \in V - T$, $|x| \le 2$, and $F \ne \emptyset$ implies $\max(F) = 1$.

(iii) $(X \to Y, \{z\})$, $X, Y \in V - T$, $z \in V^2$.

Theorems 36, 37, 38, and 39 imply the following relationships of FET0L language families:

Corollary 17.

$$CF$$
$$\subset$$
$$\mathbf{FEP0L}(0) = \mathbf{FE0L}(0) = \mathbf{EP0L} = \mathbf{E0L}$$
$$\subset$$
$$\mathbf{FEP0L}(1) = \mathbf{FEPT0L}(1) = \mathbf{FE0L}(1) = \mathbf{FET0L}(1)$$
$$= \mathbf{FEPT0L}(0) = \mathbf{FET0L}(0) = \mathbf{EPT0L} = \mathbf{ET0L}$$
$$\subset$$
$$\mathbf{FEP0L}(2) = \mathbf{FEPT0L}(2) = \mathbf{FEP0L} = \mathbf{FEPT0L} = \mathbf{CS}$$
$$\subset$$
$$\mathbf{FE0L}(2) = \mathbf{FET0L}(2) = \mathbf{FE0L} = \mathbf{FET0L} = \mathbf{RE}.$$

4.2.3 Simple Semi-conditional ET0L Grammars

Simple semi-conditional ET0L grammars represent another variant of context-conditional ET0L grammars with restricted sets of context conditions. By analogy with sequential simple semi-conditional grammars (see Section 4.1.5), these grammars are context-conditional ET0L grammars in which every production contains no more than one context condition.

Definition 18. Let $G = (V, T, P_1, \ldots, P_t, S)$ be a context-conditional ET0L grammar, for some $t \geq 1$. If for all $p = (a \rightarrow x, Per, For) \in P_i$ for every $i = 1, \ldots, t$ holds $|Per| + |For| \leq 1$, G is said to be a *simple semi-conditional ET0L grammar* (*SSC-ET0L grammar* for short). If G is a propagating SSC-ET0L grammar, then G is called an *SSC-EPT0L grammar*. If $t = 1$, then G is called an *SSC-E0L grammar*; if, in addition, G is a propagating SSC-E0L grammar, G is said to be an *SSC-EP0L grammar*.

Convention 5. Let $G = (V, T, P_1, \ldots, P_t, S)$ be an SSC-ET0L grammar of degree (r, s). By analogy with *ssc*-grammars, in each production $(a \rightarrow x, Per, For) \in P_i$, $i = 1, \ldots, t$, we omit braces and instead of $\emptyset$, we write 0. For example, we write $(a \rightarrow x, EF, 0)$ instead of $(a \rightarrow x, \{EF\}, \emptyset)$.

The families of languages generated by SSC-EPT0L, SSC-ET0L, SSC-EP0L, and SSC-E0L grammars of degree (r, s) are denoted by **SSC-EPT0L**(r, s), **SSC-ET0L**(r, s), **SSC-EP0L**(r, s), and **SSC-E0L**(r, s), respectively. Furthermore, the families of languages generated by SSC-EPT0L, SSC-ET0L, SSC-EP0L, and SSC-E0L grammars of any degree are denoted by **SSC-EPT0L**, **SSC-ET0L**, **SSC-EP0L**, and **SSC-E0L**, respectively.

Next, let us investigate the generative power of SSC-ET0L grammars. The following lemma proves that every recursively enumerable language can be defined by an SSC-E0L grammar of degree $(1, 2)$:

Lemma 20. RE $\subseteq$ SSC-E0L$(1, 2)$.

Proof. Let

$$G = (N_{CF} \cup N_{CS} \cup T, T, P, S)$$

be a phrase-structure grammar of the form of Lemma 5. Then, let $V = N_{CF} \cup N_{CS} \cup T$ and m be the cardinality of V. Let f be an arbitrary (but fixed) bijection from V to $\{1, \ldots, m\}$, and f^{-1} be the inverse of f. Set

$$
\begin{aligned}
M \;=\; & \{\#\} \cup \\
& \{\langle A, B, C\rangle :\; AB \to AC \in P, A, C \in N_{CF}, B \in N_{CS}\} \cup \\
& \{\langle A, B, C, i\rangle :\; AB \to AC \in P, A, C \in N_{CF}, B \in N_{CS}, 1 \le i \le m + 2\}
\end{aligned}
$$

and

$$W = \{[A, B, C] :\; AB \to AC \in P, A, C \in N_{CF}, B \in N_{CS}\}.$$

Next, construct an SSC-E0L grammar of degree $(1, 2)$

$$G' = (V', T, P', S'),$$

where

$$V' = V \cup M \cup W \cup \{S'\}.$$

Without any loss of generality, we assume that V, M, W, and $\{S'\}$ are pairwise disjoint. The set of productions P' is constructed in the following way:

1. Add $(S' \to \#S, 0, 0)$ to P'.

2. For all $A \to x \in P$, $A \in N_{CF}$, $x \in \{\varepsilon\} \cup N_{CS} \cup T \cup N_{CF}^2$, add $(A \to x, \#, 0)$ to P'.

3. For every $AB \to AC \in P$, $A, C \in N_{CF}$, $B \in N_{CS}$, add the following productions to P':

   (a) $(\# \to \langle A, B, C\rangle, 0, 0)$.
   (b) $(B \to [A, B, C], \langle A, B, C\rangle, 0)$.
   (c) $(\langle A, B, C\rangle \to \langle A, B, C, 1\rangle, 0, 0)$.
   (d) $([A, B, C] \to [A, B, C], 0, \langle A, B, C, m + 2\rangle)$.
   (e) $(\langle A, B, C, i\rangle \to \langle A, B, C, i + 1\rangle, 0, f^{-1}(i)[A, B, C])$ for all $1 \le i \le m$, $i \ne f(A)$.
   (f) $(\langle A, B, C, f(A)\rangle \to \langle A, B, C, f(A) + 1\rangle, 0, 0)$.
   (g) $(\langle A, B, C, m + 1\rangle \to \langle A, B, C, m + 2\rangle, 0, [A, B, C]^2)$.
   (h) $(\langle A, B, C, m + 2\rangle \to \#, 0, \langle A, B, C, m + 2\rangle[A, B, C])$.
   (i) $([A, B, C] \to C, \langle A, B, C, m + 2\rangle, 0)$.

4. For all $X \in V$, add $(X \to X, 0, 0)$ to P'.

5. Add $(\# \to \#, 0, 0)$ and $(\# \to \varepsilon, 0, 0)$ to P'.

Basic Idea. Let us explain how G' works. During the simulation of a derivation in G, every sentential form starts with an auxiliary symbol from M, called the master. This symbol determines the current simulation mode and controls the next derivation step. Initially, the master is set to $\#$ (see (1) in the definition of P'). In this mode, G' simulates context-free productions (see (2)); notice that symbols from V can always be rewritten to themselves by (4). To start the simulation of a non-context-free production of the form $AB \to AC$, G' rewrites the master to $\langle A, B, C \rangle$. In the following step, chosen occurrences of B are rewritten to $[A, B, C]$; no other productions can be used except productions introduced in (4). At the same time, the master is rewritten to $\langle A, B, C, i \rangle$ with $i = 1$ (see (3c)). Then, i is repeatedly incremented by one until i is greater than the cardinality of V (see productions (3e) and (3f)). Simultaneously, the master's conditions make sure that for every i such that $f^{-1}(i) \neq A$, no $f^{-1}(i)$ appears as the left neighbor of any occurrence of $[A, B, C]$. Finally, G' checks that there are no two adjoining $[A, B, C]$ (see (3g)) and that $[A, B, C]$ does not appear as the right neighbor of the master (see (3h)). At this point, the left neighbors of $[A, B, C]$ are necessarily equal to A and every occurrence of $[A, B, C]$ is rewritten to C. In the same derivation step, the master is rewritten to $\#$.

Observe that in every derivation step, the master allows G' to use only a subset of productions according to the current mode. Indeed, it is not possible to combine context-free and non-context-free simulation modes. Furthermore, no two different non-context-free productions can be simulated at the same time. The simulation ends when $\#$ is erased by $(\# \to \varepsilon, 0, 0)$. After this erasure, no other production can be used.

The following three claims demonstrate some important properties of derivations in G' to establish $L(G) = L(G')$:

Claim 31. *$S' \Rightarrow_{G'}^{+} w'$ implies that $w' \in M(V \cup W)^*$ or $w' \in (V \cup W)^*$. Furthermore, if $w' \in M(V \cup W)^*$, every v' such that $S' \Rightarrow_{G'}^{+} v' \Rightarrow_{G'}^{*} w'$ belongs to $M(V \cup W)^*$ as well.*

Proof. When deriving w', G' first rewrites S' to $\#S$ by using $(S' \to \#S, 0, 0)$, where $\# \in M$ and $S \in V$. Next, inspect P' to see that every symbol from M is always rewritten to a symbol belonging to M or, in the case of $\#$, erased by $(\# \to \varepsilon, 0, 0)$. Moreover, there are no productions generating new occurrences of symbols from $(M \cup \{S'\})$. Thus, all sentential forms derived from S' belong either to $M(V \cup W)^*$ or to $(V \cup W)^*$. In addition, if a sentential form belongs to $M(V \cup W)^*$, all previous sentential forms (except for S') are also from $M(V \cup W)^*$.   □

Claim 32. *Every successful derivation in G' is of the form*

$$S' \Rightarrow_{G'} \#S \Rightarrow_{G'}^{+} \#u' \Rightarrow_{G'} w' \Rightarrow_{G'}^{*} w',$$

where $u' \in V^*$, $w' \in T^*$.

Proof. From Claim 31 and its proof, every successful derivation has the form

$$S' \Rightarrow_{G'} \#S \Rightarrow_{G'}^{+} \#u' \Rightarrow_{G'} v' \Rightarrow_{G'}^{*} w',$$

where $u', v' \in (V \cup W)^*$, $w' \in T^*$. This claim shows that

$$\#u' \Rightarrow_{G'} v' \Rightarrow_{G'}^* w'$$

implies $u' \in V$ and $v' = w'$.

Consider

$$\#u' \Rightarrow_{G'} v' \Rightarrow_{G'}^* w',$$

where $u', v' \in (V \cup W)^*$, $w' \in T^*$. Assume that u' contains a nonterminal $[A, B, C] \in W$. There are two productions rewriting $[A, B, C]$: $p_1 = ([A, B, C] \rightarrow [A, B, C], 0, \langle A, B, C, m+2 \rangle)$ and $p_2 = ([A, B, C] \rightarrow C, \langle A, B, C, m+2 \rangle, 0)$. Because of its permitting condition, p_2 cannot be applied during $\#u' \Rightarrow_{G'} v'$. If $[A, B, C]$ is rewritten by p_1—that is, $[A, B, C] \in \mathrm{alph}(v')$—$[A, B, C]$ necessarily occurs in all sentential forms derived from v'. Thus, no u' containing a nonterminal from W results in a terminal string; hence, $u' \in V^*$. By analogical considerations, establish that also $v' \in V^*$. Next, assume that v' contains some $A \in N_{CF}$ or $B \in N_{CS}$. The first one can be rewritten by $(A \rightarrow z, \#, 0)$, $z \in V^*$, and the second one by $(B \rightarrow [A, B, C], \langle A, B, C \rangle, 0)$, $[A, B, C] \in W$, $\langle A, B, C \rangle \in M$. In both cases, the permitting condition forbids an application of the production. Consequently, $v' \in T^*$. It suffices to show that $v' = w'$. Indeed, every production rewriting a terminal is of the form $(a \rightarrow a, 0, 0)$, $a \in T$. $\square$

Claim 33. $S' \Rightarrow_{G'}^n Zx'$, $Z \in M$, $x' \in (V \cup W)^*$, $n \geq 1$, implies that Zx' has one of the following forms:

(I) $Z = \#$, $x' \in V^*$.

(II) $Z = \langle A, B, C \rangle$, $x' \in V^*$, for some $A, C \in N_{CF}$, $B \in N_{CS}$.

(III) $Z = \langle A, B, C, i \rangle$, $x' \in (V \cup \{[A, B, C]\})^*$, $1 \leq i \leq m+1$, and $\{f^{-1}(j)[A, B, C]: 1 \leq j < i,\ j \neq f(A)\} \cap \mathrm{sub}(x') = \emptyset$ for some $A, C \in N_{CF}$, $B \in N_{CS}$.

(IV) $Z = \langle A, B, C, m + 2 \rangle$, $x' \in (V \cup \{[A, B, C]\})^*$, $\{X[A, B, C] : X \in V,\ X \neq A\} \cap \mathrm{sub}(x') = \emptyset$, and $[A, B, C]^2 \not\subseteq \mathrm{sub}(x')$ for some $A, C \in N_{CF}$, $B \in N_{CS}$.

Proof. This claim is proved by induction on the length of derivations.

Basis: Let $n = 1$. Then, $S' \Rightarrow_{G'} \#S$, where $\#S$ is of type (I).

Induction Hypothesis: Suppose that the claim holds for all derivations of length n or less, for some $n \geq 1$.

Induction Step: Consider a derivation of the form

$$S' \Rightarrow_{G'}^{n+1} Qx',$$

$Q \in M$, $x' \in (V \cup W)^*$. Because $n + 1 \geq 2$, by Claim 31, there exists $Zy' \in M(V \cup W)^*$ and a sequence of productions $p_0, p_1, \ldots, p_q$, where $p_i \in P'$, $0 \leq i \leq q$, $q = |y'|$, such that

$$S' \Rightarrow_{G'}^n Zy' \Rightarrow_{G'} Qx' \ [p_0, p_1, \ldots, p_q].$$

Let $y' = a_1 a_2 \ldots a_q$, where $a_i \in (V \cup W)$ for all $i = 1, \ldots, q$. By the induction hypothesis, the following cases (i) through (iv) cover all possible forms of Zy':

(i) Let $Z = \#$ and $y' \in V^*$ (form (I)). According to the definition of P', p_0 is either $(\# \rightarrow \langle A, B, C \rangle, 0, 0)$, $A, C \in N_{CF}$, $B \in N_{CS}$, or $(\# \rightarrow \#, 0, 0)$, or $(\# \rightarrow \varepsilon, 0, 0)$, and every p_i is either of the form $(a_i \rightarrow z, \#, 0)$, $z \in \{\varepsilon\} \cup N_{CS} \cup T \cup N_{CF}^2$, or $(a_i \rightarrow a_i, 0, 0)$. Obviously, y' is always rewritten to a string $x' \in V^*$. If $\#$ is rewritten to $\langle A, B, C \rangle$, we get $\langle A, B, C \rangle x'$ that is of form (II). If $\#$ remains unchanged, $\#x'$ is of type (I). In case that $\#$ is erased, the resulting sentential form does not belong to $M(V \cup W)^*$ required by this claim (which also holds for all strings derived from x' (see Claim 31)).

(ii) Let $Z = \langle A, B, C \rangle$, $y' \in V^*$, for some $A, C \in N_{CF}$, $B \in N_{CS}$ (form (II)). In this case, $p_0 = (\langle A, B, C \rangle \rightarrow \langle A, B, C, 1 \rangle, 0, 0)$ and every p_i is either $(a_i \rightarrow [A, B, C], \langle A, B, C \rangle, 0)$ or $(a_i \rightarrow a_i, 0, 0)$ (see the definition of P'). It is easy to see that $\langle A, B, C, 1 \rangle x'$ belongs to (III).

(iii) Let $Z = \langle A, B, C, j \rangle$, $y' \in (V \cup \{[A, B, C]\})^*$, and y' satisfies

$$\{f^{-1}(k)[A, B, C] : 1 \leq k < j, \ k \neq f(A)\} \cap \mathrm{sub}(y') = \emptyset,$$

$1 \leq j \leq m + 1$, for some $A, C \in N_{CF}$, $B \in N_{CS}$ (form (III)). The only productions rewriting symbols from y' are $(a_i \rightarrow a_i, 0, 0)$, $a_i \in V$, and $([A, B, C] \rightarrow [A, B, C], 0, \langle A, B, C, m + 2 \rangle)$; thus, y' is rewritten to itself. By inspection of P', p_0 can be of the following three forms:

(a) If $j \neq f(A)$ and $j < m + 1$,

$$p_0 = (\langle A, B, C, j \rangle \rightarrow \langle A, B, C, j + 1 \rangle, 0, f^{-1}(j)[A, B, C]).$$

Clearly, p_0 can be used only when $f^{-1}(j)[A, B, C] \notin \mathrm{sub}(Zy')$. As

$$\{f^{-1}(k)[A, B, C] : 1 \leq k < j, \ k \neq f(A)\} \cap \mathrm{sub}(y') = \emptyset,$$

it also

$$\{f^{-1}(k)[A, B, C] : 1 \leq k \leq j, \ k \neq f(A)\} \cap \mathrm{sub}(y') = \emptyset.$$

Since $\langle A, B, C, j \rangle$ is rewritten to $\langle A, B, C, j + 1 \rangle$ and y' is unchanged, we get $\langle A, B, C, j + 1 \rangle y'$ with

$$\{f^{-1}(k)[A, B, C] : 1 \leq k < j + 1, \ k \neq f(A)\} \cap \mathrm{sub}(y') = \emptyset,$$

which is of form (III).

(b) If $j = f(A)$,

$$p_0 = (\langle A, B, C, f(A) \rangle \rightarrow \langle A, B, C, f(A) + 1 \rangle, 0, 0).$$

As before, $Qx' = \langle A, B, C, j+1 \rangle y'$. Moreover, because

$$\{f^{-1}(k)[A, B, C] : \ 1 \le k < j, \ k \neq f(A)\} \cap \mathrm{sub}(y') = \emptyset$$

and $j = f(A)$,

$$\{f^{-1}(k)[A, B, C] : \ 1 \le k < j+1, \ k \neq f(A)\} \cap \mathrm{sub}(x') = \emptyset.$$

Consequently, Qx' belongs to (III) as well.

(c) If $j = m+1$,

$$p_0 = (\langle A, B, C, m+1 \rangle \to \langle A, B, C, m+2 \rangle, 0, [A, B, C]^2).$$

Then, $Qx' = \langle A, B, C, m+2 \rangle y'$. The application of p_0 implies that $[A, B, C]^2 \notin \mathrm{sub}(x')$. In addition, observe that for $j = m+1$,

$$\{f^{-1}(k)[A, B, C] : \ 1 \le k < j, \ k \neq f(A)\}$$
$$= \{X[A, B, C] : \ X \in V, \ X \neq A\}.$$

Hence,

$$\{X[A, B, C] : \ X \in V, \ X \neq A\} \cap \mathrm{sub}(x') = \emptyset.$$

As a result, Qx' is of form (IV).

(iv) Let $Z = \langle A, B, C, m+2 \rangle$, $y' \in (V \cup \{[A, B, C]\})^*$, $[A, B, C]^2 \notin \mathrm{sub}(y')$, and

$$\{X[A, B, C] : \ X \in V, \ X \neq A\} \cap \mathrm{sub}(y') = \emptyset,$$

for some $A, C \in N_{CF}$, $B \in N_{CS}$ (form (IV)). Inspect P' to see that

$$p_0 = (\langle A, B, C, m+2 \rangle \to \#, 0, \langle A, B, C, m+2 \rangle [A, B, C])$$

and p_i is either

$$(a_i \to a_i, 0, 0), \ a_i \in V,$$

or

$$([A, B, C] \to C, \langle A, B, C, m+2 \rangle, 0),$$

$1 \le i \le q$. According to the right-hand sides of these productions, $Qx' \in \{\#\}V^*$; that is, Qx' belongs to (I).

In cases (i) through (iv), we have demonstrated that every sentential form obtained in $n+1$ derivation steps satisfies the statement of this claim. Therefore, we have finished the induction step and established Claim 33. $\square$

To prove the following claims, define a finite substitution g from V^* into $(V \cup W)^*$ as

$$g(X) = \{X\} \cup \{[A, B, C] \in W : \ A, C \in N_{CF}, \ B \in N_{CS}\}$$

for all $X \in V$. Let g^{-1} be the inverse of g.

Claim 34. *Let* $y' = a_1 a_2 \ldots a_q$, $a_i \in (V \cup W)^*$, $q = |y'|$, *and* $g^{-1}(a_i) \Rightarrow^{h_i}_G g^{-1}(x'_i)$ *for all* $i \in \{1, \ldots, q\}$ *and some* $h_i \in \{0, 1\}$, $x'_i \in (V \cup W)^*$. *Then,* $g^{-1}(y') \Rightarrow^h_G g^{-1}(x')$ *such that* $x' = x'_1 x'_2 \ldots x'_q$, $h = \sum_{i=1}^q h_i$, $h \leq q$.

Proof. First, consider a derivation

$$g^{-1}(X) \Rightarrow^l_G g^{-1}(u),$$

$X \in (V \cup W)$, $u \in (V \cup W)^*$, $l \in \{0, 1\}$. If $l = 0$, $g^{-1}(X) = g^{-1}(u)$. Let $l = 1$. Then, there surely exists a production $p = g^{-1}(X) \to g^{-1}(u) \in P$ such that

$$g^{-1}(X) \Rightarrow_G g^{-1}(u) \; [p].$$

Return to the statement of this claim. We can construct a derivation

$$
\begin{aligned}
g^{-1}(a_1) g^{-1}(a_2) \ldots g^{-1}(a_q) &\Rightarrow^{h_1}_G g^{-1}(x'_1) g^{-1}(a_2) \ldots g^{-1}(a_q) \\
&\Rightarrow^{h_2}_G g^{-1}(x'_1) g^{-1}(x'_2) \ldots g^{-1}(a_q) \\
&\vdots \\
&\Rightarrow^{h_q}_G g^{-1}(x'_1) g^{-1}(x'_2) \ldots g^{-1}(x'_q),
\end{aligned}
$$

where $g^{-1}(y') = g^{-1}(a_1) \ldots g^{-1}(a_q)$ and $g^{-1}(x'_1) \ldots g^{-1}(x'_q) = g^{-1}(x'_1 \ldots x'_q) = g^{-1}(x')$. In such a derivation, each $g^{-1}(a_i)$ is either left unchanged (if $h_i = 0$) or rewritten to $g^{-1}(x'_i)$ by the corresponding production $g^{-1}(a_i) \to g^{-1}(x'_i)$. Obviously, the length of this derivation is $\sum_{i=1}^q h_i$. □

Claim 35. $S \Rightarrow^*_G x$ *if and only if* $S' \Rightarrow^+_{G'} Qx'$, *where* $g^{-1}(x') = x$, $Q \in M$, $x \in V^*$, $x' \in (V \cup W)^*$.

Proof.

Only if: By induction on the length of derivations in G, we show that

$$S \Rightarrow^n_G x \quad \text{implies} \quad S' \Rightarrow^+_{G'} \#x,$$

where $x \in V^*$, $n \geq 0$. Clearly, $g^{-1}(x) = x$.

Basis: Let $n = 0$. Then, $S \Rightarrow^0_G S$. In G', $S' \Rightarrow_{G'} \#S$ by using $(S' \to \#S, 0, 0)$.

Induction Hypothesis: Assume that the claim holds for all derivations of length n or less, for some $n \geq 0$.

Induction Step: Consider a derivation

$$S \Rightarrow^{n+1}_G x.$$

As $n + 1 \geq 1$, there exists $y \in V^*$ and $p \in P$ such that

$$S \Rightarrow^n_G y \Rightarrow_G x \; [p].$$

Let $y = a_1 a_2 \ldots a_q$, $a_i \in V$ for all $1 \leq i \leq q$, where $q = |y|$. By the induction hypothesis,

$$S' \Rightarrow^+_{G'} \#y.$$

The following cases investigate all possible forms of p:

(i) $p = A \rightarrow z$, $A \in N_{CF}$, $z \in \{\varepsilon\} \cup N_{CS} \cup T \cup N_{CF}^2$. Then, $y = y_1 A y_3$ and $x = y_1 z y_3$, $y_1, y_3 \in V^*$. Let $l = |y_1| + 1$. In this case, we can construct

$$S' \Rightarrow_{G'}^+ \#y \Rightarrow_{G'} \#x \ [p_0, p_1, \ldots, p_q]$$

such that $p_0 = (\# \rightarrow \#, 0, 0)$, $p_l = (A \rightarrow z, \#, 0)$, and $p_i = (a_i \rightarrow a_i, 0, 0)$ for all $1 \leq i \leq q$, $i \neq l$.

(ii) $p = AB \rightarrow AC$, $A, C \in N_{CF}$, $B \in N_{CS}$. Then, $y = y_1 A B y_3$ and $x = y_1 A C y_3$, $y_1, y_3 \in V^*$. Let $l = |y_1| + 2$. At this point, there exists the following derivation:

$$
\begin{array}{ll}
S' & \Rightarrow_{G'}^+ \quad \#y_1 A B y_3 \\
& \Rightarrow_{G'} \quad \langle A, B, C \rangle y_1 A B y_3 \\
& \Rightarrow_{G'} \quad \langle A, B, C, 1 \rangle y_1 A [A, B, C] y_3 \\
& \Rightarrow_{G'} \quad \langle A, B, C, 2 \rangle y_1 A [A, B, C] y_3 \\
& \quad \vdots \\
& \Rightarrow_{G'} \quad \langle A, B, C, f(A) \rangle y_1 A [A, B, C] y_3 \\
& \Rightarrow_{G'} \quad \langle A, B, C, f(A) + 1 \rangle y_1 A [A, B, C] y_3 \\
& \quad \vdots \\
& \Rightarrow_{G'} \quad \langle A, B, C, m + 1 \rangle y_1 A [A, B, C] y_3 \\
& \Rightarrow_{G'} \quad \langle A, B, C, m + 2 \rangle y_1 A [A, B, C] y_3 \\
& \Rightarrow_{G'} \quad \#y_1 A C y_3.
\end{array}
$$

If: The if-part establishes that

$$S' \Rightarrow_{G'}^n Qx' \quad \text{implies} \quad S \Rightarrow_{G'}^* x,$$

where $g^{-1}(x') = x$, $Q \in M$, $x' \in (V \cup W)^*$, $x \in V^*$, $n \geq 1$. This claim is proved by induction on the length of derivations in G'.

Basis: Assume that $n = 1$. Because the only production that can rewrite S' is $(S' \rightarrow \#S, 0, 0)$, $S' \Rightarrow_{G'} \#S$. Clearly, $S \Rightarrow_G^0 S$ and $g^{-1}(S) = S$.

Induction Hypothesis: Suppose that the claim holds for any derivation of length n or less, for some $n \geq 1$.

Induction Step: Consider

$$S' \Rightarrow_{G'}^{n+1} Qx',$$

$Qx' \in M(V \cup W)^*$. Since $n + 1 \geq 2$, by Claim 31, there exists a derivation

$$S' \Rightarrow_{G'}^+ Zy' \Rightarrow_{G'} Qx' \ [p_0, p_1, \ldots, p_q],$$

where $Zy' \in M(V \cup W)^*$, and $p_i \in P'$ for all $i \in \{0, 1, \ldots, q\}$, $q = |y'|$. By the induction hypothesis, there is also a derivation

$$S \Rightarrow_{G'}^* y,$$

where $y \in V^*$, $g^{-1}(y') = y$. Let $y' = a_1 a_2 \ldots a_q$. Claim 33 says that Zy' has one of the following forms:

(i) Let $Z = \#$ and $y' \in V^*$. Then, there are two forms of productions rewriting a_i in y'.

(a) $(a_i \to a_i, 0, 0)$, $a_i \in V$. In this case,

$$g^{-1}(a_i) \Rightarrow_G^0 g^{-1}(a_i).$$

(b) $(a_i \to x_i, \#, 0)$, $x_i \in \{\varepsilon\} \cup N_{CS} \cup T \cup N_{CF}^2$. Because $a_i = g^{-1}(a_i)$, $x_i = g^{-1}(x_i)$ and $a_i \to x_i \in P$,

$$g^{-1}(a_i) \Rightarrow_G g^{-1}(x_i) \ [a_i \to x_i].$$

We see that for all a_i, there exists a derivation

$$g^{-1}(a_i) \Rightarrow_G^{h_i} g^{-1}(x_i)$$

for some $h_i \in \{0, 1\}$, where $x_i \in V^*$, $x' = x_1 x_2 \ldots x_q$. Therefore, by Claim 34, we can construct

$$S' \Rightarrow_G^* y \Rightarrow_G^h x,$$

where $0 \leq h \leq q$, $x = g^{-1}(x')$.

(ii) Let $Z = \langle A, B, C \rangle$, $y' \in V^*$, for some $A, C \in N_{CF}$, $B \in N_{CS}$. At this point, the following two forms of productions can be used to rewrite a_i in y':

(a) $(a_i \to a_i, 0, 0)$, $a_i \in V$. As in case (i.a),

$$g^{-1}(a_i) \Rightarrow_G^0 g^{-1}(a_i).$$

(b) $(a_i \to [A, B, C], \langle A, B, C \rangle, 0)$, $a_i = B$. Since $g^{-1}([A, B, C]) = g^{-1}(B)$, we have

$$g^{-1}(a_i) \Rightarrow_G^0 g^{-1}([A, B, C]).$$

Thus, there exists the derivation

$$S \Rightarrow_G^* y \Rightarrow_G^0 x, \ x = g^{-1}(x').$$

(iii) Let $Z = \langle A, B, C, j \rangle$, $y' \in (V \cup \{[A, B, C]\})^*$, and

$$\{f^{-1}(k)[A, B, C] : \ 1 \leq k < j, \ k \neq f(A)\} \cap \mathrm{sub}(y') = \emptyset,$$

$1 \leq j \leq m + 1$, for some $A, C \in N_{CF}$, $B \in N_{CS}$. Then, the only productions rewriting symbols from y' are

$$(a_i \to a_i, 0, 0), \ a_i \in V,$$

and

$$([A, B, C] \to [A, B, C], 0, \langle A, B, C, m + 2 \rangle);$$

hence, $x' = y'$. Because we have

$$S \Rightarrow_G^* y, \ g^{-1}(y') = y,$$

it also holds $g^{-1}(x') = y$.

(iv) Let $Z = \langle A, B, C, m+2 \rangle$, $y' \in (V \cup \{[A, B, C]\})^*$, $[A, B, C]^2 \notin \mathrm{sub}(y')$,

$$\{X[A, B, C] : X \in V, \ X \neq A\} \cap \mathrm{sub}(y') = \emptyset,$$

for some $A, C \in N_{CF}$, $B \in N_{CS}$. G' rewrites $\langle A, B, C, m+2 \rangle$ by using

$$(\langle A, B, C, m+2 \rangle \to \#, 0, \langle A, B, C, m+2 \rangle[A, B, C]),$$

which forbids $\langle A, B, C, m+2 \rangle[A, B, C]$ as a substring of Zy'. As a result, the left neighbor of every occurrence of $[A, B, C]$ in $\langle A, B, C, m+2 \rangle y'$ is A. Inspect P' to see that a_i can be rewritten either by $(a_i \to a_i, 0, 0)$, $a_i \in V$, or by $([A, B, C] \to C, \langle A, B, C, m+2 \rangle, 0)$. Therefore, we can express:

$$
\begin{aligned}
y' &= y_1 A[A, B, C]y_2 A[A, B, C]y_3 \ldots y_l A[A, B, C]y_{l+1}, \\
y &= y_1 ABy_2 ABy_3 \ldots y_l ABy_{l+1}, \\
x' &= y_1 ACy_2 ACy_3 \ldots y_l ACy_{l+1},
\end{aligned}
$$

where $l \geq 0$, $y_k \in V^*$, $1 \leq k \leq l+1$. Since we have $p = AB \to AC \in P$, there is a derivation

$$
\begin{aligned}
S &\Rightarrow_G^* y_1 ABy_2 ABy_3 \ldots y_l ABy_{l+1} \\
&\Rightarrow_G y_1 ACy_2 ABy_3 \ldots y_l ABy_{l+1} \quad [p] \\
&\Rightarrow_G y_1 ACy_2 ACy_3 \ldots y_l ABy_{l+1} \quad [p] \\
&\ \vdots \\
&\Rightarrow_G y_1 ACy_2 ACy_3 \ldots y_l ACy_{l+1} \quad [p].
\end{aligned}
$$

Because cases (i) through (iv) cover all possible forms of y', we have completed the induction and established Claim 35.

$\square$

Let us finish the proof of Lemma 20. Consider a derivation

$$S \Rightarrow_G^* w, \ w \in T^*.$$

From Claim 35, it follows that

$$S' \Rightarrow_{G'}^+ \#w$$

because $g(a) = \{a\}$ for every $a \in T$. Then, as shown in Claim 32,

$$S' \Rightarrow_{G'}^+ \#w \Rightarrow_{G'} w,$$

and hence

$$S \Rightarrow_G^* w \quad \text{implies} \quad S' \Rightarrow_{G'}^+ w$$

for all $w \in T^*$. To prove the converse implication, consider a successful derivation of the form

$$S' \Rightarrow_{G'}^+ \#u \Rightarrow_{G'} w \Rightarrow_{G'}^* w,$$

$u \in V^*$, $w \in T^*$ (see Claim 32). Observe that by the definition of P', for every

$$S' \Rightarrow_{G'}^{+} \#u \Rightarrow_{G'} w$$

there also exists a derivation

$$S' \Rightarrow_{G'}^{+} \#u \Rightarrow_{G'}^{*} \#w \Rightarrow_{G'} w.$$

Then, according to Claim 35, $S \Rightarrow_{G}^{*} w$. Consequently, we get for every $w \in T^*$,

$$S \Rightarrow_{G}^{*} w \quad \text{if and only if} \quad S' \Rightarrow_{G'}^{*} w;$$

therefore, $L(G) = L(G')$. $\qquad\qquad\square$

Lemma 21. SSC-ET0L$(r, s) \subseteq$ **RE** *for any* $r, s \geq 0$.

Proof. By Lemma 12, **CET0L** $\subseteq$ **RE**. Because **SSC-ET0L**$(r, s) \subseteq$ **CET0L** for all $r, s \geq 0$ (see Definition 18), **SSC-ET0L**$(r, s) \subseteq$ **RE** for all $r, s \geq 0$ as well. $\quad\square$

Inclusions established in Lemmas 20 and 21 result in the following theorem:

Theorem 40. SSC-E0L$(1, 2) =$ **SSC-ET0L**$(1, 2) =$ **SSC-E0L** $=$ **SSC-ET0L** $=$ **RE**.

Proof. From Lemmas 20 and 21, **RE** $\subseteq$ **SSC-E0L**$(1, 2)$ and **SSC-ET0L**$(r, s) \subseteq$ **RE** for any $r, s \geq 0$. By the definitions, it also holds that **SSC-E0L**$(1, 2) \subseteq$ **SSC-ET0L**$(1, 2) \subseteq$ **SSC-ET0L** and **SSC-E0L**$(1, 2) \subseteq$ **SSC-E0L** $\subseteq$ **SSC-ET0L**. Hence, **SSC-E0L**$(1, 2) =$ **SSC-ET0L**$(1, 2) =$ **SSC-E0L** $=$ **SSC-ET0L** $=$ **RE**. $\blacksquare$

Next, let us investigate the generative power of propagating SSC-ET0L grammars.

Lemma 22. CS $\subseteq$ **SSC-EP0L**$(1, 2)$.

Proof. We can base this proof on the same technique as in Lemma 20. However, we have to make sure that the construction produces no erasing productions. This requires some modifications of the original algorithm; in particular, we have to elliminate the production $(\# \to \varepsilon, 0, 0)$.

Let L be a context-sensitive language generated by a grammar

$$G = (V, T, P, S)$$

of the normal form of Lemma 4, where

$$V = N_{CF} \cup N_{CS} \cup T.$$

Let m be the cardinality of V. Define a bijection f from V to $\{1, \ldots, m\}$. Let f^{-1} be the inverse of f. Set

$$
\begin{aligned}
M \;=\; & \{\langle \#\,|\,X\rangle : X \in V\} \cup \\
& \{\langle A, B, C\,|\,X\rangle : AB \to AC \in P,\ X \in V\} \cup \\
& \{\langle A, B, C, i\,|\,X\rangle : AB \to AC \in P,\ 1 \le i \le m+2,\ X \in V\}, \\
W \;=\; & \{[A, B, C, X] : AB \to AC \in P,\ X \in V\}, \text{ and} \\
V' \;=\; & V \cup M \cup W,
\end{aligned}
$$

where V, M, and W are pairwise disjoint. Then, construct the SSC-EP0L grammar of degree $(1, 2)$,

$$
G' = (V', T, P', \langle \#\,|\,S\rangle),
$$

with the set of productions P' defined as follows:

1. For all $A \to x \in P$, $A \in N_{CF}$, $x \in T \cup N_{CS} \cup N_{CF}^2$,

   (a) for all $X \in V$, add $(A \to x, \langle \#\,|\,X\rangle, 0)$ to P';

   (b) if $x \in T \cup N_{CS}$, add $(\langle \#\,|\,A\rangle \to \langle \#\,|\,x\rangle, 0, 0)$ to P';

   (c) if $x = YZ$, $YZ \in N_{CF}^2$, add $(\langle \#\,|\,A\rangle \to \langle \#\,|\,Y\rangle Z, 0, 0)$ to P'.

2. For all $X \in V$ for every $AB \to AC \in P$, $A, C \in N_{CF}$, $B \in N_{CS}$, add the following productions to P':

   (a) $(\langle \#\,|\,X\rangle \to \langle A, B, C\,|\,X\rangle, 0, 0)$.

   (b) $(B \to [A, B, C, X], \langle A, B, C\,|\,X\rangle, 0)$.

   (c) $(\langle A, B, C\,|\,X\rangle \to \langle A, B, C, 1\,|\,X\rangle, 0, 0)$.

   (d) $([A, B, C, X] \to [A, B, C, X], 0, \langle A, B, C, m+2\rangle X)$.

   (e) $(\langle A, B, C, i\,|\,X\rangle \to \langle A, B, C, i+1\,|\,X\rangle, 0, f^{-1}(i)[A, B, C, X])$ for all $1 \le i \le m$, $i \ne f(A)$.

   (f) $(\langle A, B, C, f(A)\,|\,X\rangle \to \langle A, B, C, f(A)+1\,|\,X\rangle, 0, 0)$.

   (g) $(\langle A, B, C, m+1\,|\,X\rangle \to \langle A, B, C, m+2\,|\,X\rangle, 0, [A, B, C, X]^2)$.

   (h) $(\langle A, B, C, m+2\,|\,X\rangle \to \langle \#\,|\,X\rangle, 0, 0)$ for $X = A$,
   $(\langle A, B, C, m+2\,|\,X\rangle \to \langle \#\,|\,X\rangle, 0, \langle A, B, C, m+2\,|\,X\rangle [A, B, C, X])$ otherwise.

   (i) $([A, B, C, X] \to C, \langle A, B, C, m+2\,|\,X\rangle, 0)$.

3. For all $X \in V$, add $(X \to X, 0, 0)$ to P'.

4. For all $X \in V$, add $(\langle \#\,|\,X\rangle \to \langle \#\,|\,X\rangle, 0, 0)$ and $(\langle \#\,|\,X\rangle \to X, 0, 0)$ to P'.

Basic Idea. Consider this construction and the construction used in Lemma 20. Observe that the present construction does not attach the master as an extra symbol before sentential forms. Instead, the master is incorporated with its right neighbor into one composite symbol. For example, if G generates $AabCadd$, the corresponding sentential form in G' is $\langle \# \mid A \rangle abCadd$, where $\langle \# \mid A \rangle$ is one symbol. At this point, we need no production erasing $\#$; the master is simply rewritten to the symbol with which it is incorporated (see productions of (4)). In addition, this modification involves some changes to the algorithm: First, G' can rewrite symbols incorporated with the master (see productions of (1b) and (1c)). Second, conditions of the productions depending on the master refer to the composite symbols. Finally, G' can make context-sensitive rewriting of the composite master's right neighbor (see productions of (2h)). For instance, if

$$ABadC \Rightarrow_G ACadC \ [AB \rightarrow AC]$$

in G, G' derives

$$\langle \# \mid A \rangle BadC \Rightarrow_{G'}^{+} \langle \# \mid A \rangle CadC.$$

Based on the observations above, the reader can surely establish $L(G) = L(G')$ by analogy with the proof of Lemma 20. Thus, the rigorous proof is omitted. $\square$

Lemma 23. SSC-EPT0L$(r, s) \subseteq$ **CS** *for all* $r, s \geq 0$.

Proof. By Lemma 11, **CEPT0L**$(r, s) \subseteq$ **CS**, for any $r \geq 0$, $s \geq 0$. Since every SSC-EPT0L grammar is a special case of a CEPT0L grammar (see Definition 18), we obtain **SSC-EPT0L**$(r, s) \subseteq$ **CS** for all $r, s \geq 0$. $\square$

Theorem 41. CS = SSC-EP0L$(1, 2) =$ **SSC-EPT0L**$(1, 2) =$ **SSC-EP0L** = **SSC-EPT0L**.

Proof. By Lemma 22, we have **CS** $\subseteq$ **SSC-EP0L**$(1, 2)$. Lemma 23 says that **SSC-EPT0L**$(r, s) \subseteq$ **CS** for all $r, s \geq 0$. From the definitions it follows that **SSC-EP0L**$(1, 2) \subseteq$ **SSC-EPT0L**$(1, 2) \subseteq$ **SSC-EPT0L** and **SSC-EP0L**$(1, 2) \subseteq$ **SSC-EP0L** $\subseteq$ **SSC-EPT0L**. Hence, **SSC-EP0L**$(1, 2) =$ **SSC-EPT0L**$(1, 2) =$ **SSC-EP0L** = **SSC-EPT0L** = **CS**. $\blacksquare$

The following corollary summarizes the established relationships between the language families generated by SSC-ET0L grammars:

Corollary 18.

CF

$\subset$

SSC-EP0L$(0, 0) =$ **SSC-E0L**$(0, 0) =$ **EP0L** = **E0L**

$\subset$

SSC-EPT0L$(0, 0) =$ **SSC-ET0L**$(0, 0) =$ **EPT0L** = **ET0L**

$\subset$

SSC-EP0L$(1, 2) =$ **SSC-EPT0L**$(1, 2) =$ **SSC-EP0L** = **SSC-EPT0L** = **CS**

$\subset$

SSC-E0L$(1, 2) =$ **SSC-ET0L**$(1, 2) =$ **SSC-E0L** = **SSC-ET0L** = **RE**.

Open Problems. Notice that Corollary 18 does not include some related language families. For instance, it contains no language families generated by SSC-ET0L grammars with degrees $(1,1)$, $(1,0)$, and $(0,1)$. What is their generative power? What is the generative power of SSC-ET0L grammars of degree $(2,1)$? Are they as powerful as SSC-ET0L grammars of degree $(1,2)$?

4.3 Global Context Conditional Grammars

As a matter of fact, in the present section, we go beyond the topic of this chapter. Indeed, rather than associate context conditions with grammatical rules, we associate them with a grammar as a whole.

Definition 19. Let r be a natural number. A *global context conditional grammar* (a *gcc-grammar* for short) *of degree* r is a sixtuple,

$$G = (V, T, P, S, Per, For),$$

where (V, T, P, S) is a context-free grammar, $For \subseteq V$, and $Per \subseteq V^+$ such that $y \in Per$ implies $|y| \leq r$. G is said to be *propagating* if $A \to x \in P$ implies $x \neq \varepsilon$.

Let $u, v \in V^*$, $p \in P$, $p = A \to x$, $u = u_1 A u_2$, $v = u_1 x u_2$, for some $A \in (V - T)$, $x, u_1, u_2 \in V^*$, then we write

(a) $u \ ^{\mathrm{P}}\!\!\Rightarrow_G v \ [p]$ if $A \in \mathrm{alph}(\mathrm{sub}(u) \cap Per)$;

(b) $u \ ^{\mathrm{f}}\!\!\Rightarrow_G v \ [p]$ if $\mathrm{alph}(u) \cap For = \emptyset$;

(c) $u \Rightarrow_G v \ [p]$ if $u \ ^{\mathrm{P}}\!\!\Rightarrow_G v \ [p]$ or $u \ ^{\mathrm{f}}\!\!\Rightarrow_G v \ [p]$.

Roughly speaking, such a production as $A \to x \in P$ can be applied to a sentential form w provided that (a) A occurs in a permitting word from Per which is a subword of w or (b) no forbidding symbol from For occurs in w. Note that (a) requires any occurrence of A to appear in a permitting word that is a subword of u; but not necessarily the occurrence of A, which is rewritten in a given derivation step $u \ ^{\mathrm{P}}\!\!\Rightarrow_G v$.

In the standard manner, we define $\Rightarrow_G^i$ for $i \geq 0$, $\Rightarrow_G^+$, and $\Rightarrow_G^*$. The language of G, denoted by $L(G)$, is defined as

$$L(G) = \{w \in T^* : \ S \Rightarrow_G^* w\}.$$

The family of languages generated by *gcc*-grammars of degree r is denoted by **GCC**(r). Furthermore,

$$\mathbf{GCC} = \bigcup_{i=0}^{\infty} \mathbf{GCC}(i).$$

We use prefix **prop-** if we consider only propagating *gcc*-grammars. That is, **prop-GCC**(r) and **prop-GCC** denote the family of languages generated by propagating *gcc*-grammars of degree r and by propagating *gcc*-grammars of any degree, respectively.

Next, we prove two fundamental results regarding the generative power of *gcc*-grammars:

(i) A language is context-sensitive if and only if it is generated by a propagating *gcc*-grammar of degree 2.

(ii) A language is recursively enumerable if and only if it is generated by a *gcc*-grammar of degree 2.

Theorem 42. CS = prop-GCC(2).

Proof. It is straightforward to prove that **prop-GCC(2) $\subseteq$ CS**, so it suffices to prove the converse inclusion.

Let L be a context-sensitive language. Without any loss of generality, we can assume that L is generated by a context-sensitive grammar

$$G = (N_{CF} \cup N_{CS} \cup T, T, P, S)$$

of the form described in Lemma 4. Let $V = N_{CF} \cup N_{CS} \cup T$. Set

$$For = \{\langle A, B, C \rangle : \; AB \to AC \in P, \; A, C \in N_{CF}, \; B \in N_{CS}\}.$$

The propagating *gcc*-grammar G' of degree 2 is defined as

$$G' = (V', T, P', S, Per, For),$$

where $V' = V \cup For$ and

$$Per = \{A\langle A, B, C \rangle : \; A \in N_{CF}, \; \langle A, B, C \rangle \in For\}.$$

The set of productions P' is defined in the following way:

1. If $A \to x \in P$, $A \in N_{CF}$, $x \in N_{CS} \cup T \cup N_{CF}^2$, then add $A \to x$ to P'.

2. If $AB \to AC \in P$, $A, C \in N_{CF}$, $B \in N_{CS}$, then add the following two productions $B \to \langle A, B, C \rangle$, $\langle A, B, C \rangle \to C$ to P'.

Obviously, G' is a propagating *gcc*-grammar of degree 2. Moreover, observe that G is supposed to be of the form described by Lemma 4, so N_{CF} and N_{CS} are two disjoint alphabets. Thus, considering the construction of G', we should see that there is at most one occurrence of a symbol from For in any word derived from S; that is,

$$S \Rightarrow_{G'}^* x \quad \text{implies} \quad \#_{For} x \leq 1.$$

The formal proof is left to the reader.

Next, define a finite letter-to-letters substitution g from V^* into $(V \cup For)^*$ such that for all $Y \in V$,

$$g(Y) = \{Y\} \cup \{\langle X, Y, Z \rangle : \; \langle X, Y, Z \rangle \in For, \; X, Z \in N_{CF}\}.$$

Let g^{-1} be the inverse of g.

To show that $L(G) = L(G')$, we prove that

$$S \Rightarrow_G^m x \quad \text{if and only if} \quad S \Rightarrow_{G'}^n x',$$

where $x' \in g(x)$, $x \in V^+$, for some $m, n \geq 0$.

Only if: This is established by induction on the length m of derivations; that is, we have to demonstrate that

$$S \Rightarrow_G^m x \quad \text{implies} \quad S \Rightarrow_{G'}^* x'$$

for some $x' \in g(x)$, $x \in V^+$. This is our claim.

Basis: Let $m = 0$. The only x is S because $S \Rightarrow_G^0 S$. Clearly, $S \Rightarrow_{G'}^0 S$ in G' and $S \in g(S)$.

Induction Hypothesis: Suppose that our claim holds for all derivations of length at most m, for some $m \geq 0$.

Induction Step: Let us consider a derivation

$$S \Rightarrow_G^{m+1} x, \ x \in V^+.$$

Since $m + 1 \geq 1$, there is some $y \in V^+$ and $p \in P$ such that

$$S \Rightarrow_G^m y \Rightarrow_G x \ [p],$$

and by the induction hypothesis, there is also a derivation

$$S \Rightarrow_{G'}^n y'$$

for some $y' \in g(y)$.

(i) Let us assume that $p = D \rightarrow y_2 \in P$, $D \in N_{CF}$, $y_2 \in N_{CS} \cup T \cup N_{CF}^2$, $y = y_1 D y_3$, $y_1, y_3 \in V^*$, and $x = y_1 y_2 y_3$. Since from the definition of g it is clear that $g(Z) = \{Z\}$ for all $Z \in N_{CF}$, we can express $y' = y_1' D y_3'$, where $y_1' \in g(y_1)$ and $y_3' \in g(y_3)$. Clearly, $D \rightarrow y_2 \in P'$; see (1) in the definition of P'.

  (a) If $For \cap \text{alph}(y_1' D y_3') = \emptyset$, then

  $$S \Rightarrow_{G'}^n y_1' D y_3' \ {}^f\!\!\Rightarrow_{G'} y_1' y_2 y_3' \ [D \rightarrow y_2]$$

  and $y_1' y_2 y_3' \in g(y_1 y_2 y_3) = g(x)$.

  (b) If $For \cap \text{alph}(y_1' D y_3') \neq \emptyset$, then $\#_{For} y_1' D y_3' = 1$. Next, suppose that $\langle X, Y, Z \rangle \in \text{alph}(y_1' D y_3') \cap For$, $XY \rightarrow XZ \in P$, $X, Z \in N_{CF}$, $Y \in N_{CS}$; then, by (2), we have $Y \rightarrow \langle X, Y, Z \rangle \in P'$. Clearly, we can express the derivation

  $$S \Rightarrow_{G'}^n y_1' D y_3'$$

in the following way:

$$S \Rightarrow_{G'}^{n-1} g^{-1}(y_1' D y_3') \ {}^f\!\Rightarrow_{G'} y_1' D y_3' \ [Y \to \langle X, Y, Z \rangle],$$

where

$$\mathrm{alph}(g^{-1}(y_1' D y_3')) \cap For = \emptyset \text{ and } g^{-1}(y_1' D y_3') = y_1 D y_3.$$

Thus,

$$S \Rightarrow_{G'}^{n-1} y_1 D y_3 \Rightarrow_{G'} y_1 y_2 y_3 \ [D \to y_2]$$

and $y_1 y_2 y_3 \in g(x)$.

(ii) Let $p = AB \to AC \in P$, $A, C \in N_{CF}$, $B \in N_{CS}$, $y = y_1 AB y_2$, $y_1, y_2 \in V^*$, $x = y_1 AC y_2$, $y' = y_1' XY y_2'$, $y_1' \in g(y_1)$, $y_2' \in g(y_2)$, $X \in g(A)$, $Y \in g(B)$. Clearly,

$$\{ B \to \langle A, B, C \rangle, \langle A, B, C \rangle \to C \} \subseteq P'$$

(see (2) in the definition of P').

(a) If $For \cap \mathrm{alph}(y_1' XY y_2') = \emptyset$, then $y_1' XY y_2' = y_1 AB y_2$, and so

$$
\begin{array}{lll}
S & \Rightarrow_{G'}^n & y_1 AB y_2 \\
& {}^f\!\Rightarrow_{G'} & y_1 A \langle A, B, C \rangle y_2 & [B \to \langle A, B, C \rangle] \\
& {}^p\!\Rightarrow_{G'} & y_1 AC y_2 & [\langle A, B, C \rangle \to C]
\end{array}
$$

and $y_1 AC y_2 \in g(x)$.

(b) Let $For \cap \mathrm{alph}(y_1' XY y_2') \neq \emptyset$. By analogy with (i), we can find the derivation

$$S \Rightarrow_{G'}^{n-1} y_1 AB y_2$$

in G', and so

$$S \Rightarrow_{G'}^{n-1} y_1 AB y_2 \Rightarrow_{G'} y_1 A \langle A, B, C \rangle y_2 \Rightarrow_{G'} y_1 AC y_2,$$

where $y_1 AC y_2 \in g(x)$.

Thus, the only-if part now follows by the principle of induction.

If: This is also established by induction, but in this case on n. We have to demonstrate that

$$S \Rightarrow_{G'}^n x' \quad \text{implies} \quad S \Rightarrow_G^* x,$$

where $x \in V^+$, $x = g^{-1}(x')$, and $n \geq 0$.

Basis: For $n = 0$ the only x' is S because $S \Rightarrow_{G'}^0 S$. Since $S = g^{-1}(S)$, we have $x = S$. Clearly, $S \Rightarrow_G^0 S$ in G.

Induction Hypothesis: Assume that the claim holds for all derivations of length at most n, for some $n \geq 0$.

Induction Step: Consider a derivation

$$S \Rightarrow_{G'}^{n+1} x',$$

where $x = g^{-1}(x')$ for some $x \in V^+$. Since $n + 1 \geq 1$, there is some $y \in V^+$, $y = g^{-1}(y')$, and $p \in P'$ such that

$$S \Rightarrow_{G'}^n y' \Rightarrow_{G'} x' \; [p]$$

in G'. By the induction hypothesis,

$$S \Rightarrow_G^* y.$$

Let $y' = r'Ds'$, $y = rBs$, $r = g^{-1}(r')$, $s = g^{-1}(s')$, $r, s \in V^*$, $B = g^{-1}(D)$, $x' = r'z's'$ and $p = D \rightarrow z' \in P'$. Moreover, let us consider the following three cases:

(i) Let $g^{-1}(z') = B$; see (2). Then, $g^{-1}(x') = g^{-1}(r'z's') = rBs$. By the induction hypothesis, we have

$$S \Rightarrow_G^* rBs.$$

(ii) Let $z' \in T \cup N_{CS} \cup N_{CF}^2$, $D = B \in N_{CF}$. Then, there is a production $B \rightarrow z' \in P$; see (1). Hence,

$$S \Rightarrow_G^* rBs \Rightarrow_G rz's \; [B \rightarrow z'].$$

Since $z' = g^{-1}(z')$, we have $x = rz's$ such that $g^{-1}(x') = x$.

(iii) Let $z' = C$, $D = \langle A, B, C \rangle \in For$; see (2). Clearly,

$$y' \; ^P\!\Rightarrow_{G'} x' \; [p]$$

and $A\langle A, B, C \rangle \in \mathrm{sub}(y')$. By the definition of For, there is a production $AB \rightarrow AC \in P$. Since $\#_{For} y' \leq 1$, we have $r' = u'A$, $r = uA$, where $g^{-1}(u') = u$ and $u \in V^*$. Thus,

$$S \Rightarrow_G^* uABs \Rightarrow_G uACs \; [AB \rightarrow AC],$$

where $uACs = rCs$. Since $C = g^{-1}(C)$, we get $x = rCs$ such that $g^{-1}(x') = x$.

By inspection of P', we have considered all possible derivations of the form

$$S \Rightarrow_{G'}^n y' \Rightarrow_{G'} x'$$

in G'. Thus, by the principle of induction, we have established that

$$S \Rightarrow_{G'}^* x' \quad \text{implies} \quad S \Rightarrow_G^* x,$$

where $x \in V^+$, $g^{-1}(x') = x$, and $n \geq 0$.

The equivalence of G and G' immediately follows from the statement above. Indeed, by the definition of g, we have $g(a) = \{a\}$ for all $a \in T$. Therefore, we have for any $w \in T^*$,

$$S \Rightarrow_G^* w \quad \text{if and only if} \quad S \Rightarrow_{G'}^* w;$$

that is, $L(G) = L(G')$. Hence, **prop-GCC**$(2) = $ **CS**. ∎

Next, we turn to the investigation of *gcc*-grammars of degree 2 with erasing productions. We show that these grammars generate precisely the family of recursively enumerable languages.

Theorem 43. RE = GCC(2).

Proof. Clearly, **GCC**$(2) \subseteq $ **RE**. Hence, it suffices to show that **RE** $\subseteq$ **GCC**(2). This inclusion can be proved by the technique used in Theorem 42, because every language $L \in$ **RE** can be generated by a phrase-structure grammar whose productions are of the form $AB \rightarrow AC$ or $A \rightarrow x$, where $A, B, C \in V - T$ and $x \in \{\varepsilon\} \cup T \cup (V - T)^2$ (see Lemmas 3 and 5). The details are left to the reader. ∎

The following corollary summarizes results established in Theorems 42 and 43:

Corollary 19.
$$\textbf{prop-GCC}(2) = \textbf{prop-GCC} = \textbf{CS}$$
$$\subset$$
$$\textbf{GCC}(2) = \textbf{GCC} = \textbf{RE}.$$

Open Problem. Consider an alternative definition of *gcc*-grammars. Specifically, define the notion of a forbidding *gcc*-grammar of degree r (for some natural number r) as a sixtuple $G = (V, T, P, S, Per, For)$, where (V, T, P, S) is a context-free grammar, $For \subseteq V^+$ such that $x \in For$ implies $|x| \leq r$, $Per \subseteq V$, and a production $A \rightarrow x$ can be applied to a word w when $Per \subseteq \text{alph}(w)$ or $\emptyset = V^*\{A\}V^* \cap For \cap \text{sub}(w)$. What is the language generating power of these grammars?

Chapter 5

Context Conditions Placed on the Neighborhood of Rewritten Symbols

This chapter studies grammars with context conditions placed on the neighborhood of rewritten symbols. In Section 5.1, we investigate grammars with context conditions that strictly require a continuous neighborhood of the rewritten symbols. We discuss both sequential and parallel grammars of this kind. The discussion of sequential grammars naturally leads to the study of classical context-dependent grammars, such as context-sensitive and phrase-structure grammars. Regarding parallel grammars, we base this discussion on EIL grammars. In Section 5.2, we study scattered context grammars in which rewriting depends on symbols occurring in the sentential form, but these symbols may not form a continuous substring of the sentential form. Rather, these symbols, which are simultaneously rewritten during a single derivation step, may be scattered throughout the sentential form. In all grammars discussed in this chapter, we make their context-dependency uniform, reduced and easy-to-use in theory and practice.

5.1 Continuous Context

Consider the phrase-structure grammars based on productions of the form $xAy \rightarrow xuy$, where A is a nonterminal and x, y, u are strings (see Chapter 2). By using $xAy \rightarrow xuy$, we rewrite A with u on the condition that in the current sentential form x and y are substrings neighboring with the rewritten symbol A from the left and from the right, respectively. Consequently, the phrase-structure grammars can be quite naturally interpreted as grammars with context condition placed on the substrings neighboring with the rewritten symbols (see the note preceding Definition 2 in Section 2.2). Therefore, we discuss them in this chapter, although we are fully aware of the problems and difficulties that their use bring about (see Chapter 1). In fact, we intentionally concentrate our attention on some of the difficulties in order to make them more acceptable from both theoretical and practical viewpoint.

More specifically, a phrase-structure grammar can produce a very broad variety of quite different sentential forms during the generation of their languages. This inconsistent generation represents a highly undesirable grammatical phenomenon.

In theory, the demonstration of properties concerning languages generated in this way lead to extremely tedious proofs. In practice, the inconsistent generation of languages is uneasy to analyze. Therefore, we next investigate how to make this generation of languages more uniform. Specifically, the phrase-structure grammars are transformed so that they generate only words that have a uniform permutation-based form. More precisely, in Section 5.1.1, we demonstrate that every recursively enumerable language L can be generated by a phrase-structure grammar so that during the generation of any sentence from L, every sentential form is based on a sequence of substrings, each of which represents a permutation of symbols over a very small alphabet.

Besides phrase-structure grammars, we achieve analogical results for EIL grammars, which represent major parallel grammars with context condition placed on substrings continuously neighboring with the rewritten symbols (see Section 5.1.2).

5.1.1   Sequential Uniform Rewriting

The present section demonstrates that for every phrase-structure grammar G, there exists an equivalent phrase-structure grammar, $G' = (\{S, 0, 1\} \cup T, T, P, S)$ so that every $x \in F(G')$ satisfies

$$x \in T^* \Pi(w)^*,$$

where $w \in \{0, 1\}^*$. Then, it makes this conversion so that for every $x \in F(G)$,

$$x \in \Pi(w)^* T^*.$$

Let

$$G = (V, T, P, S)$$

be a phrase-structure grammar. Notice that $\mathrm{alph}(L(G)) \subseteq T$. If $a \in T - \mathrm{alph}(L(G))$, so a actually acts as a pseudoterminal because it appears in no word of $L(G)$. Every transformation described in this section assumes that its input grammar contains no pseudoterminals of this kind, and does not contain any useless nonterminals either.

Let j be a natural number. Set

> **PS[.j]** $= \{L : L = L(G),$ where $G = (V, T, P, S)$ is a phrase-structure grammar such that $|\mathrm{alph}(F(G)) - T| = j$ and $F(G) \subseteq T^* \Pi(w)^*$, where $w \in (V - T)^*\}$.

Analogously, set

> **PS[j.]** $= \{L : L = L(G),$ where $G = (V, T, P, S)$ is a phrase-structure grammar such that $|\mathrm{alph}(F(G)) - T| = j$ and $F(G) \subseteq \Pi(w)^* T^*$, where $w \in (V - T)^*\}$.

Lemma 24. *Let G be a phrase-structure grammar. Then, there exists a phrase-structure grammar, $G' = (\{S, 0, 1\} \cup T, T, P, S)$, satisfying $L(G') = L(G)$ and $F(G') \subseteq T^* \Pi(1^{n-2} 00)^*$.*

Proof. Let

$$G = (V, T, Q, \$)$$

be a phrase-structure grammar, where V is the alphabet of G, T is the terminal alphabet of G, Q is the set of productions of G, and $\$$ is the start symbol of G. Without any loss of generality, assume that $V \cap \{0,1\} = \emptyset$. The following construction produces an equivalent phrase-structure grammar:

$$G' = (\{S, 0, 1\} \cup T, T, P, S)$$

such that $F(G') \subseteq T^*\Pi(1^{n-2}00)^*$, for some natural number n.

For some integers m, n such that $m \geq 3$ and $2m = n$, introduce an injective homomorphism β from V to $(\{1\}^m\{1\}^*\{0\}\{1\}^*\{0\} \cap \{0,1\}^n) - \{1^{n-2}00\}$. Extend the domain of β to V^*. Define the phrase-structure grammar, $G' = (\{S, 0, 1\} \cup T, T, P, S)$, with

$$\begin{aligned}
P = \{&S \to 1^{n-1}00\beta(\$)1^{n-1}00\} \cup \\
&\{\beta(x) \to \beta(y) : x \to y \in Q\} \cup \\
&\{1^{n-2}00\beta(a) \to a1^{n-2}00 : a \in T\} \cup \\
&\{1^{n-2}001^{n-2}00 \to \varepsilon\}.
\end{aligned}$$

Claim 36. *Let* $S \Rightarrow^h_{G'} w$, *where* $w \in V^*$ *and* $h \geq 1$. *Then,* $w \in T^*(\{\varepsilon\} \cup \{1^{n-2}00\}(\beta(V))^*\{1^{n-2}00\})$.

Proof. The claim is proved by induction on h, $h \geq 1$.

Basis: Let $h = 1$. That is,

$$S \Rightarrow_{G'} 1^{n-1}00\beta(\$)1^{n-1}00 \quad [\$ \to 1^{n-1}00\beta(\$)1^{n-1}00].$$

As

$$1^{n-2}00\beta(S)1^{n-2}00 \in T^*(\{1^{n-2}00\}(\beta(V))^*\{1^{n-2}00\} \cup \{\varepsilon\}),$$

the basis holds.

Induction Hypothesis: Suppose that for some $k \geq 0$, if $S \Rightarrow^i_{G'} w$, where $i = 1, \ldots, k$ and $w \in V^*$, then $w \in T^*(\{1^{n-2}00\}(\beta(V))^*\{1^{n-2}00\} \cup \{\varepsilon\})$.

Induction Step: Consider

$$S \Rightarrow^{k+1}_{G'} w,$$

where $w \in V^* - T^*$. Express $S \Rightarrow^{k+1}_{G'} w$ as

$$\begin{aligned}
S \quad &\Rightarrow^k_{G'} \quad u\mathrm{lhs}(p)v \\
&\Rightarrow_{G'} \quad u\mathrm{rhs}(p)v \quad [p],
\end{aligned}$$

where $p \in P$ and $w = u\mathrm{rhs}(p)v$. Less formally, after k steps, G' derives $u\mathrm{lhs}(p)v$. Then, by using p, G' replaces $\mathrm{lhs}(p)$ with $\mathrm{rhs}(p)$ in $u\mathrm{lhs}(p)v$, so it obtains $u\mathrm{rhs}(p)v$. By the induction hypothesis,

$$u\mathrm{lhs}(p)v \in T^*(\{1^{n-1}00\}(\beta(V))^*\{1^{n-2}00\} \cup \{\varepsilon\}).$$

As $\mathrm{lhs}(p) \notin T^*$, $u\mathrm{lhs}(p)v \notin T^*$. Therefore,

$$u\mathrm{lhs}(p)v \in T^*\{1^{n-2}00\}(\beta(V))^*\{1^{n-2}00\}.$$

Let

$$u\mathrm{lhs}(p)v \in T^*\{1^{n-2}00\}(\beta(V))^j\{1^{n-2}00\}$$

in G', for some $j \geq 1$. By the definition of P, p satisfies one of these three properties:

(i) Let $\mathrm{lhs}(p) = \beta(x)$ and $\mathrm{rhs}(p) = \beta(y)$, where $x \to y \in Q$, At this point,

$$u \in T^*\{1^{n-2}00\}\{\beta(V)\}^r,$$

for some $r \geq 0$, and

$$v \in \{\beta(V)\}^{(j-|\mathrm{lhs}(p)|-r)}\{1^{n-2}00\}.$$

Distinguish between these two cases: $|x| \leq |y|$ and $|x| > |y|$.

(a) Let $|x| \leq |y|$. Set $s = |y| - |x|$. Observe that

$$u\mathrm{rhs}(p)v \in T^*\{1^{n-2}00\}(\beta(V))^{(j+s)}\{1^{n-2}00\}.$$

As $w = u\mathrm{rhs}(p)v$,

$$w \in T^*(\{1^{n-2}00\}(\beta(V))^*\{1^{n-2}00\} \cup \{\varepsilon\}).$$

(b) Let $|x| > |y|$. By analogy with (a), prove that

$$w \in T^*(\{1^{n-2}00\}(\beta(V))^*\{1^{n-2}00\} \cup \{\varepsilon\}).$$

(ii) Assume that $\mathrm{lhs}(p) = 1^{n-1}00\beta(a)$ and $\mathrm{rhs}(p) = a1^{n-2}00$, for some $a \in T$. Notice that

$$u\mathrm{lhs}(p)v \in T^*\{1^{n-2}00\}(\beta(V))^j\{1^{n-2}00\}$$

implies $u \in T^*$ and

$$v \in (\beta(V))^{(j-1)}\{1^{n-2}00\}.$$

Then,

$$u\mathrm{rhs}(p)v \in T^*\{a\}\{1^{n-2}00\}(\beta(V))^{(j-1)}\{1^{n-2}00\}.$$

As $w = u\mathrm{rhs}(p)v$,

$$w \in T^*(\{1^{n-2}00\}(\beta(V))^*\{1^{n-2}00\} \cup \{\varepsilon\}).$$

(iii) Assume that $\mathrm{lhs}(p) = 1^{n-2}001^{n-2}00$ and $\mathrm{rhs}(p) = \varepsilon$. Then, $j = 0$ in

$$T^*\{1^{n-2}00\}(\beta(V))^j\{1^{n-2}00\},$$

so

$$u\mathrm{lhs}(p)v \in T^*\{1^{n-2}00\}\{1^{n-2}00\}$$

and $u\mathrm{rhs}(p)v \in T^*$. As $w = u\mathrm{rhs}(p)v$,

$$w \in T^*(\{1^{n-2}00\}(\beta(V))^*\{1^{n-2}00\} \cup \{\varepsilon\}).$$

$\square$

Claim 37. *Let* $S \Rightarrow^+_{G'} u \Rightarrow^*_{G'} z$, *where* $z \in T^*$. *Then,* $u \in T^*\Pi(1^{n-2}00)^*$.

Proof. Let $S \Rightarrow^+_{G'} u \Rightarrow^*_{G'} z$, where $z \in T^*$. By Claim 36, $u \in T^*(\{1^{n-2}00\}(\beta(V))^*$ $\{1^{n-2}00\} \cup \{\varepsilon\})$, and by the definition of β, $u \in T^*\Pi(1^{n-2}00)^*$. $\square$

Claim 38. *Let* $\$ \Rightarrow^m_G w$, *for some* $m \geq 0$. *Then* $S \Rightarrow^+_{G'} 1^{n-2}00\beta(w)1^{n-2}00$ *in* G'.

Proof. The claim is proved by induction on m, $m \geq 0$.

Basis: Let $m = 0$. That is, $\$ \Rightarrow^0_G \$$. As

$$S \Rightarrow_{G'} 1^{n-1}00\beta(\$)1^{n-1}00 \; [S \to 1^{n-1}00\beta(\$)1^{n-1}00],$$

the basis holds.

Induction Hypothesis: Suppose that for some $j \geq 1$, if $\$ \Rightarrow^i_G w$, where $i = 1, \ldots, j$ and $w \in V^*$, then $S \Rightarrow^*_{G'} \beta(w)$.

Induction Step: Let $\$ \Rightarrow^{j+1}_G w$. Express $\$ \Rightarrow^{j+1}_G w$ as

$$\$ \Rightarrow^j_G uxv \Rightarrow_G uyv \; [x \to y],$$

where $x \to y \in Q$ and $w = uyv$. By the induction hypothesis,

$$S \Rightarrow^+_{G'} 1^{n-2}00\beta(uxv)1^{n-2}00.$$

Express $\beta(uxv)$ as $\beta(uxv) = \beta(u)\beta(x)\beta(v)$. As $x \to y \in P$, $\beta(x) \to \beta(y) \in P$. Therefore,

$$S \quad \Rightarrow^+_{G'} \quad 1^{n-2}00\beta(u)\beta(x)\beta(v)1^{n-2}00$$
$$\Rightarrow_{G'} \quad 1^{n-2}00\beta(u)\beta(y)\beta(v)1^{n-2}00 \quad [\beta(x) \to \beta(y)].$$

Because $w = uyv$, $\beta(w) = \beta(u)\beta(y)\beta(v)$, so

$$S \Rightarrow^+_{G'} 1^{n-2}00\beta(w)1^{n-2}00.$$

$\square$

Claim 39. $L(G) \subseteq L(G')$.

Proof. Let $w \in L(G)$. Thus, $\$ \Rightarrow^*_G w$ with $w \in T^*$. By Claim 38,

$$S \Rightarrow^+_{G'} 1^{n-2}00\beta(w)1^{n-2}00.$$

Distinguish between these two cases: $w = \varepsilon$ and $w \neq \varepsilon$.
  (i) If $w = \varepsilon$, $1^{n-2}00\beta(w)1^{n-2}00 = 1^{n-2}001^{n-2}00$. As $1^{n-2}001^{n-2}00 \to \varepsilon \in P$,

$$S \quad \Rightarrow^*_{G'} \quad 1^{n-2}001^{n-2}00$$
$$\Rightarrow_{G'} \quad \varepsilon \; [1^{n-2}001^{n-2}00 \to \varepsilon].$$

Thus, $w \in L(G')$.

(ii) Assume that $w \neq \varepsilon$. Express w as $w = a_1 a_2 \ldots a_{n-1} a_n$ with $a_i \in T$ for $i = 1, \ldots, n$, $n \geq 0$. Because

$$(\{1^{n-2}00\beta(a) \to a1^{n-2}00 : a \in T\} \cup \{1^{n-2}001^{n-2}00 \to \varepsilon\}) \subseteq P,$$

there exists

$$
\begin{aligned}
S \quad &\Rightarrow_{G'}^* \quad 1^{n-2}00\beta(a_1)\beta(a_2)\ldots\beta(a_{n-1})\beta(a_n)1^{n-2}00 \\
&\Rightarrow_{G'} \quad a_1 1^{n-2}00\beta(a_2)\ldots\beta(a_{n-1})\beta(a_n)1^{n-2}00 \\
&\qquad [1^{n-2}00\beta(a_1) \to a_1 1^{n-2}00] \\
&\Rightarrow_{G'} \quad a_1 a_2 1^{n-2}00\beta(a_3)\ldots\beta(a_{n-1})\beta(a_n)1^{n-2}00 \\
&\qquad [1^{n-2}00\beta(a_2) \to a_2 1^{n-2}00] \\
&\vdots \\
&\Rightarrow_{G'} \quad a_1 a_2 \ldots a_{n-2} 1^{n-2}00\beta(a_{n-1})\beta(a_n)1^{n-2}00 \\
&\qquad [1^{n-2}00\beta(a_{n-2}) \to a_{n-2} 1^{n-2}00] \\
&\Rightarrow_{G'} \quad a_1 a_2 \ldots a_{n-2} a_{n-1} 1^{n-2}00\beta(a_n)1^{n-2}00 \\
&\qquad [1^{n-2}00\beta(a_{n-1}) \to a_{n-1} 1^{n-2}00] \\
&\Rightarrow_{G'} \quad a_1 a_2 \ldots a_{n-2} a_{n-1} a_n 1^{n-2}001^{n-2}00 \\
&\qquad [1^{n-2}00\beta(a_n) \to a_n 1^{n-2}00] \\
&\Rightarrow_{G'} \quad a_1 a_2 \ldots a_{n-2} a_{n-1} a_n \\
&\qquad [1^{n-2}001^{n-2}00 \to \varepsilon].
\end{aligned}
$$

Therefore, $w \in L(G')$. □

Claim 40. *Let* $S \Rightarrow_{G'}^m 1^{n-2}00w1^{n-2}00$, *where* $w \in \{0,1\}^*$, *for some* $m \geq 1$. *Then,* $\$ \Rightarrow_G^* \beta^{-1}(w)$.

Proof. This claim is proved by induction on m.

Basis: Let $m = 1$. That is,

$$S \Rightarrow_{G'} 1^{n-2}00w1^{n-2}00,$$

where $w \in \{0,1\}^*$. Then, $w = \beta(\$)$. As $\$ \Rightarrow_G^0 \$$, the basis holds.

Induction Hypothesis: Suppose that for some $j \geq 1$, if $S \Rightarrow_{G'}^i 1^{n-2}00w1^{n-2}00$, where $i = 1, \ldots, j$ and $w \in \{0,1\}^*$, then $\$ \Rightarrow_G^+ \beta^{-1}(w)$.

Induction Step: Let

$$S \Rightarrow_{G'}^{j+1} 1^{n-2}00w1^{n-2}00,$$

where $w \in \{0,1\}^*$. As $w \in \{0,1\}^*$,

$$S \Rightarrow_{G'}^{j+1} 1^{n-2}00w1^{n-2}00$$

can be expressed as

$$
\begin{aligned}
S \quad &\Rightarrow_{G'}^j \quad 1^{n-2}00u\beta(x)v1^{n-2}00 \\
&\Rightarrow_{G'} \quad 1^{n-2}00u\beta(y)v1^{n0}200 \quad [\beta(x) \to \beta(y)],
\end{aligned}
$$

where $x, y \in V^*$, $x \to y \in Q$, and $w = u\beta(y)v$. By the induction hypothesis,

$$S \Rightarrow_{G'}^+ 1^{n-2}00\beta^{-1}(u\beta(x)v)1^{n-2}00.$$

Express $\beta^{-1}(u\beta(x)v)$ as

$$\beta^{-1}(u\beta(x)v) = \beta^{-1}(u)x\beta^{-1}(v).$$

Since $x \to y \in Q$,

$$
\begin{aligned}
\$ &\Rightarrow_G^+ & \beta^{-1}(u)x\beta^{-1}(v) \\
&\Rightarrow_G & \beta^{-1}(u)y\beta^{-1}(v) \quad [x \to y].
\end{aligned}
$$

Because $w = u\beta(y)v$, $\beta^{-1}(w) = \beta^{-1}(u)y\beta^{-1}(v)$, so

$$\$ \Rightarrow_G^+ \beta^{-1}(w).$$

$\square$

Claim 41. $L(G') \subseteq L(G)$.

Proof. Let $w \in L(G')$. Distinguish between $w = \varepsilon$ and $w \neq \varepsilon$.

(i) Let $w = \varepsilon$. Observe that G' derives ε as

$$
\begin{aligned}
S &\Rightarrow_{G'}^* & 1^{n-2}001^{n-2}00 \\
&\Rightarrow_{G'} & \varepsilon \; [1^{n-2}001^{n-2}00 \to \varepsilon].
\end{aligned}
$$

Because

$$S \Rightarrow_{G'}^* 1^{n-2}001^{n-2}00,$$

Claim 40 implies that $\$ \Rightarrow_G^* \varepsilon$. Therefore, $w \in L(G)$.

(ii) Assume that $w \neq \varepsilon$. Let $w = a_1a_2 \ldots a_{n-1}a_n$ with $a_i \in T$ for $i = 1, \ldots, n$, where $n \geq 1$. Examine P to see that in G' there exists this derivation:

$$
\begin{aligned}
S &\Rightarrow_{G'}^* & 1^{n-2}00\beta(a_1)\beta(a_2)\ldots\beta(a_{n-1})\beta(a_n)1^{n-2}00 \\
&\Rightarrow_{G'} & a_1 1^{n-2}00\beta(a_2)\ldots\beta(a_{n-1})\beta(a_n)1^{n-2}00 \\
& & [1^{n-2}00\beta(a_1) \to a_1 1^{n-2}00] \\
&\Rightarrow_{G'} & a_1 a_2 1^{n-2}00\beta(a_3)\ldots\beta(a_{n-1})\beta(a_n)1^{n-2}00 \\
& & [1^{n-2}00\beta(a_2) \to a_2 1^{n-2}00] \\
& \vdots & \\
&\Rightarrow_{G'} & a_1 a_2 \ldots a_{n-2} 1^{n-2}00\beta(a_{n-1})\beta(a_n)1^{n-2}00 \\
& & [1^{n-2}00\beta(a_{n-2}) \to a_{n-2} 1^{n-2}00] \\
&\Rightarrow_{G'} & a_1 a_2 \ldots a_{n-2}a_{n-1} 1^{n-2}00\beta(a_n)1^{n-2}00 \\
& & [1^{n-2}00\beta(a_{n-1}) \to a_{n-1} 1^{n-2}00] \\
&\Rightarrow_{G'} & a_1 a_2 \ldots a_{n-2}a_{n-1}a_n 1^{n-2}001^{n-2}00 \\
& & [1^{n-2}00\beta(a_n) \to a_n 1^{n-2}00] \\
&\Rightarrow_{G'} & a_1 a_2 \ldots a_{n-2}a_{n-1}a_n \\
& & [1^{n-2}001^{n-2}00 \to \varepsilon]
\end{aligned}
$$

Because

$$S \Rightarrow_{G'}^* 1^{n-2}00\beta(a_1)\beta(a_2)\ldots\beta(a_{n-1})\beta(a_n)1^{n-2}00,$$

Claim 40 implies that

$$\$ \Rightarrow_G^* a_1 a_2 \ldots a_{n-1} a_n,$$

so $w \in L(G)$.

$\square$

By Claims 39 and 41, $L(G) = L(G')$. By Claim 37, $F(G') \subseteq T^*\Pi(1^{n-2}00)^*$. Thus, Lemma 24 holds. $\square$

Theorem 44. PS[.2] = RE.

Proof. Clearly, **PS[.2]** $\subseteq$ **RE**. By Lemma 24, **RE** $\subseteq$ **PS[.2]**. Therefore, this theorem holds. ∎

Lemma 25. *Let G be a phrase-structure grammar. Then, there exists a phrase-structure grammar $G' = (\{S, 0, 1\} \cup T, T, P, S)$ satisfying $L(G) = L(G')$ and $F(G') \subseteq \Pi(1^{n-2}00)^*T^*$, for some $n \geq 1$.*

Proof. Let

$$G = (V, T, Q, \$)$$

be a phrase-structure grammar, where V is the total alphabet of G, T is the terminal alphabet of G, Q is the set of productions of G, and $\$$ is the start symbol of G. Without any loss of generality, assume that $V \cap \{0, 1\} = \emptyset$. The following construction produces an equivalent phrase-structure grammar:

$$G' = (\{S, 0, 1\} \cup T, T, P, S)$$

such that $F(G') \subseteq \Pi(1^{n-2}00)^*T^*$, for some $n \geq 1$.

For some $m \geq 3$ and n such that $2m = n$, introduce an injective homomorphism β from V to $(\{1\}^m\{1\}^*\{0\}\{1\}^* \cap \{0, 1\}^n) - \{1^{n-2}00\}$. Extend the domain of β to V^*. Define the phrase-structure grammar $G' = (T \cup \{S, 0, 1\}, P, S, T)$ with

$$
\begin{aligned}
P = \quad &\{S \rightarrow 1^{n-1}00\beta(\$)1^{n-1}00\} \cup \\
&\{\beta(x) \rightarrow \beta(y) : x \rightarrow y \in Q\} \cup \\
&\{\beta(a)1^{n-2}00 \rightarrow 1^{n-2}00a : a \in T\} \cup \\
&\{1^{n-2}001^{n-2}00 \rightarrow \varepsilon\}.
\end{aligned}
$$

Complete this proof by analogy with the proof of Lemma 24. $\square$

Theorem 45. PS[2.] = RE.

Proof. Clearly, **PS[2.]** $\subseteq$ **RE**. By Lemma 25, **RE** $\subseteq$ **PS[2.]**. Therefore, this theorem holds. ∎

Corollary 20. PS[.2] = PS[2.] = RE.

Open Problems. There are some open problem areas related to the results above. Recall that in this section we converted any phrase-structure grammar, G, to an equivalent phrase-structure grammar, $G' = (V, T, P, S)$, so that for every $x \in F(G')$, $x \in T^*\Pi(w)^*$, where w is a word over $V - T$. Then, we made this conversion so that for every $x \in F(G')$, $x \in \Pi(w)^*T^*$. Take into account the length of w. More precisely, for $j, k \geq 1$ set

> **PS[.j,k]** $= \{L : L = L(G),$ where $G = (V, T, P, S)$ is a phrase-structure grammar such that $|\text{alph}(F(G)) - T| = j$ and $F(G) \subseteq T^*\Pi(w)^*$, where $w \in (V - T)^*$ and $|w| = k\}$.

Analogously, set

> **PS[j,k.]** $= \{L : L = L(G),$ where $G = (V, T, P, S)$ is a phrase-structure grammar such that $|\text{alph}(F(G)) - T| = j$ and $F(G) \subseteq \Pi(w)^*T^*$, where $w \in (V - T)^*$ and $|w| = k\}$.

Reconsider Section 5.1.1 in terms of these families of languages.

5.1.2 Parallel Uniform Rewriting

The present section converts any EIL grammar G to an equivalent EIL grammar $G' = (\{S, 0, 1\} \cup T, T, P, S)$, so that for every $x \in F(G')$,

$$x \in T^*\Pi(w)^*,$$

where $w \in \{0, 1\}^*$. Then, it makes this conversion so that for every $x \in F(G')$,

$$x \in \Pi(w)^*T^*.$$

Note that by analogy with Section 5.1.1, every transformation presented in this section assumes that its input grammar contains neither pseudoterminals nor useless nonterminals. Let $j \geq 0$. Set

> **EIL[.j]** $= \{L : L = L(G),$ where $G = (V, T, P, S)$ is an EIL grammar such that $|\text{alph}(F(G)) - T| = j$ and $F(G) \subseteq T^*\Pi(w)^*$, where $w \in (V - T)^*\}$.

Analogously, define

> **EIL[j.]** $= \{L : L = L(G),$ where $G = (V, T, P, S)$ is an EIL grammar such that $|\text{alph}(F(G)) - T| = j$ and $F(G) \subseteq \Pi(w)^*T^*$, where $w \in (V - T)^*\}$.

Lemma 26. *Let G be an $E(1,0)L$ grammar. Then, there exists an EIL grammar $G' = (\{S, 0, 1\} \cup T, T, P, S)$ such that $L(G) = L(G')$ and $F(G') \subseteq T^*\Pi(1^{n-2}00)^*$, for some $n \geq 1$.*

Proof. Let

$$G = (V, T, Q, \$)$$

be an $E(1,0)L$ grammar. For some natural numbers m and n such that $m \geq 3$ and $2m = n$, introduce an injective homomorphism β from V to $(\{1\}^m\{1\}^*\{0\}\{1\}^*\{0\} \cap \{0,1\}^n) - \{1^{n-2}00\}$; in addition, introduce an injective homomorphism χ from T to $(\{1\}^m\{1\}^*\{0\}\{1\}^*\{0\} \cap \{0,1\}^n) - \{1^{n-2}00\}$ so that $\{\chi(a) : a \in T\} \cap \{\beta(A) : A \in V\} = \emptyset$. Extend the domain of β and the domain of χ to V^* and T^*, respectively. Define the $E(2n-1, 0)L$ grammar

$$G' = (T \cup \{S, 0, 1\}, T, P, S)$$

with

$$P = P_\beta \cup P_\chi \cup P_\delta,$$

where

$$
\begin{aligned}
P_\beta = \ & \{S \rightarrow \beta(\$)\} \\
& \cup \{(\beta(X)x, 0) \rightarrow \beta(y) : X \in V \cup \{\varepsilon\}, \ x \in \{0,1\}^{n-1}, \ y \in V^*, \\
& \quad x0 = \beta(Y) \text{ for some } Y \in V \text{ such that } (X, Y) \rightarrow y \in Q\} \\
& \cup \{(\beta(a)x, 0) \rightarrow \chi(b) : a \in T \cup \{\varepsilon\}, \ x \in \{0,1\}^{n-1}, \\
& \quad x0 = \beta(b) \text{ for some } b \in T\} \\
P_\chi = \ & \{(yx, 0) \rightarrow a : a \in T, \ y \in T^*, \ x \in \{0,1\}^*, \\
& \quad |yx| \leq 2n-1, \ x0 = \chi(a)\} \\
& \cup \{(yx, y) \rightarrow \varepsilon : Y \in \{0,1\}, \ y \in T^*, \ x \in \{0,1\}^*, \\
& \quad |x| \leq n-2, \ |yx| \leq 2n-1\} \\
& \cup \{(yx, Y) \rightarrow Y : Y \in \{0,1\}, \ y \in T^*, \ x \in \{0,1\}^*, \\
& \quad |x| \geq n, \ |yx| \leq 2n-1\} \\
& \cup \{(x, a) \rightarrow a : a \in T, \ |x| \leq 2n-1\}, \\
P_\delta = \ & \{(x, X) \rightarrow 1^{n-2}00 : x \in (T \cup \{0,1\})^{2n-1}, \ X \in (T \cup \{0,1\}), \\
& \quad (P_\beta \cup P_\chi) \cap \{(x, X) \rightarrow z : z \in (T \cup \{0,1\})^*\} = \emptyset\}.
\end{aligned}
$$

Claim 42. *Let* $S \Rightarrow_{G'}^m w$, *where* $w \in V^*$ *and* $m \geq 1$. *Then,* $w \in T^*\Pi(1^{n-2}00)^*$.

Proof. The claim is proved by induction on m, $m \geq 1$.

Basis: Let $m = 1$. That is, $S \Rightarrow_{G'} \beta(\$)$ $[S \rightarrow \beta(\$)]$. As $T^*\Pi(1^{n-2}00)^*$ contains $\beta(\$)$, the basis holds.

Induction Hypothesis: Suppose that for all $i = 1, \ldots, k$, where $k \geq 1$, if $S \Rightarrow_{G'}^i w$, then $w \in T^*\Pi(1^{n-2}00)^*$.

Induction Step: Consider

$$S \Rightarrow_{G'}^{k+1} w,$$

where $w \in V^*$. Express $S \Rightarrow_{G'}^{k+1} w$ as

$$S \Rightarrow_{G'}^k u \Rightarrow_{G'} v \ [p],$$

where $p \in P$. By the induction hypothesis, $u \in T^*\Pi(1^{n-2}00)^*$. Examine P to see that $v \in T^*\Pi(1^{n-2}00)^*$ if $u \in T^*\Pi(1^{n-2}00)^*$; the details are left to the reader. $\square$

Claim 43. *Let* $\$ \Rightarrow_G^m w$, *for some* $m \geq 0$. *Then,* $S \Rightarrow_{G'}^+ \beta(w)$.

Proof. This claim is proved by induction on m, $m \geq 0$.

Basis: Let $m = 0$. That is, $\$ \Rightarrow_G^0 \$$. Observe that $S \Rightarrow_{G'} \beta(\$)$ $[S \rightarrow \beta(\$)]$, so the basis holds.

Induction Hypothesis: Suppose that for some $j \geq 1$, if $\$ \Rightarrow_G^i w$, where $i = 1, \ldots, j$, and $w \in V^*$, then $S \Rightarrow_{G'}^* \beta(w)$.

Induction Step: Consider a derivation

$$\$ \Rightarrow_G^{j+1} y.$$

Express $\$ \Rightarrow_G^{j+1} y$ as

$$\$ \Rightarrow_G^j x \Rightarrow_G y.$$

Furthermore, express x as $x = X_1 X_2 \ldots X_k$, where $k = |x|$ and $X_j \in V$, for $j = 1, \ldots, k$. Assume that G makes

$$X_1 X_2 \ldots X_k \Rightarrow_G y$$

according to $(\varepsilon, X_1) \rightarrow y_1, (X_1, X_2) \rightarrow y_2, \ldots, (X_{k-1}, X_k) \rightarrow y_k$ so $y = y_1 y_2 \ldots y_k$. By the induction hypothesis,

$$S \Rightarrow_{G'}^+ \beta(x).$$

Express $\beta(x)$ as

$$\beta(x) = \beta(X_1)\beta(X_2) \ldots \beta(X_k),$$

where $X_j \in V$, for $j = 1, \ldots, k$. Return to P_β. Observe that P_β contains $(x_1, 0) \rightarrow \beta(y_1)$, where $x_1 0 = \beta(X_1)$, and $(\beta(X_{i-1})x_i, 0) \rightarrow \beta(y_i)$, where $x_i 0 = \beta(X_i)$ for $i = 2, \ldots, k$. Thus,

$$\beta(X_1)\beta(X_2) \ldots \beta(X_k) \Rightarrow_{G'} \beta(y_1)\beta(y_2) \ldots \beta(y_k).$$

As $y = y_1 y_2 \ldots y_k$, $\beta(x) \Rightarrow_{G'} \beta(y)$. Consequently,

$$S \Rightarrow_{G'}^+ \beta(y).$$

$\square$

Claim 44. $L(G) \subseteq L(G')$.

Proof. Let $w \in L(G')$. Thus, $S \Rightarrow_{G'}^* w$ and $w \in T^*$. By Claim 43, $S \Rightarrow_{G'}^+ \beta(w)$. Recall that P_β contains

$$\{(\beta(a)x, 0) \rightarrow \chi(b) : a \in T, \ x \in \{0,1\}^{n-1}, \ x0 = \beta(b) \text{ for some } b \in T\} \subseteq P_\beta.$$

Therefore,

$$\beta(w) \Rightarrow_{G'} \chi(w).$$

Examine P_χ to see that

$$\chi(w) \Rightarrow_{G'}^* w.$$

Hence, Claim 44 holds.

$\square$

Claim 45. $L(G') \subseteq L(G)$.

Proof. Let $w \in L(G')$, and let $w = a_1 a_2 \ldots a_{n-1} a_n$ with $a_i \in T$ for $i = 1, \ldots, n$, where n is a nonnegative integer ($w = \varepsilon$ if $n = 0$). Observe that

$$
\begin{aligned}
S \quad &\Rightarrow_{G'}^* \quad \beta(a_1)\beta(a_2)\ldots\beta(a_{n-1})\beta(a_n) \\
&\Rightarrow_{G'} \quad \chi(a_1)\chi(a_2)\ldots\chi(a_{n-1})\chi(a_n) \\
&\Rightarrow_{G'} \quad a_1\chi(a_2)\ldots\chi(a_{n-1})\chi(a_n) \\
&\Rightarrow_{G'} \quad a_1 a_2 \chi(a_3)\ldots\chi(a_{n-1})\chi(a_n) \\
&\quad\vdots \\
&\Rightarrow_{G'} \quad a_1 a_2 \ldots \chi(a_{n-1})\chi(a_n) \\
&\Rightarrow_{G'} \quad a_1 a_2 \ldots a_{n-1}\chi(a_n) \\
&\Rightarrow_{G'} \quad a_1 a_2 \ldots a_{n-1} a_n.
\end{aligned}
$$

In greater detail, by using productions from P_β, G' makes

$$
\begin{aligned}
S \quad &\Rightarrow_{G'}^* \quad \beta(a_1)\beta(a_2)\ldots\beta(a_{n-1})\beta(a_n) \\
&\Rightarrow_{G'} \quad \chi(a_1)\chi(a_2)\ldots\chi(a_{n-1})\chi(a_n),
\end{aligned}
$$

and by using productions from P_χ, G' makes the rest of this derivation. Examine P_β to see that if G' makes

$$
\begin{aligned}
S \quad &\Rightarrow_{G'}^* \quad \beta(a_1)\beta(a_2)\ldots\beta(a_{n-1})\beta(a_n) \\
&\Rightarrow_{G'} \quad \chi(a_1)\chi(a_2)\ldots\chi(a_{n-1})\chi(a_n)
\end{aligned}
$$

by using productions from P_β, then $\$ \Rightarrow_G^* a_1 a_2 \ldots a_{n-1} a_n$ in G. Because $w = a_1 a_2 \ldots a_{n-1} a_n$, $w \in L(G)$, so Claim 45 holds. $\square$

By Claims 44 and 45, $L(G') = L(G)$, so Lemma 26 holds. $\square$

Theorem 46. **EIL[.2]** = **RE**.

Proof. Clearly, **EIL[.2]** $\subseteq$ **RE**. By Theorem 6.1.3 in [155], for every $L \in$ **RE**, there exists an E(1,0)L grammar, G, such that $L = L(G)$. Thus, by Lemma 26, **RE** $\subseteq$ **EIL[.2]**. As **EIL[.2]** $\subseteq$ **RE** and **RE** $\subseteq$ **EIL[.2]**, **RE** = **EIL[.2]**.   ∎

Lemma 27. *Let G be an E(0,1)L grammar. Then, there exists an EIL grammar $G' = (\{S, 0, 1\}, T, P, S)$ such that $L(G) = L(G')$ and $F(G') \subseteq \Pi(1^{n-2}00)^* T^*$, for some $n \geq 6$.*

Proof. Let

$$G = (V, T, Q, \$)$$

be an E(0,1)L grammar. For some natural numbers m and n such that $m \geq 3$ and $2m = n$, introduce an injective homomorphism β from V to $(\{0\}\{1\}^*\{0\}\{1\}^* \{1\}^m \cap \{0,1\}^n) - \{1^{n-2}00\}$; in addition, introduce an injective homomorphism χ from T to $(\{0\}\{1\}^*\{0\}\{1\}^*\{1\}^m \cap \{0,1\}^n) - \{1^{n-2}00\}$ so $\{\chi(a) : a \in T\} \cap \{\beta(A) :$

$A \in V\} = \emptyset$. Extend the domain of β and the domain of χ to V^* and T^*, respectively. Define the $E(0, 2n-1)L$ grammar,

$$G' = (T \cup \{S, 0, 1\}, T, P, S),$$

with

$$P = P_\beta \cup P_\chi \cup P_\delta,$$

where

$$
\begin{aligned}
P_\beta \;=\;& \{S \to \beta(\$)\} \\
& \cup \{(0, x\beta(X)) \to \beta(y) : X \in V \cup \{\varepsilon\},\ x \in \{0,1\}^{n-1},\ y \in V^*, \\
& \quad 0x = \beta(Y) \text{ for some } Y \in V \text{ such that } (Y, X) \to y \in Q\} \\
& \cup \{(0, x\beta(a)) \to \chi(b) : a \in T \cup \{\varepsilon\},\ x \in \{0,1\}^{n-1}, \\
& \quad 0x = \beta(b) \text{ for some } b \in T\}, \\
P_\chi \;=\;& \{(0, xy) \to a : a \in T,\ y \in T^*,\ x \in \{0,1\}^*, \\
& \quad |xy| \leq 2n-1,\ 0x = \chi(a)\} \\
& \cup \{(Y, xy) \to \varepsilon : Y \in \{0,1\},\ y \in T^*,\ x \in \{0,1\}^*, \\
& \quad |x| \leq n-2,\ |xy| \leq 2n-1\} \\
& \cup \{(Y, xy) \to Y : Y \in \{0,1\},\ y \in T^*,\ x \in \{0,1\}^*, \\
& \quad |x| \geq n,\ |xy| \leq 2n-1\} \\
& \cup \{(a, x) \to a : a \in T,\ |x| \leq 2n-1\}, \\
P_\delta \;=\;& \{(X, x) \to 1^{n-2}00 : x \in (T \cup \{0,1\})^{2n-1},\ X \in (T \cup \{0,1\}), \\
& \quad (P_\beta \cup P_\chi) \cap \{(X, x) \to z : z \in (T \cup \{0,1\})^*\} = \emptyset\}.
\end{aligned}
$$

Complete this proof by analogy with the proof of Lemma 26.   □

Theorem 47. $\mathbf{EIL}[2.] = \mathbf{RE}$.

Proof. Clearly, $\mathbf{EIL}[2.] \subseteq \mathbf{RE}$. By Theorem 6.1.3 in [155], for every $L \in \mathbf{RE}$ there exists an $E(0,1)L$ grammar G such that $L = L(G)$. Thus, by Lemma 27, $\mathbf{RE} \subseteq \mathbf{EIL}[2.]$. As $\mathbf{EIL}[2.] \subseteq \mathbf{RE}$ and $\mathbf{RE} \subseteq \mathbf{EIL}[2.]$, $\mathbf{EIL}[2.] = \mathbf{RE}$.   □

Corollary 21. $\mathbf{EIL}[.2] = \mathbf{EIL}[.2] = \mathbf{RE}$.

5.2 Scattered Context

The concept of scattered context was introduced by Greibach and Hopcroft in [75]. Scattered context grammars are semi-parallel grammars whose productions simultaneously rewrite several symbols in parallel. These symbols must occur in a certain order that is given by the applied production. However, as opposed to the phrase-structure grammars, these symbols may not form a continuous sequence in the rewritten sentential form.

We concentrate our attention on the reduction of scattered context grammars with respect to several measures of descriptional complexity. Moreover, we demonstrate that by analogy with continuous-context grammars studied in Section 5.1, scattered context grammars can generate their languages in a uniform and succint way.

5.2.1   Scattered Context Grammars and Their Reduction

Definition 20. A *scattered context grammar* (see [75], [110], [122], [123], [127], [128]) is a quadruple $G = (V, T, P, S)$, where V is the total alphabet, T is a finite set of terminals $(T \subseteq V)$, and $S \in V - T$ is the axiom. P is a finite set of productions of the form

$$(A_1, A_2, \ldots, A_n) \to (x_1, x_2, \ldots, x_n)$$

where $n \geq 1$, and for all $i = 1, 2, \ldots, n$, $A_i \in V - T$ and $x_i \in V^*$. Instead of $(A_1, A_2, \ldots, A_n) \to (x_1, x_2, \ldots, x_n)$, the literature sometimes writes

$$(A_1 \to x_1, A_2 \to x_2, \ldots, A_n \to x_n).$$

Let $p = (A_1, A_2, \ldots, A_n) \to (x_1, x_2, \ldots, x_n) \in P$, $n \geq 1$. Then, $\mathrm{scleft}(p) = A_1 A_2 \ldots A_n$ and $\mathrm{scright}(p) = x_1 x_2 \ldots x_n$. If $x_i \in V^+$ for all $i = 1, \ldots, n$, G is said to be *propagating*. Set $\pi(p) = n$. If $\pi(p) \geq 2$, p is said to be a *context-sensitive* production. If $\pi(p) = 1$, p is said to be *context-free*. Consider $p = (A_1, A_2, \ldots, A_n) \to (x_1, x_2, \ldots, x_n) \in P$ and $u, v \in V^*$ of the form

$$u = u_1 A_1 u_2 A_2 \ldots u_n A_n u_{n+1}$$
$$v = u_1 x_1 u_2 x_2 \ldots u_n x_n u_{n+1}$$

where $u_i \in V^*$ for $i = 1, 2, \ldots, n$, $n \geq 1$. Then, u *directly derives* v in G, or simply

$$u \Rightarrow_G v \ [p].$$

In the standard way, $\Rightarrow_G$ can be extended to $\Rightarrow_G^n$ $(n \geq 0)$, $\Rightarrow_G^+$, and $\Rightarrow_G^*$, respectively. The *language of G, $L(G)$*, is defined as

$$L(G) = \{w \in T^* : \ S \Rightarrow_G^* w\}.$$

The family of languages generated by scattered context grammars is denoted by **SCAT**.

Theorem 48. RE = SCAT.

Proof. Let $L \in \mathbf{RE}$. By the first corollary on page 245 in [75], there exists a propagating scattered context grammar

$$G = (V, T, P, S),$$

and a homomorphism h such that $L = h(L(G))$. Without any loss of generality, assume $\mathrm{alph}(L) \cap T = \emptyset$. Define the scattered context grammar

$$G' = (V \cup T \cup \mathrm{alph}(L), \mathrm{alph}(L), P \cup P', S),$$

where

$$P' = \{(a) \to (h(a)) : \ a \in T\}.$$

Clearly, $L(G') = L$. Therefore, $\mathbf{RE} \subseteq \mathbf{SCAT}$. Obviously, $\mathbf{SCAT} \subseteq \mathbf{RE}$, so $\mathbf{RE} = \mathbf{SCAT}$. ∎

Next, we investigate the descriptional complexity of scattered context grammars. To do so, we first introduce several measures of this complexity.

If $G = (V, T, P, S)$ is a scattered context grammar, then its *nonterminal complexity* is the number of nonterminals in G. If G is a scattered context grammar, then its *degree of context-sensitivity*, symbolically written as δ-$\mathrm{CS}(G)$, is defined as the number of context-sensitive productions in G. The *maximum context sensitivity* of G is the greatest number in $\{\pi(p_i) - 1 : 1 \le i \le |P|\}$, symbolically denoted by max-$\mathrm{CS}(G)$. The *overall context sensitivity* of G, denoted by sum-$\mathrm{CS}(G)$, is the sum of all members in $\{\pi(p_i) - 1 : 1 \le i \le |P|\}$.

Lemma 28 (see [128]). *There exists a scattered context grammar G such that G defines a non-context-free language and δ-$\mathrm{CS}(G) = $ max-$\mathrm{CS}(G) = $ sum-$\mathrm{CS}(G) = 1$.*

Proof. Consider a scattered context grammar

$$G = (\{S, A, B, C, D\}, \{a, b, c\}, P, S),$$

where the set of productions P is defined as

$$P = \{(S) \to (AC),$$
$$(A) \to (aAbB),$$
$$(A) \to (\varepsilon),$$
$$(C) \to (cCD),$$
$$(C) \to (\varepsilon),$$
$$(B, D) \to (\varepsilon, \varepsilon)\}.$$

It is easy to verify that $L(G) = \{a^n b^n c^n : n \ge 0\}$ and δ-$\mathrm{CS}(G) = $ max-$\mathrm{CS}(G) = $ sum-$\mathrm{CS}(G) = 1$. $\square$

Let **SCAT**$[k, l, m, n]$ denote the family of languages such that a language L is in **SCAT**$[k, l, m, n]$ if and only if there exists a scattered context grammar G such that $L(G) = L$ and G's nonterminal complexity is k or less, δ-$\mathrm{CS}(G) \le l$, max-$\mathrm{CS}(G) \le m$, and sum-$\mathrm{CS}(G) \le n$. In this book, we consider parameters k and l as the two major measures of descriptional complexity; on the other hand, parameters m and n are less important.

First, we demonstrate that the number of nonterminals can be reduced to three or less. The proof of this statement makes use of a normal form of queue grammars (see Definition 6), which is established in the following lemma:

Lemma 29. *For any queue grammar Q' there exists an equivalent queue grammar $Q = (V, T, W, F, R, g)$ such that Q generates every $z \in L(Q)$ by the derivation of the form $R \Rightarrow_Q^i u \Rightarrow_Q v \Rightarrow_Q^k w \Rightarrow_Q z$, where $i, k \ge 1$, and the derivation satisfies the following properties:*

1. Each derivation step in $R \Rightarrow_Q^i u$ has the form

$$a'y'b' \Rightarrow_Q y'x'c' \ [(a', b', x', c')],$$

where $a' \in V - T$, $b', c' \in W - F$, $x', y' \in (V - T)^*$.

2. *In greater detail, the derivation step $u \Rightarrow_Q v$ has this form*

$$a''y''b'' \Rightarrow_Q y''h''x''c'' \ [(a'', b'', h''x'', c'')],$$

where $a' \in V - T$, $b', c' \in W - F$, $h'', y'' \in (V - T)^*$, $x'' \in T^*$.

3. *Each derivation step in $v \Rightarrow_Q^k w$ has the form*

$$a'''y'''h'''b''' \Rightarrow_Q y'''h'''x'''c''' \ [(a''', b''', x''', c''')],$$

where $a''' \in V - T$, $b''', c''' \in W - F$, $y''' \in (V - T)^*$, $x''', y''' \in T^*$.

4. *In greater detail, the derivation step $w \Rightarrow_Q z$ has the form*

$$a''''y''''b'''' \Rightarrow_Q y''''x''''c'''' \ [(a'''', b'''', x'''', c'''')],$$

where $a'''' \in V - T$, $b'''' \in W - F$, $y'''', x'''' \in T^*$, $w = a''''y''''b''''$, $z = y''''x''''$.

Proof. Let

$$Q' = (V', T', W', F', R', g')$$

be any queue grammar. Introduce these four pairwise disjoint alphabets U, X, Y, and $\{@, \$, \#, \perp\}$ so that $|U| = |V'|$ and $|X| = |Y| = |W'|$. Introduce any bijection α from $(V' \cup U')$ onto $(U \cup X)$. Furthermore, introduce another bijection β from W' to Y. Set $V = U \cup T' \cup \{@, \#\}$, $T = T'$, $W = X \cup Y \cup \{\$, \perp\}$, $F = \{\perp\}$, and $R = @\$$. Define the queue grammar $Q = (V, T, W, F, R, g)$ with g constructed in the following five-step way:

I. If $R' = ab$ with $a \in V - T$ and $b \in W - F$, then add $(@, \$, a, b)$ to g.

II. For every $(a, b, x, c) \in g'$ with $a \in V$, $x \in V^*$, and $b, c \in W$, add $(\alpha(a), \alpha(b), \alpha(x), \alpha(c))$ to g.

III. For every $(a, b, xy, c) \in g'$ with $a \in V$, $x \in V^*$, $y \in T^*$, $b, c \in W$, add $(\alpha(a), \alpha(b), \alpha(x)\#y, \beta(c))$ to g.

IV. For every $(a, b, y, c) \in g'$ with $a \in V$, $y \in T^*$, and $b, c \in W$, add $(\alpha(a), \beta(b), y, \beta(c))$ to g.

V. For every $c \in F'$, add $(\#, \beta(b), \varepsilon, \perp)$ to g.

A formal proof that Q satisfies the properties required by this lemma is left to the reader. $\square$

Theorem 49. RE = SCAT$[3, \infty, \infty, \infty]$.

Proof. Obviously, **SCAT**$[3, \infty, \infty, \infty] \subseteq$ **RE**. Next, we prove the converse inclusion. Let L be a recursively enumerable language. By Theorem 2.1 in [88], there exists a queue grammar

$$Q = (V, T, W, F, R, g)$$

such that $L = L(Q)$. Witout any loss of generality, assume that Q satisfies the properties described in Lemma 29. The next construction produces a three-nonterminal scattered context grammar G satisfying $L(G) = L(Q)$.

Set $n = |V \cup W| + 2$. Introduce a bijection β from $(V \cup W)$ to $(\{1\}^+\{0\}\{1\}^+ \cap \{0,1\}^n)$. In the standard manner, extend the domain of β to $(V \cup W)^*$. Without any loss of generality, assume that $(V \cup W) \cap \{0,1,2\} = \emptyset$. Define the scattered context grammar

$$G = (T \cup \{0,1,2\}, T, P, 2),$$

where P is constructed in the following six-step way:

I. If $R = ab$ with $a \in V - T$ and $b \in W - F$, then add

$$(2) \to (01^{n-1}\beta(b)22\beta(a)20)$$

to P.

II. For every $(a, b, x, c) \in g$ with $a \in V - T$, $x \in (V - T)^*$, and $b, c \in W - F$, add

$$(d_1, \ldots, d_n, b_1, \ldots, b_n, 2, a_1, \ldots, a_{n-1}, a_n, 2, 2) \to$$
$$(d_1, \ldots, d_n, c_1, \ldots, c_n, e_1, e_2, \ldots, e_n, 2, 2, \beta(x)2)$$

to P, where $d_1 \ldots d_n = 01^{n-1}$ (that is, $d_1 = 0$ and $d_h = 1$ for $h = 2, \ldots, n$), $b_1 \ldots b_n = \beta(b)$, $a_1 \ldots a_n = \beta(a)$, $c_1 \ldots c_n = \beta(c)$, $e_i = \varepsilon$ for $i = 1, \ldots, n$.

III. For every $(a, b, xy, c) \in g$ with $a \in V - T$, $x \in (V - T)^*$, $y \in T^*$, and $b, c \in W - F$, add

$$(d_1, \ldots, d_n, b_1, \ldots, b_n, 2, a_1, \ldots, a_{n-1}, a_n, 2, 2) \to$$
$$(f_1, \ldots, f_n, c_1, \ldots, c_n, e_1, e_2, \ldots, e_n, 2, 2, \beta(x)y2)$$

to P, where $d_1 \ldots d_n = 01^{n-1}$ (that is, $d_1 = 0$ and $d_h = 1$ for $h = 2, \ldots, n$), $f_1 \ldots f_n = 1^{n-1}0$ (that is, $f_n = 0$ and $f_h = 1$ for $h = 1, \ldots, n-1$), $b_1 \ldots b_n = \beta(b)$, $a_1 \ldots, a_n = \beta(a)$, $c_1 \ldots c_n = \beta(c)$, $e_i = \varepsilon$ for $i = 1, \ldots, n$.

IV. For every $(a, b, y, c) \in g$ with $a \in V - T$, $y \in T^*$, and $b, c \in W - F$, add

$$(f_1, \ldots, f_n, b_1, \ldots, b_n, 2, a_1, \ldots, a_{n-1}, a_n, 2, 2) \to$$
$$(f_1, \ldots, f_n, c_1, \ldots, c_n, e_1, e_2, \ldots, e_n, 2, 2, y2)$$

to P, where $f_1 \ldots f_n = 1^{n-1}0$ (that is, $f_n = 0$ and $f_h = 1$ for $h = 1, \ldots, n-1$), $b_1 \ldots, b_n = \beta(b)$, $a_1, \ldots, a_n = \beta(a)$, $c_1 \ldots c_n = \beta(c)$, $e_i = \varepsilon$ for $i = 1, \ldots, n$.

V. For every $(a, b, y, c) \in g$ with $a \in V - T$, $y \in T^*$, $b \in W - F$, and $c \in F$, add

$$(f_1, \ldots, f_n, b_1, \ldots, b_n, 2, a_1, \ldots, a_{n-1}, a_n, 2, 2) \to$$
$$(e_1, \ldots, e_n, e_{n+1}, \ldots, e_{2n}, e_{2n+1}, e_{2n+2}, \ldots, e_{3n}, \varepsilon, \varepsilon, y)$$

to P, where $f_1 \ldots f_n = 1^{n-1}0$ (that is, $f_n = 0$ and $f_h = 1$ for $h = 1, \ldots, n-1$), $b_1 \ldots b_n = \beta(b)$, $a_1 \ldots a_n = \beta(a)$, $e_i = \varepsilon$ for $i = 1, \ldots, 3n$.

VI. Add $(2, 2, a, 2) \rightarrow (2, \varepsilon, a2, 2)$ to P, where $a \in \{0, 1\}$.

To keep this proof readable, we omit some obvious details from the rest of this proof whose completion is left to the reader.

Claim 46. *Let $2 \Rightarrow_G^* x$ be a derivation in G during which G uses the productions introduced in step (I) i times, for some $i \geq 1$. Then $\#_2 w = (1 + 2i) - 3j$, $\#_1 x = (n-1)k$, and $\#_0 x = k + i - j$, where k is a nonnegative integer and j is the number of applications of a production introduced in step (V) during $2 \Rightarrow_G^* x$ such that $j \geq 1$ and $(1 + 2i) \geq 3j$.*

Proof. The proof of this claim is left to the reader. □

Claim 47. *Let $2 \Rightarrow_G^* x$ be a derivation in G during which G uses the production introduced in step (I) two or more times. Then, $x \notin T^*$.*

Proof. Let $2 \Rightarrow_G^* x$. If G uses the production introduced in step (I) two or more times, then the previous claim implies that x contains some occurrences of 0. Thus, $x \notin T^*$ because 0 is a nonterminal. □

Claim 48. *G generates every $w \in L(G)$ as $2 \Rightarrow_G u \ [p] \Rightarrow_G^* v \Rightarrow_G w \ [q]$, where p is the production introduced in (I), q is a production introduced in (V), during $u \Rightarrow_G^* v$, G makes every derivation step by a production introduced in (II)–(IV), or (VI).*

Proof. Let $w \in L(G)$. Then, $2 \Rightarrow_G^* w$ and $w \in T^*$. By Claim 46, as $w \in T^*$, G uses the production introduced in (I) once. Because $2 \Rightarrow_G^* w$ begins from 2, we can express $2 \Rightarrow_G^* w$ as

$$2 \Rightarrow_G u \ [p] \Rightarrow_G^* w,$$

where p is the production introduced in (I), and during $u \Rightarrow_G^* w$, G never uses the production introduced in (I). Observe that every production r introduced in (II)–(IV), and (VI) satisfies $\#_2 \text{scleft}(r) = 3$ and $\#_2 \text{scright}(r) = 3$. Furthermore, notice that every production q introduced in (V) satisfies $\#_2 \text{scleft}(q) = 3$ and $\#_2 \text{scright}(q) = 0$. These observations imply

$$2 \Rightarrow_G u \ [p] \Rightarrow_G^* v \Rightarrow_G w \ [q],$$

where p is the production introduced in (I), q is a production introduced in (V), and during $u \Rightarrow_G^* v$, G makes every step by a production introduced in (II)–(IV), or (VI). □

Basic Idea. Before describing the form of every successful derivation in G in greater detail, we make some observations about the use of productions introduced in (VI).

During any successful derivation in G, a production introduced in step (VI) is always applied after using a production introduced in steps (I)–(IV) (the use of these productions is described below). More precisely, to continue the derivation after applying a production introduced in (I)–(IV), G has to shift the second appearance of 2 right in the current sentential form. G makes this shift by using productions introduced in (VI) to generate a sentential form having precisely n appearances of d ($d \in \{0,1\}$) between the first appearance of 2 and the second appearance of 2. Indeed, the sentential form has to contain exactly n appearances of d between the first appearance of 2 and the second appearance of 2; otherwise, the successfulness of the derivation is contradicted by Observations 1 and 2, which follow next.

Observation 1. If there exist fewer than n ds between the first appearance of 2 and the second appearance of 2, no production introduced in (I)–(V) can be used, so the derivation ends. If the last sentential form contains nonterminals and if the derivation is not successful, it is a contradiction.

Observation 2. Assume that there exist more than n ds between the first appearance of 2 and the second appearance of 2. Then, after the next application of a production introduced in (I)–(V), more than $3n$ ds ($d \in \{0,1\}$) appear before the first appearance of 2. Return to the construction of productions in G to make the following observations:

(i) The production introduced in step (I) is always used only in the first step of a successful derivation (see Claim 48).

(ii) All productions introduced in steps (II)–(IV) rewrite $3n$ nonterminals preceding the first appearance of 2 with other $3n$ nonterminals.

(iii) Recall that a production introduced in step (V) is always used in the last derivation step (see Claim 48); furthermore, observe that this production erases precisely $3n$ nonterminals preceding the first appearance of 2.

By Observation 2, the occurrence of more than $3n$ ds between the first and the second appearance of 2 gives rise to a contradiction of the successfulness of the derivation.

By Observations 1 and 2, we see that the sentential form has to contain precisely n appearances of d between the first and the second appearances of 2.

Except for the use of productions introduced in step (VI) (this use is explained above), every successful derivation in G is made as

$$2 \Rightarrow_G \mathrm{rhs}(p_1)\ [p_1] \Rightarrow_G^i u \Rightarrow_G v\ [p_3] \Rightarrow_G^k w \Rightarrow_G z\ [p_5],$$

where $i, k \geq 1$, and the derivation satisfies the following properties (A) through (D):

(A) Each derivation step in $\mathrm{rhs}(p_1) \Rightarrow_G^i u$ has this form

$$01^{n-1}\beta(b')2\beta(a')2\beta(y')20 \Rightarrow_G 01^{n-1}\beta(c')22\beta(y'x')20\ [p_2],$$

where p_2 is a production introduced in (II), $(a', b', x', c') \in g$, $y' \in (V - T)^*$.

(B) In greater detail, the derivation step $u \Rightarrow_G v$ [p_3] has this form

$$01^{n-1}\beta(b'')2\beta(a'')2\beta(h'')20 \Rightarrow_G 1^{n-1}0\beta(c'')22\beta(h''y'')x''20 \ [p_3],$$

where $u = 01^{n-1}\beta(b'')2\beta(a'')2\beta(h'')20$, $v = 1^{n-1}0\beta(c'')22\beta(h''y'')x''20$, p_3 is a production introduced in (III), $(a'', b'', y''x'', c'') \in g$, $h'', y'' \in (V - T)^*$, $x'' \in T^*$.

(C) Each derivation step in $v \Rightarrow_G^k w$ has this form

$$1^{n-1}0\beta(b''')2\beta(a''')2\beta(y''')t'''20 \Rightarrow_G 1^{n-1}0\beta(c')22\beta(y''')t'''x'''20 \ [p_4],$$

where p_4 is a production introduced in (IV), $(a''', b''', x''', c''') \in g$, $y''' \in (V - T)^*$, $t''', x''' \in T^*$.

(D) In greater detail, the derivation step $w \Rightarrow_G z$ [p_5] has this form

$$1^{n-1}0\beta(b'''')2\beta(a'''')2t''''20 \Rightarrow_G t''''x'''' \ [p_5],$$

where $w = 1^{n-1}0\beta(b'''')2\beta(a'''')2t''''20$, $z = t''''x''''$, p_5 is a production introduced in (V), $(a'''', b'''', x'''', c'''') \in g$ with $c'''' \in F$.

Let

$$2 \Rightarrow_G \mathrm{rhs}(p_1) \ [p_1] \Rightarrow_G^i u \Rightarrow_G v \ [p_3] \Rightarrow_G^k w \Rightarrow_G z \ [p_5]$$

be any successful derivation in G such that this derivation satisfies the properties above. Observe that at this point

$$R \Rightarrow_Q^i a''y''b'' \Rightarrow_Q \ \Rightarrow_Q y''x''b''' \Rightarrow_Q^k a''''t''''b'''' \Rightarrow_Q z$$

in Q, so $z \in L(Q)$. Consequently, $L(G) \subseteq L(Q)$.

A proof demonstrating that $L(Q) \subseteq L(G)$ is left to the reader. Since $L(Q) = L(G)$ and G has only three nonterminals 0, 1, and 2, $\mathbf{RE} \subseteq \mathbf{SCAT}[3, \infty, \infty, \infty]$. Having $\mathbf{SCAT}[3, \infty, \infty, \infty] \subseteq \mathbf{RE}$, we get $\mathbf{SCAT}[3, \infty, \infty, \infty] = \mathbf{RE}$, and the theorem holds. ∎

Rigorous proofs of the remaining theorems given in this section are tedious, so we describe them rather informally. In the next theorem, we demonstrate that the number of context-sensitive productions can be reduced to two or less (see [127]).

Theorem 50. $\mathbf{SCAT}[\infty, 2, 3, 6] = \mathbf{RE}$.

Proof. It is well known that every recursively enumerable language $L \subseteq \Sigma^*$ can be represented as $L = h(L_1 \cap L_2)$, where h is a homomorphism from T^* onto Σ^* and L_1 and L_2 are two context-free languages (see [79]). Let $T = \{a_1, \ldots, a_n\}$ and $0, 1, \$ \notin (T \cup \Sigma)$ be three new symbols. Let $g(a_i) = 10^i 1$ and $f(a_i) = h(a_i)g(a_i)$ for all $i \in \{1, \ldots, n\}$. By the closure properties of context-free languages, there are context-free grammars G_1 and G_2 that generate $f(L_1)$ and $f(L_2^R)$, respectively. Note that L_2^R denotes the reversal of L_2. Without any loss of generality, assume that the nonterminal alphabets of these grammars are disjoint. Let S_1 and S_2 be the start symbols of G_1 and G_2, respectively. Define another context-free grammar, G', by putting together G_1 and G_2 and adding a new production of the form $S \to \$S_1 1111 S_2\$$, where $\$$ and S are new nonterminals (S is the start symbol of G'). Observe that

$$L(G') = \$f(L_1)1111g(L_2^R)\$.$$

If we now consider the productions of G' as belonging to the scattered context grammar G, where $0, 1, \$$ are interpreted as nonterminal symbols and where we have three additional productions, namely $r_1 = (\$, 0, 0, \$) \to (\varepsilon, \$, \$, \varepsilon)$, $r_2 = (\$, 1, 1, \$) \to (\varepsilon, \$, \$, \varepsilon)$, and $r_3 = (\$) \to (\varepsilon)$, then $L(G) = L$ is rather evident.

Indeed, consider a word $w \in L$. There is a word $v \in L_1 \cap L_2$ such that $w = h(v)$. Hence, $u = \$f(v)1111g(v^R)\$ \in L(G')$. By the construction, u is generated by the scattered context grammar G. The productions r_1, r_2, and r_3 of G allow us to remove all occurrences of 0, 1 and $\$$ to obtain w from u. Thus, $L \subseteq L(G)$.

To prove $L(G) \subseteq L$, consider any $w \in L(G)$. Since 0, 1, and $\$$ are terminals in G' on which G is based, we can assume that some generation of w exists that uses, in a first phase, only productions from G' and then, in a second phase, the productions r_1, r_2, and r_3. By the construction, there never exist more than two occurrences of $\$$ in any sentential form generated by G. Since the productions r_1 and r_2 test for the presence of two occurrences of $\$$, r_3 has to be the last production that is used.

If r_1 is applied so it does not rewrite the left-most or right-most appearance of 0, then $\$$ serves as a delimiter so that no terminal word is derivable. An analogical observation applies to r_2. Hence, we can assume that in the second phase of the derivation of w, the productions r_1 and r_2 are used to test whether the word $e(v)$ is a palindrome, where $\$v\$$ is generated by the first derivation phase and e is the homomorphism erasing all letters from V and mapping 0 and 1 to 0 and 1, respectively. Only in this case the second phase succeeds.

By the way the codification of f and g works, this means that the first phase ends with $\$v\$ = \$f(u)1111g(u^R)\$$. Hence, G_1 derives $f(u)$ and G_2 derives $g(u^R)$, yielding $u \in L_1 \cap L_2$. Moreover, the codification ensures that $w = h(u)$. Thus, $L(G) \subseteq L$.

As a result, $L(G) = L$. Observe that apart from r_1 and r_2, all productions in G are context-free. Moreover, max-CS$(G) = 3$ and sum-CS$(G) = 6$. So, $L(G) \in$ **SCAT**$[\infty, 2, 3, 6]$. Consequently, the theorem holds. ∎

Unfortunately, in the construction of the proof of Theorem 50, the number of nonterminals is unbounded. The following theorem demonstrates how to simultaneously reduce both the number of context-sensitive productions and the number of nonterminals (see [128]).

Theorem 51. **SCAT**$[8, 5, 5, 17] =$ **RE**.

Proof. Let $L \subseteq \Sigma^*$ be a recursively enumerable language. L can be represented as $L = h(L_1 \cap L_2)$, where h is a homomorphism from T^* to Σ^* and L_1 and L_2 are two context-free languages (see [79]). Let $T = \{a_1, \ldots, a_n\}$ and $0, 1, 2, 3, 4, \#, \$, S \notin$

$(T \cup \Sigma)$ be eight new symbols. Let $c(a_i) = 10^i 1$ and $f(a_i) = h(a_i)c(a_i)$ for all $a_i \in T$, $1 \leq i \leq n$. By the definition, c is a coding; that is, it is injective. By the closure properties of context-free languages, there are context-free grammars G_1 and G_2 that generate $f(L_1)$ and $f(L_2^R)$, respectively. More precisely, let

$$G_i = (V_i, T, P_i, S_i)$$

for $i = 1, 2$. Let $N_1 = (V_1 - T)$, $N_2 = (V_2 - T)$. Without any loss of generality, assume that the nonterminal alphabets N_1 and N_2 are disjoint. Let $N = N_1 \cup N_2$ and let C be a coding from N to $\{43^i 4 : 1 \leq i \leq |N|\}$. Next, we extend the codings C and c in two different ways. Let C_1 be a homomorphism defined as $C_1(A) = C(A)2$ for all $A \in N_1$ and $C(a) = f(a)$ for every $a \in T$. Moreover, let C_2 be a homomorphism such that $C_2(A) = C(A)2$ for all $A \in N_2$ and $C_2(a) = c(a)$ for all $a \in T$. Now consider the context-free grammar

$$G = (V, \Sigma \cup \{0, 1, 3, 4, \#, \$\}, P, S)$$

with $V - (\Sigma \cup \{0, 1, 3, 4, \#, \$\}) = \{S, 2\}$ and where P contains the following productions:

1. $S \to \$ C_1(S_1)1111 C_2(S_2)\#\#\$$.

2. $2 \to C(A)C_i(w)$ if $A \to w \in P_i$ for $i = 1, 2$.

A word in $L(G)$ starts with $\$$ and ends with $\#\#\$$. Moreover, it cannot contain any 2, which means that the simulations of G_1 and G_2 have come to an end (no unresolved codings of nonterminals of the simulated grammars remain). The two simulations of G_1 and G_2 are separated by a sequence of four 1's, which cannot occur elsewhere by construction. The coding $C(A)$ of the nonterminal A, which actually has to be replaced according to G_i, is placed before the coding $C_i(w)$ of the right-hand side w of the production $A \to w \in P_i$. Therefore, a correct simulation can be detected by a sequence of two codings of A in the terminal word of G. Next, let n be a homomorphism from $\Sigma \cup \{0, 1, 3, 4, \#, \$\}$ to $\{3, 4\}$, where $n(3) = 3$, $n(4) = 4$, and $n(a) = \varepsilon$ for $a \notin \{3, 4\}$. Furthermore, let t be a homomorphism from $\Sigma \cup \{0, 1, 3, 4, \#, \$\}$ to Σ defined as $t(a) = a$ for every $a \in \Sigma$ and $t(A) = \varepsilon$ for all $A \notin \Sigma$. Finally, let t' be a homomorphism from $\Sigma \cup \{0, 1, 3, 4, \#, \$\}$ to $\{0, 1\}$, where $t'(a) = a$, $a \in \{0, 1\}$, and $t'(A) = \varepsilon$, $A \notin \{0, 1\}$.

Considering homomorphisms n, t, and t', we can state: $\$w_1 1111 w_2 \#\#\$ \in L(G)$ represents a correct simulation of G_i if

$$n(w_i) \in \{C(A)C(A) : A \in N_i\}^+.$$

If both w_1 and w_2 represent a correct simulation, then $t'(w_i) = c(x_i)$ for a terminal word x_i derivable by G_i, and, moreover, $t(w_1) = h(x_1)$ in that case. Summarizing, we conclude that

$$h(L_1 \cap L_2) = \{t(w) : w = \$w_1 1111 w_2 \#\#\$ \text{ represents a correct simulation}$$
$$\text{both of } G_1 \text{ and of } G_2 \text{ and } t'(w_1) = t'(w_2^R) = (t'(w_2))^R\}.$$

We will now design a scattered context grammar based on G that checks the conditions mentioned above. Consider the scattered context grammar

$$G' = (V', \Sigma, P', S)$$

with

$$V' = \{0, 1, 2, 3, 4, \#, \$, S\} \cup \Sigma.$$

P' contains, besides all the productions from P, the following checking productions:

1. $r_a = (\$, a, a, \$) \to (\varepsilon, \$, \$, \varepsilon)$ for $a = 0, 1$ allows G' to skip the codings of terminal symbols; more precisely, if w is a word derived by G, then the zeros and ones are erased synchronously from both ends of the subwords w_1 and w_2, this way checking whether $t'(w_1) = t'(w_2)$. The four ones in the middle of the word are necessary to also check the boundary between the w_1- and the w_2-parts.

2. $r_{init} = (4, 4, 4, \#, \#) \to (\#, 4, \#, \varepsilon, \varepsilon)$ initializes the check of "neighbored codings" of nonterminals.

3. $r_3 = (\#, 3, 4, 3, \#) \to (\varepsilon, \#, 4, \#, \varepsilon)$ and $r_4 = (\#, 4, 4, \#) \to (\#\#, \varepsilon, \varepsilon, \varepsilon)$ for checking the neighbored codings.

The checking of the codings of terminal strings works as in the case proved in Theorem 50. The checking of codings of neighbored nonterminals is performed by a right-to-left scan over the word derived by G. Assume that we are confronted with a word $\xi = w43^i443^j4x\#y\#z$ before applying r_{init}, where x does not contain any occurrence of a 4. If w contains some occurrences of 4's and one of them is selected when applying r_{init}, then the indicated substring 43^i443^j4 is at least partially skipped, meaning that at least some of the occurrences of 4's or 3's cannot be erased anymore.

When applying r_{init} to $\xi = w43^i443^j4x\#y\#z$ by replacing the three displayed right-most 4's, we arrive at $w43^i\#43^j4\#xyz$. Then, none of the productions r_{init}, r_3, r_4 are applicable. The replacement of the three displayed left-most 4's can be symmetrically treated.

Hence, the only possible next sentential form ξ' derivable from ξ by applying r_{init} which might finally lead to a terminal word in G' yields $\xi' = w\#3^i443^j\#xyz$. Now, a sequence of applications of r_3 leads to $\xi'' = w\#44\#xyz$ if and only if $i = j$. In that case, applying r_4 once yields $\xi''' = w\#\#xyz$, and the checking can proceed by going into the next cycle. Assume that $\xi'' = w\#3^\ell44\#xyz$ or $\xi'' = w\#443^\ell\#xyz$ for some $\ell > 0$ (this corresponds to the error case when neighbored codings do not coincide). Applying now r_4 would skip over some occurrences of 3's (in the left direction) so that those 3's would never be erased anymore. r_3 and r_{init} are not applicable here.

Moreover, the simulating grammar contains context-free productions to get rid of the markers, $(\$) \to (\varepsilon)$ and $(\#) \to (\varepsilon)$.

Observe that the construction works even if derivations of G are interleaved with checking steps in the derivation of G'. ∎

At the expense of a larger context-sensing ability, we can merge both markers
\$ and # in the construction above, which gives us the following corollary:

Corollary 22. SCAT$[7, 5, 6, 27]$ = RE.

Proof. We only indicate the necessary modifications and comment on the correctness of the construction. In doing so, we make use of the same abbreviations as in the proof of the preceding theorem, especially regarding G_1, G_2, G, and G'.

The start production of G' and of G equals $(S) \to (\$C_1(S_1)1111C_2(S_2)\$\$\$)$. G' contains the following context-sensitive productions:

1. $(\$, 0, 0, \$, \$, \$) \to (\varepsilon, \$, \$\$\$, \varepsilon, \varepsilon, \varepsilon)$.

2. $(\$, 1, 1, \$, \$, \$) \to (\varepsilon, \$, \$\$\$, \varepsilon, \varepsilon, \varepsilon)$.

3. $(\$, 4, 4, 4, \$, \$, \$) \to (\$, \$, 4, \$, \varepsilon, \varepsilon, \$)$.

4. $(\$, \$, 3, 4, 3, \$, \$) \to (\$, \varepsilon, \$, 4, \$, \varepsilon, \$)$.

5. $(\$, \$, 4, 4, \$, \$) \to (\$, \$\$, \varepsilon, \varepsilon, \varepsilon, \$)$.

$\square$

At a further additional cost of enlarged context-sensing abilities and with a further context-sensitive production, we can improve the nonterminal complexity. To do that, however, we have to modify the construction of Theorem 51 considerably.

Theorem 52. SCAT$[6, 6, 12, 44]$ = RE.

Proof. We start again with the representation of a recursively enumerable language $L \subseteq \Sigma^*$ as $L = h(L_1 \cap L_2)$, where h is a homomorphism from T^* to Σ^* and L_1 and L_2 are two context-free languages. Let $T = \{a_1, \ldots, a_n\}$ and $0, 1, 2, 3, \$, S \notin (T \cup \Sigma)$ be six new symbols. Let c and f be two homomorphisms defined as $c(a_i) = (10)^i$ and $f(a_i) = h(a_i)c(a_i)$ for all $a_i \in T$, $1 \leq i \leq n$. Let

$$G_i = (V_i, T, P_i, S_i)$$

for $i = 1, 2$ be two context-free grammars with $L(G_1) = L_1\#$ and $L(G_2) = (L_2)^R\#$ and $\# \notin T$. Let $N_1 = V_1 - T$ and $N_2 = V_2 - T$. Assume, without any loss of generality, that G_1 and G_2 are in Chomsky normal form and that $N_1 \cap N_2 = \emptyset$. We modify G_1 slightly so that we add a further production $S_1' \to S_1$ to P_1 and take S_1' as new start symbol of G_1. Let us call this modified grammar again $G_1 = (V_1, T, P_1, S_1')$ in what follows. Let C be a coding that maps symbols from N_1 to $\{0^i : 1 \leq i \leq |N_1|\}$ and symbols from N_2 to $\{1^i : 1 \leq i \leq |N_2|\}$.

The scattered context grammar that generates L is defined as

$$G' = (V', T, P', S)$$

with

$$V' = \{0, 1, 2, 3, \$, S\} \cup T$$

and P' constructed as follows:

1. The start production is $(S) \rightarrow (\$\$C(S_1')2\$C(S_2)2\$)$.

2. The simulation productions are defined as:

   (a) for each $A \rightarrow XY \in P_1 \cup P_2$, introduce $(2) \rightarrow (\$C(A)\$C(X)3C(Y)3)$ into P';

   (b) for each $A \rightarrow a \in P_1$ with $\# \neq a$, put $(2) \rightarrow (\$C(A)\$h(a)c(a))$ into P';

   (c) for each $A \rightarrow a \in P_2$ with $\# \neq a$, add $(2) \rightarrow (\$C(A)\$(c(a))^R)$ into P';

   (d) for every production $A \rightarrow \# \in P_1 \cup P_2$, add $(2) \rightarrow (\$C(A)\$3\$^3)$ into P';

   (e) add $(2, \$, \$, \$, \$, \$, \$) \rightarrow (\$C(S_1')\$3C(S_1)3, \$, \$, \varepsilon, \varepsilon, \varepsilon, \varepsilon)$ to P'.

3. Checking rules for matching nonterminals are:
   $(\$, \$, 0, \$, 0, \$, 3, \$) \rightarrow (\$, \varepsilon, \$, \$, \$, \varepsilon, 3, \$)$,
   $(\$, \$, 1, \$, 1, \$, 3, \$) \rightarrow (\$, \varepsilon, \$, \$, \$, \varepsilon, 3, \$)$,
   $(\$, \$, \$, \$, 3, \$) \rightarrow (\$, \varepsilon, \varepsilon, \varepsilon, \$2, \$)$.

4. Checking rules for matching terminals are:
   $(\$, 1, \$, \$, \$, 1, \$) \rightarrow (\varepsilon, \$^6, \$, \$, \$, \$, \varepsilon)$,
   $(\$, \$, \$, \$, \$, \$, 0, \$, \$, \$, \$, 0, \$) \rightarrow (\varepsilon, \varepsilon, \varepsilon, \varepsilon, \varepsilon, \varepsilon, \$, \$, \$, \$, \$, \$, \varepsilon)$.

5. Erasing productions are $(\$) \rightarrow (\varepsilon)$ and $(2) \rightarrow (\varepsilon)$.

The simulation proceeds again in several phases, different from the simulation described in the proof of Theorem 51.

We start with the simulation of G_2. Observe that the simulation of G_1 cannot start at this point, since there are no 6 occurrences of $\$$ to the right-hand side of any symbol 2 as required by the production designed to initiate a derivation of G_1. Basically, a left-most derivation of G_2 is mimicked. This is accomplished in the following way: after applying $(2) \rightarrow (\$C(A)\$C(X)3C(Y)3)$, $(2) \rightarrow (\$C(A)\$(c(a))^R)$ or $(2) \rightarrow (\$C(A)\$3\$^3)$, there is no 2 needed to go on simulating G_2. Therefore, a checking production for matching nonterminals is to be applied. Then, $(\$, \$, \$, \$, 3, \$) \rightarrow (\$, \varepsilon, \varepsilon, \varepsilon, \$2, \$)$ terminates the checking phase and starts a new possible simulation with one of the productions having 2 as the left-hand side. If the checking phase fails or is ended prematurely, then there are leftover 1's. These 1's will not be removed anymore, since the checking productions for matching terminals are designed in a way that only strings with an equal number of zeros and ones, occurring alternatively, pass this test.

The simulation of grammar G_1 starts after having applied $(2) \rightarrow (\$C(A)\$3\$^3)$, the checking productions for nonterminals, and the erasing production $(2) \rightarrow (\varepsilon)$ to end the simulation of G_2. Observe that the chosen codings of nonterminals for N_1 and for N_2 prevent that the use of nonterminal checking productions mingles simulations of G_1 and G_2. Most important, check that starting the simulation of G_1 immediately after applying $(2) \rightarrow (\$C(A)\$3\$^3)$ will lead to an error situation, since there is a 3 to the right of the right-most occurrence of $\$$ that cannot be removed, so no successful derivation exists in this way. The simulation of grammar G_1 is also mimicking a left-most derivation.

Finally, we can apply alternatingly both terminal checking productions. The production designed for checking 0's cannot be applied twice in a row because too many $'s are erased.   ∎

Open Problems. Recall that $\mathbf{SCAT}[1, \infty, \infty, \infty] \subset \mathbf{RE}$; in fact, the one-nonterminal scattered context grammars cannot even generate some context-sensitive languages (see [120]). In Theorem 49, we prove that $\mathbf{SCAT}[3, \infty, \infty, \infty] = \mathbf{RE}$. What is the generative power of two-nonterminal scattered context grammars?

By Theorem 50, scattered context grammars with two context-sensitive productions characterize $\mathbf{RE}$. What is the generative power of scattered context grammars with one context-sensitive production?

Theorems 50 through 52 reduce the number of context-sensitive productions and nonterminals of scattered context grammars in terms of the characterization of every recursively enumerable language, L, by two context-free languages, L_1 and L_2, and a homomorphism, h, so that $L = h(L_1 \cap L_2)$ (see [79]). Reconsider these results in terms of another characterizations of recursively enumerable languages. For instance, in [68], [69], and [70], Geffert established several normal forms of phrase-structure grammars with a significantly reduced number of context-sensitive productions and nonterminals. Perhaps most interesting, some of these normal forms require only one context-sensitive production to characterize $\mathbf{RE}$. Is it possible to improve the results above by using these normal forms?

5.2.2   Semi-parallel Uniform Rewriting

In this section, we discuss the uniform generation of languages by scattered context grammars (see [121]). More precisely, we demonstrate that for every recursively enumerable language, L, there exists a scattered context grammar, G, and two equally long words, $z_1 \in \{A, B, C\}^*$ and $z_2 \in \{A, B, D\}^*$, where A, B, C, and D are G's nonterminals, so that G generates L and every word appearing in a generation of a sentence from L has the form $y_1 \ldots y_m u$, where u is a word of terminals and each y_i is a permutation of z_j, where $j \in \{1, 2\}$. Furthermore, we achieve an analogical result so that u precedes $y_1 \ldots y_m$.

Recall that by $\mathbf{SCAT}$, we denote the family of languages generated by scattered context grammars. Set

$\mathbf{SCAT}[.\mathbf{i}/\mathbf{j}] = \{L : L = L(G), \text{ where } G = (V, T, P, S) \text{ is a scattered context}$
$\text{grammar such that } \Delta(G) \subseteq T^*\Pi(K)^*, \text{ where } K \text{ is}$
$\text{a finite language consisting of equally long words}$
$\text{with } |K| = i \text{ and } |\text{alph}(K)| = j\},$

and

> **SCAT[i/j.]** $= \{L : L = L(G)$, where $G = (V, T, P, S)$ is a scattered context
> grammar such that $\Delta(G) \subseteq \Pi(K)^* T^*$, where K is
> a finite language consisting of equally long words
> with $|K| = i$ and $|\text{alph}(K)| = j\}$.

Lemma 30. *Let $L \in \mathbf{RE}$. Then, there exists a queue grammar Q (see Definition 6, [88]), $Q = (V, T, W, F, R, g)$, satisfying these two properties:*

(I) $L = L(G)$.

(II) Q derives every $w \in L(Q)$ in this way

$$
\begin{aligned}
R \quad &\Rightarrow_Q^i \quad a_1 u_1 b_1 \\
&\Rightarrow_Q \quad u_1 x_1 y_1 c_1 \quad [(a_1, b_1, x_1 y_1, c_1)] \\
&\Rightarrow_Q^j \quad y_1 z_1 d,
\end{aligned}
$$

where $i, j \geq 1$, $w = y_1 z_1$, $x_1, u_1 \in V^*$, $y_1, z_1 \in T^*$, $b_1, c_1 \in W$ and $d \in F$.

Proof. Let L be a recursively enumerable language. By Theorem 2.1 in [88], there exists a queue grammar

$$Q' = (V, T, W, F, R, g)$$

such that Q' derives every $w \in L(Q')$ as

$$
\begin{aligned}
R \quad &\Rightarrow_{Q'}^i \quad a_1 u_1 b_1 \\
&\Rightarrow_{Q'} \quad u_1 x_1 y_1 c_1 \quad [(a_1, b_1, x_1 y_1, c_1)] \\
&\Rightarrow_{Q'}^j \quad y_1 z_1 d,
\end{aligned}
$$

where $i, j \geq 0$, $w = y_1 z_1$, $x_1, u_1 \in V^*$, $y_1, z_1 \in T^*$, $b_1, c_1 \in W$, and $d \in F$ ($i = 0$ implies $a_1 u_1 b_1 = u_1 x_1 y_1 c_1$ and $j = 0$ implies $u_1 x_1 y_1 c_1 = y_1 z_1 d$). Transform Q' to an equivalent queue grammar, Q, so that Q generates every $w \in L(Q')$ by a derivation of the form above, where $i \geq 1$ and $j \geq 1$. A detailed version of this simple modification is left to the reader. □

Lemma 31. *Let $L \in \mathbf{RE}$. Then, there exists a scattered context grammar $G = (\{A, B, C, D, S\} \cup T, T, P, S)$ so that $L(G) = \text{rev}(L)$ and $\Delta(G) \subseteq \Pi(\{A^t B^{n-t} C, A^t B^{n-t} D\})^* T^*$ for some $t, n \geq 1$.*

Proof. Let $L \in \mathbf{RE}$. By Lemma 30, without any loss of generality, assume that there exists a queue grammar

$$Q = (V, T, W, F, R, q)$$

such that $L = L(Q)$ and Q derives every $w \in L(Q)$ in this way

$$
\begin{aligned}
R \quad &\Rightarrow_Q^i \quad a_1 u_1 b_1 \\
&\Rightarrow_Q \quad u_1 x_1 y_1 c_1 \quad [(a_1, b_1, x_1 y_1, c_1)] \\
&\Rightarrow_Q^j \quad y_1 z_1 d,
\end{aligned}
$$

where $i, j \geq 1$, $w = y_1 z_1$, $x_1, u_1 \in V^*$, $y_1, z_1 \in T^*$, $b_1, c_1 \in W$ and $d \in F$. The following construction produces a scattered context grammar

$$G = (\{A, B, C, D, S\} \cup T, T, P, S)$$

satisfying

$$L(G) = \mathrm{rev}(L(Q))$$

and

$$\Delta(Q) \subseteq \Pi(\{A^t B^{n-t} C, A^t B^{n-t} D\})^* T^*$$

for some $t, n \geq 1$.

For some $n \geq 2^{|V \cup W|}$ and $t \in \{1, \dots, n-1\}$, introduce an injective homomorphism β from $(V \cup W)$ to Z, where

$$Z = \{w : \ w \in (\{A, B\}^n - (\{A\}^t \{B\}^{n-t} \cup \{B\}^t \{A\}^{n-t})), \ \#_A w = t\}.$$

Intuitively, β represents $(V \cup W)$ in binary. Furthermore, let χ be the homomorphism from $(V \cup W)$ to $Z\{D\}$ defined as $\chi(a) = \beta(a)\{D\}$ for all $a \in (V \cup W)$. Extend the domain of β and χ to $(V \cup W)^*$ in the standard manner. Define the scattered context grammar $G = (\{A, B, C, D, S\} \cup T, T, P, S)$ with P constructed by performing the next six steps:

1. For $a \in V - T$ and $b \in W - F$ such that $ab = R$, add

$$(S \to A^t B^{n-t} C b_1 \dots b_n C a_1 \dots a_n C C A^t B^{n-t})$$

   to P, where $b_i, a_i \in \{A, B\}$ for $i = 1, \dots, n$, $b_1 \dots b_n = \beta(b)$, $a_1 \dots a_n = \beta(a)$.

2. For every $(a, b, x, c) \in g$, add

$$(d_1, \dots, d_n, C, b_1, \dots, b_n, C, a_1, \dots, a_n, C, C, d_1, \dots, d_n) \to$$
$$(d_1, \dots, d_n, C, e_1, \dots, e_n, \varepsilon, e_1, \dots, e_n, \beta(c) C A^t B^{n-t} C, \chi(x) C, d_1, \dots, d_n)$$

   to P, where $e_i = \varepsilon$, $d_i, b_i, a_i \in \{A, B\}$ for $i = 1, \dots, n$, $d_1 \dots d_n = A^t B^{n-t}$, $b_1 \dots b_n = \beta(b)$, $a_1 \dots a_n = \beta(a)$.

3. For every $(a, b, xy, c) \in g$ with $x \in V^+$ and $y \in T^*$, add

$$(d_1, \dots, d_n, C, b_1, \dots, b_n, C, a_1, \dots, a_n, C, C, d_1, \dots, d_n) \to$$
$$(f_1, \dots, f_n, C, e_1, \dots, e_n, \varepsilon, e_1, \dots, e_n, \beta(c) C A^t B^{n-t} C,$$
$$\chi(x) A^t B^{n-t} C \mathrm{rev}(y), e_1, \dots, e_n)$$

   to P, where $e_i = \varepsilon$, $d_i, f_i, b_i, a_i \in \{A, B\}$ for $i = 1, \dots, n$, $d_1 \dots d_n = A^t B^{n-t}$, $f_1 \dots f_n = B^t A^{n-t}$, $b_1 \dots b_n = \beta(b)$, $a_1 \dots a_n = \beta(a)$.

4. For every $(a, b, y, c) \in g$ with $y \in T^*$ and $c \in W - F$, add

$$(f_1, \dots, f_n, C, b_1, \dots, b_n, C, a_1, \dots, a_n, C, C) \to$$
$$(f_1, \dots, f_n, C, e_1, \dots, e_n, \varepsilon, e_1, \dots, e_n, \beta(c) C A^t B^{n-t} C, C \mathrm{rev}(y))$$

   to P, where $e_i = \varepsilon$, $f_i, b_i, a_i \in \{A, B\}$ for $i = 1, \dots, n$, $f_1 \dots f_n = B^t A^{n-t}$, $b_1 \dots b_n = \beta(b)$, $a_1 \dots a_n = \beta(a)$.

5. For every $(a, b, y, c) \in g$ with $y \in T^*$ and $c \in F$, add

$$(f_1, \ldots, f_n, C, b_1, \ldots, b_n, C, a_1, \ldots, a_n, C, d_1, \ldots, d_n, C) \rightarrow$$
$$(e_1, \ldots, e_n, \varepsilon, e_1, \ldots, e_n, \varepsilon, e_1, \ldots, e_n, \varepsilon, e_1, \ldots, e_n, \mathrm{rev}(y))$$

to P, where $e_i = \varepsilon$, $f_i, b_i, a_i, d_i \in \{A, B\}$ for $i = 1, \ldots, n$, $d_1 \ldots d_n = A^t B^{n-t}$, $f_1 \ldots f_n = B^t A^{n-t}$, $b_1 \ldots b_n = \beta(b)$, $a_1 \ldots a_n = \beta(a)$.

6. Add

$$(C, C, d_1, \ldots, d_n, C, f, C) \rightarrow (C, C, e_1, \ldots, e_n, \varepsilon, fC, C)$$

to P, where $e_i = \varepsilon$, $f, d_i \in \{A, B\}$ for $i = 1, \ldots, n$, $d_1 \ldots d_n = A^t B^{n-t}$.

Next, we prove that $\Delta(G) \subseteq \Pi(\{A^t B^{n-t} C, A^t B^{n-t} D\})^* T^*$ and $L(G) = \mathrm{rev}(L)$. For brevity, we omit some details in this proof; a complete version of this proof is left to the reader.

Consider any $z \in L(G)$. G generates z in this way:

$$
\begin{aligned}
S \quad &\Rightarrow_G \quad A^t B^{n-t} C b_{1_1} \ldots b_{1_n} C a_{1_1} \ldots a_{1_n} C C A^t B^{n-t} \quad [p_1] \\
&\Rightarrow_G^j \quad u \\
&\Rightarrow_G \quad v \\
&\Rightarrow_G^k \quad w \\
&\Rightarrow_G \quad \mathrm{rev}(w_5) \; [p_5],
\end{aligned}
$$

where $j, k \geq 0$, $z = \mathrm{rev}(w_5)$, and the five subderivations satisfy the following properties:

(i) In

$$S \Rightarrow_G A^t B^{n-t} C b_{1_1} \ldots b_{1_n} C a_{1_1} \ldots a_{1_n} C C A^t B^{n-t} \; [p_1],$$

p_1 is of the form

$$(S \rightarrow A^t B^{n-t} C b_{1_1} \ldots b_{1_n} C a_{1_1} \ldots a_{1_n} C C A^t B^{n-t}),$$

where $a_{1_i}, b_{1_i} \in \{A, B\}$ for $i = 1, \ldots, n$, $b_{1_1} \ldots b_{1_n} = \beta(b_1)$ with $b_1 \in W$, $a_{1_1} \ldots a_{1_n} = \beta(a_1)$ with $a_1 \in V$, and $a_1 b_1 = R$ (see (1) in the construction of P).

(ii) In

$$A^t B^{n-t} C b_{1_1} \ldots b_{1_n} C a_{1_1} \ldots a_{1_n} C C A^t B^{n-t} \Rightarrow_G^j u,$$

every derivation step that is not made by a production introduced in (6) has the form

$$
\begin{aligned}
&A^t B^{n-t} C b_{2_1} \ldots b_{2_n} C a_{2_1} \ldots a_{2_n} C \chi(u_2) C A^t B^{n-t} \Rightarrow_G \\
&A^t B^{n-t} C c_{2_1} \ldots c_{2_n} C A^t B^{n-t} C \chi(u_2 x_2) C A^t B^{n-t} \; [p_2],
\end{aligned}
$$

where p_2 is of the form

$$
\begin{aligned}
&(d_{2_1}, \ldots, d_{2_n}, C, b_{2_1}, \ldots, b_{2_n}, C, a_{2_1}, \ldots, a_{2_n}, C, C, d_{2_1}, \ldots, d_{2_n}) \rightarrow \\
&(d_{2_1}, \ldots, d_{2_n}, C, e_{2_1}, \ldots, e_{2_n}, \varepsilon, e_{2_1}, \ldots, e_{2_n}, \beta(c) C A^t B^{n-t} C, \\
&\chi(x_2) C, d_{2_1}, \ldots, d_{2_n}),
\end{aligned}
$$

where $e_{2_i} = \varepsilon$, $a_{2_i}, b_{2_i}, d_{2_i} \in \{A, B\}$ for $i = 1, \ldots, n$, $a_{2_1} \ldots a_{2_n} = \beta(a_2)$ with $a_2 \in V$, $b_{2_1} \ldots b_{2_n} = \beta(b_2)$ with $b_2 \in W$, $d_{2_1} \ldots b_{2_n} = A^t B^{n-t}$ (see (2) in the construction of P).

Thus,

$$A^t B^{n-t} C b_{1_1} \ldots b_{1_n} C a_{1_1} \ldots a_{1_n} CC A^t B^{n-t} \Rightarrow_G^j u$$

can be expressed as

$$A^t B^{n-t} C b_{1_1} \ldots b_{1_n} C a_{1_1} \ldots a_{1_n} CC A^t B^{n-t} \Rightarrow_G$$

$$\vdots$$

$$\Rightarrow_G A^t B^{n-t} C b_{2_1} \ldots b_{2_n} C a_{2_1} \ldots a_{2_n} C \chi(u_2) C A^t B^{n-t}$$
$$\Rightarrow_G A^t B^{n-t} C c_{2_1} \ldots c_{2_n} C A^t B^{n-t} C \chi(u_2 x_2) C A^t B^{n-t}$$

$$\vdots$$

$$\Rightarrow_G A^t B^{n-t} C b_{3_1} \ldots b_{3_n} C a_{3_1} \ldots a_{3_n} C A^t B^{n-t} C \chi(u_3) C A^t B^{n-t},$$

where

$$u = A^t B^{n-t} C b_{3_1} \ldots b_{3_n} C a_{3_1} \ldots a_{3_n} C A^t B^{n-t} C \chi(u_3) C A^t B^{n-t}.$$

(iii) Step $u \Rightarrow_G v$ has the following form:

$$A^t B^{n-t} C b_{3_1} \ldots b_{3_n} C a_{3_1} \ldots a_{3_n} C A^t B^{n-t} C \chi(u_3) C A^t B^{n-t} \Rightarrow_G$$
$$B^t A^{n-t} C c_{3_1} \ldots c_{3_n} C A^t B^{n-t} C \chi(u_3 x_3) A^t B^{n-t} C \mathrm{rev}(y_3) \; [p_3],$$

where

$$v = B^t A^{n-t} C c_{3_1} \ldots c_{3_n} C A^t B^{n-t} C \chi(u_3 x_3) A^t B^{n-t} C \mathrm{rev}(y_3)$$

and p_3 is of the form

$$(d_{3_1}, \ldots, d_{3_n}, C, b_{3_1}, \ldots, b_{3_n}, C, a_{3_1}, \ldots, a_{3_n}, C, C, d_{3_1}, \ldots, d_{3_n}) \rightarrow$$
$$(f_{3_1}, \ldots, f_{3_n}, C, e_{3_1}, \ldots, e_{3_n}, \varepsilon, e_{3_1}, \ldots, e_{3_n}, \beta(c) C A^t B^{n-t} C,$$
$$\chi(x_3) A^t B^{n-t} C \mathrm{rev}(y_3), e_{3_1}, \ldots, e_{3_n}),$$

where $e_{3_i} = \varepsilon$, $a_{3_i}, b_{3_i}, d_{3_i}, f_{3_i} \in \{A, B\}$ for $i = 1, \ldots, n$, $a_{3_1} \ldots a_{3_n} = \beta(a_3)$ with $a_3 \in V$, $b_{3_1} \ldots b_{3_n} = \beta(b_3)$ with $b_3 \in W$, $d_{3_1} \ldots d_{3_n} = A^t B^{n-t}$, $f_{3_1} \ldots f_{3_n} = B^t A^{n-t}$ (see (3) in the construction of P).

(iv) In $v \Rightarrow_G^k w$, any derivation step that is not made by a production introduced in (6) has the following form:

$$B^t A^{n-t} C b_{4_1} \ldots b_{4_n} C a_{4_1} \ldots a_{4_n} C \chi(u_4) A^t B^{n-t} C \mathrm{rev}(v_4) \Rightarrow_G$$
$$B^t A^{n-t} C c_{4_1} \ldots c_{4_n} C A^t B^{n-t} C \chi(u_4) A^t B^{n-t} C \mathrm{rev}(y_4) \mathrm{rev}(v_4), \; [p_4]$$

where p_4 is of the form

$$(f_{4_1}, \ldots, f_{4_n}, C, b_{4_1}, \ldots, b_{4_n}, C, a_{4_1}, \ldots, a_{4_n}, C, C) \rightarrow$$
$$(f_{4_1}, \ldots, f_{4_n}, C, e_{4_1}, \ldots, e_{4_n}, \varepsilon, e_{4_1}, \ldots, e_{4_n}, \beta(c_4) C A^t B^{n-t} C, C \mathrm{rev}(y)),$$

where $e_{4_i} = \varepsilon$, $a_{4_i}, b_{4_i}, f_{4_i} \in \{A, B\}$ for $i = 1, \ldots, n$, $f_{4_1} \ldots f_{4_n} = B^t A^{n-t}$, $b_{4_1} \ldots b_{4_n} = \beta(b_4)$ with $b_4 \in W$, $a_{4_1} \ldots a_{4_n} = \beta(a_4)$ with $a_4 \in V$, $c_{4_1} \ldots c_{4_n} = \beta(c_4)$ with $c_4 \in W$.

As a result, $v \Rightarrow_G^k w$ can be expressed as

$$B^t A^{n-t} C c_{3_1} \ldots c_{3_n} C A^t B^{n-t} C \chi(u_3 x_3) A^t B^{n-t} C \mathrm{rev}(y_3)$$

$$\vdots$$

$$\Rightarrow_G B^t A^{n-t} C b_{4_1} \ldots b_{4_n} C a_{4_1} \ldots a_{4_n} C \chi(u_4) A^t B^{n-t} C \mathrm{rev}(v_4)$$
$$\Rightarrow_G B^t A^{n-t} C c_{4_1} \ldots c_{4_n} C A^t B^{n-t} C \chi(u_4) A^t B^{n-t} C \mathrm{rev}(y_4) \mathrm{rev}(v_4) \ [p_4]$$

$$\vdots$$

$$\Rightarrow_G B^t A^{n-t} C b_{5_1} \ldots b_{5_n} C a_{5_1} \ldots a_{5_n} C A^t B^{n-t} C \mathrm{rev}(w_5),$$

where

$$w = B^t A^{n-t} C b_{5_1} \ldots b_{5_n} C a_{5_1} \ldots a_{5_n} C A^t B^{n-t} C \mathrm{rev}(w_5).$$

and p_5 is of the form

$$(f_{5_1}, \ldots, f_{5_n}, C, b_{5_1}, \ldots, b_{5_n}, C, a_{5_1}, \ldots, a_{5_n}, C, d_{5_1}, \ldots, d_{5_n}, C) \rightarrow$$
$$(e_{5_1}, \ldots, e_{5_n}, \varepsilon, e_{5_1}, \ldots, e_{5_n}, \varepsilon, e_{5_1}, \ldots, e_{5_n}, \varepsilon, e_{5_1}, \ldots, e_{5_n}, \mathrm{rev}(y_5)),$$

where $e_{5_i} = \varepsilon$, $a_{5_i}, b_{5_i}, d_{5_i}, f_{5_i} \in \{A, B\}$ for $i = 1, \ldots, n$, $a_{5_1} \ldots a_{5_n} = \beta(a_5)$ with $a_5 \in V$, $b_{5_1} \ldots b_{5_n} = \beta(b_5)$ with $b_5 \in W$, $d_{5_1} \ldots d_{5_n} = A^t B^{n-t}$, $f_{5_1} \ldots f_{5_n} = B^t A^{n-t}$ (see (5) in the construction of P').

In addition, during

$$A^t B^{n-t} C b_{1_1} \ldots b_{1_n} C a_{1_1} \ldots a_{1_n} C C A^t B^{n-t} \Rightarrow_G^j u$$

and

$$v \Rightarrow_G^k w,$$

G uses a production introduced in (6) to generate a sentential form that contains exactly n hs, where $h \in \{A, B\}$, between the second appearance of C and the third appearance of C, so G can use p_2 and p_4 as described above. Observe that in the previous generation of z by G, every sentential form belongs to $\Pi(\{A^t B^{n-t} C, A^t B^{n-t} D\})^* T^*$, so

$$\Delta(G) \subseteq \Pi(\{A^t B^{n-t} C, A^t B^{n-t} D\})^* T^*.$$

Furthermore, the form of this generation and the construction of P imply that

$$R \Rightarrow_Q^* \mathrm{rev}(z) d$$

with $d \in F$. Consequently, $L(Q)$ contains $\mathrm{rev}(L(G))$, so $L(G)$ is in $\mathrm{rev}(L(Q))$. Because $L = L(Q)$, $L(G) = \mathrm{rev}(L)$. $\qquad \square$

Lemma 32. RE $\subseteq$ SCAT[2/4.]

Proof. Let L be a recursively enumerable language. Set $L' = \text{rev}(L)$. As **RE** is closed under reversal, L' is a recursively enumerable language. By Lemma 31, there exists a scattered context grammar

$$G = (\{A, B, C, D, S\} \cup T, T, P, S)$$

so that

$$\Delta(G) \subseteq \Pi(\{A^t B^{n-t} C, A^t B^{n-t} D\})^* T^*$$

and $L(G) = \text{rev}(L')$. Observe that $L(G)$, $\text{rev}(L(Q))$, $\text{rev}(L')$, $\text{rev}(\text{rev}(L))$, and L coincide. As $L(G) \in$ **SCAT[2/4.]**, this lemma holds. $\qquad\square$

Theorem 53. SCAT[2/4.] = RE.

Proof. Clearly, **SCAT[2/4.] $\subseteq$ RE**. By Lemma 32, **RE $\subseteq$ SCAT[2/4.]**. Thus, **SCAT[2/4.] = RE**. $\qquad\blacksquare$

Lemma 33. RE $\subseteq$ SCAT[.2/4].

Proof. Let L be a recursively enumerable language. By Lemma 31, there exists a scattered context grammar,

$$G' = (V, T, P', S),$$

satisfying $L(G') \in$ **SCAT[2/4.]** and $L(G') = \text{rev}(L)$. Introduce a scattered context grammar

$$G = (V, T, P, S),$$

where P is defined by the equivalence

$$(A_1, \ldots, A_n) \to (x_1, \ldots, x_n) \in P$$

if and only if

$$(A_n, \ldots, A_1) \to (\text{rev}(x_n), \ldots, \text{rev}(x_1)) \in P'.$$

Observe that $L(G) \in$ **SCAT[.2/4]** and $L(G) = \text{rev}(\text{rev}(L))$. As $\text{rev}(\text{rev}(L)) = L$, this lemma holds. $\qquad\square$

Theorem 54. SCAT[.2/4] = RE.

Proof. Clearly, **SCAT[.2/4] $\subseteq$ RE**. By Lemma 33, **RE $\subseteq$ SCAT[.2/4]**. Thus, **SCAT[.2/4] = RE**. $\qquad\blacksquare$

Open Problem. All the uniform rewriting discussed in this chapter is obtained for grammars with erasing productions. In the techniques by which we achieved this uniform rewriting, these productions fulfill a crucial role. Therefore, we believe that these techniques cannot be straightforwardly adapted for grammars without erasing productions. Can we achieve some uniform rewriting for grammars without erasing productions by using completely different techniques?

Chapter 6

Grammatical Transformations and Derivation Simulations

The previous parts of this book contain various transformations of some grammars with context conditions to other grammars so that both the input and the output grammars are equivalent. Taking a closer look at these grammars, we intuitively see that some grammars generate the language in a more similar way than others. Indeed, consider two grammars of this kind. If we can find a suitable substitution by which we change each string of every derivation in one grammar so that the sequence of strings resulting from this change represents a derivation in the other grammar, we tend to consider them as two grammars that closely simulate each other. On the other hand, if a substitution of this kind cannot be found, we do not consider them in this way. In the present chapter, we formalize this intuitive understanding of equivalent grammars that make similar derivations. First, we introduce the basic concept of a derivation simulation. Making use of this concept, we rigorously describe what we intuitively mean by grammatical transformations that convert some grammars to other equivalent grammars so that the output grammars closely simulate the input grammars. Specifically, we discuss this kind of grammatical transformations in terms of EIL grammars (see Chapter 2), pointing out that an analogical discussion can be made for any equivalent grammars. Then, we present a grammatical transformation of EIL grammars to equivalent symbiotic E0L grammars (see Section 3.2) in order to illustrate the concept of close simulation.

6.1 Derivation Simulation

In this section, we conceptualize the derivation similarity of language models.

Definition 21. A *string-relation system* is a quadruple

$$\Psi = (W, \Rightarrow, W_0, W_F),$$

where W is a language, $\Rightarrow$ is a binary relation on W, $W_0 \subseteq W$ is a set of *start strings*, and $W_F \subseteq W$ is a set of *final strings*.

Every string, $w \in W$, represents a 0-step string-relation sequence in Ψ. For every $n \geq 1$, a sequence

$$w_0, w_1, \ldots w_n,$$

$w_i \in W$, $0 \leq i \leq n$, is an *n-step string-relation sequence*, symbolically written as

$$w_0 \Rightarrow w_1 \Rightarrow \ldots \Rightarrow w_n$$

if, for each $0 \leq i \leq n-1$, $w_i \Rightarrow w_{i+1}$.

If there is a string-relation sequence $w_0 \Rightarrow w_1 \Rightarrow \ldots \Rightarrow w_n$, where $n \geq 0$, we write $w_0 \Rightarrow^n w_n$. Furthermore, $w_0 \Rightarrow^* w_n$ means that $w_0 \Rightarrow^n w_n$ for some $n \geq 0$, and $w_0 \Rightarrow^+ w_n$ means that $w_0 \Rightarrow^n w_n$ for some $n \geq 1$. Obviously, from the mathematical point of view, $\Rightarrow^+$ and $\Rightarrow^*$ are the transitive closure of $\Rightarrow$ and the transitive and reflexive closure of $\Rightarrow$, respectively.

Let $\Psi = (W, \Rightarrow, W_0, W_F)$ be a string-relation system. A string-relation sequence in Ψ, $u \Rightarrow^* v$, where $u, v \in W$, is called a *yield sequence* if $u \in W_0$. If $u \Rightarrow^* v$ is a yield sequence and $v \in W_F$, $u \Rightarrow^* v$ is *successful*.

Let $D(\Psi)$ and $SD(\Psi)$ denote the set of all yield sequences and all successful yield sequences in Ψ, respectively.

Example 9. To illustrate the way we use string-relation systems, consider a context-free grammar

$$G = (V, T, P, S),$$

where V, T, P, and S are the total alphabet, the terminal alphabet, the set of productions, and the start symbol, respectively. In the standard way (see [118]), define the direct derivation $\Rightarrow$ on V^*, the set of G's sentential forms $F(G)$, and the language of G, $L(G)$. Then, introduce a string-relation system

$$\Psi = (V^*, \Rightarrow, \{S\}, T^*).$$

Observe that $w_0 \Rightarrow w_1 \Rightarrow \ldots \Rightarrow w_n$ is a yield sequence in Ψ if and only if $w_n \in F(G)$. Furthermore, $w_0 \Rightarrow w_1 \Rightarrow \ldots \Rightarrow w_n$ is a successful yield sequence if and only if $w_n \in L(G)$.

Definition 22. Let $\Psi = (W, \Rightarrow_\Psi, W_0, W_F)$ and $\Omega = (W', \Rightarrow_\Omega, W'_0, W'_F)$ be two string-relation systems, and let σ be a substitution from W' to W. Furthermore, let d be a yield sequence in Ψ of the form

$$w_0 \Rightarrow_\Psi w_1 \Rightarrow_\Psi \ldots \Rightarrow_\Psi w_{n-1} \Rightarrow_\Psi w_n,$$

where $w_i \in W$, $0 \leq i \leq n$, for some $n \geq 0$. A yield sequence h, in Ω, *simulates* d *with respect to* σ, symbolically written as

$$h \vartriangleright_\sigma d,$$

if h is of the form

$$y_0 \Rightarrow_\Omega^{m_1} y_1 \Rightarrow_\Omega^{m_2} \ldots \Rightarrow_\Omega^{m_{n-1}} y_{n-1} \Rightarrow_\Omega^{m_n} y_n,$$

where $y_j \in W'$, $0 \leq j \leq n$, $m_k \geq 1$, $1 \leq k \leq n$, and $w_i \in \sigma(y_i)$ for all $0 \leq i \leq n$. In addition, if there exists $m \geq 1$ such that $m_k \leq m$ for each $1 \leq k \leq n$, then h *m-closely simulates* d *with respect to* σ, symbolically written as

$$h \vartriangleright_\sigma^m d.$$

Definition 23. Let $\Psi = (W, \Rightarrow_\Psi, W_0, W_F)$ and $\Omega = (W', \Rightarrow_\Omega, W'_0, W'_F)$ be two string-relation systems, and let σ be a substitution from W' to W. Let $X \subseteq D(\Psi)$ and $Y \subseteq D(\Omega)$. Y *simulates* X *with respect to* σ, written as $Y \rhd_\sigma X$, if the following two conditions hold:

1. For every $d \in X$, there is $h \in Y$ such that $h \rhd_\sigma d$.

2. For every $h \in Y$, there is $d \in X$ such that $h \rhd_\sigma d$.

Let m be a positive integer. Y *m-closely simulates* X *with respect to* σ, $Y \rhd_\sigma^m X$, provided that:

1. For every $d \in X$, there is $h \in Y$ such that $h \rhd_\sigma^m d$.

2. For every $h \in Y$, there is $d \in X$ such that $h \rhd_\sigma^m d$.

Definition 24. Let $\Psi = (W, \Rightarrow_\Psi, W_0, W_F)$ and $\Omega = (W', \Rightarrow_\Omega, W'_0, W'_F)$ be two string-relation systems. If there exists a substitution σ from W' to W such that $D(\Omega) \rhd_\sigma D(\Psi)$ and $SD(\Omega) \rhd_\sigma SD(\Psi)$, then Ω is said to be Ψ's *derivation simulator* and *successful-derivation simulator*, respectively. Furthermore, if there is an integer, $m \geq 1$, such that $D(\Omega) \rhd_\sigma^m D(\Psi)$ and $SD(\Omega) \rhd_\sigma^m SD(\Psi)$, Ω is called an *m-close derivation simulator* and *m-close successful-derivation simulator* of Ψ, respectively. If there exists a homomorphism ρ from W' to W such that $D(\Omega) \rhd_\rho D(\Psi)$, $SD(\Omega) \rhd_\rho SD(\Psi)$, $D(\Omega) \rhd_\rho^m D(\Psi)$, and $SD(\Omega) \rhd_\rho^m SD(\Psi)$, then Ω is Ψ's *homomorphic derivation simulator*, *homomorphic successful-derivation simulator*, *m-close homomorphic derivation simulator* and *m-close homomorphic successful-derivation simulator*, respectively.

Example 10. Let us demonstrate the idea of derivation simulations on grammars generating the language $L = \{a^n b^n : n \geq 1\}$. Consider

$$
\begin{aligned}
G_1 &= (V_1, \{a, b\}, P_1, S), \text{ where} \\
V_1 &= \{S, a, b\}, \\
P_1 &= \{S \to ab, \ S \to aSb\}.
\end{aligned}
$$

Clearly, every derivation in G_1 has the form

$$S \Rightarrow_{G_1} aSb \Rightarrow_{G_1} aaSbb \Rightarrow_{G_1} \cdots \Rightarrow_{G_1} a^{n-1}Sb^{n-1} \Rightarrow_{G_1} a^n b^n$$

for some $n \geq 1$. The language of G_1 is L. Next, consider

$$
\begin{aligned}
G_2 &= (V_2, \{a, b\}, P_2, S), \text{ where} \\
V_2 &= \{S, A, B, a, b\}, \\
P_2 &= \{S \to aB, \ B \to Ab, \ A \to aB, \ B \to b\}.
\end{aligned}
$$

G_2 makes every derivation in this way

$$S \Rightarrow_{G_2} aB \Rightarrow_{G_2} aAb \Rightarrow_{G_2} aaBb \Rightarrow_{G_2} aaAbb \Rightarrow_{G_2} \cdots \Rightarrow_{G_2} a^n Bb^{n-1} \Rightarrow_{G_2} a^n Ab^n,$$

where $n \geq 1$. Furthermore, every sentential form $a^n B b^{n-1}$ can be rewritten to $a^n b^n$. Obviously, $L(G_2) = L(G_1) = L$.

Investigate the derivations in G_1 and G_2 in terms of derivation simulations. To do so, introduce the corresponding string-relation systems

$$\Psi_1 = (V_1^*, \Rightarrow_{G_1}, \{S\}, \{a,b\}^*) \quad \text{and} \quad \Psi_2 = (V_2^*, \Rightarrow_{G_2}, \{S\}, \{a,b\}^*)$$

by analogy with Example 9. Notice that Ψ_1 and Ψ_2 are defined so that their yield sequences correspond to the derivations above in G_1 and G_2. Then, introduce a homomorphism σ_2 from V_2^* to V_1^* as

1. $\sigma_2(S) = \sigma_2(A) = S$;

2. $\sigma_2(B) = \sigma_2(b) = b$;

3. $\sigma_2(a) = a$.

Let us show that Ψ_2 is a 2-close homomorphic derivation simulator of Ψ_1 with respect to σ_2. First, inspect all steps of yield sequences in Ψ_1:

1. For $S \Rightarrow_{G_1} ab$, there is $S \Rightarrow_{G_2} aB \Rightarrow_{G_2} ab$.

2. For $S \Rightarrow_{G_1} aSb$, Ψ_2 makes $S \Rightarrow_{G_2} aB \Rightarrow_{G_2} aAb$, where $\sigma_2(aAb) = aSb$.

3. For $a^{n-1} S b^{n-1} \Rightarrow_{G_1} a^n S b^n$, $n \geq 2$, there is

$$a^{n-1} A b^{n-1} \Rightarrow_{G_2} a^n B b^{n-1} \Rightarrow_{G_2} a^n A b^n,$$

   where $\sigma_2(a^{n-1} A b^{n-1}) = a^{n-1} S b^{n-1}$, $\sigma_2(a^n A b^n) = a^n S b^n$.

4. For $a^{n-1} S b^{n-1} \Rightarrow_{G_1} a^n b^n$, $n \geq 2$, there exists

$$a^{n-1} A b^{n-1} \Rightarrow_{G_2} a^n B b^{n-1} \Rightarrow_{G_2} a^n b^n$$

   with $\sigma_2(a^{n-1} A b^{n-1}) = a^{n-1} S b^{n-1}$ and $\sigma_2(a^n b^n) = a^n b^n$.

That is, every step in any yield sequence from Ψ_1 can be simulated by two steps in Ψ_2. Hence, by induction on the length of yield sequences in Ψ_1, prove that every $d \in D(\Psi_1)$ is 2-close-simulatable by some $h \in D(\Psi_2)$ with respect to σ_2; in symbols, $h \rhd_{\sigma_2}^2 d$. Next, observe that every $h \in D(\Psi_2)$ is a 2-close homomorphic simulation of some $d \in D(\Psi_1)$. Indeed, $S \Rightarrow_{G_2}^* a^n A b^n$ and $S \Rightarrow_{G_2}^* a^n b^n$, $n \geq 1$, are 2-close simulations of yield sequences from Ψ_1. The other forms of yield sequences in Ψ_2 are of the forms $S \Rightarrow_{G_2} aB$ and

$$S \Rightarrow_{G_2}^+ a^n A b^n \Rightarrow_{G_2} a^{n+1} B b^n,$$

$n \geq 1$. Because $\sigma_2(B) = b$, the first sequence is a 1-close simulation of $S \Rightarrow_{G_1} ab$ and the second sequence is a 2-close simulation of

$$S \Rightarrow_{G_1}^+ a^n S b^n \Rightarrow_{G_2} a^{n+1} b^{n+1}.$$

Hence, for every $h \in D(\Psi_2)$, there exists $d \in D(\Psi_1)$ such that $h \rhd^2_{\sigma_2} d$. As a result, $D(\Psi_2) \rhd^2_{\sigma_2} D(\Psi_1)$; that is, Ψ_2 is a 2-close homomorphic derivation simulator of Ψ_1.

Return to the grammars G_1 and G_2. Intuitively, the 2-closeness of their derivations means that the grammars generate their sentential forms in a very similar way. Indeed, while G_1 inserts new occurrences of symbols a and b in one derivation step, G_2 does the same in two steps.

Example 11. Consider G_1 from Example 10. Let us demonstrate that the following grammar G_3 homomorphically simulates G_1, but the closeness of this simulation is not limited by any number:

$$\begin{aligned} G_3 &= (V_3, \{a, b\}, P_3, S), \text{ where} \\ V_3 &= \{S, M, A, B, X, Z, a, b\}, \end{aligned}$$

and the set of productions P_3 is defined as

$$\begin{aligned} P_3 = \{ &S \to ZXMXZ, \\ &ZA \to ZXa, \ BZ \to bXZ, \\ &Xa \to aX, \ bX \to Xb, \\ &XMX \to AMB, \ XMX \to AB, \\ &aA \to Aa, \ Bb \to bB, \\ &ZA \to a, \ BZ \to b\}. \end{aligned}$$

Introduce a string-relation system

$$\Psi_3 = (V_3^*, \Rightarrow_{G_3}, \{S\}, \{a, b\}^*)$$

and a homomorphism σ_3 from V_3 to V_1 as:

1. $\sigma_3(S) = \sigma_3(M) = S$;

2. $\sigma_3(A) = \sigma_3(a) = a$;

3. $\sigma_3(B) = \sigma_3(b) = b$;

4. $\sigma_3(X) = \sigma_3(Z) = \varepsilon$.

Inspect the definition of P_3 to see that for every derivation step

$$a^{n-1}Sb^{n-1} \Rightarrow_{G_1} a^n S a^n, \ n \geq 1,$$

G_3 makes a derivation

$$\begin{aligned} ZXa^{n-1}Mb^{n-1}XZ \quad &\Rightarrow^{2n-2}_{G_3} \quad Za^{n-1}XMXb^{n-1}Z \\ &\Rightarrow_{G_3} \quad Za^{n-1}AMBb^{n-1}Z \\ &\Rightarrow^{2n-2}_{G_3} \quad ZAa^{n-1}Mb^{n-1}BZ \\ &\Rightarrow^2_{G_3} \quad ZXa^n Mb^n XZ. \end{aligned}$$

Analogously, for every

$$a^{n-1}Sb^{n-1} \Rightarrow_{G_1} a^n b^n, \ n > 0,$$

there is

$$
\begin{aligned}
ZXa^{n-1}Mb^{n-1}XZ \quad &\Rightarrow_{G_3}^{2n-2} & &Za^{n-1}XMXb^{n-1}Z \\
&\Rightarrow_{G_3} & &Za^{n-1}ABb^{n-1}Z \\
&\Rightarrow_{G_3}^{2n-2} & &ZAa^{n-1}Mb^{n-1}BZ \\
&\Rightarrow_{G_3}^{2} & &a^n b^n
\end{aligned}
$$

in G_3. Informally, while G_1 inserts new occurrences of symbols a and b in the middle of a sentential form, G_3 adds as and bs to the ends of the corresponding sentential form. It is rather easy to prove that if $d \in D(\Psi_1)$, there exists $h \in D(\Psi_3)$ such that $h \rhd_{\sigma_3} d$. Furthermore, it can be demonstrated that for every $h \in D(\Psi_3)$, there is some $d \in D(\Psi_1)$ such that $h \rhd_{\sigma_3} d$. However, observe that G_3 simulates every derivation step of G_1 by a sequence of steps whose number depends on the length of the rewritten sentential form. Therefore, $D(\Psi_3) \rhd_{\sigma_3} D(\Psi_1)$, but there exists no m satisfying $D(\Psi_3) \rhd_{\sigma_3}^m D(\Psi_1)$.

Consider three string-relation systems Ψ, Ω, and Θ. Assume, for instance, that Ω is a q-close derivation simulator of Ψ and Θ is a r-close derivation simulator of Ω. The following two theorems establish a simulation-based relationship between Ψ and Θ.

Theorem 55. *Let $\Psi = (W, \Rightarrow_\Psi, W_0, W_F)$, $\Omega = (W', \Rightarrow_\Omega, W_0', W_F')$, and $\Theta = (W'', \Rightarrow_\Theta, W_0'', W_F'')$ be string-relation systems, σ be a substitution from W' to W, and τ be a substitution from W'' to W'. If for some $X \subseteq D(\Psi)$, $Y \subseteq D(\Omega)$, $Z \subseteq D(\Theta)$ holds $Y \rhd_\sigma^q X$ and $Z \rhd_\tau^r Y$, $q, r \geq 1$, there exists a substitution ϕ from W'' to W such that $Z \rhd_\phi^{qr} X$.*

Proof.

(i) Let $d \in X$. Then, there exist some $g \in Y$ and $h \in Z$ such that $g \rhd_\sigma^q d$ and $h \rhd_\tau^r g$. From the definition of $g \rhd_\sigma^q d$, d and g can be expressed as

$$d = x_0 \Rightarrow_\Psi x_1 \Rightarrow_\Psi \ldots \Rightarrow_\Psi x_m$$

and

$$g = y_0 \Rightarrow_\Omega^+ y_1 \Rightarrow_\Omega^+ \ldots \Rightarrow_\Omega^+ y_m,$$

where $x_i \in W$, $y_i \in W'$, $x_i \in \sigma(y_i)$ for all $0 \leq i \leq m$; furthermore, every $y_k \Rightarrow_\Omega^+ y_{k+1}$, $0 \leq k \leq m-1$, consists of q or fewer steps. Therefore, each $y_k \Rightarrow_\Omega^+ y_{k+1}$ is a string-relation sequence

$$y_{k0} \Rightarrow_\Omega y_{k1} \Rightarrow_\Omega \ldots \Rightarrow_\Omega y_{kq_k},$$

where $y_k = y_{k0}$, $y_{k+1} = y_{kq_k}$, $1 \leq q_k \leq q$. Because $h \rhd_\tau^r g$, it holds that

$$h = z_{00} \Rightarrow_\Theta^+ z_{01} \Rightarrow_\Theta^+ \ldots \Rightarrow_\Theta^+ z_{(m-1)q_{m-1}}$$

such that for every $y_{ki} \Rightarrow_\Omega y_{k(i+1)}$, $0 \le k \le m-1$, $0 \le i \le q_k$, $y_{ki} = \tau(z_{ki})$, and every $z_{ki} \Rightarrow_\Theta^+ z_{k(i+1)}$ has r or fewer steps. Putting the simulations together, we get for every $x_k \Rightarrow_\Psi x_{k+1}$ a string-relation sequence

$$z_{k0} \Rightarrow_\Theta^+ z_{k1} \Rightarrow_\Theta^+ \cdots \Rightarrow_\Theta^+ z_{kq_k}$$

with at most qr steps so that $x_k \in \sigma(\tau(z_{k0}))$ and $x_{k+1} \in \sigma(\tau(z_{kq_k}))$. Consequently,

$$h \rhd_\phi^{qr} d,$$

where ϕ is defined as

$$\phi(a) = \{v \in \sigma(u) : u \in \tau(a)\}$$

for all $a \in W''$.

(ii) Let $h \in Z$. By the definition of $Z \rhd_\tau^r Y$, there exists $g \in Y$ such that $h \rhd_\tau^r g$. Moreover, because $Y \rhd_\sigma^q X$, there is some $d \in X$ such that $g \rhd_\sigma^q d$. Hence, by analogy with (i),

$$h \rhd_\phi^{qr} d.$$

From (i) and (ii), for every $d \in X$ there is $h \in Z$ such that $h \rhd_\phi^{qr} d$, and for every $h \in Z$ there exists some $d \in X$ such that $h \rhd_\phi^{qr} d$. As a result,

$$Z \rhd_\phi^{qr} X.$$

■

Theorem 56. *Let* $\Psi = (W, \Rightarrow_\Psi, W_0, W_F)$, $\Omega = (W', \Rightarrow_\Omega, W_0', W_F')$, *and* $\Theta = (W'', \Rightarrow_\Theta, W_0'', W_F'')$ *be string-relation systems,* σ *be a homomorphism from* W' *to* W, *and* τ *be a homomorphism from* W'' *to* W'. *If for some* $X \subseteq D(\Psi)$, $Y \subseteq D(\Omega)$, $Z \subseteq D(\Theta)$ *holds* $Y \rhd_\sigma^q X$ *and* $Z \rhd_\tau^r Y$, $q, r \ge 1$, *there exists a homomorphism* ϕ *from* W'' *to* W *such that* $Z \rhd_\phi^{qr} X$.

Proof. By Theorem 55, $Z \rhd_\phi^{qr} X$, where ϕ is a substitution from W'' to W defined as

$$\phi(a) = \{v \in \sigma(u) : u \in \tau(a)\}$$

for all $a \in W''$. Clearly, if both σ and τ are homomorphisms, ϕ is a homomorphism as well. ■

6.2 Grammatical Simulation

Return to Examples 10 and 11. To study the closeness of derivations in grammars G_1 and G_2, the corresponding string-relation systems Ψ_1 and Ψ_2 were introduced. More precisely, for grammars $G_1 = (V_1, T_1, P_1, S_1)$ and $G_2 = (V_2, T_2, P_2, S_2)$, Ψ_1 and Ψ_2 were defined as $\Psi_1 = (V_1^*, \Rightarrow_{G_1}, \{S_1\}, T_1^*)$ and $\Psi_2 = (V_2^*, \Rightarrow_{G_2}, \{S_2\}, T_2^*)$. That is, in both Ψ_1 and Ψ_2, the set of start strings contained only the axiom and the set of final strings was defined as a set of all words over the terminal alphabet. As demonstrated next, however, the study of grammatical simulations frequently requires a more general approach.

Consider a typical transformation of a grammar G_1 to another equivalent grammar G_2; for example, see Theorems 19 and 21 in Section 4.1.3, Theorem 30 in Section 4.1.5, or Lemma 19 in Section 4.2.2.

As a rule, G_2 simulates derivations in G_1 by performing these three phases:

(A) *Initialization* that produces a string of a desired form by making a few initial steps.

(B) *Main phase* that actually makes the derivation simulation.

(C) *Conclusion* that removes various auxiliary symbols.

Phase (B) almost always fulfills a crucial role while the other two phases are usually much less important. Furthermore, phases (A) and (C) usually correspond to no derivation steps in terms of this simulation. As a result, the simulation as a whole is less close than the main phase. Therefore, we next introduce string-relation systems that allow us to formally express phase (B) and, simultaneously, suppress the inessential phases (A) and (C).

Making use of the notions introduced in the previous section, we formalize the grammatical simulation in terms of EIL grammars because this formalization is discussed throughout Section 6.3. Let us point out, however, that analogically this simulation can be formalized in terms of any grammatical models.

Definition 25. Let $G = (V, T, P, s)$ be an EIL grammar. Let $\Rightarrow_G$ be the direct derivation relation in G. For $\Rightarrow_G$ and every $l \geq 0$, set

$$\Delta(\Rightarrow_G, l) = \{x \Rightarrow_G y : \ x \Rightarrow_G y \Rightarrow_G^i w, \ x, y \in V^*, \ w \in T^*, \ i+1 = l, \ i \geq 0\}.$$

Next, let $G_1 = (V_1, T_1, P_1, s_1)$ and $G_2 = (V_2, T_2, P_2, s_2)$ be EIL grammars. Let $\Rightarrow_{G_1}$ and $\Rightarrow_{G_2}$ be the derivation relations of G_1 and G_2, respectively. Let σ be a substitution from V_2 to V_1. G_2 *simulates* G_1 *with respect to* σ, $D(G_2) \triangleright_\sigma D(G_1)$ in symbols, if there exists two natural numbers $k, l \geq 0$ so that the following conditions hold:

1. $\Psi_1 = (V_1^*, \Rightarrow_{G_1}, \{s_1\}, T_1^*)$ and $\Psi_2 = (V_2^*, \Rightarrow_{\Psi_2}, W_0, W_F)$ are string-relation systems corresponding to G_1 and G_2, respectively, where $W_0 = \{x \in V_2^* : s_2 \Rightarrow_{G_2}^k x\}$ and $W_F = \{x \in V_2^* : x \Rightarrow_{G_2}^l w, \ w \in T_2^*, \ \sigma(w) \subseteq T_1^*\}$.

2. Relation $\Rightarrow_{\Psi_2}$ coincides with $\Rightarrow_{G_2} - \Delta(\Rightarrow_{G_2}, l)$.

3. $D(\Psi_2) \triangleright_\sigma D(\Psi_1)$.

In case that $SD(\Psi_2) \triangleright_\sigma SD(\Psi_1)$, G_2 *simulates successful derivations of* G_1 *with respect to* σ; in symbols, $SD(G_2) \triangleright_\sigma SD(G_1)$.

Definition 26. Let G_1 and G_2 be EIL grammars with total alphabets V_1 and V_2, terminal alphabets T_1 and T_2, and axioms S_1 and S_2, respectively. Let σ be a substitution from V_2 to V_1. G_2 *m-closely simulates* G_1 *with respect to* σ if $D(G_2) \triangleright_\sigma D(G_1)$ and there exists $m \geq 1$ such that the corresponding string-relation systems Ψ_1 and Ψ_2 satisfy $D(\Psi_2) \triangleright_\sigma^m D(\Psi_1)$. In symbols, $D(G_2) \triangleright_\sigma^m D(G_1)$.

Analogously, G_2 *m-closely simulates successful derivations of* G_1 *with respect to* σ, denoted by $SD(G_2) \triangleright_\sigma^m SD(G_1)$, if $SD(\Psi_2) \triangleright_\sigma^m SD(\Psi_1)$ and there exists $m \geq 1$ such that $SD(G_2) \triangleright_\sigma^m SD(G_1)$.

Definition 27. Let G_1 and G_2 be two EIL grammars. If there exists a substitution σ such that $D(G_2) \triangleright_\sigma D(G_1)$, then G_2 is said to be G_1's *derivation simulator*.

By analogy with Definition 27, the reader can also define *homomorphic, m-close*, and *successful-derivation simulators* of EIL grammars.

6.3   Simulation of E(0,1)L Grammars

In this section, we investigate E(0,1)L grammars and symbiotic E0L grammars (see Section 3.2) in terms of the grammatical simulation. Recall that by Theorem 10 and [155], these two types of EIL grammars have the same generative power. Indeed, both E(0,1)L grammars and symbiotic E0L grammars generate **RE**. From the simulation point of view, however, there exists no transformation of an E(0,1)L grammar to an equivalent symbiotic E0L grammar that closely simulates the input one. Therefore, we improve the results concerning the generative power of these EIL grammars by proving that for any E(0,1)L grammar, there exists an equivalent symbiotic E0L grammar that 1-closely simulates the input grammar.

First, we introduce a construction that transforms any E(0,1)L grammar, $G = (V, T, P, s)$, satisfying $s \notin T^*$, to a symbiotic E0L grammar, (G', W). After that, we establish Theorems 57 and 58. Theorem 57 proves that $L(G) = L(G', W)$. Theorem 58 demonstrates that (G', W) is a 1-close homomorphic simulator of G. Then, we modify the construction for any $s \in V^*$ and show that the statements of Theorems 57 and 58 hold for G with $s \in T^*$ as well.

Construction 1.

Input: An E(0,1)L grammar, $G = (V, T, P, s)$, where $s \notin T^*$.

Output: A symbiotic E0L grammar, (G', W).

Algorithm: Introduce a new alphabet, V', defined as

$$V' = V \cup \{@, \#, S'\} \cup \bar{V} \cup \widehat{V} \cup \widetilde{T}, \quad \text{where}$$
$$\bar{V} = \{\bar{a} : a \in V \cup \{@, \#\}\},$$
$$\widehat{V} = \{\widehat{a} : a \in V \cup \{@, \#\}\},$$
$$\widetilde{T} = \{\widetilde{a} : a \in T\}.$$

Let τ be a homomorphism from T to $\widetilde{T}$ such that $\tau(a) = \widetilde{a}$ for all $a \in T$. Define a language W over V' as

$$W = V \cup \{@, \#, S'\} \cup \widetilde{T} \cup (\{\bar{a}\bar{a}, \widehat{a}\widehat{a}, @\bar{a}, @\widehat{a} : a \in V \cup \{@, \#\}\} - \{@\bar{\#}\}).$$

Then, construct a symbiotic E0L grammar (G', W) with $G' = (V', T, P', S')$, where the set of productions is defined in the following way:

1. Add $S' \to @s\#$ to P'.

2. For every $(a, b) \to x \in P$, add $a \to \bar{a}x\bar{b}$ to P'.

3. For every $(a, \varepsilon) \to x \in P$, add $a \to \bar{a}x\bar{\#}$ to P'.

4. For every $(a, b) \to t \in P$, $t \in T^*$, add $a \to \widehat{a}\tau(t)\widehat{b}$ to P'.

5. For every $(a, \varepsilon) \to t \in P$, $t \in T^*$, add $a \to \widehat{a}\tau(t)\widehat{\#}$ to P'.

6. Add $@ \to @\bar{@}$, $\# \to \bar{\#}\#$, $@ \to \widehat{@}$, $\# \to \widehat{\#}$ to P'.

7. For every $\bar{a} \in \bar{V}$, add $\bar{a} \to \varepsilon$ to P'.

8. For every $\widehat{a} \in \widehat{V}$, add $\widehat{a} \to \varepsilon$ to P'.

9. For all $a \in T$, add $\widetilde{a} \to a$ to P'.

Theorem 57. *Let $G = (V, T, P, s)$ be an E(0,1)L grammar satisfying $s \notin T^*$. Let (G', W) be a symbiotic E0L grammar constructed by using Construction 1 with G as its input. Then, $L(G) = L(G', W)$.*

Proof. Let ω be a homomorphism from V' to $V' - (\bar{V} \cup \widehat{V})$ defined as $\omega(a) = \varepsilon$ for all $a \in \bar{V} \cup \widehat{V}$ and $\omega(a) = a$ for every $a \in V' - (\bar{V} \cup \widehat{V})$. Furthermore, let $\widetilde{\omega}$ be a homomorphism from V' to V such that $\widetilde{\omega}(a) = a$ for all $a \in V$, $\widetilde{\omega}(\widetilde{a}) = a$ for all $\widetilde{a} \in \widetilde{T}$, and $\widetilde{\omega}(a) = \varepsilon$ for all $V' - (V \cup \widetilde{T})$. Informally, ω removes all occurrences of symbols of the forms $\bar{a}$ and $\widehat{a}$. In addition, $\widetilde{\omega}$ also removes $@$ and $\#$; moreover, it converts tilde-versions of terminals back to their originals.

Claim 49. *For every $w \in W^*$,*

(I) $S' \Rightarrow^+_{(G', W)} w$ if and only if $@s\# \Rightarrow^*_{(G', W)} w$;

(II) $S' \Rightarrow^+_{(G', W)} w$ implies $S' \notin \mathrm{sub}(w)$.

Proof. By the definition of P', it is easy to see that the very first derivation step always rewrites S' to $@s\#$. Moreover, no productions generate S'; thus, S' appears in no sentential form derived from S'. $\square$

Claim 50. *For all $u, v \in W^*$, $S' \notin \mathrm{sub}(uv)$,*

$$u \Rightarrow_{(G', W)} v \quad \text{if and only if} \quad \omega(u) \Rightarrow_{(G', W)} v.$$

Proof. Examine the definition of P'. Clearly, all occurrences of symbols from $\bar{V} \cup \widehat{V}$ are always erased during $u \Rightarrow_{(G', W)} v$, so they play no role in the generation of v. By the definition of W and ω, $\omega(u) \in W^*$; therefore, $\omega(u) \Rightarrow_{(G', W)} v$ is a valid derivation in (G', W).

Note that this property of derivations in (G', W) allows us to ignore symbols of forms $\bar{a}$ and $\widehat{a}$ occurring in left-hand sides of derivation steps. $\square$

In Claims 51 and 52, we investigate some rewritings of sentential forms that belong to $\{@\}V^*\{\#\}$.

Claim 51. *Let* $@y\# \Rightarrow_{(G', W)} @x\#$, *where* $y = a_1 a_2 \ldots a_n$ *for some* $a_i \in V$, $x \in W^*$, $n \geq 0$. *Then,* $@x\# = @\bar{@}\bar{a}_1 x_1 \bar{a}_2 \bar{a}_2 x_2 \bar{a}_3 \ldots \bar{a}_n x_n \bar{\#}\bar{\#}\#$, *where* $x_i \in V^*$ *for all* $i = 1, \ldots, n$.

Proof. Since x is surrounded by $@$ and $\#$ in $@x\#$, (G', W) surely rewrites $@y\#$ in such a way that $@$ is rewritten to $@\bar{@}$ and $\#$ is rewritten to $\bar{\#}\#$ (see the definition of P'). Every a_i can be rewritten either to $\bar{a}_i x_i \bar{b}_i$ or $\widehat{a}_i \tau(t_i) \widehat{b}_i$, where $b_i \in V$, $x_i \in V^*$, and $t_i \in T^*$. Thus,

$$@x\# = @\bar{@}\alpha_1 z_1 \beta_1 \alpha_2 z_2 \beta_2 \ldots \alpha_n z_n \beta_n \bar{\#}\#$$

with $\alpha_i = \bar{a}_i$, $z_i = x_i$, and $\beta_i = \bar{b}_i$ or $\alpha_i = \widehat{a}_i$, $z_i = \tau(t_i)$, and $\beta_i = \widehat{b}_i$ for all $i = 1, \ldots, n$. However, $@x\#$ must be a string over W. Inspect the definition of W to see that $@x\# \in W^*$ if and only if $\alpha_1 = \bar{a}_1$, $\beta_1 = \alpha_2 = \bar{a}_2$, $\beta_2 = \alpha_3 = \bar{a}_3$, ..., $\beta_{n-1} = \alpha_n = \bar{a}_n$, and $\beta_n = \bar{\#}$. As a result, we get

$$@x\# = @\bar{@}\bar{a}_1 x_1 \bar{a}_2 \bar{a}_2 x_2 \bar{a}_3 \ldots \bar{a}_n x_n \bar{\#}\bar{\#}\#.$$

$\square$

Claim 52. *Let* $@y\# \Rightarrow_{(G', W)} x$, *where* $y = a_1 a_2 \ldots a_n$ *and* $\{@, \#\} \cap \mathrm{sub}(x) = \emptyset$ *for some* $a_i \in V$, $x \in W^*$, $n \geq 0$. *Then,* $x = \widehat{@}\widehat{a}_1 \tau(t_1)\widehat{a}_2 \widehat{a}_2 \tau(t_2)\widehat{a}_3 \ldots \widehat{a}_n \tau(t_n)\widehat{\#}\widehat{\#}$, *where* $t_i \in T^*$ *for all* $i = 1, \ldots, n$.

Proof. Prove this claim by analogy with the proof of Claim 51. $\square$

The following claim shows that Claims 51 and 52 cover all possible ways of rewriting a string having the form $@y\#$, $y \in V^*$, in (G', W).

Claim 53. *Let* $@y\# \Rightarrow_{(G', W)} u$, $y \in V^*$. *Then, either* $u = @x\#$, $x \in W^*$, *or* $u \in W^*$, $\omega(u) \in \widetilde{T}^*$, *and* $\{@, \#\} \cap \mathrm{sub}(u) = \emptyset$.

Proof. Return to the proof of Claim 51. Suppose that $@$ is rewritten to $@\bar{@}$ and $\#$ is rewritten to $\widehat{\#}$. Inspect the resulting sentential form to see that either $\alpha_1 \in \widehat{V}$ or $\beta_n \in \bar{V}$ or there exists $i \in \{1, \ldots, n-1\}$ such that $\beta_i \alpha_{i+1} \in \bar{V}\widehat{V}$; in all cases, the sentential form does not belong to W^*. Analogously, suppose that $@$ is rewritten to $\widehat{@}$ and $\#$ is rewritten to $\bar{\#}\#$. As before, such a sentential form is out of W. $\square$

Claim 54. *Every derivation in* (G', W) *is a beginning of*

$$
\begin{aligned}
S' &\Rightarrow_{(G',W)} && @w_0\# \\
&\Rightarrow_{(G',W)} && @w_1\# \\
&\quad\vdots \\
&\Rightarrow_{(G',W)} && @w_n\# \\
&\Rightarrow_{(G',W)} && u \\
&\Rightarrow_{(G',W)} && t,
\end{aligned}
$$

where $w_0 = s$, $w_i \in W^*$, $\omega(u) = \tau(t)$, $t \in T^*$, $0 \le i \le n$, $n \ge 0$.

Proof. By the proof of Claim 49, S' is always rewritten to $@w_0\#$, where $w_0 = s$. Then, Claim 53 tells us that there are two possible forms of derivations rewriting $\omega(@w_i\#)$ and, hence, $@w_i\#$. First, (G', W) can generate a sequence of n sentential forms that belong to $\{@\}W^*\{\#\}$, for some $n \ge 0$ (their form is described in Claim 51). Second, (G', W) can rewrite $@w_n\#$ to $u \in W^*$, satisfying $\omega(u) \in \widetilde{T}^*$ (see Claim 52). By the definition of P', $\widetilde{a} \to a$ is the only production that can rewrite $\widetilde{a} \in \widetilde{T}$. Therefore, $u \Rightarrow_{(G',W)} t$ such that $t \in T^*$ and $\omega(u) = \tau(t)$. After that, no other derivation step can be made from t because P' contains no production that rewrites terminals. $\qquad\square$

Claim 55. *For all* $x, y \in V^*$, $u \in W^*$, *it holds that*

$$
y \Rightarrow_G x \quad \text{if and only if} \quad @y\# \Rightarrow_{(G',W)} @u\#,
$$

where $x = \omega(u)$.

Proof.

Only if: Let $y \Rightarrow_G x$. Express y and x as $y = a_1 a_2 \ldots a_n$ and $x = x_1 x_2 \ldots x_n$, respectively, so that $(a_i, a_{i+1}) \to x_i \in P$ and $(a_n, \varepsilon) \to x_n \in P$ are applied during $y \Rightarrow_G x$, $i = 1, \ldots, n-1$, $n \ge 0$. Then, for every $(a_i, a_{i+1}) \to x_i$, there exists $a_i \to \bar{a}_i x_i \bar{a}_{i+1} \in P'$, and for $(a_n, \varepsilon) \to x_n$, there exists $a_n \to \bar{a}_n x_n \bar{\#} \in P'$. Therefore, taking into account Claim 51, we can construct

$$
@y\# \Rightarrow_{(G',W)} @\bar{@}\bar{a}_1 x_1 \bar{a}_2 \bar{a}_2 x_2 \bar{a}_3 \ldots \bar{a}_n x_n \bar{\#} \bar{\#} \#.
$$

Obviously,

$$
\omega(\bar{@}\bar{a}_1 x_1 \bar{a}_2 \bar{a}_2 x_2 \bar{a}_3 \ldots \bar{a}_n x_n \bar{\#} \bar{\#}) = x_1 x_2 \ldots x_n = x.
$$

If: Let $@y\# \Rightarrow_{(G',W)} @u\#$. Express y as $y = a_1 a_2 \ldots a_n$, $a_i \in V$, $n \ge 0$. By the proof of Claim 51, every a_i is rewritten to $\bar{a}_i x_i \bar{a}_{i+1}$, $x_i \in V^*$, $0 \le i \le n-1$, a_n is rewritten to $\bar{a}_n x_n \bar{\#}$, $x_n \in V^*$, and

$$
@u\# = @\bar{@}\bar{a}_1 x_1 \bar{a}_2 \bar{a}_2 x_2 \bar{a}_3 \ldots \bar{a}_n x_n \bar{\#} \bar{\#} \#.
$$

Examine the definition of P'. For every $a_i \to \bar{a}_i x_i \bar{a}_{i+1}$, there exists $(a_i, a_{i+1}) \to x_i \in P$, and for $a_n \to \bar{a}_n x_n \bar{\#}$, there is $(a_n, \varepsilon) \to x_n$ in P. Hence, G can derive $y \Rightarrow_G x$ such that $x = x_1 x_2 \ldots x_n = \omega(u)$. $\qquad\square$

Claim 56. *For all $t \in T^*$, $y \in V^*$, $u \in W^*$, it holds that*

$$y \Rightarrow_G t \quad \text{if and only if} \quad @y\# \Rightarrow_{(G',W)} u,$$

where $\tau(t) = \omega(u)$.

Proof. Prove by analogy with the proof of Claim 55. □

From the claims above, it is easy to prove that

$$s \Rightarrow_G^* t \quad \text{if and only if} \quad S' \Rightarrow_{(G',W)}^+ t$$

for all $t \in T^*$.

Only If: Let

$$s \Rightarrow_G v_1 \Rightarrow_G v_2 \Rightarrow_G \ldots \Rightarrow_G v_n \Rightarrow_G t$$

for some $n \geq 0$. Then, there exists

$$S' \Rightarrow_{(G',W)} @s\# \Rightarrow_{(G',W)} @w_1\# \Rightarrow_{(G',W)} @w_2\# \Rightarrow_{(G',W)} \cdots$$
$$\Rightarrow_{(G',W)} @w_n\# \Rightarrow_{(G',W)} u \Rightarrow_{(G',W)} t,$$

where $v_i = \omega(w_i)$ for all $i = 1, \ldots, n$ and $\tau(t) = \omega(u)$.

If: By Claim 54, $S' \Rightarrow_{(G',W)}^+ t$ has the form

$$S' \Rightarrow_{(G',W)} @s\# \Rightarrow_{(G',W)} @w_1\# \Rightarrow_{(G',W)} @w_2\# \Rightarrow_{(G',W)} \cdots$$
$$\Rightarrow_{(G',W)} @w_n\# \Rightarrow_{(G',W)} u \Rightarrow_{(G',W)} t,$$

where $n \geq 0$. For this derivation, we can construct

$$s \Rightarrow_G v_1 \Rightarrow_G v_2 \Rightarrow_G \ldots \Rightarrow_G v_n \Rightarrow_G t$$

so that $v_i = \omega(w_i)$ for all $i = 1, \ldots, n$.

Therefore, $L(G) = L(G', W)$, and the theorem holds. ∎

Theorem 58. *Let $G = (V, T, P, s)$ be an $E(0, 1)L$ grammar satisfying $s \notin T^*$. Let (G', W) with $G' = (V', T, P', S')$ be a symbiotic E0L grammar constructed by using Construction 1 with G as its input. Then, there exists a homomorphism $\widetilde{\omega}$ such that $D(G', W) \triangleright_{\widetilde{\omega}}^{\frac{1}{}} D(G)$ and $SD(G', W) \triangleright_{\widetilde{\omega}}^{\frac{1}{}} SD(G)$.*

Proof. Let

$$\Psi = (V^*, \Rightarrow_G, \{s\}, T^*)$$

be a string-relation system corresponding to G. Let $\widetilde{\omega}$ be the homomorphism defined in the proof of Theorem 57. Let

$$\Psi' = ((V')^*, \Rightarrow_{\Psi'}, W_0, W_F)$$

be a string-relation system corresponding to (G', W), where

$$\Rightarrow_{\Psi'} = \Rightarrow_{(G',W)} - \{\widehat{@}\widehat{a}_1\tau(t_1)\widehat{a}_2\widehat{a}_2\tau(t_2)\widehat{a}_3\ldots\widehat{a}_n\tau(t_n)\widehat{\#}\widehat{\#} \Rightarrow_{(G',W)} t_1t_2\ldots t_n :$$
$$a_i \in V, \ t_i \in T^*, \ 1 \leq i \leq n, \ n \geq 0\};$$
$$W_0 = \{@s\#\};$$
$$W_F = \{\widehat{@}\widehat{a}_1\tau(t_1)\widehat{a}_2\widehat{a}_2\tau(t_2)\widehat{a}_3\ldots\widehat{a}_n\tau(t_n)\widehat{\#}\widehat{\#} : \ a_i \in V, \ t_i \in T^*, \ 1 \leq i \leq n,$$
$$n \geq 0\}.$$

It is easy to verify that Ψ and Ψ' satisfy (1) through (3) of Definition 25; of course, $S' \Rightarrow^1_{(G',W)} @s\#$ and for every $u \in W_F$, $u \Rightarrow^1_{(G',W)} t$, where $t \in T^*$ (see Claim 54 in the proof of Theorem 57). Next, we show that $D(\Psi') \rhd^1_{\widetilde{\omega}} D(\Psi)$. By Definition 23, we have to establish that:

(1) for every $d \in D(\Psi)$, there exists $h \in D(\Psi')$ such that $h \rhd^1_{\widetilde{\omega}} d$;

(2) for every $h \in D(\Psi')$, there exists $d \in D(\Psi)$ such that $h \rhd^1_{\widetilde{\omega}} d$.

(Note that most of this proof is based on substitutions and claims introduced in the proof of Theorem 57).

(1) Let $d \in D(\Psi)$. Express d as

$$d = v_0 \Rightarrow_G v_1 \Rightarrow_G v_2 \Rightarrow_G \ldots \Rightarrow_G v_n,$$

where $v_0 = s$, for some $n \geq 0$. For $n = 0$, there is $@s\# \in \Psi'$ such that the zero-length derivations s and $@s\#$ satisfy $s \rhd^1_{\widetilde{\omega}} @s\#$. Assume that $n > 0$. Then, according to Claims 50 and 55,

$$v_i \Rightarrow_G v_{i+1} \quad \text{if and only if} \quad @w_i\# \Rightarrow_{(G',W)} @w_{i+1}\#,$$

where $v_{i+1} = \omega(w_{i+1}) = \widetilde{\omega}(@w_{i+1}\#)$, $w_i, w_{i+1} \in W^*$, $0 \leq i \leq n-1$. Moreover, by the definition of Ψ',

$$@w_i\# \Rightarrow_{\Psi'} @w_{i+1}\#$$

for all $i = 0, \ldots, n-1$. Hence, by induction on the length of derivations in G, the reader can easily establish that for every $d \in D(\Psi)$, there exists $h \in D(\Psi')$ such that $h \rhd^1_{\widetilde{\omega}} d$.

(2) Let $h \in D(\Psi)$. By the definition of $\Rightarrow_{\Psi'}$ and Claim 54, every yield sequence in Ψ' is a prefix of

$$@w_0\# \Rightarrow_{\Psi'} @w_1\# \Rightarrow_{\Psi'} \ldots \Rightarrow_{\Psi'} @w_n\# \Rightarrow_{\Psi'} u,$$

where $w_0 = s$, $w_i \in W^*$, $u \in W_F$, $0 \leq i \leq n$, $n \leq 0$. The zero-length derivation $@s\#$ is a 1-close simulation of s from G. Claims 50 and 55 imply that for every $@w_i\# \Rightarrow_{\Psi'} @w_{i+1}\#$, there exists $v_i \Rightarrow_G v_{i+1}$ for some $v_i, v_{i+1} \in V^*$, $v_{i+1} = \omega(w_{i+1}) = \widetilde{\omega}(@w_{i+1}\#)$, $0 \leq i \leq n-1$. Furthermore, according to Claims 52 and 56, for $@w_n\# \Rightarrow_{\Psi'} u$, there exists $v_n \Rightarrow_G t$ such that $t \in T^*$, $\tau(t) = \omega(u)$; that is, $\widetilde{\omega}(u) = t$. Clearly, every derivation step in h is a simulation of a corresponding derivation step in d; as a result, $h \rhd^1_{\widetilde{\omega}} d$.

Next, we prove that $SD(G', W) \rhd^1_{\widetilde{\omega}} SD(G)$. From (2), it follows that every successful yield sequence $h \in SD(\Psi')$ is a 1-close simulation of a derivation $s \Rightarrow^*_G t$ with $t \in T^*$. To prove that for every $d \in SD(\Psi)$ there exists $h \in SD(\Psi')$ such that $h \rhd^1_{\widetilde{\omega}} d$, return to case (1) in this proof. Assume that $v_0 \Rightarrow^n_G v_n$, $v_n \in T^*$, $n \geq 1$. Then, there exists a derivation $@w_{n-1}\# \Rightarrow_{\Psi'} u$, $u \in W_F$ (see Claim 56) such that $\tau(v_n) = \omega(u)$, which implies $\widetilde{\omega}(u) = v_n$. Therefore, we get $h \rhd^1_{\widetilde{\omega}} d$, so $SD(G', W) \rhd^1_{\widetilde{\omega}} SD(G)$.   ∎

Theorems 57 and 58 show that for every E(0, 1)L grammar $G = (V, T, P, s)$, $s \notin T^*$, there exists a symbiotic E0L grammar (G', W) with $G' = (V', T, P', S')$ such that:

1. $L(G) = L(G', W)$;

2. (G', W) is a 1-close homomorphic derivation simulator of G;

3. (G', W) is a 1-close homomorphic successful-derivation simulator of G;

4. To simulate G, (G', W) uses one initial derivation step $S' \Rightarrow_{(G',W)} @s\#$, and one derivation step that removes auxiliary symbols:

$$\widehat{@}\widehat{a}_1\tau(t_1)\widehat{a}_2\widehat{a}_2\tau(t_2)\widehat{a}_3 \ldots \widehat{a}_n\tau(t_n)\widehat{\#}\widehat{\#} \Rightarrow_{(G',W)} t_1 t_2 \ldots t_n, \ a_i \in V, \ t_i \in T^*.$$

To cover the entire family of E(0, 1)L grammars, however, we have to demonstrate that the results above can also be established for any G with $s \in T^*$. First, introduce the following new part to Construction 1: if $s \in T^*$, add $S' \to \widehat{@}\widehat{a}\tau(s)\widehat{\#}\widehat{\#}$, where $a \in V$, to P'. Then, use this construction to create (G', W). $S' \to \widehat{@}\widehat{a}\tau(s)\widehat{\#}\widehat{\#}$ adds the following new derivations $S' \Rightarrow_{(G',W)} \widehat{@}\widehat{a}\tau(s)\widehat{\#}\widehat{\#}$ and $S' \Rightarrow_{(G',W)} \widehat{@}\widehat{a}\tau(s)\widehat{\#}\widehat{\#} \Rightarrow_{(G',W)} s$ to (G', W). By analogy with Theorem 57, it is easy to see that $L(G) = L(G', W)$. Inspect the corresponding string-relation system Ψ' defined by analogy with Ψ' in the proof of Theorem 58. Clearly, the only difference is that W_0 and W_F contain $\widehat{@}\widehat{a}\tau(s)\widehat{\#}\widehat{\#}$. However, because $\widetilde{\omega}(\widehat{@}\widehat{a}\tau(s)\widehat{\#}\widehat{\#}) = s$, the zero-length yield sequence $\widehat{@}\widehat{a}\tau(s)\widehat{\#}\widehat{\#}$ is a 1-close simulation of s. Therefore, all results established for E(0, 1)L grammars with $s \notin T^*$ also hold for E(0, 1)L grammars with any axiom.

Chapter 7

Applications and Implementation

Although this book primarily represents a theoretically oriented treatment, most grammars discussed in the previous chapters have realistic applications. Indeed, these grammars are useful to every scientific field that formalizes its results by some strings and studies how these strings are produced from one another under some permitting or, in contrast, forbidding conditions. As numerous areas of science formalize and study their results in this way, any description of applications that cover more than one of these areas would be unbearably sketchy, if not impossible. Therefore, we concentrate our attention on a single application area—*microbiology*, which appears of great interest at present. In this intensively investigated scientific field, we give three case studies that make use of L grammars with context conditions (see Chapter 4.2). Section 7.1 presents two case studies of biological organisms whose development is affected by some abnormal conditions, such as a virus infection. From a more practical point of view, Section 7.2 discusses parametric 0L grammars (see [150]), which represent a powerful and elegant implementation tool in the area of biological simulation and modeling today. More specifically, we extend parametric 0L grammars by context conditions and demonstrate their use in models of growing plants.

7.1 Applications

Case Study 1. Consider a cellular organism in which every cell divides itself into two cells during every single step of healthy development. However, when a virus infects some cells, all of the organism stagnates until it is cured again. During the stagnation period, all of the cells just reproduce themselves without producing any new cells. To formalize this development by a suitable simple semi-conditional L grammar (see Section 4.2.3), we denote a healthy cell and a virus-infected cell by A and B, respectively, and introduce the simple semi-conditional 0L grammar, $G = (\{A, B\}, P, A)$, where P contains the following productions:

$$(A \rightarrow AA, 0, B), \quad (B \rightarrow B, 0, 0),$$
$$(A \rightarrow A, B, 0), \quad (B \rightarrow A, 0, 0),$$
$$(A \rightarrow B, 0, 0).$$

Figure 7.1 describes G simulating a healthy development while Figure 7.2 gives a development with a stagnation period caused by the virus. □

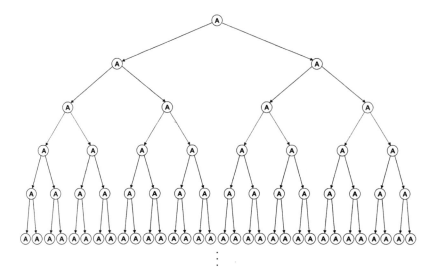

Figure 7.1: Healthy development.

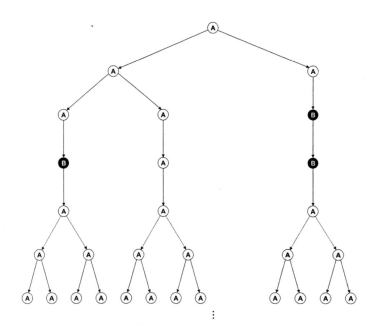

Figure 7.2: Development with a stagnation period.

In the next case study, we discuss an 0L grammar that simulates the developmental stages of a red alga (see [161], [166]). Using context conditions, we can modify this grammar so that it describes some unhealthy development of this alga that leads to its partial death or degeneration.

Case Study 2. Consider an 0L grammar

$$G = (V, P, 1),$$

where

$$V = \{1, 2, 3, 4, 5, 6, 7, 8, [,]\}$$

and the set of productions P contains

$$
\begin{array}{lllll}
1 \to 23, & 2 \to 2, & 3 \to 24, & 4 \to 54, & [\to [, \\
5 \to 6, & 6 \to 7, & 7 \to 8[1], & 8 \to 8, &] \to].
\end{array}
$$

From a *biological viewpoint*, expressions in fences represent branches whose position is indicated by 8s. These branches are shown as attached at alternate sides of the branch on which they are born. Figure 7.3 gives a biological interpretation of the developmental stages formally specified by the next derivation, which contain 13 strings corresponding to stages (a) through (m) in the figure.

$$
\begin{array}{rl}
1 & \Rightarrow_G \quad 23 \\
& \Rightarrow_G \quad 224 \\
& \Rightarrow_G \quad 2254 \\
& \Rightarrow_G \quad 22654 \\
& \Rightarrow_G \quad 227654 \\
& \Rightarrow_G \quad 228[1]7654 \\
& \Rightarrow_G \quad 228[23]8[1]7654 \\
& \Rightarrow_G \quad 228[224]8[23]8[1]7654 \\
& \Rightarrow_G \quad 228[2254]8[224]8[23]8[1]7654 \\
& \Rightarrow_G \quad 228[22654]8[2254]8[224]8[23]8[1]7654 \\
& \Rightarrow_G \quad 228[227654]8[22654]8[2254]8[224]8[23]8[1]7654 \\
& \Rightarrow_G \quad 228[228[1]7654]8[227654]8[22654]8[2254]8[224]8[23]8[1]7654.
\end{array}
$$

Death. Let us assume that the red alga occurs in some unhealthy conditions under which only some of its parts survive while the rest dies. This dying process starts from the newly born, marginal parts of branches, which are too young and weak to survive, and proceeds toward the older parts, which are strong enough to live under these conditions. To be quite specific, all the red alga parts become gradually dead except for the parts denoted by 2s and 8s. This process is specified by the following 0L grammar, G, with forbidding conditions. Let $W = \{a' : a \in V\}$. Then,

$$G = (V \cup W, P, 1),$$

where the set of productions P contains:

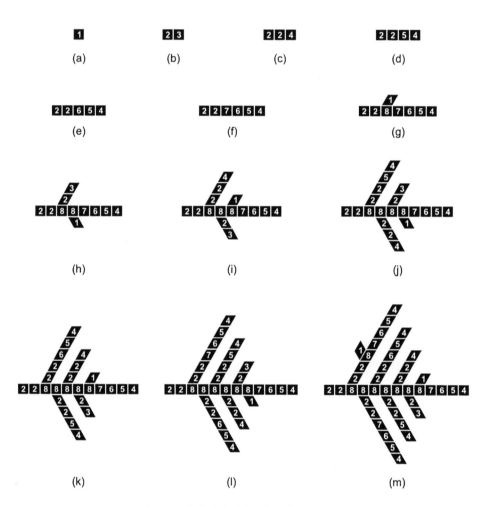

Figure 7.3: Healthy development.

$$(1 \to 23, W), \qquad (1' \to 2', \{3', 4', 5', 6', 7'\}),$$
$$(2 \to 2, W), \qquad (2' \to 2', \emptyset),$$
$$(3 \to 24, W), \qquad (3' \to \varepsilon, \{4', 5', 6', 7'\}),$$
$$(4 \to 54, W), \qquad (4' \to \varepsilon, \emptyset),$$
$$(5 \to 6, W), \qquad (5' \to \varepsilon, \{4'\}),$$
$$(6 \to 7, W), \qquad (6' \to \varepsilon, \{4', 5'\}),$$
$$(7 \to 8[1], W), \qquad (7' \to \varepsilon, \{4', 5', 6'\}),$$
$$(8 \to 8, W),$$
$$([\to [, \emptyset),$$
$$(] \to], \emptyset),$$

and for every $a \in V$,

$$(a \to a', \emptyset), \qquad (a' \to a', \emptyset).$$

Figure 7.4 pictures the dying process corresponding to the next derivation, whose last eight strings correspond to stages (a) through (h) in the figure.

$$1 \Rightarrow_G^* 228[228[1]7654]8[227654]8[22654]8[2254]8[224]8[23]8[1]7654$$
$$\Rightarrow_G 2'2'8'[2'2'8'[1']7'6'5'4']8'[2'2'7'6'5'4']8'[2'2'6'5'4']8'[2'2'5'4']8'[2'2'4']$$
$$\qquad 8'[2'3']8'[1']7'6'5'4'$$
$$\Rightarrow_G 2'2'8'[2'2'8'[1']7'6'5']8'[2'2'7'6'5']8'[2'2'6'5']8'[2'2'5']8'[2'2']8'[2'3']$$
$$\qquad 8'[1']7'6'5'$$
$$\Rightarrow_G 2'2'8'[2'2'8'[1']7'6']8'[2'2'7'6']8'[2'2'6']8'[2'2']8'[2'2']8'[2'3']8'[1']7'6'$$
$$\Rightarrow_G 2'2'8'[2'2'8'[1']7']8'[2'2'7']8'[2'2']8'[2'2']8'[2'2']8'[2'3']8'[1']7'$$
$$\Rightarrow_G 2'2'8'[2'2'8'[1']]8'[2'2']8'[2'2']8'[2'2']8'[2'2']8'[2'3']8'[1']$$
$$\Rightarrow_G 2'2'8'[2'2'8'[1']]8'[2'2']8'[2'2']8'[2'2']8'[2'2']8'[2'8'[1']$$
$$\Rightarrow_G 2'2'8'[2'2'8'[2']]8'[2'2']8'[2'2']8'[2'2']8'[2'2']8'[2']8'[2'].$$

Degeneration. Imagine a situation where the red alga has degenerated. During this degeneration, only the main stem was able to give a birth to new branches while all the other branches lengthened themselves without any branching out. This degeneration is specified by the forbidding 0L grammar $G = (V \cup \{D, E\}, P, 1)$, with P containing

$$(1 \to 23, \emptyset), \qquad (2 \to 2, \emptyset), \qquad (3 \to 24, \emptyset), \qquad (4 \to 54, \emptyset),$$
$$(5 \to 6, \emptyset), \qquad (6 \to 7, \emptyset), \qquad (7 \to 8[1], \{D\}), \qquad (8 \to 8, \emptyset),$$
$$([\to [, \emptyset), \qquad (] \to], \emptyset), \qquad (7 \to 8[D], \emptyset),$$
$$(D \to ED, \emptyset), \qquad (E \to E, \emptyset).$$

Figure 7.5 pictures the degeneration specified by the following derivation, in which the last 10 strings correspond to stages (a) through (j) in the figure:

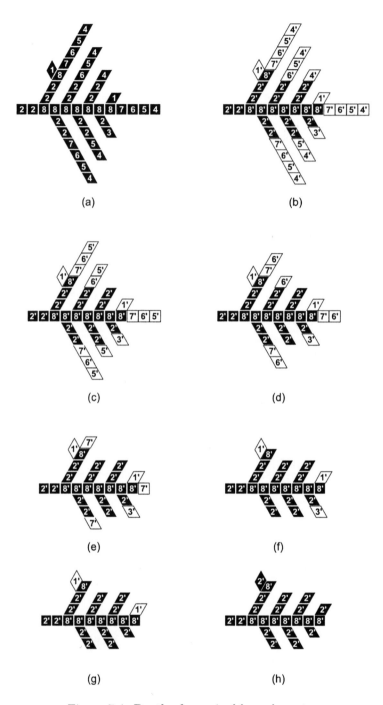

Figure 7.4: Death of marginal branch parts.

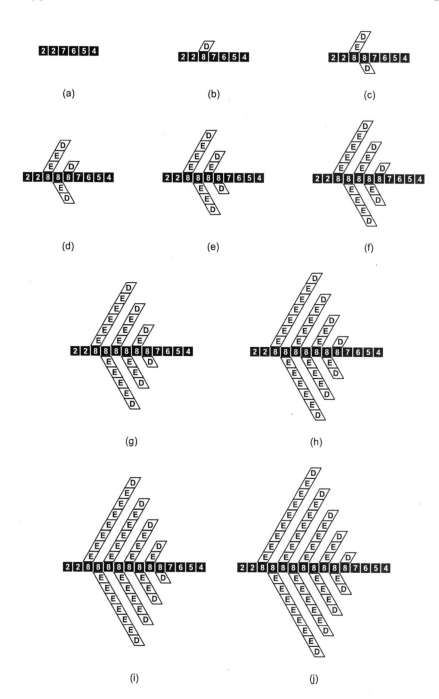

Figure 7.5: Degeneration.

$1 \Rightarrow^*_G 227654$

$\quad \Rightarrow_G 228[D]7654$

$\quad \Rightarrow_G 228[ED]8[D]7654$

$\quad \Rightarrow_G 228[E^2D]8[ED]8[D]7654$

$\quad \Rightarrow_G 228[E^3D]8[E^2D]8[ED]8[D]7654$

$\quad \Rightarrow_G 228[E^4D]8[E^3D]8[E^2D]8[ED]8[D]7654$

$\quad \Rightarrow_G 228[E^5D]8[E^4D]8[E^3D]8[E^2D]8[ED]8[D]7654$

$\quad \Rightarrow_G 228[E^6D]8[E^5D]8[E^4D]8[E^3D]8[E^2D]8[ED]8[D]7654$

$\quad \Rightarrow_G 228[E^7D]8[E^6D]8[E^5D]8[E^4D]8[E^3D]8[E^2D]8[ED]8[D]7654$

$\quad \Rightarrow_G 228[E^8D]8[E^7D]8[E^6D]8[E^5D]8[E^4D]8[E^3D]8[E^2D]8[ED]8[D]7654.$

$\square$

7.2   Implementation

In this section, we describe *parametric 0L grammars* (see [150]) and their extension by context conditions. We make this description from a purely practical point of view to clearly demonstrate how these grammars are implemented and used.

Case Study 3. *Parametric 0L grammars* (see [150], [149]) operate on strings of modules called *parametric words*. A *module* is a symbol from an alphabet with an associated sequence of *parameters* belonging to the set of real numbers. Productions of parametric 0L grammars are of the form

$$predecessor \; [\; : \; logical \; expression \;] \; \rightarrow \; successor.$$

The *predecessor* is a module having a sequence of formal parameters instead of real numbers. The *logical expression* is any expression over predecessor's parameters and real numbers. If the logical expression is missing, the logical truth is assumed. The *successor* is a string of modules containing expressions as parameters; for example,

$$A(x) \; : \; x < 7 \; \rightarrow \; A(x+1)D(1)B(3-x).$$

Such a production *matches* a module in a parametric word provided that the symbol of the rewritten module is the same as the symbol of the predecessor module, both modules have the same number of parameters, and the value for the logical expression is true. Then, the module can be rewritten by the given production. For instance, consider $A(4)$. This module matches the above production since A is the symbol of production's predecessor, there is one actual parameter, 4, in $A(4)$, that corresponds to the formal parameter x in $A(x)$, and the value for the logical expression $x < 7$ with $x = 4$ is true. Thus, $A(4)$ can be rewritten to $A(5)D(1)B(-1)$.

As usual, a parametric 0L grammar can rewrite a parametric word provided that there exists a matching production for every module that occurs in it. Then, all modules are simultaneously rewritten, and we obtain a new parametric word.

Parametric 0L grammars with context conditions. Next, we extend the parametric 0L grammars by permitting context conditions. Each production of a *parametric 0L grammar with permitting conditions* has the form

$$predecessor \ [\ ?\ context\ conditions]\ [\ :\ logical\ expression]\ \rightarrow\ successor,$$

where the *predecessor*, the *logical expression*, and the *successor* have the same meaning as in parametric 0L grammars, and *context conditions* are some permitting context conditions separated by commas. Each condition is a string of modules with formal parameters. For example, consider

$$A(x)\ ?\ B(y),\ C(r,z)\ :\ x < y + r\ \rightarrow\ D(x)E(y + r).$$

This production matches a module in a parametric word w provided that the predecessor $A(x)$ matches the rewritten module with respect to the symbol and the number of parameters and there exist modules matching to $B(y)$ and $C(r,z)$ in w such that the value for logical expression $x < y + r$ is true. For example, this production matches $A(1)$ in $C(3,8)D(-1)B(5)H(0,0)A(1)F(3)$ because there are $C(3,8)$ and $B(5)$ such that $1 < 5 + 3$ is true. If there are more substrings matching the context condition, any of them can be used.

Having described the parametric 0L grammars with permitting conditions, we next show how to use them to simulate the development of some plants.

In nature, developmental processes of multicellular structures are controlled by the quantity of substances exchanged between modules. In the case of plants, growth depends on the amount of water and minerals absorbed by the roots and carried upward to the branches. The model of branching structures making use of the resource flow was proposed by Borchert and Honda in [24]. The model is controlled by a *flux* of resources that starts at the base of the plant and propagates the substances toward the apexes. An apex accepts the substances, and when the quantity of accumulated resources exceeds a predefined threshold value, the apex bifurcates and initiates a new lateral branch. The distribution of the flux depends on the number of apexes that the given branch supports and on the type of the branch—plants usually carry greater amount of resources to straight branches than to lateral branches (see [24] and [149]).

The following two examples illustrate the idea of plants simulated by parametric 0L grammars with permitting conditions:

(I) Consider the model

$$axiom:\ I(1,1,e_{root})\,A(1)$$
$$p_1:\quad A(id)\ ?\ I(id_p,c,e)\ :\ id == id_p \wedge e \geq e_{th}$$
$$\rightarrow\ [+(\alpha)\,I(2 * id + 1, \gamma, 0)\,A(2 * id + 1)]/(\pi)\,I(2 * id, 1 - \gamma, 0)\,A(2 * id)$$
$$p_2:\quad I(id,c,e)\ ?\ I(id_p,c_p,e_p)\ :\ id_p == \lfloor id/2 \rfloor$$
$$\rightarrow\ I(id,c,c * e_p)$$

This L grammar describes a simple plant with a constant resource flow from its roots and with a fixed distribution of the stream between lateral and straight branches. It operates on the following types of modules:

- $I(id, c, e)$ represents an internode with a unique identification number id, a distribution coeficient c, and a flux value e.

- $A(id)$ is an apex growing from the internode with identification number equal to id.

- $+(\phi)$ and $/(\phi)$ rotate the segment orientation by angle ϕ (for more information, consult [149]).

- [and] enclose the sequence of modules describing a lateral branch.

We standardly assume that if no production matches a given module $X(x_1, \ldots, x_n)$, the module is rewritten by an implicit production of the form

$$X(x_1, \ldots, x_n) \to X(x_1, \ldots, x_n);$$

that is, it remains unchanged.

At the beginning, the plant consists of one internode $I(1, 1, e_{root})$ with apex $A(1)$, where e_{root} is a constant flux value provided by the root. The first production, p_1, simulates the bifurcation of an apex. If an internode preceding the apex $A(id)$ reaches a sufficient flux $e \geq e_{th}$, the apex creates two new internodes I terminated by apexes A. The lateral internode is of the form $I(2 * id + 1, \gamma, 0)$ and the straight internode is of the form $I(2 * id, 1 - \gamma, 0)$. Clearly, the identification numbers of these internodes are unique. Moreover, every child internode can easily calculate the identification number of its parent internode; the parent internode has $id_p = \lfloor id/2 \rfloor$. The coefficient γ is a fraction of the parent flux to be directed to the lateral internode. The second production, p_2, controls the resource flow of a given internode. Observe that the permitting condition $I(id_p, c_p, e_p)$ with $id_p = \lfloor id/2 \rfloor$ matches only the parent internode. Thus, p_2 changes the flux value e of $I(id, c, e)$ to $c * e_p$, where e_p is the flux of the parent internode, and c is either γ for lateral internodes or $1 - \gamma$ for straight internodes. Therefore, p_2 simulates the transfer of a given amount of parent's flux into the internode. Figure 7.6 pictures 12 developmental stages of this plant, with e_{root}, e_{th}, and γ set to 12, 0.9, and 0.4, respectively. The numbers indicate the flow values of internodes.

It is easy to see that this model is unrealistically simple. Since the model ignores the number of apexes, its flow distribution does not depend on the size of branches, and the basal flow is set to a constant value. However, it sufficiently illustrates the technique of communication between adjacent internodes. Thus, it can serve as a template for more sophisticated models of plants, such as the following model.

(II) We discuss a plant development with a resource flow controlled by the number

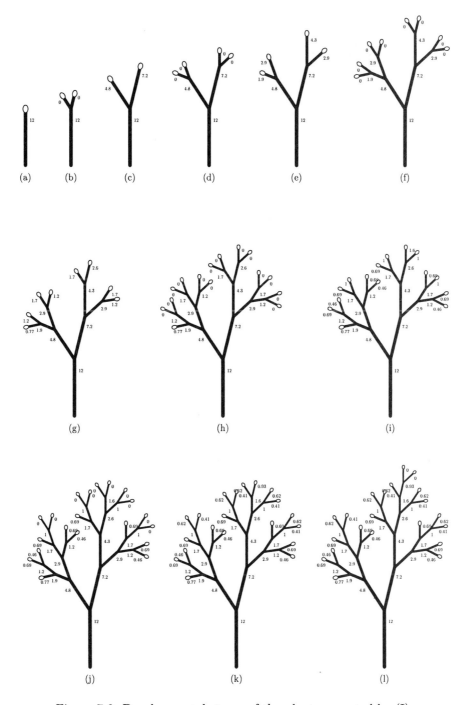

Figure 7.6: Developmental stages of the plant generated by (I).

of apexes. This example is based on Example 17 in [149].

$$
\begin{array}{ll}
axiom: & N(1)\,I(1,straight,0,1)\,A(1) \\
p_1: & N(k) \;\to\; N(k+1) \\
p_2: & I(id,t,e,c)\;?\;N(k),\;A(id) \\
& :\;id == 1 \\
& \to\; I(id,t,\sigma_0 2^{(k-1)\eta^k},1) \\
p_3: & I(id,t,e,c)\;?\;N(k),\;I(id_s,t_s,e_s,c_s),\;I(id_l,t_l,e_l,c_l) \\
& :\;id == 1\;\wedge\;id_s == 2*id\;\wedge\;id_l == 2*id+1 \\
& \to\; I(id,t,\sigma_0 2^{(k-1)\eta^k},c_s+c_l) \\
p_4: & I(id,t,e,c)\;?\;I(id_p,t_p,e_p,c_p),\;I(id_s,t_s,e_s,c_s),\;I(id_l,t_l,e_l,c_l) \\
& :\;id_p == \lfloor id/2 \rfloor\;\wedge\;id_s == 2*id\;\wedge\;id_l == 2*id+1 \\
& \to\; I(id,t,\delta(t,e_p,c_p,c),c_s+c_l) \\
p_5: & Id(id,t,e,c)\;?\;I(id_p,t_p,e_p,c_p),\;A(id_a) \\
& :\;id_p == \lfloor id/2 \rfloor\;\wedge\;id_a == id \\
& \to\; I(id,t,\delta(t,e_p,c_p,c),1) \\
p_6: & A(id)\;?\;I(id_p,t_p,e_p,c_p) \\
& :\;id == id_p\;\wedge\;e_p \geq e_{th} \\
& \to\; [+(\alpha)\,I(2*id+1,lateral,e_p*(1-\lambda),1)\,A(2*id+1)] \\
& \quad /(\pi)\,I(2*id,straight,e_p*\lambda,1)\,A(2*id)
\end{array}
$$

This L grammar uses the following types of modules:

- $I(id,t,e,c)$ is an internode with a unique identification number id, where t is a type of this internode, $t \in \{straight, lateral\}$, e is a flux value, and c is a number of apexes the internode supports.

- $A(id)$ is an apex terminating the internode id.

- $N(k)$ is an auxiliary module, where k is the number of a developmental cycle to be done by the next derivation.

- $+(\phi)$, $/(\phi)$, [and] have the same meaning as in the previous example.

The flux distribution function, δ, is defined as

$$
\delta(t,e_p,c_p,c) = \begin{cases} e_p - e_p(1-\lambda)((c_p-c)/c) & \text{if } t = straight, \\ e_p(1-\lambda)(c/(c_p-c)) & \text{if } t = lateral. \end{cases}
$$

The development starts from the axiom $N(1)\,I(1,straight,0,1)\,A(1)$ containing one straight internode with one apex. In each derivation step, by application of p_4, every inner internode $I(id,t,e,c)$ gets the number of apexes of its straight ($I(id_s,t_s,e_s,c_s)$) and lateral ($I(id_l,t_l,e_l,c_l)$) descendant. Then, this number is stored in c. Simultaneously, it accepts a given part of the flux e_p provided by its parent internode $I(id_p,t_p,e_p,c_p)$. The distribution function δ depends on the number of apexes in the given branch and in the sibling branch, and on the type of this branch (straight or lateral). The distribution factor λ determines the amount

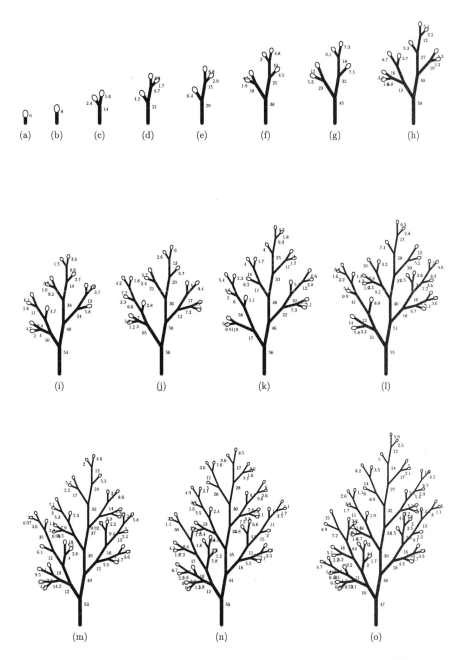

Figure 7.7: Developmental stages of the plant generated by (II).

of the flux that reaches the straight branch in case that both branches support the same number of apexes. Otherwise, the fraction is also affected by the ratio of apex counts. Productions p_2 and p_3 rewrite the basal internode, calculating its input flux value. The expression used for this purpose, $\sigma_0 2^{(k-1)\eta^k}$, was introduced by Borchert and Honda to simulate a sigmoid increase of the input flux; σ_0 is an initial flux, k is a developmental cycle, and η is a constant value scaling the flux change. Production p_5 rewrites internodes terminated by apexes. It keeps the number of apexes set to 1, and by analogy with p_4, it loads a fraction of parent's flux by using the δ function. The last production, p_6, controls the addition of new segments. By analogy with p_1 in the previous example, it erases the apex and generates two new internodes terminated by apexes. Figure 7.7 shows 15 developmental stages of a plant simulation based on this model.

Obviously, there are two concurrent streams of information in this model. The bottom-up (acropetal) stream carries and distributes the substances required for the growth. The top-down (basipetal) flow propagates the number of apexes that is used for the flux distribution. A remarkable feature of this model is the response of a plant to a pruning. Indeed, after a branch removal, the model redirects the flux to the remaining branches and accelerates their growth.

Let us note that this model is a simplified version of the model described in [149], which is very complex. Under this simplification, however, $c_p - c$ may be equal to zero as the denominator in the distribution function δ. If this happens, we change this zero value to the proper non-zero value so that the number of apexes supported by the parent internode corresponds to the number of apexes on the straight and lateral branches growing from the parent internode. Consult [149] for a more appropriate, but also complicated solution of this problem.

From the presented examples, we see that with permitting conditions, parametric 0L grammars can describe sophisticated models of plants in a very natural way. Particularly, compared to the context-sensitive L grammars, they allow one to refer to modules that are not adjacent to the rewritten module, and this property makes them more adequate, succint, and elegant. □

Chapter 8

Concluding and Bibliographical Notes

Summary. The classical context-dependent grammars, such as context-sensitive and phrase-structure grammars, represent powerful generators of languages. However, their strict conditions placed on the context surrounding the rewritten symbol during the generation of languages complicate their use both in theory and in practice. Therefore, in this book, we discuss a large variety of grammars with much less restrictive context conditions that are placed on derivation domains, use of productions, or the neighborhood of rewritten symbols. All the grammars under discussion also use context-independent productions so as to simplify the language generation process. Perhaps most important, we demonstrate that most of the grammars with alternative context conditions are as powerful as the classical context-dependent grammars. That is, they have the same generative power as the phrase-structure grammars, and if erasing productions are ruled out, they are as powerful as the context-sensitive grammars. As a result, the grammars studied in this book represent language generators based on context-independent productions and very simple context conditions, yet they maintain the power of context-dependent grammars. All these advantages make their use obviously preferable to the classical context-dependent grammars both from a theoretical and practical point of view. From a theoretical viewpoint, they simplify the language generation and its analysis, which usually turns out unbearably tedious and clumsy in terms of the classical context-dependent grammars. From a practical viewpoint, these easy-to-use grammars with flexible context conditions have their important applications in reality as we demonstrate in examples from microbiology.

Historical Notes. Conditional grammars were introduced in [64]. Several variants of these grammars were discussed in [41], [44], [52], [53], [84], [85], [87], [91], [141], [145], [146], [154], [158], [173], and [174]. The crucial concepts of these grammars and results concerning them are summarized in [126].

General References. Although the present treatment of conditional grammars is selfcontained, it assumes some background in the formal language theory. For an introduction to this theory, consult [7], [8], [16], [72], [79], [81], [86], [118], [157], [160], [161], [162], or [182].

Future Investigation. We suggest the following new directions of investigation concerning grammars with context conditions.

(1) By context conditions, the grammars dicussed in this book actually restrict their derivations. In this sense, they are strongly related to regulated grammars, which make this restriction by various regulating mechanisms. Study how to replace some of these mechanisms by suitable context conditions and vice versa. Regulated grammars are investigated, for instance, in [1], [2], [58], [83], [101], [102], [103], [108], [111], [113], [115], [125], [129], [130], [145], [152], [153], [154], and [157]. A good introduction to regulated grammars is [43].

(2) Introduce automata with context conditions. Concentrate on pushdown automata with some context conditions placed on their stacks. For a detailed discussion of automata, consult [4], [7], [8], [12], [16], [32], [34], [54], [55] [56], [71], [78], [79], [80], [81], [86], [92], [124], [132], [134], [151], [157], [160], [163], [171], or [182].

(3) Adapt the language models with context conditions for translation. Develop translation grammars and automata working under these conditions. For an essential discussion of the translation models, see [4], [5], [6], [7], [8], [9], [22], [27], [31], [35], [59], [60], [76], [82], [89], [90], [98], [143], [144], [164], or [183].

(4) Chapter 7 concentrates its attention on applications in terms of microbiology. Study some other applications of the language and translation models with context conditions. Specifically, apply these models in some classical application areas of computer science, such as the applications included in [3], [4], [9], [10], [11], [13], [14], [15], [17], [18], [19], [20], [21], [23], [25], [26], [28], [29], [30], [31], [32], [33], [35], [36], [37], [38], [39], [40], [42], [45], [46], [47], [48], [49], [50], [51], [57], [59], [61], [62], [63], [65], [66], [67], [74], [93], [94], [95], [96], [97], [99], [139], [140], [142], [159], [165], [172], [176], [177], [178], [179], [180], [181], and [183].

Bibliography

[1] S. Abraham. Compound and serial grammars. *Information and Control*, 20:432–438, 1972.

[2] A. V. Aho. Indexed grammars: An extension of context-free grammars. *Journal of the ACM*, 15:647–671, 1968.

[3] A. V. Aho. *Currents in the Theory of Computing*. Prentice-Hall, Englewood Cliffs, New Jersey, 1973.

[4] A. V. Aho. Pattern matching in strings. In R.V., ed., *Formal Language Theory: Perspectives and Open Problems*. Academic Press, New York, 1980, pp. 325–247.

[5] A. V. Aho and J. D. Ullman. Properties of syntax directed relations. *Journal of Computer and System Sciences*, 3:319–334, 1969.

[6] A. V. Aho and J. D. Ullman. Syntax directed translations and the pushdown assembler. *Journal of Computer and System Sciences*, 3:37–56, 1969.

[7] A. V. Aho and J. D. Ullman. *The Theory of Parsing, Translation and Compiling, Volume I: Parsing*. Prentice-Hall, Englewood Cliffs, New Jersey, 1972.

[8] A. V. Aho and J. D. Ullman. *The Theory of Parsing, Translation and Compiling, Volume II: Compiling*. Prentice-Hall, Englewood Cliffs, New Jersey, 1973.

[9] A. V. Aho and J. D. Ullman. *Principles of Compiler Design*. Addison-Wesley, Reading, Massachusetts, 1977.

[10] S. Alagic and M. A. Arbib. *The Design of Well-structured and Correct Programs*. Springer-Verlag, Heidelberg, 1978.

[11] R. B. Anderson. *Proving Programs Correct*. Wiley, New York, 1979.

[12] M. A. Arbib, A. J. Kfoury, and R. N. Moll. *A Basis for Theoretical Computer Science*. Springer-Verlag, New York, 1981.

[13] E. A. Ashcroft and W. W. Wadge. Lucid, a formal system for writing and proving programs. *SIAM Journal on Computing*, 5:336–354, 1976.

[14] J. W. Backus. The syntax and semantics of the proposed international algebraic language of the Zurich ACM-GAMM conference. In *Proceedings of the International Conference on Information Processing*. UNESCO, 1959, pp. 125–132.

[15] C. B. Becker. *Software Testing Techniques*. Van Nostrand Reinhold, New York, 1983.

[16] R. Beigel and R. W. Floyd. *The Language of Machines*. Freeman, New York, 1994.

[17] R. E. Bellmann and S. E. Dreyfus. *Applied Dynamic Programming*. Princeton University Press, Princeton, 1962.

[18] J. L. Bentley and Th. Ottmann. The complexity of manipulating hierarchically defined sets of rectangles. In *Mathematical Foundations of Computer Science 1981*. Springer-Verlag, Heidelberg, 1981, pp. 1–15.

[19] J. L. Bentley, Th. Ottmann, and P. Widmayer. The complexity of manipulating hierarchically defined sets of rectangles. In F. P. Preparata, ed., *Advances in Computing Research 1*. JAI Press, Greenwich, Connecticut, 1983, pp. 127–158.

[20] R. Berger. The undecidability of the domino problem. In *Memoirs of the American Mathematical Society*, vol. 66. American Mathematical Society, Providence, Rhode Island, 1966.

[21] E. R. Berlekamp, J. H. Conway, and R. K. Guy. *Winning Ways, Volume 2: Games in Particular*. Academic Press, New York, 1982.

[22] J. Berstel. *Transductions and Context-Free Languages*. Teubner, Stuttgart, 1979.

[23] J. Berstel and L. Boasson. Une suite decroissante de cones rationnels. *Springer-Verlag Lecture Notes in Computer Science*, 14:383–397, 1974.

[24] R. Borchert and H. Honda. Control of development in the bifurcating branch system of *Tabebuia Rosea*: A computer simulation. *Botanical Gazette*, 145(2):184–195, 1984.

[25] S. R. Bourne. *The UNIX System*. Addison-Wesley, Reading, Massachussetts, 1983.

[26] P. Braffort and D. Hirschberg (eds.). *Computer Programming and Formal Systems*. North-Holland, Amsterdam, 1963.

[27] J. G. Brookshear. *Theory of Computation*. Benjamin/Cummings, Redwood City, California, 1989.

[28] J. A. Brzozowski. A survey of regular expressions and their applications. *IEEE Transactions on Electronic Computers*, 11:324–335, 1962.

[29] J. A. Brzozowski and E. J. McCluskey Jr. Signal flow graph techniques for sequential circuit state diagrams. *IEEE Transactions on Electronic Computers*, EC-12:67–76, 1963.

[30] J. A. Brzozowski and M. Yoeli. *Digital Networks*. Prentice-Hall, Englewood Cliffs, New Jersey, 1976.

[31] W. Bucher and H. A. Maurer. *Teoretische Grundlagen der Programmiersprachen: Automatem und Sprachen*. Bibliographisches Institut, Zurich, 1984.

[32] A. W. Burks. *Essays in Cellular Automata*. University of Illinois Press, Champaign, 1970.

[33] A. W. Burks, W. D. Warren, and J. B. Wright. An analysis of a logical machine using parenthesis-free notation. *Mathematical Tables and Other Aids to Computation*, 8:55–57, 1954.

[34] J. Carroll and D. Long. *Theory of Finite Automata*. Prentice-Hall, Englewood Cliffs, 1989.

[35] N. Chomsky. *Syntactic Structures*. The Hague, Netherlands, 1957.

[36] A. Church. The calculi of lambda-conversion. In *Annals of Mathematics Studies 6*. Princeton University Press, Princeton, New Jersey, 1941.

[37] W. F. Clocksin and C. S. Mullish. *Programming in PROLOG*. Springer-Verlag, Heidelberg, 1981.

[38] A. Cobham. The intrinsic computational difficulty of functions. In *Proceedings of 1964 Congress for Logic, Mathematics, and Philosophy of Science*. North-Holland, Amsterdam, 1964, pp. 24–30.

[39] M. E. Conway. Design of a separable transition-diagram compiler. *Communications of the ACM*, 6:396–408, 1963.

[40] S. A. Cook. Linear-time simulation of deterministic two-way pushdown automata. In *Proceeding of the 1971 IFIP Congress*. North-Holland, Amsterdam, 1971, pp. 75–80.

[41] E. Csuhaj-Varju. On grammars with local and global context conditions. *International Journal of Computer Mathematics*, 47:17–27, 1992.

[42] G. B. Dantzig. On the significance of solving linear programming problems with integer variables. *Econometrica*, 28:30–44, 1960.

[43] J. Dassow and Gh. Paun. *Regulated Rewriting in Formal Language Theory*. Akademie-Verlag, Berlin, 1989.

[44] J. Dassow, Gh. Paun, and A. Salomaa. Grammars based on patterns. *International Journal of Foundations of Computer Science*, 4(1):1–14, 1993.

[45] J. W. de Bakker. Semantics of programming languages. In J. Tou, ed., *Advances in Information Systems and Sciences*, vol. 2. Plenum Press, New York, 1969, pp. 173–227.

[46] R. A. DeMillo, D. P. Dobkin, A. K. Jones, and R. J. Lipton (eds.). *Foundations of Secure Computation*. Academic Press, New York, 1978.

[47] R. A. DeMillo, R. J. Lipton, and A. J. Perlis. Social processes and proofs of theorems and programs. *Communications of the ACM*, 22:271–280, 1979.

[48] A. K. Dewdney. Computer recreations: A computer trap for the busy beaver, the hardest-working turing machine. *Scientific American*, 251:19–23, 1984.

[49] A. K. Dewdney. Computer recreations. *Scientific American*, 252:23, 1985.

[50] E. W. Dijkstra. *A Discipline of Programming*. Prentice-Hall, Englewood Cliffs, New Jersey, 1976.

[51] J. Edmonds. Covers and packings in a family of sets. *Bulletin of the American Mathematical Society*, 68:494–499, 1962.

[52] A. Ehrenfeucht, J. Kleijn, and G. Rozenberg. Adding global forbidding context to context-free grammars. *Theoretical Computer Science*, 37:337–360, 1985.

[53] A. Ehrenfeucht, P. Pasten, and G. Rozenberg. Context-free text grammars. *Acta Informatica*, 31:161–206, 1994.

[54] S. Eilenberg. *Automata, Languages, and Machines*, vol. A. Academic Press, New York, 1974.

[55] S. Eilenberg. *Automata, Languages, and Machines*, vol. B. Academic Press, New York, 1976.

[56] J. Engelfriet, E. M. Schmidt, and J. van Leeuwen. Stack machines and classes of nonnested macro languages. *Journal of the ACM*, 27:6–17, 1980.

[57] J. Evey. Application of pushdown store machines. In *Proceedings 1963 Fall Joint Computer Conference*. AFIPS Press, Montvale, New Jersey, 1963, pp. 215–227.

[58] M. J. Fischer. Grammars with macro-like productions. In *Proceedings of the Ninth Annual Symposium on Switching and Automata Theory*. IEEE, Schenectady, New York, 1968, pp. 131–142.

[59] R. W. Floyd. The syntax of programming languages–a survey. *IEEE Transactions on Electronic Computers*, EC-13:346–353, 1964. Reprinted in S. Rosen (ed.), Programming Systems and Languages, McGraw-Hill, New York, 1967; and B. W. Pollack, Compiler Techniques, Auerbach Press, Philadelphia, Pensylvania, 1972.

[60] R. W. Floyd and J. D. Ullman. The compilation of regular expressions into integrated circuits. *Journal of the ACM*, 29:603–622, 1984.

[61] L. D. Fosdick and L. J. Osterweil. Data flow analysis in software reliability. *Computing Surveys*, 8:305–330, 1976.

[62] J. M. Foster. A syntax-improving program. *Computer Journal*, 11:31–34, 1968.

[63] J. M. Foster. *Automatic Syntactic Analysis*. American Elsevier, New York, 1970.

[64] I. Fris. Grammars with partial ordering of the rules. *Information and Control*, 12:415–425, 1968.

[65] B. A. Galler and A. J. Perlis. *A View of Programming Languages*. Addison-Wesley, Reading, Massachusetts, 1970.

[66] M. Gardner. *Wheels, Life and Other Mathematical Amusements*. Freeman, San Francisco, 1983.

[67] M. Gardner. The traveling saleman's travail. *Discover*, 6:87–90, 1985.

[68] V. Geffert. Context-free-like forms for the phrase-structure grammars. In *Proceedings of the Mathematical Foundations of Computer Science 1988*. Springer-Verlag, New York, 1988, pp. 309–317.

[69] V. Geffert. How to generate languages using only two pairs of parentheses. *Journal of Information Processes in Cybernetics EIK*, 27:303–315, 1991.

[70] V. Geffert. Normal forms for phrase-structure grammars. *Informatique théorique et Applications/Theoretical Informatics and Applications*, 25(5):473–496, 1991.

[71] F. Gesceg and M. Steinby. *Tree Automata*. Akademia Kiado, Budapest, 1984.

[72] S. Ginsburg. *The Mathematical Theory of Context-Free Languages*. McGraw-Hill, New York, 1966.

[73] J. Gonczarowski and M. K. Warmuth. Scattered and context-sensitive rewriting. *Acta Informatica*, 20:391–411, 1983.

[74] M. G. Gouda and L. E. Rosier. Priority networks of communicating finite state machines. *SIAM Journal on Computing*, 14:569–584, 1985.

[75] S. Greibach and J. Hopcroft. Scattered context grammars. *Journal of Computer and System Sciences*, 3:233–247, 1969.

[76] D. Gries. *Compiler Construction for Digital Computers*. Wiley, New York, 1971.

[77] J. Gruska. On a classification of context-free languages. *Kybernetika*, 13:22–29, 1967.

[78] M. Harrison. *Introduction to Switching and Automata Theory*. McGraw-Hill, New York, 1965.

[79] M. Harrison. *Introduction to Formal Language Theory*. Addison-Wesley, Reading, Massachusetts, 1979.

[80] J. E. Hopcroft. An $n \log n$ algorithm for minimizing the states in a finite automaton. In Z. Kohavi and A. Paz, eds., *Theory of Machines and Computations*. Academic Press, New York, 1971, pp. 189–196.

[81] J. E. Hopcroft and J. D. Ullman. *Introduction to Automata Theory, Languages, and Computation*, 2nd ed. Addison-Wesley, Reading, Massachusetts, 1979.

[82] P. M. Lewis II, D. J. Rosenkrantz, and R. E. Stearns. *Compiler Design Theory*. Addison-Wesley, Reading, Massachusetts, 1976.

[83] J. H. Johnson. *Formal Models for String Similarity*. PhD thesis, Department of Computer Science, University of Waterloo, 1983.

[84] J. Kelemen. Conditional grammars: Motivations, definition, and some properties. In I. Peak and J. Szep, eds., *Proceedings on Automata, Languages and Mathematical Systems*. K. Marx University of Economics, Budapest, 1984, pp. 110–123.

[85] J. Kelemen. Measuring cognitive resources use (a grammatical approach). *Computers and Artificial Intelligence*, 8(1):29–42, 1989.

[86] D. Kelley. *Automata and Formal Languages*. Prentice-Hall, Englewood Cliffs, New Jersey, 1995.

[87] H. C. M. Kleijn and G. Rozenberg. Context-free-like restrictions on selective rewriting. *Theoretical Computer Science*, 16:237–239, 1981.

[88] H. C. M. Kleijn and G. Rozenberg. On the generative power of regular pattern grammars. *Acta Informatica*, 20:391–411, 1983.

[89] D. E. Knuth. On the translation of languages from left to right. *Information and Control*, 8:611–618, 1967.

[90] A. J. Korenjak and J. E. Hopcroft. Simple deterministic languages. In *Proceedings of the Seventh Annual Symposium on Switching and Automata Theory*. IEEE, Berkeley, California, 1966, pp. 36–46.

[91] J. Kral. A note on grammars with regular restrictions. *Kybernetika*, 9(3):159–161, 1973.

[92] W. Kuich and A. Salomaa. *Semirings, Automata, Languages*. Springer-Verlag, New York, 1985.

[93] L. C. Larson. *Problem-Solving through Problems*. Springer-Verlag, New York, 1983.

[94] P. E. Lauer, P. R. Torrigiani, and M. W. Shields. Cosy: A system specification language based on paths and processes. *Acta Informatica*, 12:109–158, 1979.

[95] R. C. Linger, H. D. Mills, and B. I. Witt. *Structured Programming: Theory and Practice*. Addison-Wesley, Reading, Massachusetts, 1979.

[96] J. Loeckxx and K. Sieber. *The Foundations of Program Verification*. Wiley, New York, 1978.

[97] J. S. Mallozi and N. J. De Lillo. *Computability with PASCAL*. Prentice-Hall, Englewood Cliffs, New Jersey, 1984.

[98] J. McCarthy. A basis for a mathematical theory of computation. In P. Braffort and D. Hirschberg, eds., *Programming and Formal Systems*. North-Holland, Amsterdam, 1963, pp. 33–70.

[99] W. S. McCulloch and W. Pitts. A logical calculus of the ideas immanent in nervous activity. *Bulletin of Mathematical Biophysics*, 5:115–133, 1943.

[100] A. Meduna. A note on exponential density of ET0L languages. *Kybernetika*, 22:514–518, 1986.

[101] A. Meduna. Characterization of the Chomsky hierarchy through sequential-parallel grammars. *Rostocker Mathematische Kolloquium*, 32:4–14, 1987.

[102] A. Meduna. Evaluated grammars. *Acta Cybernetika*, 8:169–176, 1987.

[103] A. Meduna. Context-free derivations on word monoids. *Acta Informatica*, 27:781–786, 1990.

[104] A. Meduna. Generalized forbidding grammars. *International Journal of Computer Mathematics*, 36:31–38, 1990.

[105] A. Meduna. Symbiotic E0L systems. *Acta Cybernetica*, 10:165–172, 1992.

[106] A. Meduna. Canonical scattered rewriting. *International Journal of Computer Mathematics*, 51:122–129, 1993.

[107] A. Meduna. A formalization of sequential, parallel and continuous rewriting. *International Journal of Computer Mathematics*, 47:153–161, 1993.

[108] A. Meduna. Matrix grammars under leftmost and rightmost restrictions. In Gh. Paun, ed., *Mathematical Linguistics and Related Topics*. Romanian Academy of Sciences, Bucharest, 1994, pp. 243–257.

[109] A. Meduna. Syntactic complexity of scattered context grammars. *Acta Informatica*, 32:285–298, 1995.

[110] A. Meduna. A trivial method of characterizing the family of recursively enumerable languages by scattered context grammars. *EATCS Bulletin*, 56:104–106, 1995.

[111] A. Meduna. Syntactic complexity of context-free grammars over word monoids. *Acta Informatica*, 33:457–462, 1996.

[112] A. Meduna. Four-nonterminal scattered context grammars characterize the family of recursively enumerable languages. *International Journal of Computer Mathematics*, 63:67–83, 1997.

[113] A. Meduna. On the number of nonterminals in matrix grammars with leftmost derivations. *LNCS*, 1217:27–38, 1997.

[114] A. Meduna. Six-nonterminal multi-sequential grammars characterize the family of recursively enumerable languages. *International Journal of Computer Mathematics*, 65:179–189, 1997.

[115] A. Meduna. Descriptional complexity of multi-continuous grammars. *Acta Cybernetica*, 13:375–384, 1998.

[116] A. Meduna. Economical transformation of phrase-structure grammars to scattered context grammars. *Acta Cybernetica*, 13:225–242, 1998.

[117] A. Meduna. Prefix pushdown automata. *International Journal of Computer Mathematics*, 71:215–228, 1999.

[118] A. Meduna. *Automata and Languages: Theory and Applications*. Springer, London, 2000.

[119] A. Meduna. Generative power of three-nonterminal scattered context grammars. *Theoretical Computer Science*, 246:276–284, 2000.

[120] A. Meduna. Terminating left-hand sides of scattered context productions. *Theoretical Computer Science*, 237:423–427, 2000.

[121] A. Meduna. Uniform generation of languages by scattered context grammars. *Fundamenta Informaticae*, 44:231–235, 2001.

[122] A. Meduna. Descriptional complexity of scattered rewriting and multirewriting: An overview. *Journal of Automata, Languages and Combinatorics*, 7:571–577, 2002.

[123] A. Meduna. Coincidental extension of scattered context languages. *Acta Informatica*, 39:307–314, 2003.

[124] A. Meduna. Simultaneously one-turn two-pushdown automata. *International Journal of Computer Mathematics*, 80:679–687, 2003.

[125] A. Meduna, C. Crooks, and M. Sarek. Syntactic complexity of regulated rewriting. *Kybernetika*, 30:177–186, 1994.

[126] A. Meduna and E. Csuhaj-Varju. Grammars with context conditions. *EATCS Bulletin*, 32:112–124, 1993.

[127] A. Meduna and H. Fernau. On the degree of scattered context-sensitivity. *Theoretical Computer Science*, 290:2121–2124, 2003.

[128] A. Meduna and H. Fernau. A simultaneous reduction of several measures of descriptional complexity in scattered context grammars. *Information Processing Letters*, 86:235–240, 2003.

[129] A. Meduna and A. Gopalaratnam. On semi-conditional grammars with productions having either forbidding or permitting conditions. *Acta Cybernetica*, 11:307–323, 1994.

[130] A. Meduna and G. Horvath. On state grammars. *Acta Cybernetica*, 8:237–245, 1988.

[131] A. Meduna and D. Kolář. Descriptional complexity of multi-parallel grammars with respect to the number of nonterminals. In *Grammars and Automata for String Processing: from Mathematics and Computer Science to Biology and Back*. Francis and Taylor, London, 2000, pp. 724–732.

[132] A. Meduna and D. Kolář. Regulated pushdown automata. *Acta Cybernetica*, 18:653–664, 2000.

[133] A. Meduna and D. Kolář. Homogenous grammars with a reduced number of non-context-free productions. *Information Processing Letters*, 81:253–257, 2002.

[134] A. Meduna and D. Kolář. One-turn regulated pushdown automata and their reduction. *Fundamenta Informaticae*, 16:399–405, 2002.

[135] A. Meduna and M. Švec. Reduction of simple semi-conditional grammars with respect to the number of conditional productions. *Acta Cybernetica*, 15:353–360, 2002.

[136] A. Meduna and M. Švec. Descriptional complexity of generalized forbidding grammars. *International Journal of Computer Mathematics*, 80(1):11–17, 2003.

[137] A. Meduna and M. Švec. Forbidding ET0L grammars. *Theoretical Computer Science*, 306:449–469, 2003.

[138] A. Meduna and P. Vurm. Multisequential grammars with homogeneous selectors. *Fundamenta Informaticae*, 34:1–7, 2001.

[139] G. B. Moore, J. L. Kuhns, J. L. Trefftzs, and C. A. Montgomery. *Accessing Individual Records from Personal Data Files Using Non-Unique Identifiers*. NBS Special Publication 500-2, US Department of Commerce, National Bureau of Standards, Washington, DC, 1977.

[140] P. Naur. Report on the algorithmic language ALGOL 60. *Communications of the ACM*, 3:299–314, 1960. Revised in Communications of the ACM 6 (1963), 1–17.

[141] E. Navrátil. Context-free grammars with regular conditions. *Kybernetika*, 6(2):118–125, 1970.

[142] W. Newman and R. Sproul. *Principles of Interactive Computer Graphics*, 2nd ed. McGraw-Hill, New York, 1979.

[143] A. G. Oettinger. Automatic syntactic analysis and pushdown store. In *Proceedings of the Symposia in Applied Mathematics*, vol. 12. American Mathematical Society, Providence, Rhode Island, 1961, pp. 104–109.

[144] F. G. Pagan. *Formal Specification of Programming Languages L: A Panoramic Primer*. Prentice-Hall, Englewood Cliffs, New Jersey, 1981.

[145] Gh. Paun. On the generative capacity of conditional grammars. *Information and Control*, 43:178–186, 1979.

[146] Gh. Paun. A variant of random context grammars: Semi-conditional grammars. *Theoretical Computer Science*, 41:1–17, 1985.

[147] M. Penttonen. One-sided and two-sided context in formal grammars. *Information and Control*, 25:371–392, 1974.

[148] M. Penttonen. ET0L-grammars and N-grammars. *Information Processing Letters*, 4:11–13, 1975.

[149] P. Prusinkiewicz, M. Hammel, J. Hanan, and R. Měch. L-systems: From the theory to visual models of plants. In M. T. Michalewicz, ed., *Proceedings of the 2nd CSIRO Symposium on Computational Challenges in Life Sciences*. CSIRO Publishing, Collingwood, Victoria, Australia, 1996.

[150] P. Prusinkiewicz and A. Lindenmayer. *The Algorithmic Beauty of Plants*. Springer-Verlag, New York, 1990.

[151] G. E. Revesz. *Introduction to Formal Language Theory*. McGraw-Hill, New York, 1983.

[152] D. J. Rosenkrantz. Matrix equations and normal forms for contex-free grammars. *Journal of the ACM*, 14:501–507, 1967.

[153] D. J. Rosenkrantz. Programmed grammars and classes of formal languages. *Journal of the ACM*, 16:107–131, 1969.

[154] G. Rozenberg. Selective substitution grammars (towards a framework for rewriting systems), Part I: Definitions and examples. *Journal of Information Processes in Cybernetics*, 13:455–463, 1977.

[155] G. Rozenberg and A. Salomaa. *The Mathematical Theory of L Systems.* Academic Press, New York, 1980.

[156] G. Rozenberg and A. Salomaa. *The Book of L.* Springer-Verlag, Berlin, 1986.

[157] G. Rozenberg and A. Salomaa. *Handbook of Formal Languages*, vols. 1–3. Springer, Berlin, 1997.

[158] G. Rozenberg and S. H. von Solms. Priorities on context conditions in rewriting systems. *Information Sciences*, 14:15–50, 1978.

[159] R. Rustin. *Formal Semantics of Programming Languages.* Prentice-Hall, Englewood Cliffs, New Jersey, 1972.

[160] A. Salomaa. *Theory of Automata.* Pergamon Press, London, 1969.

[161] A. Salomaa. *Formal Languages.* Academic Press, New York, 1973.

[162] A. Salomaa. *Computation and Automata.* Cambridge University Press, Cambridge, 1985.

[163] C. E. Shannon and J. McCarthy (eds.). *Automata Studies.* Princeton University Press, Princeton, New Jersey, 1956.

[164] S. Sippu and E. Soisalon-Soininen. *Parsing Theory.* Springer-Verlag, New York, 1987.

[165] A. R. Smith. Plants, fractals, and formal languages. *Computer Graphics*, 18:1–10, 1984.

[166] S. H. von Solms. Modelling the growth of simple biological organisms using formal language theory. *Manuscript.*

[167] S. H. von Solms. Random context grammars with sequential rewriting and priorities on conditions. *Manuscript.*

[168] S. H. von Solms. Rewriting systems with limited distance permitting context. *International Journal of Computer Mathematics*, 8, 1979.

[169] S. H. von Solms. Random context array grammars. *Information Processing*, 80:59–64, 1980.

[170] S. H. von Solms. Rewriting systems with limited distance forbidding context. *International Journal of Computer Mathematics*, 15:39–49, 1984.

[171] T. A. Sudkamp. *Languages and Machines.* Addison-Wesley, Reading, Massachusetts, 1988.

[172] R. E. Tarjan. A unified approach to path problems. *Journal of the ACM*, 28:577–593, 1981.

[173] F. J. Urbanek. A note on conditional grammars. *Revue Roumaine de Mathématiques Pures at Appliquées*, 28:341–342, 1983.

[174] G. Vaszil. On the number of conditional rules in simple semi-conditional grammars. *Theoretical Computer Science*, 2004 (in press).

[175] A. P. J. van der Walt. Random context grammars. In *Proceedings of the Symposium on Formal Languages*, 1970.

[176] P. Wegner. Programming language semantics. In R. Rustin, ed., *Formal Semantics of Programming Languages*. Prentice-Hall, Englewood Cliffs, New Jersey, 1972, pp. 149–248.

[177] A. van Wijngaarden, B. J. Mailloux, J. E. L. Peck, C. H. A. Koster, M. Sintzoff, C. H. Lindsey, L. G. L. T. Meertens, and R. G. Fisker (eds.). Revised report on the algorithmic language ALGOL 68. *Acta Informatica*, 5:1–236, 1974.

[178] P. H. Winston. *Artificial Intelligence*. Addison-Wesley, Reading, Massachusetts, 1977.

[179] N. Wirth. *Systematic Programming: An Introduction*. Prentice-Hall, Englewood Cliffs, New Jersey, 1973.

[180] N. Wirth. Data structures and algorithms. *Scientific American*, 251:60–69, 1984.

[181] D. Wood. *Paradigms and Programming with PASCAL*. Computer Science Press, Rockville, Maryland, 1984.

[182] D. Wood. *Theory of Computation*. Harper and Row, New York, 1987.

[183] D. H. Younger. Recognition and parsing of context-free languages in time n 3. *Information and Control*, 10:189–208, 1976.

Denotations of Language Families

CE0L	context-conditional E0L grammars (CE0L grammars)
CEP0L	propagating CE0L grammars (CEP0L grammars)
CEPT0L	propagating CET0L grammars (CEPT0L grammars)
CET0L	context-conditional ET0L grammars (CET0L grammars)
CF	context-free grammars
CG	context-conditional grammars
CS	context-sensitive grammars
EIL[.i], EIL[i.]	EIL grammars with uniform rewriting
E0L	E0L grammars
EP0L	propagating E0L grammars (EP0L grammars)
EPT0L	propagating ET0L grammars (EPT0L grammars)
ET0L	ET0L grammars
F	forbidding grammars
FE0L	forbidding E0L grammars (FE0L grammars)
FEP0L	propagating FE0L grammars (FEP0L grammars)
FEPT0L	propagating FET0L grammars (FEPT0L grammars)
FET0L	forbidding ET0L grammars (FET0L grammars)
GCC	global context conditional grammars
GF	generalized forbidding grammars
prop-CG	propagating context-conditional grammars
prop-F	propagating forbidding grammars
prop-GCC	propagating global context conditional grammars
prop-GF	propagating generalized forbidding grammars
prop-RC	propagating *rc*-grammars
prop-RC(ac)	propagating *rc*-grammars with appearance checking
prop-SC	propagating semi-conditional grammars
prop-SSC	propagating simple semi-conditional grammars
prop-WM	propagating context-free grammars over word monoids
PS[.i], PS[i.]	phrase-structure grammars with uniform rewriting
RC	random-context grammars
RC(ac)	random-context grammars with appearance checking
RE	phrase-structure grammars
SE0L	symbiotic E0L grammars (**SE0L = WME0L**(2))
SEP0L	propagating symbiotic E0L grammars
SC	semi-conditional grammars
SCAT	scattered context grammars
SCAT[.i/j]	scattered context grammars with uniform rewriting
SSC	simple semi-conditional grammars
SSC-E0L	simple semi-conditional E0L grammars

SSC-EP0L	propagating SSC-E0L grammars (SSC-EP0L grammars)
SSC-EPT0L	propagating SSC-ET0L grammars (SSC-EPT0L grammars)
SSC-ET0L	simple semi-conditional ET0L grammars
WM	context-free grammars over word monoids
WME0L	E0L grammars over word monoids
WMEP0L	propagating E0L grammars over word monoids

Subject Index